# Stronger Together

## The Story of SEIU

By Don Stillman

Design by Katerina Barry:  www.katerinabarry.com
Additional Writing and Editing by Margie Snider
Research/Fact-Checking by Eli Staub
Photo Research/Credits by David Sachs
Production Editing by Dan Giosta

Printed in the United States of America

First printing, May 2010

Library of Congress Cataloging-in-Publication Data

Stillman, Donald Dennis, 1945-
Stronger together : the story of SEIU / by Don Stillman ; design by Katerina Barry ;
additional writing and editing by Margie Snider ; research and fact-checking by Eli Staub.
    p. cm.
Includes bibliographical references.
ISBN 978-0-578-05461-2
1.  Service Employees International Union. 2.  Labor unions--United States--History.
3.  Service industries workers--Labor unions--History. 4. Social change--United States--History.  I. Title.

HD6475.S45S75 2010
331.88'11000973--dc22

2010015160

Chelsea Green Publishing                    Service Employees International Union (SEIU), CTW, CLC
P.O. Box 428                                1800 Massachusetts Avenue, NW
White River Junction, VT  05001             Washington, DC  20036
(802) 295 6300                              (800) 424 8592
www.chelseagreen.com                        www.seiu.org

# Stronger Together

## The Story of SEIU

By Don Stillman

Design by Katerina Barry

Additional Writing and Editing by Margie Snider

Research and Fact-Checking by Eli Staub

Chelsea Green Publishing, White River Junction, Vermont

# Table of Contents

# Acknowledgments

This book was done with the support and authorization of SEIU's International Executive Board and the union's leadership, including Mary Kay Henry, Andy Stern, Anna Burger, Eliseo Medina, Tom Woodruff, Gerry Hudson, Dave Regan, Mitch Ackerman, and Bruce Raynor. Their commitment to seeing that the SEIU story would be available to a new generation of labor activists and members was at the core of this book.

Tom Chabolla did a superb job coordinating the project. Margie Snider played a crucial role in the preparation of the book, including writing and editing. Much of the content of this book reflects her talent and work. Eli Staub, researcher for the union's Public Services Division, did excellent research and fact-checking. Our thanks go to Katerina Barry, a superb graphic artist, who designed this book.

Thanks to Kirk Adams for his ideas and assistance. David Sachs assisted with photograph research and credits. Norm Gleichman, deputy general counsel, coordinated the legal review with help from Orrin Baird, John Sullivan, Maryann Parker, Dora Chen, and Alvin Velazquez. Thanks go also to Cheryl Alston for her help. Stephen Chavers, Michelle Miller, and Kris Price provided help with graphic images. Stephen Lerner provided relevant documents and advice. We drew heavily on Barbara Shulman's research on SEIU organizing from 1996-2009. Kay Anderson, J.J. Johnson, and Belinda Gallegos of 1199SEIU provided materials and photographs for the chapter dealing with 1199. Mike Fishman, Larry Engelstein, Matt Nerzig, and Cassandra Waters of SEIU Local 32BJ as well as Leyla Vural of *Building Strength* magazine provided documents,

photographs, and other help. Thanks as well to David Rolf for help on the Los Angeles home care workers' organizing and to Jess Walsh, a leader of the Victoria State Branch of the Liquor, Hospitality & Miscellaneous Workers Union in Australia. Christy Hoffman, Jessica Champagne, Scott Shumaker, and Carl Leinonen provided materials for the segment on global union partnerships. Christine Miller and Linda Mackenzie-Nicholas of SEIU in Canada assisted with materials and photographs. Thanks to Bob Hauptman, Bill Pritchett, Meg Casey, John Adler, Dennis Short, Travis Stein, Brian Olney, Christy Coleman, Bob Lawson, Susan Galvan, Then Tran, and Bruce Colburn. Our great appreciation goes to Glenn Adler and Carmen Caneda, both of whom read the manuscript. Dan Giosta provided valuable copy editing and proofreading help, as did Susan Burke. Thanks as well to Adrienne Eaton, Janice Fine, Saul Rubinstein, all professors at Rutgers University, and Allison Porter. They examined organizational change at SEIU. David Snapp, who worked with the Rutgers group, reviewed a draft of this book. Our thanks go as well to all of the photographers listed on pages 268-269.

SEIU published an early history titled *A Need For Valor: The Roots Of The Service Employees International Union* in 1984. That volume was updated in a second edition issued by the union in 1992. We owe a great debt to those who wrote and edited *A Need For Valor* and have drawn heavily on their work in the first three chapters of this book. Our thanks go to labor historians Grace Palladino and Pat Cooper, who did much of the research for the *Valor* books, and to the late Tom Beadling and Peter Pieragostini, then on the SEIU staff, who edited the material. Dr. Palladino is co-editor of the Samuel Gompers Papers and a member of the history faculty at the University of Maryland. Dr. Cooper chairs the Gender and Women's Studies Department at the University of Kentucky. Thanks, too, to David Sheridan, who managed the 1992 revision. Although significant events in the life of the union through 1992 that appear in this volume are adapted from the work of those above, they are not responsible for any errors or misinterpretations herein. For the Canada chapter, we wish to credit *Building A Dream: The History Of A Union For Canadian Service Workers 1943-1988* by Albert G. Hearn published by SEIU in 1988.

The Walter P. Reuther Library of Labor and Urban Affairs at Wayne State University is the largest labor archive in North America. SEIU's historical records, papers, and photographs are at the Reuther Library. Thanks to Mike Smith, the director of the Reuther Library, and to Louis Jones, the SEIU archivist there. Jones provided many documents, photographs, and other materials used in the preparation of this book and did a superb job. Thanks, too, to Steve Babson for his photo research.

*SEIU Action* magazine chronicled important developments in the union for years, as did its predecessors. We relied heavily on that magazine for much of this book and major sections, particularly worker stories and comments, come directly from *SEIU Action*. We want to thank SEIU writers and editors who worked on the magazine, including Margie Snider, Peter Pieragostini, Hans Johnson, Kris Price, Micki Francis, Cindy Reymer, Dan Giosta, Bill Pritchett, Tula Connell, Nicole Crawford, and Peter Pocock.

Our thanks goes also to Chelsea Green Publishing, which published *Stronger Together*. We particularly appreciate the support of Margo Baldwin, Chelsea Green's president, as well as Bill Bokermann and Jeffrey Slayton.

Finally, we must note that, while we've done our best to ensure accuracy and fairness throughout, we apologize for any errors that may have crept in and note that such mistakes or other shortcomings are not the responsibility of the SEIU leaders, staff, and others listed above. The huge scope of this project, spanning more than a century, inevitably means that errors will occur. If you spot an inaccuracy or other problem, please email: seiu.book@gmail.com. Any and all royalties from the sale of this book will be donated to the SEIU Education and Support Fund.

This book tells much of the story of SEIU, but far more remains to be told. Every SEIU local has its own rich history that deserves to be documented for future generations of union members. *Stronger Together* does not attempt to be a formal history of SEIU—that task awaits academic historians who offer their own independent judgments and analysis in the years ahead. This book seeks instead to provide a window into a number of the worker struggles and debates that have defined the union.

# Introduction

SEIU is a union born in struggle. From seven small local unions of janitors in Chicago in 1921, SEIU grew to more than 2.2 million members today in the United States, Canada, and Puerto Rico.

Those building service workers were joined by hospital workers and then public employees who dared to dream they could build better lives for themselves and their families by uniting in a union.

They faced hostile employers and anti-union politicians. Many got fired for their work building the union, some ended up jailed. But they kept fighting.

Although of many different nationalities, races, religions, and creeds, the pioneers of what became today's SEIU all knew one thing: they were STRONGER TOGETHER.

Uniting 2.2 million members in SEIU has allowed workers to achieve progress at the bargaining table and the ballot box. The union's growth has enabled it to achieve big economic gains for SEIU workers. And its political work has resulted in programs and policies that have benefited all Americans.

The chapters that follow tell some of the stories that have made SEIU, now led by President Mary Kay Henry, one of the largest and most effective progressive advocacy groups in North America.

They describe the early achievements of the union's pioneers and tell the story of how SEIU transformed itself into the preeminent and fastest-growing labor union in North America. They describe SEIU's fight to realize economic, social, and political justice for its members and to help restore the American Dream for all working families.

In recent years, as most unions suffered major membership declines, the SEIU story has been one of remarkable growth. From 1996 to 2010, 1.2 million new members united with SEIU. That new strength translated into better wages and benefits for huge numbers of janitors, security officers, healthcare workers, public employees, home care and child care workers, and others—many of whom were immigrants, women, and people of color who suffered previously from low wages and lack of dignity on the job.

SEIU's restructuring since 1996 under President Andy Stern and its willingness to adapt to meet new challenges have made the union a driving force pressing for a new social contract for working people—one that leaves behind the old role of effective advocacy on behalf of a union elite and replaces that with a progressive thrust on behalf of improving standards for all workers—here and abroad.

Much of what the union has achieved occurred during periods of sustained assault on workers' ability to form unions. Under President George W. Bush and earlier under his father, President George H.W. Bush, there was a concerted and often successful effort to weaken labor laws and a failure to enforce the few worker protections that did exist. Much of corporate America pursued anti-worker policies that made it extremely difficult for workers to join unions.

The growth of multinational corporations and the increased globalization of the world economy meant SEIU and the entire labor movement faced new and hostile conditions for organizing and bargaining. Employers that once had been local or regional became national or international firms that used their size and power to fight labor.

Even before the economic collapse of late 2008, real median household income had declined and the secure, middle-class life many workers once enjoyed had slipped further out of reach for much of the population.

Against this backdrop, the achievements of SEIU stand in sharp contrast. It's worth examining briefly where the union is today so as to better understand the history that brought us here.

Perhaps the key to SEIU's recent success can be found in three components:

- huge organizing gains during an extremely anti-labor period;
- bargaining success that has resulted in substantial wage and benefit gains for SEIU families; and
- political victories that have helped the union both stave off harsh anti-worker proposals and achieve some of what SEIU has struggled for over the years.

Since new leadership in 1996 launched a process of focusing the union's resources at all levels on organizing, SEIU's membership more than doubled. In 2010, the union represents more than 2.2 million workers, up from 1 million just 15 years before.

Each of SEIU's core sectors faced unique challenges from 1996 to 2010, yet each expanded substantially, and the workers who united in SEIU bettered their standard of living as a result.

Janitors, for example, transformed an industry that used to be driven by a "race to the bottom" on wages to one in which many contractors had to adhere to area standards on compensation. The union also forced employers to do their fair share to provide affordable healthcare, rather than shifting those costs onto taxpayers and strapped local governments.

More than 40,000 janitors have united in SEIU since 1996 and about 151,000 janitors were members of the union in 2010. Approximately 44 percent of all janitors in 25 of the 30 largest commercial office markets in the United States are SEIU members.

Achieving that union density helped SEIU janitors in New York City enjoy pay of $920 per week in 2008, compared to nonunion janitors whose weekly pay averaged $412. SEIU janitors in Chicago got $592 per week and those in Los Angeles $527 per week during that period—far more than their nonunion counterparts.

In the healthcare sector, some 150,000 hospital workers have united in SEIU since 1996; about 500,000 hospital workers were SEIU members in 2010. The union's success came as hospital chains consolidated and focused on harsh cost-cutting and other restructuring aimed at lowering labor costs and reducing staffing for patient care to help the bottom line.

Again, organizing victories translated into bargaining clout, as hospital workers won major economic gains. Workers, for example, at all of HCA's hospitals in California were unionized in 2010, as were those in Nevada. SEIU members at HCA won across-the-board raises totaling 29.6 percent between 2007 and 2010, as well as step increases based on experience. Some licensed vocational nurses in 2001 who earned $14 per hour before HCA workers joined SEIU went on to get $17 per hour in the first contract and by 2010 received $19.50 per hour.

Home care workers also have benefited from SEIU organizing progress. About 450,000 home care workers have united in SEIU since 1996 and about 40 percent of all independent provider home care workers in the United States belonged to the union. They received wages that were 10 percent higher than nonunion workers. Union home care aides were almost twice as likely to have health insurance as nonunion home care aides and more than twice as likely to have some kind of pension or retirement plan.

SEIU members employed in nursing homes (56,000 have united with the union since 1996 to bring total membership to

160,000 by 2010) have also won major contract gains. So, too, have those in sectors where the union has focused its efforts in recent years, such as child care providers, security officers, and multiservice workers.

In 2010, SEIU represented a total of one million public service workers, with some 330,000 uniting with the union since 1996. Major breakthroughs came through innovative organizing models based on solution-oriented partnerships with state and local governments. These centered around the fact that front-line public employees often have the best ideas for improving services on which taxpayers rely.

With the economic collapse in 2008, governments at all levels faced budget deficits that put great pressure on public employees, yet SEIU members repeatedly have staved off cuts through skillful advocacy and creative approaches aimed at protecting much-needed public services.

The organizing successes and the bargaining victories that followed increased the public and political profile of SEIU over recent years. Beginning with the union's earliest political campaigns in Illinois, members seem to have always known that the path to a better life requires success both at the bargaining table and in the political arena.

As the chapters that follow make clear, SEIU members transitioned from a fairly modest political involvement to become, in recent years, an incredibly effective political force. SEIU's political action committee raised less than $5 million in voluntary donations in the 1996 election cycle, and in preceding years the union had not achieved a strong record in involving members in elections.

But that began to change in 1996 when the union fielded thousands of members who pledged to spend five days on political work, such as voter registration and get-out-the-vote activities. By 2004, SEIU had deployed more than 2,000 "Heroes"—members who worked full-time on political advocacy for months in battleground states—as well as some 50,000 part-time member volunteers in the field. And SEIU made the largest investment by any single organization in the history of American politics through 2004—a total of $65 million.

And all that was a warm-up for SEIU's biggest political success to date: its role in the election of Barack Obama as President in 2008, along with Democratic majorities in both the U.S. House and Senate. SEIU backed Obama early in the primary/caucus season and ultimately put more than 3,000 members, as well as local and national staff, into 19 battleground states to work full-time during the 2008 campaign. More than 100,000 nurses, janitors, home care providers, and other SEIU members volunteered countless hours after work and on weekends to help elect Obama as President.

In addition to the grassroots impact, SEIU put some $70 million into the 2008 campaign season. From a political action committee (PAC) that ranked 35th among unions in 1995, SEIU in 2010 had one of the largest and most effective PACs in the country.

After eight years of George W. Bush and his Republican and corporate allies waging war on working people, candidate Obama promised "HOPE" and "CHANGE."

With an Obama victory, the interests and concerns of SEIU members on a wide range of issues from healthcare reform, job creation and growth, labor law reform, immigration legislation, and many others finally began to get attention in the White House and the halls of Congress.

Soon after the 2009 inauguration, President Obama began tackling the huge problems inherited from the Bush years with SEIU strongly allied with the new agenda of hope and change. At the same time, the union knew well the ability of anti-worker forces to delay and obstruct the path to progress—with millions spent by corporate lobbyists seeking to block much of the legislation advocated by SEIU.

The historic passage of landmark healthcare reform legislation in March 2010 signaled a new era. That achievement could not have occurred without the hard work of SEIU members, President Obama told Andy Stern at the signing ceremony. The victory on a top legislative priority of the union held out hope for more gains on the union's full agenda.

The struggles of today and tomorrow for good jobs, fair rules enabling workers to join unions, and comprehensive immigration reform will not be won easily. SEIU's history reveals that victories are hard won and, when achieved, come because of the union's members' willingness to sacrifice and struggle against tough odds.

Nearly 90 years ago, courageous groups of janitors in Chicago joined together immigrants from many lands to struggle for a better life. They knew that through the union came strength and a meaningful voice in the workplace.

As SEIU members today look forward in their struggle for justice for all, they draw on the lesson of the past: Victories are won because workers are stronger together.

SEIU MEMBERSHIP GROWTH
1996-2009

# CHAPTER 1

# SEIU: The Early Years
## Chicago Janitors Organize A Union

Yes, they were tired. Yes, they were angry. Yes, they were fed up.

They shouted their answers to questions put to them by 24-year-old William F. Quesse, who was—like them—a janitor in one of the many apartment buildings on the South Side of Chicago.

Tired because a janitor's official workday began before 5 a.m. and, with luck, ended about 10 p.m. There were no days off.

Angry because their pay often amounted to less than $20 a month for all the cleaning, scrubbing, painting, repairing, plumbing, carpentry, and maintenance work required for the building.

Fed up because a single complaint from a tenant could end with the janitor being fired and ordered from the premises on the spot.

Quesse's next question to the 200 or so janitors gathered that night of April 6, 1902, evoked the biggest "Yes" of all: Should they band together and form a union to fight for a better life?

Workers across America, Canada, and Puerto Rico grapple today with that same question. Many thousands also have shouted "Yes" as the Service Employees International Union (SEIU) continues to add new members who, more than a century later, still join together to win gains in pay, better working conditions, and a voice on the job.

The movement to organize service workers in North America into what is now SEIU can be traced back to that April night in 1902, even though the official formation of the union that became SEIU occurred nearly two decades later in 1921.

An effort by the Knights of Labor to unionize janitors and elevator operators in New York City had failed in 1891. But Quesse and the others who cleaned and maintained apartments, or "flats" as they often were called, succeeded. In May 1902, the flat janitors' union received a federal charter (for locals unaffiliated with any international union) from the American Federation of Labor.[1]

Much like today, the media decried the very idea that workers needed unions and ridiculed the role of the janitors. *The New York Times* editorialized back then that a janitor was "nothing more than a servant" and that assertions about his or her work having value were "laughable."[2]

Four more flat janitors' locals won federal charters from the AFL later in 1902 and 1903. During this period, many of the one million members of the AFL worked in skilled trades, such as carpentry and plumbing. Much of the support for accepting janitors into the AFL came from carpenters' and plumbers' unions that frequently complained that the janitors performed work within the apartment buildings that was in their jurisdiction. Those unions saw the organizing of the flat janitors as a vehicle to expand the reach of their own work.

The five flat janitors' unions had together a total membership of about 2,500 by 1904 and had won "working agreements" with some Chicago real estate owners. These early and modest gains led window washers and office janitors to organize, as well as elevator operators who won an agreement with the Chicago Office Building Managers Association.

Building workers in other cities also saw unionization as the answer to their own exploitation. In San Francisco, theater janitors had organized in 1902 and a cemetery workers' union had formed, while in New York City a Janitors' Society began trying to organize.

By 1905, the early gains of the Chicago building service unions led them to launch the "International Union of Building Employees"—a response in part to the interest percolating in other cities. But shortly after being chartered by the AFL and electing Charles Fieldstack, the leader of office building janitors, as president, the effort collapsed in disarray.

The AFL stepped in and within a year had dissolved the International Union and both the flat janitors' and office janitors' unions disbanded. Samuel Gompers, the AFL leader, proclaimed the International Union had been "instituted prematurely and officered poorly, and its constituent locals [were] so diverse that they were unable to successfully carry on the work of the International Union."[3]

Quesse, crushed by the implosion of the janitors' and building service workers' unions, suffered an emotional collapse. He moved to the Oklahoma Territory and worked a small farm there with his wife and brother. But by 1912 he was back in Chicago working as a janitor and holding meetings with union supporters in South Side saloons—the only venues that welcomed labor agitators.

Unlike the early flat janitors' relatively easy organizing victories, Quesse found employers pushing back hard in 1914. Janitors may have been "the people that God forgot," but the real estate moguls remembered the early union gains and mobilized the police and hired thugs in their effort to thwart new unionization efforts by the service workers.

Despite the climate of intimidation, the workers fought back with their own campaigns. One recalled the effort to win agreements from the Chicago apartment owners this way:

"Lots of things would happen. Tubs wouldn't work and something would happen to the boiler until the fellow figured he had better make peace with this crowd. It wasn't rosy by any means and Sunday School or kid glove methods were probably not used."[4]

These tactics secured the flat janitors' union enough individual deals with apartment owners that in 1916 the Cook County Real Estate Board had agreed to broader contracts that provided wage scales and a reduced workload.

When World War I began the next year, the flat janitors' union, like most of American labor, supported the war effort. To maintain war production, a federal disputes board restricted strikes and the janitors agreed to moderate wage demands as part of the patriotic spirit of the times.

As WWI ended, the U.S. political leaders rewarded labor's patriotism and restraint with an unprecedented wave of anti-union persecution. Fueled in part by paranoia over the 1917 Russian Revolution, U.S. Attorney General A. Mitchell Palmer set out to break organized labor. His hysterical efforts and those of his employer allies sought to equate unions with communism and launched a union-busting theme that continues at

The first president of the Building Service Employees International Union was William Quesse, shown here conducting a strike vote of flat janitors in Chicago.

times even today. Thousands of trade unionists were jailed and some deported.

But even in this climate, the building service workers fought back. Quesse threatened to strike in Cook County in 1918 and the union won wage increases, a closed shop, and the end of the system of forcing the janitors' wives to share their husbands' workload without pay. The union also won a permanent arbitration system. In the two years that followed, janitors accepted a wage system that linked wage levels to the rents charged in a given building.

The early years of what is now SEIU stand as a testament to a union born in struggle. Then, as today, organizing took top priority as Quesse and his fellow workers started with 200 and grew membership to 2,500 in short order and to thousands more by 1920. Then, as today, employers fought back with harsh anti-union tactics…the media ridiculed workers and unions…politicians red-baited labor and used federal, state, and local power to frustrate and forestall union organizing and bargaining efforts.

Then, as today, SEIU's forebears sought support from a broader labor federation hobbled by its own internal shortcomings. Then, as today, the union embraced the diversity of its members, many of whom were African Americans and first-generation immigrants from Europe. Indeed, unlike most AFL unions of the time, the union that became today's SEIU had African Americans in top leadership posts as early as 1916.

Then, as today, women played major roles in the union, in part because until 1918 flat janitors' wives usually were forced by employers to work side-by-side with their husbands, but received no pay or benefits other than free housing. Union members went on to choose Elizabeth Grady, a longtime organizer and leader of the Chicago School Janitresses, to be one of the first officers on the Executive Board. She held the post of trustee.[5]

The union that today is SEIU was founded officially when it received a charter from the American Federation of Labor (AFL) on April 23, 1921.

Gains for service workers resulted from struggle, just as they do today. As we have seen, SEIU's roots trace back to the low-wage workers of the early 1900s, many of them immigrants, who chose to organize and fight for economic, social, and political justice.

William Quesse continued to press the AFL for an international union charter, which finally won approval at the AFL's 1920 convention in Montreal. On April 23, 1921, the union that today is SEIU was formed by representatives from seven local building service unions. They met at AFL headquarters to form the Building Service Employees International Union (BSEIU).

## Organizing Municipal Employees

By VICE-PRESIDENT WM. McFETRIDGE President Local No. 46 of the
School Janitors

In the field of organization for workers eligible to membership in the Trades Union Movement there is not one that compares with that of the Building Service Employes International Union and of the particular branches the most likely and the one which the results are more certain is that of organizing the crafts doing our particular kind of work in all City, County, State and Board of Education bodies.

It is a fact that the Janitors, Janitresses, Window Washers, and kindred crafts are all under paid, it is certain the Cities, Counties, States and Board of Education and other Municipal Bodies should be exemplary employers paying a living wage under fair working conditions. The so-called sweat shop and piece work conditions and starvation wages are un-American and all of our tax paying bodies would not knowingly foster such conditions and wages or permit such conditions to exist if

measure brought about the local Trade Union.

This field is ready for an active organization campaign by the Building Service Employes International Union, every effort should be made to bring all of these employees into various local organizations at this time.

### "This Union of Ours"

If you don't like the kind of union,
    That this union seems to be;
If doings here are tumbled around
    A way you hate to see;
If something isn't up-to-date
    Or good as things of old,
While other unions are simply great,
    Or so you have been told;
If you would like to see a place
    That's full of push and snap—
A union that hits a faster pace,
    A union that's on the map.
Yes, if a way you'd like to know

Public employees belonged to the union from the time it affiliated with the AFL in 1921. William McFetridge of Local 46 of the School Janitors wrote here about the union's organizing campaign for municipal employees. McFetridge later became president of the entire BSEIU.

Quesse, who helped launch the flat janitors' organizing efforts nearly 20 years earlier, became the first president of the BSEIU, which had seven locals, but five of them had fewer than 150 members each. The total membership numbered about 2,900.[6]

But bargaining successes won the union a following and by 1922 the BSEIU had grown to 9,400 members. Chicago was the union's center of power, and soon the city's real estate moguls had targeted Local 1 there, as well as the International Union and William Quesse himself.

Labor's successes in the post-World War I period had been met with an incredibly aggressive pushback from employers and their political allies.

It was the era of the "open shop" with employers pushing to weaken unions in construction and manufacturing through an end to union shop provisions that required that workers in organized shops belong to the union. And the early 1920s saw tough anti-union decisions handed down by the U.S. Supreme Court and many lower courts.[7]

The Illinois Legislature established a commission to probe the building trades in Chicago during this period. Some clear cases of corruption did emerge, but the broad-brush smears against all unions there soon led to widespread beatings, jailings, and intimidation of unionists.

Quesse and nine members of Local 1 were indicted on charges of conspiracy, extortion, bombing, and "committing malicious mischief." During this anti-union era, conspiracy charges often were brought against unions. Employers and politicians argued that what in fact were legitimate and legal actions by unions constituted a "conspiracy" against the interests of employers. The building service union leaders indeed had not denied the conspiracy charge, but rather argued that their activities had not been illegal.

The jury in the trial, which occurred in January 1922, had at one point voted 9-3 for acquittal, but in the end could not reach a verdict. A retrial resulted in Quesse and his colleagues being found guilty of "conspiring to extort by threat and by boycott" the owners of apartment buildings.[8] The 10 received one-to-five-year sentences.

Quesse and the other leaders of the building service union soon realized that their organizing and bargaining victories could be weakened or negated by the power of elected judges and government officials. Between his indictment and the trial date, Quesse mobilized the union to campaign for circuit court judge candidates committed to supporting organized labor.

When the appeal of the janitors' leaders was denied, Quesse expanded the union's political action effort to include a petition drive urging Illinois Governor Lennington Small to pardon the 10 who had been convicted. Local 1 mobilized politically throughout Chicago and all of Illinois and, with the help of the Chicago Federation of Labor, succeeded in winning re-election for Gov. Small in 1924.

This was one of the first broad mobilizations of the service workers on behalf of a political candidate. It paid off. Gov.

Small soon pardoned all 10 janitors' union leaders, including Quesse, on grounds that they had been denied a fair trial before an impartial tribunal.[9]

The BSEIU soon helped form the Cook County Wage Earners' League, which played a crucial role in winning political elections and remains perhaps the best early example of the effectiveness of service workers forming coalitions with other labor and community groups to elect government officials.

The harsh attacks on labor by employers and government and the onset of the Great Depression contributed to union membership in the United States dropping from five million in 1920 to just over three million by 1932. The Building Service Employees International Union defied the trend and its membership rose above 10,000 in that period.

Nurses at San Francisco General Hospital joined the union in 1935. Local 250 won a historic master agreement with the San Francisco Hospital Conference in 1941. This early healthcare organizing was a building block in what has made SEIU the largest healthcare union in North America today.

Still, there were problems. Chicago's flat janitors Local 1, which had pioneered gains others sought to emulate, did end up taking pay cuts, while other locals in the service sector disbanded altogether. Layoffs created a ripple effect, as those who lost jobs in manufacturing flooded into the building service sector.

Local 4 in St. Louis collapsed and Locals 52 in Milwaukee and 20 in Detroit saw sharp declines. The union did show some strength in the West, with gains in San Francisco's Local 9 led by Charles Hardy and in Seattle's Local 6 led by John Rankin.

But the real growth potential lay in New York City, which continued to have jurisdictional battles among various locals. One bright spot was the window cleaners in Local 8, who proved real militancy with strikes in 1926. A year later they struck for 11 weeks and won $45 a week with a 44-hour maximum workweek and gained compensation insurance as well. As the depression took hold, though, other New York City locals had to take wage cuts and some, such as Local 14 in Harlem, even disbanded.

Just when things looked bleakest, America elected a new president: Franklin Delano Roosevelt, who took office in March 1933. He appointed pro-labor officials to key governmental posts and pushed through the National Industrial Recovery Act of 1933, which for the first time guaranteed workers' rights to organize and bargain collectively. Union organizing and bargaining until then had not been illegal, but the new legislation gave those rights legal protection.

Service workers in New York City moved quickly to seek gains in this new climate. When FDR took office, New York City janitors suffered from conditions the Chicago flat janitors endured 20 years earlier: no holidays, vacations, or even days off. Janitors in apartment buildings got only $70 a month for 84 hours of work per week. Paul Krat, the BSEIU's eastern representative, had sought to dampen infighting among locals as well as factionalism, but even Local 32 had declined to fewer than 300 members.

A pivotal moment came in March 1934 when Tom Young, a West Indian active in an independent elevator union, was fired by owners of a building at 501 Seventh Avenue because he allegedly failed to say: "Down, please." All 25 building employees struck to protest Young's firing and an organizer named James Bambrick stepped in to help them win a settlement four days later.[10]

The workers soon joined what was chartered as Local 32B with Bambrick as president and Young as vice president. Soon the tiny local made demands on the New York Real Estate Board for improved wages and working conditions, only to be told: "Who ever heard of elevator operators and porters joining a union?"

Local 32B, with $250 in its treasury, launched a strike of its 500 members in New York City's garment district on Nov. 1, 1934. The workers in the International Ladies' Garment Workers' Union (ILGWU) and the Teamsters both supported

Striking elevator operators helped found Local 32B in 1934. The local's headquarters in New York City is shown here in 1954.

the strike and some 400 buildings between 23rd to 42nd streets had to shut down.[11]

"Flying Squadrons" of about 25 unionists each would enter the buildings and encourage those inside to come out and join the union. Within three days, 32B had signed up 6,000 new members. Garment manufacturers pressured New York City Mayor Fiorello LaGuardia to intervene. Employers agreed on the spot to a closed shop, with other issues sent to arbitration. Arthur Harckham, a local union leader, called the victory "the cradle of our union."

Local 32B knew it needed to act fast to take advantage of the gains in the garment district and the new climate created by President Roosevelt. Soon the local targeted eight areas of the city, and threatened to strike in them one by one. Mayor LaGuardia would intervene and the strikes would be put off. Employers were recruiting large numbers of strikebreakers and some installed armed guards in the buildings.

The time was right for the union and momentum for organizing grew when arbitrators issued the so-called "Curran Award" guaranteeing the garment district janitors a substantial wage hike and a 48-hour week.[12] By 1936, Local 32B had grown to 25,000 members and had moved on to target workers in apartment buildings in New York City. A 17-day apartment janitors' strike led to new gains similar to those won earlier by the workers in the garment district.

Local 32B had shown that big organizing and contract gains could be won by strategic targeting and shrewd use of a political climate far more open to labor than the "open shop" era a decade before.

The big organizing gains in New York City helped propel the service employees union to a membership of more than 70,000 in the late 1930s. Some of that growth came outside the union's base of janitors and building service workers, as the BSEIU expanded members among doormen, telephone

Chicago Flat Janitors Local 1 members marched in 1958 with their brooms as part of Mayor Richard Daley's annual Clean-Up Campaign.

operators, athletic and public events vendors, ticket sellers, and others.

BSEIU President William McFetridge took over in 1940 after a scandal involving George Scalise, who briefly served as president. The union then moved to strengthen its administrative structures and tighten internal procedures. It had become a loose group of often freewheeling activists and locals, but McFetridge realized a new day had come with the gains of the Roosevelt presidency and labor's growing respect nationally.

The expansion of the union's membership base outside building services had McFetridge's full support. An important test came on the West Coast during his first year in office, when Local 250 took on the San Francisco Hospital Conference, a citywide employers group. The local had started to organize at San Francisco General Hospital in 1935, largely through a community campaign emphasizing the need for a union to push for better conditions for patients within the hospital.

San Francisco's nonprofit "voluntary" hospitals were smaller, paid better wages than San Francisco General, and fought

unions with the most vicious tactics used by anti-labor employers. But BSEIU countered with a sophisticated outreach campaign to the public that developed substantial support.

Earlier, healthcare organizing efforts at Cook County Hospital in Chicago and at Illinois State Hospital had proven unsuccessful, but the BSEIU campaign in San Francisco ended in 1941 with the San Francisco Hospital Conference yielding to the union and signing a master agreement.

This was the first such contract of its kind and laid the groundwork for SEIU eventually to become the largest healthcare workers' union in the United States.

A leader of Local 144 in New York recalled the broader impact this way:

"For almost 20 years, the only union in the United States and Canada that attempted to bring the benefits of decent trade unionism to the long-exploited hospital workers was our own BSEIU. We were the pioneers. We were trying to do the difficult job back in the days when the [other] unions didn't want to bother organizing hospital employees."

Soon, BSEIU organized healthcare campaigns in Seattle and Minneapolis. In Canada—which had developed a more progressive healthcare system and had better labor laws—the Canadian BSEIU grew substantially during this period, organizing the majority of its members in healthcare facilities in Ontario and Saskatchewan.

The BSEIU magazine featured a nurse on its cover and new campaigns emerged up and down the West Coast organized by George Hardy (who would go on to become president of SEIU) seeking to unionize healthcare workers.

By 1960, the Building Service Employees International Union had grown its membership to the 250,000 mark—a reflection of President William McFetridge's commitment to both increasing emphasis on broad organizing goals and improving the union's ability to deliver for its members.

BSEIU's post-war progress came as the union not only succeeded in organizing hospital workers in San Francisco in the 1940s, but also won new members in airports, public schools, bowling alleys, shoe repair shops, and nurseries. There also had been growth among cemetery workers and even the atomic energy staff at the Argonne and Oak Ridge atomic laboratories.

The organizing gains occurred at a time when the union also suffered some erosion of membership as technological advances resulted in some members losing jobs. Some elevator operators, for example, who were a major force in New York's Local 32B, were displaced as automated self-service elevators came on the scene in the early 1950s. At bowling alleys where BSEIU began organizing in the 1940s (gaining some 10,000 new members), "pin boys" lost jobs to automatic pinsetting machines. Ticket sellers and pari-mutuel clerks at sports events and racetracks fell victim to the advent of television, as some people began to stay home from events and, from their couches, watch them on TV. And even what appeared to be growth sectors, such as atomic energy, proved less than successful for McFetridge. BSEIU remained strong in the traditional building service sector where it added some 130,000 in the 1940s, mainly in large cities such as New York, San Francisco, Chicago, and Seattle.

A Republican Congress in 1947 passed the Taft-Hartley Act, over the objections of labor. Once again, as in the early 1920s, there was a rising anti-union climate. This time the National Labor Relations Act, enacted in 1935 as part of Franklin Roosevelt's New Deal, was amended to limit many rights workers had enjoyed. For example, Taft-Hartley prohibited solidarity and political strikes, closed shops, and secondary boycotts. It also allowed states to enact so-called "right to work" laws that outlawed union shops.

Still, BSEIU remained militantly committed to organizing and to winning gains at the bargaining table. Apartment workers in New York City achieved a 40-hour workweek after a four-day strike, for example. In addition, the union had broadened its negotiating approach to benefits—building on McFetridge's achievement in 1943 of a "death benefit plan" that paid $100 to the families of members in good standing when they died. The money came from the union treasury and by the late 1940s was the biggest expense the union had. The union program ended the old days when low-paid janitors and other service workers had to pass the hat to come up with money to help families bury their dead.

By 1951, Local 32B, led by David Sullivan, had achieved pension and welfare programs for members that paid out $2.5

million annually. The local opened a "rest home" on 21 acres outside New York City that was available free to its members. Local 1's flat janitors in Chicago offered members free legal advice as well as a credit union, scholarships, and its own death gratuity on top of the International's. More than 70,000 BSEIU members had union-provided life insurance.

In the mid-1950s, BSEIU President McFetridge had served on the AFL's "no raiding" committee during merger discussions with the Congress of Industrial Organizations (CIO). But this period saw numerous jurisdictional conflicts, often with the American Federation of State, County and Municipal Employees (AFSCME) union. Going all the way back to 1937, BSEIU leader Paul David wrote that "this organization (AFSCME) has given us continual trouble all over the country."

Despite problems with AFSCME, the union won big in 1958 in Pennsylvania, where the governor signed an executive order providing state workers with the right to union recognition. BSEIU played a vital role in getting that order and promptly, under Vice President Charles Levey, had organized six locals of Pennsylvania state employees. In California, where BSEIU membership rose to 50,000 by 1959, there were 11,600 public employee members.

As the union entered the decade of the 1960s with the achievement of 250,000 members, President McFetridge announced he would not seek re-election at the union's convention. *Business Week* magazine, often at odds then with unions, paid tribute to him as "the model U.S. labor leader." It noted: "BSEIU has achieved a record of peaceful bargaining, contract observance, and wage progress that not many other unions can equal."

# Diversity Helped Build Early Janitors' Union

SEIU today is not only North America's largest and fastest-growing private sector union, but also the most diverse.

The union was founded with the knowledge that diversity brings strength and that welcoming workers of all races without discrimination was crucial.

The Chicago Flat Janitors' union, which today is SEIU Local 1, brought together both white and black janitors in one union. Most other unions in that era excluded African Americans, or forced them to join separate black locals. The Chicago Commission on Race Relations found in 1920 that the janitors' union was one of only 4 unions out of 391 that were integrated.

In addition, the Chicago Flat Janitors' union had a vice president and three members of its execu-

tive board who were African American. Seymour Miller, the vice president, won that position in 1916. There also were stewards and delegates to the Chicago Federation of Labor from the janitors' union who were black.

At the time, the janitors' union had about 1,000 African-American members—about eight percent of all black trade unionists in the city, according to historian John B. Jentz of Marquette University's Memorial Library.[13] About 20 percent of the male janitors in 1910 were black at a time when blacks made up about 2 percent of Chicago's population. A migration from the South to Chicago added substantially to the number of blacks between 1910 and 1920, and many of them hired on in jobs where they looked to the veteran black janitors for guidance.

William Quesse, who helped found

CHICAGO FLAT JANITOR'S UNION, NO. 14332          23

EXECUTIVE BOARD

J. D. SULLIVAN          E. SWANSON          E. FOSDICK

R. L. CILLEY          WILLIAM F. QUESSE
Chairman          C. SLUSSER

C. LINDSAY          S. MILLER          ALBERT JOHNSON

the janitors' movement that ultimately became SEIU, believed the union's mission would fail without unity across racial and ethnic lines.[14] "We had a lot of prejudices of various kinds to overcome," Quesse wrote.

The first *Year Book* published by the flat janitors in 1916 quoted Quesse:

"We are an organization doing business in a courteous way; and we are composed of all creeds, colors, and nationalities, and do not allow anyone to use any prejudice in the organization...."[15]

Jentz, the historian, found that the members of the Chicago janitors' union "identified themselves not only as members of different races, but also as patriotic union janitors." Some of this evolved from the class experience shaped by the effort to achieve a labor agreement in 1917, as well as by World War I, where black troops fought in Europe for democracy and freedom while denied those values at home.[16] The union's new immigrant members also rallied around the war effort—buying Liberty Bonds and conserving coal to help with shortages due to the conflict—as a way of assimilating in their adopted homeland.

The janitors' union was not free of prejudice or discrimination, of course, but it benefited from the fact that most members did the same type of work and there weren't many gradations that provided higher status work over which conflicts might have occurred.[17]

In addition, the union not only had adopted a patriotic culture around World War I that unified members, but also had introduced elements of fraternal orders popular

---

"We do not allow anyone to use any prejudice in the organization..."

---

during that era that created a form of group loyalty—secret passwords, rituals, and easy interaction among the initiated, for example. When the Chicago Commission on Race Relations investigated a race riot that occurred there, it found that unions that excluded blacks claimed that white members objected to "close physical contact" between races. But the Commission's investigator reported this was not the case in what today is SEIU Local 1.

He wrote: "New passwords were given out [at the union meeting]. All members, white and Negro, had to come before the Negro vice president, who whispered the words to each and they in turn repeated them to him. Not the slightest hesitance was noted on the part of the white members, but rather a hearty handshake or a slap on the back seemed to be the rule... At this meeting, packed to standing-room and attended by well over a thousand members, Negroes were a large percentage of those present. These were not confined to a group by themselves, but were scattered in all parts of the hall and seemed to be in cordial conversation with the white members."[18]

The Chicago Flat Janitors, like SEIU of today, was made up of many immigrants, particularly from Germany, Sweden, Ireland, Belgium, and Austria. They came together as human beings with some ethnic chauvinism and prejudice, but united as union members with a common class experience. Alongside the union's African American members, the immigrants sought economic gains as well as dignity and respect for the work they did.

That struggle still continues.

SEIU organizer Ann Spears confronts hospital authorities in 1976. By that time, she had organized more than 1,500 members of Local 50 in St. Louis as SEIU redoubled its efforts to win gains in healthcare and the public sector.

# CHAPTER 2

# SEIU Gains Healthcare Workers, Public Employees
## Organizing, Civil Rights, Jobs Key From 1960-1990

Patches of mist hugged dormant farm fields outside Selma, Alabama, on March 21, 1965, as BSEIU President David Sullivan finished his lukewarm oatmeal and joined the column of marchers.

Sullivan had come to Selma with a wide array of civil rights supporters who planned to march to the state capitol in Montgomery to demand voting rights for African Americans and to protest violent repression of earlier marches.

Dr. Martin Luther King Jr. at Brown Chapel urged the marchers to "walk together, children, don't you get weary, and it will lead us to the promised land."[19] Sullivan joined the demonstrators as they clapped and sang and waved American flags. They passed gas stations and trailer parks where crew-cut men holding Confederate flags sat on car hoods smoking.

For Sullivan, it was important that the service employees union take a strong and public stand with the sharecroppers, maids, janitors, and so many blacks in Alabama who had shown such great courage in fighting for voting rights and equality in the face of violent attacks from the Ku Klux Klan, White Citizens' Council, and various sheriffs and other authorities.

The 54-mile march route traversed Highway 80 through Lowndes County, where 81 percent of residents were black, but not one had been allowed to register to vote. At the same time, some 2,240 whites were registered, a number that made up 118 percent of the white population of the county.[19a]

The Selma-to-Montgomery march played a pivotal role in building broader public support throughout the nation for civil rights, as Americans saw images of violent attacks on demonstrators, including killings that led up to the March 21 march.

Those events resulted in a federal court injunction that enabled U.S. Army troops to protect the marchers.

Sullivan felt proud that BSEIU joined the struggle in Selma, in part because labor had been embarrassed in 1963 when AFL-CIO President George Meany and a majority of the federation had refused to endorse the March on Washington. Walter Reuther, president of the United Auto Workers, defied Meany and led a labor contingent that included more than a dozen BSEIU locals to hear Dr. King give his famous "I Have a Dream" speech. But by the time of the Selma march, Meany had come around and the AFL-CIO officially sent top union leaders to join the civil rights activists.

BSEIU had a long history of inclusion and diversity, which at times put it at odds with other forces in labor. The AFL's Samuel Gompers, for example, had criticized the early janitors' union as too diverse when he withdrew its charter in 1905.[20] Unlike many white-dominated unions, the flat janitors had elected black leaders, such as Seymour Miller, who was the union's vice president in 1916, along with Robert Ford and E. Grigsby, who served as the union's trustee and steward respectively.

After the Irish-born Sullivan won election at the union's 1960 convention, he aligned the union with John F. Kennedy's presidential candidacy and left behind the Republican-style business unionism of his predecessor, William McFetridge. Civil rights was a fundamental issue for the union, as were unemployment and automation. Sullivan, who had led Local 32B in New York City, had seen 20,000 elevator operators lose their jobs to self-service elevators. He led the call in Washington,

D.C., for job retraining, a shorter workweek, and better unemployment benefits. "The economy needs rebuilding," Sullivan said, "not just a tune-up."

In addition to pushing the union to establish civil rights committees and pursue internal efforts to create more opportunities for minority members, Sullivan also testified in 1962 on "equal pay for equal work"—an issue that became a priority for SEIU in years that followed. The union also advocated for the Anderson-King bill, which later evolved into what's known today as Medicare. And Sullivan championed a broader scholarship program for members and their children based on College Board scores and high school records. The program proved exceedingly popular with members, many of whom were immigrants who saw education as a way for their children to have a better life.

For Sullivan, all was not smooth sailing, however, with former President McFetridge and his allies who re-emerged to create political difficulties. McFetridge apparently had believed

SEIU President David Sullivan led the union in the 1960s. He pushed for measures to help elevator operators and other members displaced by new technology, including job retraining, a shorter workweek, and better unemployment benefits. In 1965, SEIU helped win the Service Contract Act that put an end to the federal government hiring cleaners at rates lower than the prevailing wage.

Sullivan would defer to him, but the new president proved a strong leader with his own sense of a new direction for the BSEIU. McFetridge launched attacks on Sullivan for problems handling Marina City, an office and apartment complex in Chicago the union invested in as both a job creation initiative and an urban revitalization effort.

And the former union president retained his local union base in Chicago at Local 1, from which he waged a jurisdictional dispute with Local 4. That led to a labor war in the Windy City until 1965, when McFetridge finally conceded.[21] A year earlier, he had tested the waters for a run against Sullivan, but found little support.

Despite the internal strife, Sullivan and the BSEIU leadership continued to advance economic priorities after the Kennedy assassination led to the presidency of Lyndon B. Johnson. One huge victory for the union came with the passage of the Service Contract Act in 1965, which put an end to the federal government's practice of hiring cleaners at rates lower than the prevailing wage. In addition, BSEIU won protection for more than one million hospital and nursing home workers who came under the minimum wage requirements of the Fair Labor Standards Act.

Although Sullivan pushed an aggressive program of social justice on domestic issues, his strong support for the war in Vietnam caused him to come under attack from members, one of whom wrote to the *Service Employee* magazine stating: "I wish you would volunteer for combat, since you say 'that we have the men'."[22]

Sullivan prioritized the organizing of public employees as a key goal and, by 1965, more than half of the BSEIU's locals included public workers. Three years later, the union's membership topped 372,000, fueled by strong growth in California and also organizing gains in Canada. The BSEIU moved the International Union's headquarters from Chicago to Washington, D.C., in 1963.

**EXECUTIVE ORDER 10988**

**FEDERAL REGISTER**

It's Your Right
To Join
A Union

# Join the
# Building Service Union

The union supported President John F. Kennedy, who went on to sign Executive Order 10988 in 1962, which guaranteed federal workers the right to organize and bargain collectively.

By 1968, in recognition of the growing membership in healthcare and public employment, an official ceremony at the union's convention dropped the word "Building" from the official name.

From that point on, the International Union was known as SEIU, the Service Employees International Union.

When he addressed the 1972 convention shortly after succeeding David Sullivan as SEIU president, George Hardy outlined an ambitious plan to double the union's membership, which at that time was 430,000. He set the goal of adding 500,000 new members "in the shortest time possible" and expanded the organizing budget by $1 million.

This wasn't just rhetoric. Hardy personally trained

some 1,500 local union organizers and 70 new organizers on the International staff in a series of 35 weeklong organizing workshops.

Hardy knew his stuff. He started work as a janitor at the San Francisco Public Library in 1935. A foreman there dropped an unlit match behind a radiator one night and, when Hardy missed it on his rounds, the library fired him. With his father, Charles Hardy, George helped form a new janitors union, Local 87. Seven years later, with widespread organizing success in San Francisco, George Hardy began organizing for BSEIU in Los Angeles, San Diego, and all along the coast.

By 1950, Hardy had organized more than one-third of the office buildings in L.A. and won 40 percent wage hikes over a four-year period. He went on to help the union win pensions and health benefits in a number of locals, and also achieved moving many part-time jobs into full-time work. Many of the gains Hardy helped win involved public workers and those in the healthcare sector.

Working with John Geagan, who had been with the Los Angeles School Union (Local 99), and Elinor Glenn, a veteran labor organizer, Hardy competed with the Los Angeles County Employees Association (LACEA), seeking bargaining rights for 50,000 county employees. SEIU won initial elections, and in 1970 LACEA affiliated with the union.

Shortly after he arrived in Washington, D.C., in 1971, Hardy saw SEIU target Pennsylvania, where Act 195 (passed in 1970) had made possible the organizing of thousands of government employees at the state and local level. Local 668 (Social Workers) and Local 675 (Employment Bureau Workers) soon won bargaining rights for 12,000 Pennsylvania government workers. Campaigns in Scranton, Allentown, and Allegheny County added additional members, raising the total to 17,000 gained in the Pennsylvania campaign.

The Canadian-born Hardy had inherited an increasingly professional and competent union staff, built in part by Tony

Weinlein and George Fairchild, and SEIU now boasted first-rate publications, education programs, and political activists.

If David Sullivan's presidency benefited from close ties to John F. Kennedy, George Hardy faced a radically more difficult political environment created by President Richard Nixon, a strong opponent of labor.

Despite his anti-union record during the first term, Nixon ran for re-election in 1972 with the union movement in disarray because AFL-CIO President George Meany and his allies refused to support the Democratic nominee, Senator George McGovern. Meany had strongly supported the Vietnam War, even after its unpopularity spread throughout the country. McGovern, however, won SEIU's strong backing—both because of Nixon's long record of anti-worker positions and because McGovern, the "peace" candidate, promised an end to the Vietnam conflict. Despite David Sullivan's early backing, Hardy and the top SEIU leadership opposed the war.

Nixon overwhelmingly defeated McGovern and Hardy led the union in vigorous efforts to counter the Republican president's anti-worker economic program at a time when large corporations had begun to move into major sectors organized by the union, such as healthcare. Against the odds, SEIU won a key victory in 1974 when workers at nonprofit hospitals won new legislative protections under the National Labor Relations Act (which they had lost under Taft-Hartley amendments exempting non-profits from federal labor law). The union geared up hospital organizing and over the next five years held 500 hospital organizing elections that added more than 30,000 healthcare workers as SEIU members.

Gains continued in the public sector, with public employee affiliations taking place at more than one a month, often adding thousands of members at a time. Of all the AFL-CIO unions, SEIU had the highest growth rate and the top record in terms of percentage of organizing election victories.

New York City still had the highest number of SEIU

More than half of the union's locals included public sector workers by 1965 thanks to organizing efforts such as this one conducted in 1958 by Local 285 that reached out to Boston city employees.

members at 109,000 in 1976, with Chicago second at 71,000 and Los Angeles third with 68,000. San Francisco/Oakland had 42,000 SEIU members and Detroit 21,000. Local 32B in New York City merged with the women janitors' Local 32J in 1977, forming the second-largest local union in the AFL-CIO with 55,000 members.[23]

With Nixon's resignation over the Watergate scandal, SEIU saw an opportunity to regain the White House for the Democrats. George Hardy backed former Oklahoma Senator Fred Harris in the primaries, but supported Jimmy Carter in his successful campaign to defeat President Gerald Ford in the 1976 general election.

Hardy did not hesitate to blast President Carter just weeks into his presidency when he embraced tax cuts for business and decontrolled oil and gas prices (which SEIU said was "an act of aggression on the American worker").

SEIU relations with Carter deteriorated further when Carter raised the issue of a military draft registration after problems developed in Iran and Afghanistan. "I for one do not want American youth to be asked to fight a war to keep the world safe for Standard Oil and a handful of dictators," Hardy said.

In 1978, SEIU joined with the American Federation of Teachers in what was a third effort to win over New York public employees who belonged to the Civil Service Employees Association (CSEA). Many workers there wanted a union, rather than an association that often failed to represent them with vigor. The joint effort of SEIU and AFT was called the Public Employees Federation (PEF), which succeeded in winning bargaining rights over the CSEA.

Further conflicts developed, however, after CSEA affiliated with the American Federation of State, County and Municipal Employees (AFSCME). But the AFL-CIO executive council upheld PEF's right to represent New York professionals, doctors, nurses, accountants, parole officers, engineers, and other workers. PEF went on in 1979 to win a 36 percent pay increase over three years.[24]

Hardy broadened the makeup of the SEIU executive board to more directly reflect the rank-and-file membership. By 1980, the union board had 33 members and 9 vice presidents with more than 75 percent of SEIU's local union members having a direct voice on the board.

Ever the populist, Hardy took on President Carter as the 1980 presidential primaries began at a time when inflation had tripled to 13 percent, energy prices had skyrocketed, and government programs had been slashed. Hardy initially supported Governor Jerry Brown from his home state of California. Brown's effort faltered and Hardy and the SEIU executive board shifted to back Senator Edward Kennedy against Carter in the primaries. Carter prevailed but went on to lose to Ronald Reagan, despite SEIU support for Carter in the general election.

George Hardy announced his retirement as SEIU president in 1980, just as the Reagan era, with its massive onslaught against American workers, commenced. As Hardy toured the country giving farewell speeches to various regional conferences, he left them with the command:

"If they're breathing, organize them."

SEIU launched a major effort in 1982 to organize Beverly Enterprises, the nation's largest nursing home chain and a favorite of Wall Street for its big profits. The company topped earnings charts by providing poor care to many residents of its homes and poor wages and working conditions for its workers.

Working together with the United Food and Commercial Workers and the AFL-CIO's Food and Beverage Trades Department, SEIU ran a corporate accountability campaign against Beverly. Innovative public relations tactics highlighted the nursing home chain's dismal record of patient care. Shareholder actions and intervention at government regulatory hearings further embarrassed Beverly.

Elinor Glenn, a leader of Local 434 and a legendary SEIU activist, helped organize ambulance crews at Martin Luther King Jr. General Hospital in the Watts area of Los Angeles in 1973.

By 1984, the company was forced to agree that its 50,000 workers had the right to organize free of company intimidation. In the year that followed, SEIU won 70 percent of the organizing elections it sought at Beverly, but the nursing home chain continued to violate the law. First contract negotiations proved particularly difficult.

SEIU had begun the decade of the 1980s with about 635,000 members. John Sweeney, who had been president of Local 32BJ, rose to the SEIU presidency in 1980 after a brief period as the union's secretary-treasurer. Elected with Sweeney was Rosemary Trump, who became SEIU's first woman vice president at age 35. Delegates also chose a new vice president: William Stodghill, a strong leader of St. Louis Local 50 and an African American.

The union's new leadership faced an incredibly hostile environment with the onset of Ronald Reagan's eight-year presidency. Reagan set the tone eight months into his first term with the firing of 13,000 striking air traffic controllers in PATCO— an act that signaled White House support for what became a decade of union busting by corporate America. The ultraconservative Reagan and his supporters in Congress set about to cut taxes for corporations and the wealthiest Americans, while dramatically increasing military spending. Domestic programs that made up the crucial "safety net" for millions were slashed or eliminated. From 1980 to 1989, union membership in the United States dropped from 22 percent of the total workforce to about 18 percent, with industrial unions taking a big hit.

In 1981, SEIU launched a campaign to organize clerical workers and chartered a new nationwide affiliate, District 925, in a partnership with 9to5, the National Organization of Working Women. The affiliate took on Equitable Life Assurance and, after a national boycott, won a contract in 1984.

The union's real growth, however, took place in a series of affiliations of public employee associations. SEIU gained more than 160,000 members between 1980 and 1984 through such affiliations. Oregon public employees chose the union in 1980, for example, while some 80,000 state workers in the California State Employees Association voted to affiliate with SEIU in 1984. The California victory came shortly after major contract victories for SEIU's public sector unions in Pennsylvania, Oregon, and Los Angeles.

During this period, the union became active internationally when it joined FIET, a global union federation of service sector workers now known as UNI Global Union. SEIU also joined PSI, the international union federation for public and healthcare workers. The union also expanded its coalition work at home with a big victory in 1984 when the federal government ordered the removal of exposed asbestos in schools and other public facilities.

Sweeney successfully proposed the creation internally of sector-based SEIU divisions at the 1984 convention to focus the work of a union that now contained not only janitors, but also workers in the public sector, healthcare, clerical, jewelry, and other sectors.

The new divisions, created in part to deal with employers' own consolidation and restructuring, were: Building Services,

George Hardy, SEIU president from 1972-1980, conducted an organizing workshop in 1978. John Geagan (right) played a major role as the union's organizing director.

Healthcare, Clerical, Public, and Allied-Industrial. Each was chaired by an International Union vice president and directed by boards made up from leaders of the big SEIU locals in the sector. For example, Ophelia McFadden of Los Angeles Local 434 and SEIU's first woman/African-American vice president led the Public Division.

A revitalized Building Services Division demanded "Justice for Janitors" at Mellon Bank in Pittsburgh where members had been locked out of their jobs when they refused to accept a 25 percent pay cut and loss of health benefits.

Other new divisions had victories as well, such as the Clerical Division's achievement of the first neutrality agreement in the insurance industry at Blue Cross/Blue Shield and the Healthcare Division's continued gains at Beverly Enterprises where, by 1988, some 120 nursing homes had been unionized and, in Michigan, a statewide contract had been achieved.

SEIU efforts at Beverly, and also in the Justice for Janitors campaigns, represented a fundamental change in the union's approach to organizing aimed at employers that once had been primarily local but now had become regional and national enterprises. The union's shift involved combining local and International Union capacity and resources, moving to national campaigns rather than taking on employers local by local, and applying innovative, nontraditional organizing tactics.

Despite SEIU's 1985 success in Pittsburgh with janitors, the union had suffered serious declines in this period as large real estate firms had contracted out much of their cleaning work.

A union report in 1985 concluded that, while SEIU building service locals were the foundation of the International Union, "that foundation is crumbling with the potential for collapse." The document described decline of the union in every city in the country except New York, San Francisco, and Chicago. Among the problems cited:

In 1973, the 4,000-member Alameda County (CA) Employees Association became SEIU Local 616. Members gathered here during contract negotiations with the county supervisors.

- Membership losses, and stagnation, in both real numbers and as a percentage of the industry;
- Growth of commercial real estate in nonunion suburbs and the South;
- Declining wages, two-tier agreements, loss of benefits, speed-ups, and part-timing of work;
- An undocumented immigrant workforce that had proved difficult to organize;
- Growth of multinational cleaning contractors that sought to expand profits through union busting and "double breasting" with both union and nonunion workforces; and
- An increasingly anti-union environment.[25]

SEIU's building services organizing director, Stephen Lerner, found that membership declines had occurred in 18 of the 21 janitors' local unions and that wages and benefits also had dropped. In earlier days, many building owners hired their own cleaning crews and, over time, developed relationships with the union. In the 1980s, the real estate owners began

SEIU President John Sweeney (left), elected in 1980, joined with United Food and Commercial Workers President William Wynn to announce the start of a campaign to organize the nation's largest chain of nursing homes, Beverly Enterprises, in 1982.

to subcontract janitors' work to companies that specialized in cleaning and often strongly opposed unionization.

The nature of the workforce also shifted, with the cleaning firms hiring fewer African Americans and whites and more Latino immigrants. SEIU, which had a positive history of inclusion and diversity, was slow during this period to communicate with and involve the new and expanding Latino/immigrant workforce.

Locals tended to devote organizing resources to the healthcare and public employee sectors, where wage levels and job stability were higher and where potential membership gains were larger.

SEIU President John Sweeney's 1984 restructuring included a mandate to invest more union resources in organizing. A few months before, he chose a young union leader from Pennsylvania, Andy Stern, to spearhead SEIU's expanded organizing effort. Stern had been president of Local 668, the Pennsylvania Social Services Union (PSSU), and earned a reputation for molding it into an innovative and militant local. He had become president of SEIU's Political Council in Pennsylvania as well, which had 45,000 members statewide.

With organizing's importance acknowledged through new SEIU funding, Stern took on the organizing job aware that it had not been a high-stature role within the union.

"Organizing new workers into unions was underfunded and undervalued," Stern later recalled. "Over time, union organizing became a low-prestige function.... Promotion, power, and glory came from being a tough bargainer and fighting for existing members who voted in union elections."[26]

With Sweeney's support, Stern set about to elevate the role of organizing and of organizers within the union. SEIU began to promote organizers who succeeded, and the union broke down old rules most other unions continue to follow by hiring young college graduates as well as rank-and-filers as organizers. Talented organizers from other unions were recruited and hired, too. Some of the new approaches succeeded and some did not, but there was a fresh willingness to explore new ideas and tactics and throw off old rules that had led to stagnation.

SEIU's ability to bluntly admit weaknesses, such as the 1985 report on the deterioration in the janitors' locals, laid the groundwork for big changes in the union's organizing strategies. "Starting from scratch and saying what we were doing was a failure gave us the freedom to look for innovative new ways to build power, leverage and beat contractors and real estate corporations," said a 1993 analysis by the union's Building Services Division.

The union adopted what became known as the "Rebuilding Resolution," which outlined a new organizational framework and set division bargaining guidelines and standards for what SEIU wanted to achieve. Local union leaders gave their approval to the resolution, and even those who lacked interest in the revitalized set of actions and goals could not afford to publicly oppose them.

The Rebuilding Resolution called for:

- Rebuilding membership support: gaining full, active, and militant support for the new janitors' campaign;
- Organizing the "new" workforce: learning how to organize immigrants, undocumented workers, and emerging minorities;
- Targeting organizing efforts: determining how the union gains real leverage in markets locally and nationally, so it can better negotiate wage and benefit levels;
- Achieving contracts through new strategies and tactics to exert pressure on employers;
- Gaining public support: SEIU cannot win without community backing; and
- Finding the resources to rebuild: International Union and locals must commit major resources to support organizing.

Three significant victories in the 1984-1987 period gave a boost to the new strategies Sweeney and Stern had started to implement.

First, the new Justice for Janitors campaign cited earlier brought support for striking janitors in Pittsburgh where a business group led by Mellon Bank interests sought a 25 percent cut in pay and a loss of health benefits for 400 members of Local 29. With the support of building service locals around the country, SEIU won a huge victory—a victory that showed the nation the union could still win contract fights for existing members even in a tough economic climate.

With so many workers being forced to make concessions in the industrial heartland, SEIU had shown it had the will and the fight to win at the bargaining table for its members, even if it was forced to strike.

Two other victories—one in Denver, the other in San Diego—proved the union could regain ground. SEIU had lost its master contracts in both of those medium-sized cities, but regained its membership base and those master agreements without going to National Labor Relations Board elections.

The revitalized organizing effort saw new tactics as well that employed creativity to win broader support within the community for the low-wage, increasingly immigrant workforce. In Denver, for example, an SEIU organizer dressed as Santa Claus paraded in the lobby of a large corporation proclaiming the disappointment the janitors' children would have when they didn't receive any presents due to the firm's low pay. With the union's victory there, the next holiday season was far sweeter for those kids.

In other campaigns, the union honed its ability to create a "David and Goliath" clarity that the struggles were about the rich and powerful versus the have-nots of our society. Large amounts of time and money went into building public support and sympathy for the union's organizing efforts to bring low-wage workers together so they could bargain for a better future for themselves and their communities.

Militancy, creative campaigns, resources, and citywide strategies weren't always enough. SEIU tried to organize Atlanta in 1987-88, but failed. The campaign sought to unionize

SEIU members at San Francisco Chinese Hospital held signs in Mandarin that combined to read: "Chinese Hospital employees agree to join union [Local] 250."

about 1,300 janitors citywide. Most were African American and about 70 percent were women with pay rates of about $3.50 an hour with no benefits.

The union targeted properties owned by John C. Portman Jr., a developer famous for hotels with atrium lobbies, such as the Hyatt Regency in Atlanta and the Bonaventure in Los Angeles. About 200 Atlanta janitors worked for companies to which Portman subcontracted janitorial work.

When SEIU leafleted at Peachtree Center, made up of a shopping mall and six office towers, Portman's management company sought and won an injunction from a Georgia state court that severely restricted the union's ability to reach out to janitors at the complex. SEIU filed charges with the National Labor Relations Board, which much later found that Peachtree had violated the union's right to organize.[27]

Internally, some Justice for Janitors staffers had argued to defy the injunction, but in the end SEIU obeyed it. A 1990 analysis of the failed Atlanta campaign and other Building Services Division internal reports contrasted that decision with the later success of the crucial Los Angeles campaign in 1990 dur-

Doctors have been an important part of SEIU membership for years. Here Dr. Howard Hu and Dr. Tony Schlaff are shown trying to "revive" a dummy representing Boston City Hospital.

ing which the union defied court injunctions.

In Atlanta, the union had a potential pressure point with 1988 Democratic Party's national convention scheduled there, but blinked when political heat was applied by top Democrats to SEIU President John Sweeney and union leaders. Andrew Young, then mayor of Atlanta, negotiated with the union, which agreed to limit protest events. An SEIU spokesman told reporters that Sweeney "decided he did not want to do anything that would hurt Mayor Young or the DNC" (Democratic National Committee).

Portman, a self-styled "progressive" business leader of the New South, used his leverage with the growing business wing of the Democratic Party, which emphasized fundraising over grassroots political organizing. He ultimately prevailed, despite some visible protest activity by Justice for Janitors at the Atlanta convention that nominated Michael Dukakis as the Democratic presidential candidate.

Despite the failure in Atlanta, SEIU organizers moved on to the campaigns in San Jose/Silicon Valley and Los Angeles having gained valuable knowledge about what was necessary to impact building owners. The union also had won valuable public attention for the janitors' struggle and some credibility with real estate firms that had seen the union's energy and militancy, even in a failed effort.

During this period, key union officials, particularly Organizing Director Andy Stern, had become convinced of the importance of unionizing an entire labor market.

When he and Stephen Lerner of the Building Services Division met with unionized employers, they heard one line over and over: "You guys can't protect the wage." The firms with SEIU contracts were losing business to the nonunion operators expanding their work into more and more buildings where they paid the minimum wage with no benefits.

"Our priority should be to contribute to our employers' success by organizing all of their competitors," Stern later wrote

An SEIU Local 105 organizer leafleted outside Mile High Stadium during a Denver Broncos football game in 1987.

in his book, *A Country That Works*. "Only then would we be able to bargain contracts that set the same minimum standards for all the competing employers and thus take wage differentials off the table.

"Either we brought up the wages and benefits of all the workers in the market, or the nonunion workers' wages and benefits were going to drag down the standards of all the workers."

Unfortunately, even companies with an enlightened and sophisticated public image often refused to work with SEIU, despite its willingness to understand the competitive realities

those firms faced in the marketplace. Apple, the computer firm now famous for the iPod and iPhone, strongly resisted SEIU organizing efforts to unionize janitors in Silicon Valley/San Jose in the early 1990s.

Union pickets and hunger strikes put pressure on Apple, as did a full-page ad in *The New York Times* highlighting charges of sexual harassment against the cleaning contractor at Apple's buildings. That pressure, combined with SEIU's outreach to Apple's European pension fund investors, finally forced the company to accept that it was responsible for the working conditions and wages of its contracted janitors. The union signed up a majority of those janitors and successfully negotiated a contract. More organizing gains followed with close to 2,000 high-tech janitors unionized in the San Jose area in 18 months.

SEIU earlier had trusteed three locals in the area and then combined them into one. Under new leadership, the local established an effective community coalition. The organizing successes that followed the Apple campaign grew out of the local's very public civil disobedience in support of the organizing and also through use of a variety of litigation strategies that nearly bankrupted targeted cleaning contractors.

L.A. SHOULD WORK...

FOR EVERYONE

JUSTICE
for
JANITORS

HOSPITAL AND SERVICE EMPLOYEES UNION LOCAL 399
1247 W. 7TH STREET • LOS ANGELES, CA 90017 • 213 680-9567

# CHAPTER 3

# Janitors And The Battle Of Century City
## SEIU Rebuilds Base, Hits One Million Members

As the decade of the 1990s opened, SEIU's effort to regain lost ground for janitors in Los Angeles began on the Olympic Boulevard bus that went from Century City to Pico Union each day at 2:30 a.m.

"It was the janitors' private bus," recalled Jono Shaffer, an SEIU organizer on the Justice for Janitors campaign in 1989. "There sure wasn't anyone else on it, and it was the one place where they could talk freely about their jobs."[28]

SEIU, which had about 5,000 members working as janitors in Los Angeles in 1978, had won contracts by 1982 that pushed wages above $12 an hour and provided full health benefits. But building owners had begun a rush to subcontract cleaning services at nonunion wages of less than $4 an hour with no benefits.

The shift to a hyper-competitive market resulted in new nonunion firms entering the business, while union companies also set up nonunion subsidiaries to compete.

SEIU soon found itself struggling to survive after the last L.A. master agreement was reached in 1983 and membership had sunk to about 1,500. A building boom had transformed the market in Los Angeles, and even downtown Local 399 had only about 30 percent of the workforce in the late 1980s.[28a]

The new SEIU effort in Los Angeles focused on Bradford, a nonunion firm eventually acquired by American Building Maintenance. SEIU Local 399 won a master agreement there in April 1989, which was the first such contract in downtown L.A. in six years.[28b]

The next Justice for Janitors campaign focused on Century City, the commercial center on the West Side of Los Angeles bordering on Beverly Hills. Fancy law firms, corporations, and film and television companies had offices there cleaned by some 400 janitors employed by nonunion cleaning subcontractors. One of those, the Danish-owned ISS, employed 250—making it the center of SEIU's efforts.

The location was somewhat self-contained, which worked to the union's advantage. In addition to riding the bus together, many of the janitors would gather at the single lunch truck that came at mealtime. The geography of the buildings worked to provide a fairly easy opportunity for organizers to make contact with janitors.[28c]

Most of the Century City janitors were Latinos, some from Mexico and others from El Salvador and elsewhere in Central America, a region many had fled during conflicts there in the 1980s. Soon rank-and-file activists and union organizers began a series of marches and demonstrations that signaled the workers' dissatisfaction. Usually, these noisy encounters involved chants, beating on drums, and aggressive activities not particularly welcomed by the business executives operating in the buildings' fancy offices.

The union did a Secretary's Day action during which thousands of carnations were passed out to the secretaries who worked in Century City offices, saying thanks, in effect, to other relatively low-wage workers who had been inconvenienced by earlier protests. All the action led to tenants complaining to the building owners about the unrest.[28d]

In May 1990, having made little headway with the building owners and the subcontractors, including ISS, SEIU took a strike vote. After announcing the results in newspaper ads, the janitors walked. For days they tied up traffic and marched through the buildings, which prompted the Los Angeles Police Department (LAPD) to declare a citywide tactical alert.

The Century City struggle's turning point came on June 15, 1990, when Justice for Janitors held a peaceful march from Beverly Hills to Century City. About 100 police wielding batons attacked the 400 or so janitors and supporters at the intersection of Olympic Boulevard and Century Park East. LAPD officers engaged in a police riot, seriously injuring about 25 people, including a pregnant woman who miscarried after the attack.

The protestors had sat in the middle of the intersection expecting to be arrested. But rather than an orderly, peaceful arrest process, the LAPD waded into the group and began hitting demonstrators with their batons. Those who attempted to get up were knocked back to the ground. Soon LAPD officers had called for backup, and dozens more arrived to do battle.[28e]

Most of the fray was filmed by numerous TV cameras as reporters looked on. Bob Baker of the *Los Angeles Times* reported that "several officers ignored calls from supervisors to stop charging the demonstrators."[29] About 40 peaceful protestors were arrested. Sgt. William de la Torre, an LAPD spokesperson, told reporters after the attack that police had "reacted with quite an amount of restraint." (Less than a year later, that same LAPD brutalized Rodney King with repeated blows by baton that were captured on videotape and led to two officers being sentenced to prison terms for their violence.)

Justice for Janitors organizers feared the aftermath of the police attack might have an intimidating effect on the struggle. But instead of staying home, the workers turned out in force. "It was just, that's it. They cannot treat us like this when we didn't do anything," wrote Rocio Saenz, an SEIU organizer at

Century City who went on to become president of SEIU Local 615 in Boston.[30]

The police riot enraged many across the country and especially in Los Angeles, where an even broader group of clergy and community leaders as well as elected officials gave new support to the union's struggle. The janitors adopted the United Farm Workers' rallying cry, "Sí Se Puede" (Yes We Can), long before it was used in President Obama's 2008 election campaign.

In the end, the Century City janitors won their fight.

> The janitors' struggle became the subject of the movie *Bread and Roses.*

The janitors' struggle at Century City—and their victory—became the subject of a major feature film directed by Ken Loach entitled *Bread and Roses.* It brought the Justice for Janitors story to a wide audience throughout the world a decade later.

Los Angeles, the city where the union had its greatest loss of membership and deepest contract concessions at the end of the 1970s and into the early 1980s, had been a successful test of SEIU's ability to organize where the workforce had shifted rapidly from African American to Latino. Janitors were able to win raises, health insurance, and other benefits, and were able to demonstrate that the union could halt the cleaning firms' expanded use of double-breasting (creating nonunion operations alongside their unionized units).

In L.A., SEIU didn't hesitate to spend money on the organizing program and to commit substantial research and organizing staff, many newly hired, to the challenge.

A key to the Century City outcome was the expansion of coordinated activity by other SEIU local unions, particularly Local 32BJ in New York, which had a bargaining relationship with ISS, the multinational based in Denmark. The firm was fully unionized in its home country, but viciously anti-union where the opportunity presented itself, such as L.A. Without pressure from Local 32BJ, it's unclear whether or not the union could have forced ISS to yield to the Century City campaign.

Led by Gus Bevona, 32BJ seldom used its power on behalf of other union locals. An internal union report in the early 1990s said that "our inability to get Local 32BJ to take the lead in using its leverage to support organizing around the country as well as in New Jersey—its own backyard and jurisdiction— has cost the union literally tens of thousands of members. It is a real question as to how long the local can maintain its power and standards, as the rest of the country continues to lag farther and farther behind."

But L.A. proved an exception (as did Washington, D.C., later). The support from 32BJ, other SEIU locals on the West Coast, and the intervention of the Danish unions pressuring ISS on its home turf, all contributed to the reorganizing of Los Angeles by the union's Justice for Janitors campaign. ISS and Bradford together represented 3,500 janitors, and others at American Building Maintenance and other big cleaning contractors followed.

The Century City win bolstered those who argued SEIU could take bold action across entire markets and didn't have to be limited to organizing a few buildings and janitors at a time.

While SEIU was winning organizing victories in Los Angeles, San Jose, and elsewhere in the early 1990s and adding tens of thousands of new members through affiliations in the public sector, much of the rest of American labor found itself in decline. Eight years under President Reagan's anti-union policies followed by another four years of George H.W. Bush had weakened the union movement.

The healthcare crisis had deepened and SEIU President Sweeney, who had chaired the AFL-CIO's Health Care Committee since 1984, pushed the union into a leading position as an advocate for reform of the nation's healthcare system. Companies such as Hospital Corporation of America (HCA) had begun offering nonprofit hospitals their brand of "for-profit" management services. Kaiser Permanente, the prominent nonprofit HMO, repeatedly took on its employees, leading to a strike at virtually every SEIU-organized Kaiser facility in the country starting in the mid-1980s.

By 1989, some 37 million Americans had no health insurance—and two-thirds of the uninsured were employed. Experts estimated that nearly 100 million people in the United States were underinsured.

Employer-based healthcare over the years had been a standard benefit for many workers, particularly those with union contracts, but that system began to erode as Republican-inspired "free market" competition helped lead to runaway inflation in the cost of health insurance.

Hospital organizing was plagued by delays in the election process due to employers contesting the makeup of bargaining units in most cases. But in 1991, the U.S. Supreme Court unanimously rejected objections by hospitals to new NLRB unit determination rules, making it easier to organize hospitals—one of SEIU's biggest legal victories.

SEIU's healthcare membership jumped by more than 50,000 in 1989 when certain districts of District 1199 outside New York City that earlier had been part of the Retail, Wholesale, and Department Store Union (RWDSU) voted to affiliate. An earlier round of merger talks in the early 1980s failed because of internal strife within RWDSU.

In 1973, District 1199 had established itself as the semi-autonomous National Union of Hospital and Health Care Employees (NUHHCE) under the militant Leon Davis, who had a reputation for aggressive organizing and left politics. NUHHCE became a "union within a union" and gained more autonomy from the RWDSU, which had retail clerks as its base. Davis supported the idea of one healthcare union for all healthcare

Century City janitors, fighting for the right to join SEIU, suffered violent attacks from Los Angeles Police Department officers in 1990.

workers and had talked with SEIU President George Hardy in the 1970s about some form of merger with SEIU.

By 1981, with 1199/NUHHCE's greater autonomy from RWDSU, a merger referendum was held with more than 75 percent of the healthcare members voting in favor of talks with SEIU that could lead to a dual affiliation for them. But RWDSU leaders trusteed 1199/NUHHCE on the grounds of "dissension," and the hopes of merging with SEIU's healthcare sector were put off. In the aftermath, 1199/NUHHCE disaffiliated from RWDSU and became independently chartered by the AFL-CIO in 1984.

The vote by key districts of 1199 to join SEIU in 1989 added healthcare workers in 12 states, the District of Columbia, and Puerto Rico. Other 1199 districts representing about 25,000 workers affiliated with AFCSME during this period.

The membership growth in the healthcare sector, the huge expansion in public employee affiliations, and the Justice for Janitors victories all poised SEIU for the incredible achievement of reaching one million members. On a fall day in 1991 in Miami, a nurses' group of Haitian, Jamaican, Puerto Rican, Filipino, Nicaraguan, Cuban, African American, and white backgrounds boosted SEIU over the million-member mark.

The success of SEIU with the achievement of one million members unfortunately was not replicated by the American labor movement, which under AFL-CIO President Lane Kirkland continued to decline in numbers and clout. Kirkland, a protégé of George Meany, had succeeded him in 1979 and presided over the long, slow decline of the labor federation.

In the industrial heartland, plant after plant closed. Other companies shook off years of decent labor relations with their unions and, taking a page out of Ronald Reagan's PATCO book, made contract demands aimed at forcing strikes. The workers then would be permanently replaced and the companies would operate nonunion going forward.

Kirkland chain-smoked cigarettes using a long yellowed holder and was prone to withering dismissal of colleagues, reporters, and anyone he disliked. His indifference to the plight of member unions in steep decline contrasted with his abiding interest in pursing an anti-communist agenda on the international stage.

SEIU's victory at Century City helped spark renewed organizing of janitors across Los Angeles and elsewhere in the early 1990s.

A supporter of the Vietnam War, Kirkland played a key role in the AFL-CIO's refusal to campaign for Democratic presidential nominee George McGovern in 1972. Later, he aligned with conservatives and neo-conservatives in forming the Committee on the Present Danger, which campaigned for large military budgets. The AFL-CIO did support the *Solidarnosc* movement in Poland, an act for which Kirkland deservedly won credit. But in many other countries, American labor was viewed with hostility for alignment with right-wing politicians and governments that often suppressed worker movements. Under Kirkland, the AFL-CIO and its various units spent more on international affairs than on organizing, civil rights, and worker health and safety.[31]

The election of Bill Clinton as U.S. President in 1992, after 12 years of Republican control of the White House, held out hope for a reversal of labor's decline under Kirkland. But during the crucial moment when a bill was under consideration on Capitol Hill that would have banned permanent replacement of strikers, Kirkland was off in Europe—a symbol for his critics of indifference to the bread-and-butter concerns of American workers.

The story of the SEIU janitors' victory at Century City became a feature film starring Adrien Brody and Pilar Padilla in 2000.

The labor movement during this period made a strategic miscalculation in delaying the legislative push for labor law reform and accepting President Clinton's proposal in 1993 to establish a study commission instead. Made up of management, labor, and government officials, the commission was chaired by John Dunlop, a Harvard law professor and noted labor expert. It took up the issues of workplace labor-management cooperation and labor law reform.

The Dunlop report did find that workers who exercised their rights under the National Labor Relations Act (NLRA) often ended up being illegally fired by employers and that about one-third of the workplaces where workers voted to join a union ended up without a collective bargaining agreement due to employer tactics. While major elements of the commission report underscored labor's case for reform of labor laws, business had no interest in making it easier for workers to join unions.

Instead of a broad consensus on reform, the Dunlop commission served to delay and diffuse the political effort to update labor laws. Meanwhile, employers continued to violate the rights of workers who sought to join unions. The delay disappointed many, including SEIU leaders and members, who had hoped the first Democratic president in 12 years would have used his clout to push labor law reform forward. (By missing this opportunity, the issue languished for more than 15 years until legislation known as the Employee Free Choice Act began to be debated as a serious option after the election of Barack Obama as President in 2008.)

For workers who had hoped for progress through the ban on permanent replacement of strikers and broader labor law reform, some disillusionment set in. Then came President Clinton's inability to move healthcare reform and his energetic push to pass the disastrous North American Free Trade Agreement (NAFTA), which was strongly opposed by labor.

In 1994, Democrats paid the price with huge losses at the polls that left both the House and Senate under Republican control.

A group of union presidents of major AFL-CIO affiliates, including SEIU President John Sweeney, began to meet privately to discuss the need to reinvigorate the labor movement, starting with replacing Kirkland. Presidents of the United Auto Workers, Teamsters, United Steelworkers, AFSCME, United Mine Workers, and other unions approached Kirkland, then age 72, and urged him to retire and clear the way for AFL-CIO Secretary-Treasurer Tom Donahue to move up. Kirkland refused and attempted to dig in. He blasted the dissidents as disloyal to him and to the concept of labor solidarity.

The union presidents formed a "Committee for Change" and decided to run a candidate against Kirkland at the federation's 1995 convention. Donahue, unwilling to oppose Kirkland, resigned as AFL-CIO secretary-treasurer, and the next day Kirkland announced he would once again be a candidate for the AFL-CIO presidency.

Under the "New Voice for American Workers" label, the Kirkland opposition made clear it wanted "an organizing president" to replace him. Rejecting AFSCME President Gerald McEntee as too polarizing, the group settled on SEIU's Swee-

ney. It soon became likely that the New Voice slate of Sweeney, Richard Trumka of the United Mine Workers, and Linda Chavez-Thompson of AFSCME would have the majority of votes at the federation's convention.

Sweeney's New Voice slate called for spending $20 million to put thousands of new organizers in the field to try to regain lost ground. They sought a "Sunbelt Organizing Fund" to expand unionization of the growing Southern and Western workforce. Taking a cue from SEIU's own organizing successes, Sweeney proposed not only a separate organizing department for the AFL-CIO, but also a "Center for Strategic Campaigns" that would bring the federation a new capability to wage corporate accountability campaigns.

The New Voice forces chose a young SEIU activist named Anna Burger to manage their campaign. Picking up additional support from some smaller unions and from central labor councils, the Sweeney forces embraced the expanded organizing effort and also a more effective political action program in the wake of Republican gains in the 1994 elections.

With the New Voice for American Workers slate gaining the backing of 21 unions representing 56 percent of the del-

AFL-CIO President Lane Kirkland (right) was pushed out in 1995 after devoting his energies to an anti-communist agenda abroad rather than building union strength in the United States. Kirkland talked here with President George H.W. Bush.

egates to the AFL-CIO convention, Lane Kirkland announced he would resign effective August 1, 1995. With Kirkland out, former Secretary-Treasurer Tom Donahue jumped into the race, but his moment had passed.

A former Local 32BJ activist, Donahue embraced some of the New Voice program after being selected as Kirkland's replacement until the convention in October 1995. But Sweeney and his New Voice allies continued to run a skillful campaign, picking up crucial support from state federations and central labor councils.

At the convention, Sweeney won the support of 34 unions with delegates representing 57 percent of the AFL-CIO's membership. It was a victory that held out great hope for a reinvigorated American labor movement that would put new resources behind organizing and political action.

And it left a vacancy in the presidency of SEIU.

Profits!

Dignity
Rights & Respect

act Now!

NION

EVERLY
BARGAIN
NOW

• jobs

SEIU Unity Pact
Locals 250, 399, 535

Dignity
Rights & Respect

NEW VOICES
for SEIU

Andy Stern, who had been fired as organizing director when he decided to run
for SEIU president, won broad grassroots support for his candidacy in 1996.

# CHAPTER 4

# 1996: Andy Stern Elected President

## 'Our Choice Is Simple: Organize Or Die'

As John Sweeney departed SEIU for the presidency of the AFL-CIO, he pushed successfully for SEIU Secretary-Treasurer Dick Cordtz to run the union on an interim basis for four months until the SEIU convention in April 1996, when delegates would elect a new president.

Cordtz, an old-line labor leader, had worked at Del Mar racetrack near San Diego where he joined SEIU and later became head of Local 79 in Detroit until elected to the union's number two position in 1980 along with Sweeney.

To many, Cordtz seemed like a leader for another time— one who might have been right for an earlier period in the union's history, rather than a figure who could build on the innovations of the Sweeney presidency. Cordtz's critics proved right, as he immediately moved to undo a number of reforms that had taken the union to one million members and a leading role in the American labor movement.

Andy Stern, then an International Union vice president (and, as director of organizing, the key strategist for many of its organizing successes), watched Cordtz and pondered his own next move.

"I was now at a personal crossroads," Stern recalled in his book *A Country That Works*. "I could continue on as organizing director and try to help SEIU move in the direction I thought was best. I could support others who were considering running," he wrote.

"I could 'wait my turn' and try to succeed President Dick Cordtz when he decided to retire. I could resign my position and leave SEIU. Or I could risk my career by running for president."

Stern and other top staff feared the direction Cordtz had charted would stall or reverse SEIU's strong momentum. "Many of us were participating in a process called the Committee on the Future at the time," Stern later recalled. "The future we were envisioning and recommending on that committee and the future with Dick Cordtz as our leader really could not be harmonized in our minds.

"I realized that, if I was not successful, the 23 years I spent in the SEIU would be over and I would no longer be welcome," he remembered. "This was a winner-take-all experience."

Stern and a like-minded group of SEIU activists analyzed the politics of that moment. Anna Burger, Tom Woodruff, Celia Wcislo, Debbie Schneider, and Mary Kay Henry were among the core group sizing up the campaign against Cordtz, who had begun to offer Stern various "deals" if he would agree not to run.

On the eve of an important meeting of SEIU leaders in the western states where locals representing more than one-third of the votes in the union election would be present, Stern made up his mind. If he did not go to California and seek support at the meeting, Cordtz might lock up critical backing from those western leaders.

Stern decided to seek the union presidency.

Unlike corporate America, where CEOs have tremendous power over workers and communities yet no accountability to them, trade unions operate under laws requiring that leaders— from local unions to executive boards and top officers—must be elected.

When rumors of Stern's candidacy surfaced, Cordtz put

aside the niceties of "may the best candidate win" and immediately fired Stern. A union politician of the old school, Cordtz sent a message with the firing to SEIU staff and leaders that anything but total loyalty to him would not be tolerated.

Making the message even clearer, Cordtz sealed shut Stern's office at union headquarters with yellow police tape.

"They fired me when I was out of the office, locked the door, put police tape across it, and made it very clear—particularly for the staff in the building—that I was never returning," Stern later recalled. "To the senior staff, they made it clear that the same fate awaited them if they chose to support me."[32]

Stern returned home to tell his wife and two young children, Matt and Cassie, that he'd lost his job for a time, but planned to seek Sweeney's old position of SEIU president.

"Daddy," his son Matt asked, "Are we going to have to sell the house?"

Stern reassured him and Cassie they would not, but "in my heart I knew that a defeated, dissident candidacy was not a resume builder."[33]

Sweeney had pushed Stern to support Cordtz and was upset that an orderly transition to his longtime friend had not gone forward.

"Everybody appreciated what John Sweeney had done for SEIU, but he also had positioned himself with one foot in each world," Stern said later. Sweeney had pushed the union in a more modern, activist direction as evidenced by the Committee on the Future. But he also moved slowly and with deference to old guard local leaders who resisted any hint of infringement on their virtual total autonomy.

Meanwhile, Stern barnstormed the country and Canada meeting with local union leaders and rank-and-file workers, many of whom were impressed with his program and his personal energy. Many of them saw Cordtz as a candidate who wouldn't really be continuing Sweeney's agenda, but rather as someone who would return SEIU to an earlier era.

On the morning of his first executive council meeting as AFL-CIO president, Sweeney attempted to cut a deal with Stern: let Dick Cordtz serve two years of the four-year term and then he'd resign and clear the way for the young SEIU leader. It didn't fly.

The "compromise" not only would have been unenforceable, but it also signaled that Stern's campaign had real momentum. In hospital corridors, public employee cafeterias, and janitors' union halls, members heard Stern's ambitious plans to expand organizing and political action. They heard others running on his slate describe the need to confront employers at the bargaining table in new and smarter ways and to take on right-wing, anti-union politicians in the voting booths.

Stern's grassroots support far outmatched that of Cordtz, who saw union politics in a more standard way. Cordtz followed the traditional path to the SEIU presidency, which was to seek support from the powerbrokers who controlled the four geographic conferences of SEIU: the eastern, central, and western states plus Canada.

"They just presumed that everyone inside of each conference would follow the direction of their conference president," Stern said later. "They kind of missed the fact that between 1950 and 1996, SEIU added hundreds of thousands of healthcare and public workers who did not understand those were the rules.

"Those members decided they were going to support who they wanted, not who they were told to back," Stern recalled. "That was a different understanding that Dick Cordtz and the old school did not quite get: the union had changed."

To his credit, Cordtz knew when he didn't have the votes. He withdrew his candidacy shortly before SEIU opened its 75th anniversary convention in Chicago.

Delegates from across the United States, Canada, and Puerto Rico elected Andy Stern SEIU's ninth and youngest president on April 21, 1996.

In his convention speech, Stern was gracious to Cordtz and praised Sweeney for all the two had achieved. But he struck a more militant and energetic tone.

"We are the ones who stood our ground against baton-wielding police on the streets of Los Angeles, and who got arrested on the bridges in Washington, D.C., to defend every worker's right to a living wage," he said.

Stern pledged to the delegates: "I will kick open every door and make sure that, regardless of the color of your skin or whether you are gay or straight, regardless of the language that you speak, your country of origin, your age, or your gender, you are welcome in SEIU!"

After working as a welfare caseworker in Philadelphia, Andy Stern became an assistant shop steward for the Pennsylvania Social Services Union, which was SEIU Local 668. Stern rose to leadership there and won some of the longest strikes in public sector history in Pennsylvania. He became SEIU's organizing director and went on to be elected president of the entire union in 1996.

The new president said that "we are up against some of the most powerful corporations on this planet; corporate giants that salute no flag but their own logos; that worship no god but the almighty dollar; and honor no obligation but their bottom line.

"In the name of maximizing profits, they will downsize their workforce, drive down wages, imperil our health and safety, and pollute our political system without a second thought. And these corporate giants have no qualms about squeezing exorbitant executive salaries out of working people's paychecks," Stern said.

Stern described what he called the **"Bold Action"** program. "There's only one way we can build the power to deliver for our members—and that is to organize the great majority of workers in our industries," the new SEIU president argued. "Our choice is simple: Organize or die."

The expanded organizing effort required resources—the large dollar amounts needed could come in part from reallocating the union's resources at all levels, Stern believed.

"If every local commits more resources to organizing, we will have $45 million more to recruit and train the best organizers in North America from the ranks of our members and from wherever we can find people with the energy and the anger, the courage and commitment to organize whole industries, to get the job done," he told delegates.

A second element of the Bold Action plan focused on politics. Like many public workers, hospital employees, janitors, and others, Stern had tired of politicians seeking union support and then walking away from labor's agenda when it came time to vote.

Politicians, he said, are going to have to act like they're our friends and vote like they're our friends, and not just talk like they're our friends. "Our members have permanent issues and permanent interests, but no permanent friends," he told the delegates. "We're not going to let one party write us off and another party take us for granted."

"We're going to use the power we have, the power of persuasion—and if that doesn't work, we're going to use the persuasion of power...and turn up the heat until the politicians see the light."

The third Bold Action challenge the new president put to the union was to find innovative ways to involve the rank-and-file membership in everything SEIU does. The union must develop fresh leadership and a plan "to make this a union that listens and learns and leads. We need to involve the members of our union in the organizational decisions that affect them—we need to stop wringing our hands and start extending them."

Delegates responded overwhelmingly by embracing the changes Stern outlined, including many recommended by the union's Committee on the Future. They also elected Betty Bednarczyk as secretary-treasurer and three leaders to newly created executive vice president positions: Eliseo Medina, Pat Ford, and Paul Policicchio.

Back at union headquarters at 1313 L Street NW in Washington, D.C., after the 1996 convention, Stern entered his new office (unimpeded by police tape) and sat looking out the windows. He reflected about how difficult it seemed to be in Washington for leaders of all sorts to remember whom they were really there to serve.

He said later he felt an enormous sense of responsibility for the one million members then in SEIU. All of the late-night talk of the past among friends and allies about leaders taking risks and setting priorities could not be ignored. "We had no one to blame anymore but ourselves," he said.[34]

"I thought about the janitor who works in the building across the street, cleaning its offices and bathrooms," Stern recalled. "He has no idea who we are, but every two weeks he sends a small part of his hard-earned paycheck to our union, hoping that we will improve his life.

"Our job is to wake up every morning and find ways to make his life—not ours—better. SEIU's mission is to live up to his trust."[35]

# SEIU Uses Art As Path Into The Union

More money for organizing was critical to the union's growth, for sure, but SEIU in 1996 also invested in a creative approach to building the union—a lively arts and cultural program. The SEIU Greenhouse program run by Nina Shapiro-Perl used an array of arts—music, photography, theater, film, storytelling, and more—to give voice to the lives and struggles of members and to bring their stories to the larger public. It recognized that the arts not only inspire people to action, but are a path into the union—a way of involving people who might otherwise not be active. The traditional sounds of labor songs such as *Solidarity Forever* were still heard at SEIU events, but the soundscape now included hip-hop, Latin, and world music—a reflection of the new and varied cultural programming being created by and for SEIU members.

One of the first projects was *Tales from the Trenches*, a video capturing the stories of member-organizers. When New York's 1199 affiliated with SEIU, the Greenhouse program entered into a partnership with 1199's Bread and Roses program, which had been created in the 1970s to merge art and social justice concerns. The first collaboration was the 1999 SEIU Women of Hope calendar, showcasing photographic portraits of courageous women from both inside and outside the labor movement, such as novelist Toni Morrison and Native American activist Wilma Mankiller. It was the first of a series of SEIU Social Justice Calendars featuring works by a diverse range of artists and marketed broadly within the progressive community.

Over the years, members got training in how to use photos, video, and other digital media to tell their stories in their own voices. One of the most exciting projects began in New York, with 100 donated cameras, volunteer professional photographers, and students who wanted to show life from their own perspective as home care workers, migrant workers, taxi drivers, restaurant workers, and other service sector employees. They took moving and provocative pictures, and had their work exhibited in venues ranging from union halls to county courthouses. The project spread to locals throughout the country, with members in Ohio, Wisconsin, and elsewhere taking part. In 2005, 300 of the images were published as the book *unseenamerica: Photos and Stories by Workers*.

Like the wider culture itself, SEIU's arts program continually evolved. By 2010, much of the work had shifted to a relatively new program in the union, called Popular Media Organizing. Its mission was to connect popular culture and the labor movement in new and compelling ways. In 2008, that included teaming up some of Hollywood's politically progressive television stars with SEIU activists who also were volunteering in the Obama campaign. Instead of the actors simply making speeches at a rally, they were out door-knocking in neighborhoods. It was a novel way to create buzz about support for Obama—and a way to get even more SEIU activists motivated to do some door-knocking, just like the stars.

SEIU leaders and members march in a 1997 strike action in California.

# CHAPTER 5

# SEIU Shifts Big Resources To Organizing
## Local Unions Adopt 10-15-20 Percent Plan

As the new leadership team took over in 1996, the union and the broader world soon found they really would force big changes. Andy Stern's goal of SEIU spending the majority of dues income on organizing required reallocation of the union's resources at all levels.

At the Washington, D.C. headquarters, Stern eliminated six departments and cut 22 management positions. Some 144 national office staffers were told they would continue to have jobs, but most had to transfer to the field where the organizing action would be. The health and safety department, for example, went from 22 staff down to 2. Education and research services popular with local unions were slashed—again with staff being offered transfers to field work. A hiring freeze was implemented.

"Nobody had done anything wrong," recalled Tom Woodruff, who had become the new director of organizing. "People were working hard. All the work they did was important. But the labor movement was dying, and to keep doing the same things was not a correct response to impending death."

The fairly radical changes occurred after consultation with the staff unions, but the decisions provoked anger among some. In December, Stern invited the headquarters staff to an informal holiday reception in his office.

"Staff, wearing black armbands, delivered their RSVPs and sang not very flattering Christmas carols about what they saw as my lack of holiday spirit," Stern remembered. "Personally, it was difficult to put my colleagues on the headquarters staff through so much anxiety so quickly after my election.

"But reorienting SEIU was not about either my life or the staff's," the SEIU president wrote in his book *A Country That Works*. "It was about the lives of our members."

Stern faced an early challenge as SEIU fought to organize janitors in Washington, D.C. In 1995, about 3,500 janitors in the nation's capital, most of them cleaners in federal office buildings, were SEIU members and had union contracts.

But thousands more janitors who cleaned commercial office buildings there were in a tough position. They had struggled for years to unite with SEIU to win wages and benefits that would lift them out of poverty. But their effort to win a citywide master contract met strong resistance from the D.C. commercial real estate industry.

The D.C. Council had been cutting funding for crucial city services and was considering favorable property tax treatment for the very real estate owners and managers opposing the janitors' attempts to win a better life.

The janitors responded with one of the most daring direct-action campaigns in years. Not once, but three times in 1995, SEIU janitors and their allies blocked rush-hour traffic on the 14th Street and other major bridges leading into D.C. from suburban Virginia. The blockades snarled traffic for hours, got the janitors called a lot of nasty epithets such as "transportation terrorists," and even led to a congressional hearing.

They used other direct-action tactics as well, including marches and sit-ins at major traffic intersections in downtown D.C. And they swung into political action, launching a successful ballot initiative providing for a fairer property tax appeals process for commercial property owners. But the janitors still found themselves without a citywide master contract.

The logjam was broken in 1996, shortly after Stern took over as SEIU's top officer. He reached out to D.C.'s commercial building owners and agreed to a "moratorium" on the union's direct-action activities.

The city's non-union cleaning contractors then began negotiations with the union. Those talks, finally, led to the victory the janitors had fought so many years to win—the first-ever master agreement, covering 5,000 janitors in D.C.'s commercial building industry.

As SEIU expanded the number of organizers and developed focus on its core sectors, the new leadership made clear its guiding operating premise: The union must organize substantial new membership in its core industries, such as healthcare, building services, and the public sector, in order to have the strength to win bargaining gains from employers and political gains, such as healthcare reform and job opportunities, from government.

Prior to the 1996 convention, SEIU had spent two years discussing where the union should be headed and at the Chicago convention had adopted the report of the "Committee on the Future." Created by John Sweeney, the committee had been chaired by Betty Bednarczyk, who then served as the union's secretary-treasurer.

Among the committee's basic findings submitted in 1996:
- Union density had peaked in 1953 at 35 percent, with more than 40 percent density at that time in the private sector and less than 10 percent in the public sector;
- Density at the end of 1995 had fallen to 14.9 percent, with 12 percent in the private sector and over 30 percent in the public sector;

- As a result of that decline, living standards for most U.S. workers were eroding;
- Income was declining for the bottom four quintiles of the population, with income increasing for only the top quintile;
- 60 percent of all new jobs created in the United States between 1979 and 1995 paid less than $8,000 annually;
- Average wages adjusted for inflation were lower than they had been in 1959;
- The number of workers covered by health insurance and pensions was declining;
- Other worker benefits, such as vacations and holidays, also were declining;
- Parents were spending 40 percent less time with their children than their parents had spent with them;
- Meanwhile, corporate profits had risen 118 percent since 1980; and
- CEO pay soared 536 percent since 1980, but the average factory wage dropped 8 percent, and the value of the minimum wage declined 15 percent from 1980 to 1995.

> ## Reform at the local union level was crucial.

The unwritten social contract following World War II had been broken. Between 1945 and 1975, average compensation rose with productivity, so that real increases in living standards were accomplished. Then, between 1975 and 1995, productivity had continued to rise equal to the previous period, but worker pay became flat and eventually fell.

A poll of SEIU members at the end of Sweeney's presidency showed that members rated the union quite high on trying hard, but quite low on accomplishing what to them was the most important union task: raising wages and standards. Some 83 percent said that they would vote to keep the union—on the surface a comforting statistic for the leadership. But members polled had reached that conclusion not because they thought the union would win improvements, but because they feared conditions might worsen without the union.[36]

The Committee on the Future had outlined some grim realities, but by facing up to the situation, the new leadership felt a better future could be charted. Key to Stern's change agenda was reform at the local union level. Many locals over time had become amalgamated general unions made up of a mix of healthcare workers, public employees, janitors, jewelry workers, etc.—all joined in one local. SEIU's new leaders began discussing the need to reorganize each around one sector and focus on that, so janitors and building services workers might be in one local union in a given geography, while public workers would be in a second local, hospital workers in a third, and so on.

SEIU's Bold Action program adopted at the 1996 convention called upon the local unions to spend 10 percent of their post per capita dues revenue on organizing in 1997, 15 percent in 1998, and 20 percent in 1999. Only *actual* organizing expenses could be counted, such as payroll for full-time organizers and real expenses for organizing. Other expenses were *disallowed*, such as a percentage of elected officials' salaries, even though they spent time on organizing, and a percentage of office rent, even though organizers worked out of those offices.

The shift of local dues income to organizing created some turmoil among local SEIU leadership. They had been elected by members to their positions—and union leaders, like any and all politicians, worry about their own re-elections, their bases of support, and what the new future might hold for them.

## In 1997, 81,000 new members joined SEIU.

Stern later recalled:

"When we thought about change, the good news was there had been a blueprint created by a committee that John Sweeney had created called the Committee on the Future. And it talked about how every local union needed to have an organizing director—how he or she had to build resources for that organizing plan...how our locals had to come together and have a united industry strategy."

"So we had a lot of the blueprints in front of us, but we had lots of resistance from our major local unions that never were for the [Committee on the Future] report or for my presidency and those locals posed a huge threat to whether or not we could really do this."[37]

But by the end of 1997, more than 86 local unions had run organizing campaigns. Using innovative strategies developed by Tom Woodruff and Mary Kay Henry, SEIU had won 81,000 members—58,000 newly organized and the remainder by affiliations.

One of those early organizing successes came about because of SEIU members such as Bridget Lewis, a certified nurse aide at St. Therese nursing home in Minneapolis.

"When we're short-staffed, we're told to prioritize, but how do you tell people who can't brush their own teeth, wash their own body, or go to the bathroom by themselves that you can't help them, because you've got to prioritize?" Lewis asked.

She got some answers from Julia Grantham, an SEIU Local 113 member organizer, who took a leave from her job as a nursing home dietary worker to work on the union's Twin Cities nursing home campaign in 1996-97.

St. Therese workers had tired of short-staffing at the nursing home and had formed an organizing committee. Their first public act was to present a set of ground rules to Sister Bernice Ebner, CEO of St. Therese, calling on management to respect workers' rights to organize without interference.

Sister Bernice had been around for the defeat of two union drives in the previous five years, and she defiantly responded that she "knew the rules" already.

"You don't understand, Sister," the organizing committee leader responded. "These are *our* rules."

Grantham learned about unions when she was nine years old. Her parents, both members of the United Auto Workers, called her into the kitchen. A strike loomed, they told her, and that bike she wanted might not be coming for her birthday. "At first I was upset," the Local 113 member organizer said. "But when my Dad explained why they had to go on strike—for a good contract and better wages—I understood," she recalled.

Grantham, another member organizer named Mary Rosas, and SEIU staffer Becky Belcore joined Bridget Lewis and other St. Therese nursing home workers to celebrate a 222 to 91 organizing victory. They had stood up to mandatory meetings where managers portrayed the union as an interfering third

party and threatened layoffs and worse if SEIU won the election. The late Senator Paul Wellstone (D-MN) had come to Local 113's big rally and told workers how proud he was that they were organizing the unorganized.

The St. Therese victory in 1997 symbolized the aggressive new mood of SEIU under the recently elected leadership team. The International Union had a small but strong core of experienced organizers and researchers, but now SEIU deployed them to train and develop local union members to go out and unionize their fellow workers.[38]

Gloria Santos, for example, was a 45-year-old single mother and Local 535 steward in California where she worked at the San Marcos Head Start program. Union leaders spotted her there and recruited her for a member organizer role, which she took reluctantly because she cared for two children and a grandson, worked a second job, and attended classes at California State for a sociology degree.

Santos answered the call in 1996 to go to Houston for two weeks to assist Local 100 in an organizing blitz among 1,000 Head Start workers. "She was irreplaceable," recalled Orell Fitzsimmons, a local union organizing director in Texas at the time. "Every time she went out, she signed people up."

Born in Mexico, Santos moved to the United States when she was 11, so her bilingual skills and her job as a Head Start worker herself impressed those she contacted in the worker-to-worker union card sign-up program. The result: Houston Head Start workers voted by a 13-1 margin to join SEIU in January 1997.[39]

Similar victories occurred around the country as SEIU organized more than 17,000 workers in the first five months of 1997. Thirteen local unions won campaigns at some 30 nursing homes with more than 3,000 new members, exceeding 1996's full-year tally of 2,400 new members organized in the nursing home sector under the union's "Dignity, Rights and Respect" campaign.

## SEIU ORGANIZING REPORT
## JANUARY – DECEMBER 1997 TOTALS

| REGION | IA | BS | HC | PS | TOTAL |
|---|---|---|---|---|---|
| EAST | 1,521 | 806 | 6,827 | 2,420 | 11,574 |
| CENTRAL | 502 | 1,245 | 6,699 | 1,980 | 10,426 |
| SOUTH | | | 903 | 5,505 | 6,408 |
| WEST | | 1,270 | 4,334 | 19,766 | 25,370 |
| PUERTO RICO | | | 266 | 918 | 1,184 |
| CANADA | 1,858 | 100 | 1,629 | 153 | 3,740 |
| SUBTOTALS | 3,881 | 3,421 | 20,658 | 30,742 | 58,702 |
| AFFILIATION | | | 23,000 | | 23,000 |
| TOTALS | 3,881 | 3,421 | 43,658 | 30,742 | 81,702 |

In addition to the member organizers, SEIU had seasoned veterans charting strategy. John Carter, for example, took a leave from his job as an executive board member of Local 1199RC and helped to organize the Nortonian Nursing Home in Rochester, New York. Other talented organizers in District 1199NE helped win victories in Hartford and Stamford, Connecticut.

SEIU's 1996 convention delegates had renewed the union's strong commitment to organizing and mandated that the International Union spend 45 percent of its budget on organizing—some $25 million in 1997 alone.

When Stern took over as president, the union had been devoting about 27 percent of per capita dues paid to the International Union to organizing, or about $18.8 million.[40] The real money in SEIU then remained with local unions, which kept about 80 percent of dues paid by members. Local union revenue in 1996 amounted to $352 million, but very little of that went to organizing.[41]

A number of local unions had met the convention goal to spend 10 percent of their budgets on organizing in 1996 and 15 percent in 1997 with the program looking ahead to 1998, when they sought to devote 20 percent to organizing. SEIU reported in September 1997 that some 94 local unions, representing more than 600,000 members, had been spending at least 15 percent of their budgets on organizing.

One incentive for locals to participate in the 10-15-20 program was a policy that authorized a 25 cents per member per month rebate to the locals that complied. But locals needed to submit organizing plans and budgets to the International Union each year—something that had never been done before.

This created an ability for Stern and his leadership team to better coordinate how the core divisions of the union interacted with local unions that had launched organizing efforts. Stern inherited a situation in which most SEIU locals were small and amalgamated, with members in a variety of different types of work at different employers in a particular local area. Indeed, of the 373 locals in existence in 1995, 218 of them had fewer than 1,000 members. In Illinois, where the union was founded, building services workers, such as janitors and doormen, were divided among three locals, for example.[42]

"We had more staff dedicated [in 1997] to organizing in the locals than at the International," Stern said at the time. "We had hundreds and hundreds of members who volunteered their time to help bring new members into SEIU, because they understood that this is the only way we are going to build the strength to improve their own wages and benefits."[43]

GRAY DAVIS GOVERNOR
Experience That Will Move Us ... Forward!

GRAY DAVIS GOVERNOR
Experience That Will Move Us ... Forward!

SEIU played a major role in electing Gray Davis as governor of California.

# CHAPTER 6

# Building An Issue-Based Political Program
## SEIU Wins Big In California In 1998

The membership poll brought bad news. SEIU leaders were off to a good start with a revitalized organizing program in 1997. And the initial effort to restructure local unions had begun. But as they turned to politics, the survey research showed a difficult task ahead.

Only 34 percent of SEIU's membership agreed that helping to elect candidates who take pro-worker positions on issues should be a priority for the union. And only 37 percent of stewards polled shared that view, while 64 percent of the top local union leadership saw politics as a priority.

The union published the results in its magazine and noted: "The numbers demonstrate some of the challenges of building a member-based political program."

On a more positive note, 71 percent of the members polled agreed that "working people can take on the system and fight for change" and 69 percent said they believed that "who gets elected directly affects my life." These findings planted seeds for change.

At the union's International Executive Board meeting in Miami Beach, Florida, in December 1996, Stern had argued that organizing could not be effective alone, because the political context in which it occurs often would determine the union's success.[44] Steve Rosenthal, then the AFL-CIO's political director and a skilled campaign strategist who later would help expand SEIU's political efforts, conducted a briefing for the board on the 1996 presidential and congressional elections. Board members, virtually all of whom were major political players in their states (and in Puerto Rico and across Canada), departed the meeting with a sense that much more would have to be done to make SEIU a political powerhouse.

Stern had set a tone at the 1996 convention with his speech pointing out that "in the world of politics, we have no permanent friends, only permanent issues." He had told delegates: "That's why we must build a strong, issues-based political program driven by grassroots action and beholden to no individual or party."

Eight years earlier, Stern had attended the Democratic Party convention in Atlanta. He had seen Democrats kick off the event with a party for dignitaries at the home of John Portman, a prominent architect and real estate mogul who had fought bitterly to keep workers employed at his properties from joining SEIU. Democratic leaders, instead of pressing Portman to accept unionization, pushed then-SEIU President John Sweeney into calling off what they thought would be embarrassing picketing at the Portman party.

"We left with hollow and vague promises to help resolve the janitors' dispute," Stern recalled. "Those promises didn't survive the week."

Stern believed that Democrats by far did more to support worker issues than Republicans and said his personal voting record was overwhelmingly Democratic. But he liked to quote Martin Luther King Jr.: "In the end, we will remember not the words of our enemies, but the silence of our friends."

As his administration set out to build a more vigorous member-based political program, Stern and many local union leaders had been critical of President Clinton's welfare changes, the push for the NAFTA trade deal, and particularly the failure to achieve the crucial healthcare reforms advocated by labor. Republicans, of course, came down vigorously on the wrong side of such key SEIU issues, but too many Democrats did as well.

"Democrats have left me frustrated with their weak and disparate voices about issues of work, and their failure to define themselves as a party that stands squarely on the side of American workers," Stern later wrote. "Everyone knows what defines Republicans: free enterprise, a strong national defense, less regulation, smaller government, corporate interests, social conservatism, and individual responsibility."

"Can voters as easily define the Democratic Party's core beliefs?" he asked.[45]

Other SEIU activists shared similar views. One official put it this way: "Too often we had made contributions in money and sweat equity to elect supposedly friendly politicians, only to receive a couple of tickets to the Inaugural Ball and then very quickly the shaft."[46]

The new SEIU leadership again turned to the Committee on the Future for the blueprint on which to build a revitalized political program. It had urged SEIU to:

- Stop relying on individual politicians or political parties to look out for workers—they abandon labor on too many issues, such as NAFTA, healthcare reform, and the right to strike;
- Ground SEIU's new political program on the issues members identify as important to them and their families; and
- Involve members more fully in every stage of the political process.[47]

A process began of refashioning the criteria under which SEIU made political contributions. The new focus: support candidates who believe strongly in workers' right to unionize and seek tighter commitments around a growth agenda that empowers workers' voices in their daily lives.[48]

Many SEIU workers, and many nonunion workers the union sought to organize, relied on government-funded programs for their jobs, such as nursing homes and hospitals paid through Medicare and Medicaid, state- and federally funded

home care and child care workers, the Head Start program, and so on. They needed to back politicians who would support and expand funding for such programs and defeat those who wanted to gut them.

SEIU got a nice victory in Rhode Island in 1997 when the state adopted the strongest legislation in the nation at that time to limit the number of for-profit hospitals in the state. The law barred Columbia/HCA, the nation's largest for-profit hospital chain, which SEIU sought to organize, from acquiring yet another acute-care public health facility, the Roger Williams Medical Center in Providence. Such wins helped members understand the important links involving political action that end with elected officials—in this case state legislators—who enact laws that benefit the public and working families.

SEIU raised less than $5 million in voluntary donations for its political action committee (PAC) in the election cycle that followed. The SEIU PAC ranked 35th compared with other labor unions' PACs. Union leaders knew the political program would have to do better if SEIU's influence and reach were to expand on the issues important to its members.[49]

The union had fielded thousands of members who pledged in 1996 to spend five days on political work, such as voter registration and get-out-the-vote activities. Just as the core of SEIU's organizing effort was built around member organizers, its new political effort would be based on MPOs—Member Political Organizers. SEIU launched its plan to "build a standing army of 10,000 trained and active members who will work on political campaigns, lobby for legislation that improves our lives, and talk to union members and our neighbors about the issues that concern us all." MPOs had to volunteer six hours a month to such activities, as well as coalition building in their communities and raising money for the union's Committee on Political Education (COPE), the political action committee funded by voluntary contributions from members.

Donald Chapman became a member political organizer in

Philadelphia, where he worked as an office building lobby attendant and belonged to Local 36. He devoted one Saturday a month to knocking on doors in Philadelphia neighborhoods encouraging people to register to vote. "I'm convinced that once you build a grassroots organization and stick to your agenda, you can really make a difference," Chapman said. "You simply listen to what people say about the problems they have and you explain how politics relates to it. Most people get it."

SEIU's political prowess under the new leadership faced one of its first big tests in California in 1998. Business interests and their conservative political allies had hired a huge army of paid signature gatherers to force a vote on Proposition 226—an anti-union initiative designed to silence the voices of working families. The measure would have required unions to get annual written permission from each member before using union dues for political action purposes. It would have stymied worker efforts to fight for legislative gains on health and safety, and against cuts in public services, workers' compensation, and other programs.

While the language sounded modest, the so-called "paycheck protection" initiative would have created a bureaucratic nightmare for unions—requiring them to contact every member virtually every time a campaign or political/legislative issue resulted in union expenditures. At the same time, corporations and nonlabor advocacy groups would remain free to spend without comparable restrictions, such as asking shareholders for approval before spending money on politics. With corporations already outspending unions 11 to 1 in the political arena, costly new bureaucratic limits on labor hardly seemed fair.

Richard Mellon Scaife, the quirky far-right multibillionaire, and Grover Norquist, a skillful conservative organizer who ran Americans for Tax Reform, raised more than $500,000 for the proposition, which they said would "crush labor as a political entity." SEIU and most of the AFL-CIO affiliates feared that a

win for Prop. 226 would give a strong boost to similar efforts in other states.

Eliseo Medina, SEIU executive vice president for the western region of the country, was a veteran of California politics going back to his early days as a top organizer and strategist for Cesar Chavez and the United Farm Workers union. He ran SEIU's political opposition to Prop. 226.

Just four months before the vote, Medina and SEIU local political activists confronted a very bleak political landscape: Support for the measure stood at a daunting 71 percent, while only 26 percent told pollsters they opposed it. Medina knew that labor would lose if the Prop. 226 effort remained a "sound bite" campaign with proponents arguing, "Who could be against allowing union members to exert control over how their dues money was spent?"

SEIU and other unions launched an intensive, well-organized member contact program through leafleting, phone calls, mail, and one-to-one meetings. Polling and focus group research helped hone the union message, and it began to resonate first with members and then with the broader public.

When the vote occurred in June 1998, Prop. 226 failed by a 54-46 margin, with the voters rejecting the effort to cripple unions by cutting off union funds for issues such as education, politics, and legislative work. In just four months, the work of some 10,000 SEIU volunteers and those of other unions had pulled off a political miracle.

*The Washington Times*, a conservative newspaper owned by the Rev. Sun Myung Moon, couldn't believe the outcome. It wrote:

"Those who campaigned heavily for Proposition 226 spent much of yesterday trying to explain how they could have blown a 50 percentage point lead in four months to lose by six points on election day."

Medina noted that opposition to the anti-worker initiative came from labor, but also from the broader public—reaffirming

SEIU's commitment to build strong allies among a wide range of organizations. Environmentalists in the Sierra Club backed labor, for example, as did the Heart and Lung associations and the League of Women Voters, which provided needed third-party validation for labor's position.

"We have sent a loud and clear message that working people want unions involved in the political process to counter the hidden—and the not-so-hidden—agendas of the monied interests," Medina said as SEIU locals celebrated the victory.

The victory in June gave the union momentum as it approached the general election in November 1998, particularly in California where SEIU supported Gray Davis, the Democrat seeking to become the first worker-friendly governor in that state in 15 years.

SEIU over the years made only modest political contributions to candidates and was not known for the size of its political action committee fund financed by voluntary contributions from members. But in support of Gray Davis, SEIU took a huge step: The union donated $1 million to his campaign, as well as providing local union activists to work for him because members

SEIU President Andy Stern joined Gray Davis on the campaign trail in 1998. As Governor of California, Davis supported pro-worker legislation.

believed his policies would change people's lives for the better. Grassroots political support and SEIU funding helped Davis to be competitive in the face of well-financed opposition from big business.

The union saw that it was crucial to have worker-friendly officials at all levels of government as a way to achieve policies and programs to benefit the broader public and also to win recognition and good contracts for workers in the public sector. SEIU had sought to unionize home care workers in California (and around the country) for 10 years or more, yet had not made needed progress.

A study by professors at Rutgers cited SEIU's support for Gray Davis as crucial to the union's growth agenda. It quoted a staff member of the International Union on the watershed moment for the union's political program:

"We gave Davis a million dollars, and that was the biggest contribution we have ever made. This was a fundamental shift. Up until then, we had done contributions the old-fashioned way, but this was a move to make a significant contribution to a governor—in this case to try to create the political environment we needed to allow what ended up being 110,000 home care workers to organize in California.

"We had organized home care workers for 10 years in the state, but we needed to come to terms with the fact that they were dependent upon a political solution. We had to play much more in the political world."[50]

SEIU's efforts in the 1998 elections paid off not only in California with Gray Davis becoming governor, but elsewhere as well. The New York State Council played a critical role in the upset win of Charles Schumer over incumbent U.S. Senator Alfonse D'Amato. SEIU members in Washington State helped elect Patty Murray to the U.S. Senate and passed Initiative 688, which not only raised the state minimum wage, but also tied it to inflation, so it rose substantially during the long period when the federal minimum wage remained stagnant.

In 1998, Anna Burger became SEIU's executive vice president for the eastern region. In that role, she marshaled union support in Maryland for pro-worker Governor Parris Glendening. Burger had begun as a rank-and-file member—a state caseworker in Pennsylvania and an activist in SEIU Local 668. She rose through the ranks to become its first woman president and helped launch the union's organizing efforts at Beverly Enterprises in Pennsylvania. She also served as executive director of the Pennsylvania State Council.

She was called to Washington, D.C., to serve as Sweeney's assistant for programs and field services, and in 1995 the SEIU president tapped Burger to manage his successful *New Voice* campaign for AFL-CIO president. She served as assistant to SEIU President Stern and as a member of the union's International Executive Board. A highly skilled union and political organizer, Burger had been a delegate to three Democratic conventions and held a seat on the Democratic National Committee at the time she became executive vice president.

Burger, daughter of a nurse and a disabled Teamster truck driver, would become the SEIU secretary-treasurer in 2001 and chair of the Change to Win federation in 2005, making her the highest-ranking woman in the U.S. labor movement.

After the 1998 elections, Stern was asked by Reba Heath, a member of Local 1984 in New Hampshire, about the union's political momentum. Stern said that "we didn't expect the election night news to be as good as it was" and called the results "another victory for our new approach to political action.

"Instead of just letting political parties define the issues, we ran our own campaign on issues our members care about: patients' rights, Social Security and Medicare, and education," Stern noted. "Instead of just making endorsements from on high, we involved thousands of working people in a grassroots campaign. And on election day, 24 percent of all voters came from union households—up from 14 percent in 1994."

"This was a major reason for the defeats of many anti-worker candidates," Stern said.

In the three years after the SEIU Committee on the Future had set goals for revitalizing the union's political program, it was clear the union no longer simply relied on making political donations to friendly (but often unaccountable) politicians and telling its members how to vote.

Instead, the successes achieved in 1998 at the ballot box came from a revamped SEIU political program, which was based on:

- building the union's political infrastructure closer to where its members live: at the state council and local union level;
- changing the way SEIU communicates with members about politics, so that they got helpful information about candidates and issues, rather than directives about who to vote for;
- changing the union's endorsement process to get members more involved in screening and endorsing candidates— which in turn increased their motivation to go out and actually vote for those candidates;
- increasing voluntary political donations from members, so that SEIU had the resources to help the candidates who support members' issues; and
- recruiting and mobilizing thousands of SEIU members to get involved in politics as member political organizers (MPOs).

Hart Research, a polling firm, found a significant jump in voting by SEIU members for pro-worker candidates in the 1998 elections. Their survey in 1994 reported that 62 percent of SEIU members voting in races for the U.S. House of Representatives cast ballots for pro-worker candidates. In 1998, that figure jumped to 77 percent.[51]

The increased SEIU backing was even greater in the Gray Davis gubernatorial race in California, Hart Research found. In 1994, 62 percent of the SEIU vote went to the Democratic candidate, while in 1998 a stunning 92 percent voted for Davis.

**SEIU** *Cooks!*

SERVICE EMPLOYEES INTERNATIONAL UNION GIFT CATALOG

SEIU worked on creating an institutional identity in part by adopting the color purple along with a new logo and other forms of branding. Members could order shirts, hats, bowling equipment, and cooking gear—in purple—from SEIU gift catalogs like this one.

CHAPTER 7

# The Color Purple
## SEIU's Branding Creates Union Identity

With SEIU's organizing successes mounting in the first two years of the Stern administration, the union still remained without much of a public profile. With more than one million members in 1997, SEIU should have been a union frequently at the center of public debate. The joke was that the union wasn't SEIU, it was "SEI-Who"?

Simply put, there was no "SEIU" brand—the union mainly was a collection of local unions with different names, most of which did not even include the word "SEIU." You had the Maine State Employees, the Hospital and Health Care Workers, Oregon Public Employees, the Committee of Interns and Residents, the Sindicato Puertorriqueno de Trabajadores (Puerto Rico), and so on. Of the 370 locals in 1997, there were 144 different names.[52]

With a lot of amalgamated locals used to nearly total autonomy, there were hundreds of different logos from union to union. For years SEIU had developed a new union logo for each convention, and locals were free to adopt it or keep their old logo. This ended in hundreds of different designs and no sense of commonality. Workers lacked the collective power of their larger movement if the public and politicians did not understand they spoke from a broad, diverse, but unified base of union members.

Other unions, such as AFSCME, had adopted a color that people identified with them—AFSCME's green T-shirts frequently could be seen en masse at its demonstrations and rallies, for example. SEIU had no "official color" and its rallies, while impressive in turnout and fervor, lacked visual theme.

"It was no surprise that I was constantly barraged by our own leaders as to why SEIU's name recognition was so low, compared to the Steelworkers', Auto Workers', or teachers' unions," Stern recalled, explaining that the lack of name recognition weakened the workers' impact in the public debate.

SEIU set a process in motion quickly to develop a "branding" strategy for the union: a common name, logo, color, mission statement, and slogans. The branding team rejected the idea of changing the union's name as too costly, so it pushed the idea of just using the abbreviation SEIU that conveniently fit well on a bumper sticker.

Designs were commissioned for a new logo from five different artists who produced 276 different options that were tested in focus groups of members, stewards, and leaders. But the team ultimately recommended a logo with a stylized path leading to a sun that had been designed by Mackie Lopez, an SEIU communications department staffer.

For a color, the union considered three, but ended up with purple—not just any purple, but Pantone 268c as the specific *shade* of purple that later would grace hundreds of thousands of T-shirts and printed materials produced by SEIU. "Every time people see jackets, T-shirts, or caps, they will recognize SEIU from the color before they see the name," a report on the change in *SEIU Action*, the union magazine, said. It noted that green, red, and blue already were identified with other unions and therefore had been ruled out in favor of purple.

The International Executive Board adopted many of the branding recommendations, but did so knowing the importance of locals buying in to the changes. To ease the transition, the IEB allowed locals to use their own names along with

"SEIU," but required that SEIU be most prominent.[53]

A group of Rutgers professors who studied the SEIU's organizational changes from 1996 to 2009 interviewed one local leader who had been unenthusiastic early on about letting go of old ways. "I was skeptical at first," he said. "But now I am amazed at how effective it has been in making us feel like one organization."[54]

To make it easier for locals to adopt, the International Union produced a starter kit with materials providing exact colors and logo copies. Each local got a supply of letterhead and banners, and three regional printers were contracted by the headquarters to produce materials for locals with the new names integrated into the new logo. SEIU also chose a central vendor to do T-shirts so as to maintain the same purple theme throughout the union.

Stern himself began regularly wearing purple shirts as part of the effort to infuse an institutional identity with brand loyalty. Soon the union magazine offered a huge variety of SEIU purple products—from purple bowling balls to purple umbrellas, megaphones, clothes, and so on.

At the time, it probably was hard for SEIU activists to know just how widespread the impact of the branding would be. SEIU had become the "purple union" and, as it grew in size and militancy, more and more purple T-shirts were seen in demonstrations and strikes around the United States, Canada, and Puerto Rico.

"Once a movement of rust brown and steel gray, Big Labor is increasingly represented at rallies and political conventions by a rising sea of purple," *The New York Times* noted some years after the SEIU identity campaign had taken hold.

> The new focus on organizing was a means to an end, and that end was a better life for SEIU members and their families.

Frank Borges, a member of Local 285 in Massachusetts, wrote to Stern after the adoption of the purple branding strategy about how it connected members:

"I thought you would like to hear what happened today," Borges said in his letter. "I was in New Hampshire at a coffee shop when three men approached me and said, 'Hi, Brother.' I looked around to see who was calling me and asked if I knew who they were.

"They said, 'You're one of the purple brothers.' I had my SEIU purple jacket on. I asked what that meant and they said they never knew how big their union was until everybody started wearing purple. Now they know they belong to SEIU. They were Department of Transportation workers in New Hampshire. I guess it really works."[55] Stern's message of "organize or die" remained the order of the day, but the branding effort also came up with slogans for the union. The initial tagline had been "Leading the Way." While SEIU indeed had begun to out-organize other AFL-CIO unions, those unions criticized the new slogan. SEIU eventually replaced it with: "Stronger Together."

On the way to a new common identity as an organizing union, the leadership also knew the union's success would be judged by how well it did at the bargaining table and the ballot box. The new focus on organizing in 1997 was a means to an end, and that end was a better life for SEIU members and their families.

To get there, SEIU had to win wages and benefit gains as well as political elections that could lead to laws and policies that would help working people.

## Purple Power [56]

by Scott Abbot
Local 535, Santa Barbara, California

**P** eople, struggling all alone,
    Have heavy burdens & very little power.
**U** nited with others though, strength
    Will blossom, like a beautiful flower.
**R** ejuvenated energies stimulate
    Organized action, and plans take root.
**P** rogress then grows, grounded in the
    United diversity, and the results bear fruit.
**L** ife is a more rewarding experience
    When we stand up together and unite!
**E** veryone wins when we join with the

**POWER of PURPLE**,
Isn't that right?

Those goals were particularly important to SEIU, because so many of its members were low-wage workers. Many of them were immigrants, women, African Americans, Latinos, and others all struggling in an economy that seemed to reward hard work less and less as the wealthiest often reaped outsized gains at their expense. SEIU campaigns echoed that theme: "Justice for Janitors" for building cleaners; "Dignity, Rights, and Respect" for nursing home workers; and "We're Worth It!" for public sector workers.

At the bargaining table in 1997, SEIU Local 25 janitors in downtown Chicago took on management in a new way. Earlier, members had called attention during the 1996 convention to what they believed to be the corrupt practices of some of the local's leaders. Stern investigated and then forced out Gene Moats, Local 25 president, and placed the local in trusteeship. The move was a shot across the bow of other "old bulls"—leaders of certain big SEIU locals who found themselves often at odds with the law and in violation of democratic accountability provisions of the SEIU constitution.

A year later, Local 25 was waging an aggressive, well-orchestrated street campaign to win contract gains. "Stewards and membership activists spent a lot of hours educating members about contract issues and getting them involved in negotiations," recalled Teresa Bajerczak, a shop steward. Management had sought wage freezes and givebacks in an effort to reduce downtown wages to the lower rates paid to janitors in the Chicago suburbs.

Some 1,000 workers staged daily protests, including dropping 300 bags of trash at management headquarters. Rebuilding after the trusteeship, Local 25's involvement of members at every step of the bargaining process proved successful. They won a substantial wage increase, large holiday bonuses, and contract language to address workload problems.[57]

Other bargaining by the union saw new gains for workers in the healthcare sector. In July 1997, SEIU workers ratified agreements at 19 Beverly Enterprises-owned nursing homes. Locals 585, 668, and 1199P won annual wage increases of between 3 percent and 5 percent. They also forced Beverly, after a long strike, to agree to a common expiration date for all 19 contracts—a unionwide bargaining goal for agreements with a common employer aimed at strengthening the union's hand in the negotiations four years later.

"I think we now have a stronger union because of this," said Bea Sutton, an LPN at Fayette Health Care Center in Uniontown, Pennsylvania.

Beverly management had replaced about 500 workers who struck over unfair labor practices. SEIU lawyers fought successfully at the National Labor Relations Board and later in federal district court to win an injunction forcing Beverly to reinstate all of the replaced workers. Sutton got her job back as a result.

SEIU's public workers won gains, too. Local 500 in Montgomery County, Maryland, faced a common problem: unorganized "part-time" employees working side by side with members. The local believed it had about 200 part-timers whose job titles were the only thing separating them from a union contract. They were stunned to find that the county had more than 2,000 part-timers working outside the SEIU contract.

The local successfully bargained new contract language giving SEIU the right to represent most of the so-called temporary workers. Under Eileen Kirlin, the International Union's public division organizing director, leaders from public employee locals adopted a strategy of "bargaining to organize" to win gains and protections for intermittent employees.

Local 347 in its contract with the city of Los Angeles had won language earlier to give the union the right to represent more than 1,000 part-time employees. And Local 715 brought 250 office clerks and typists under contract with Santa Clara County in California.

Fighting under the banner "L.A. County Needs a Raise," Local 660 workers in 1997 won their first pay raise in five years in contracts that represented many of the 40,000 public employees there. Half of the bargaining units boosted wages between 12 percent and 21 percent over three years—a major victory given that two years earlier the county's chief administrative officer proposed cutting wages and laying off 18,000 workers.

Public workers in Canada won a big victory in 1997 after SEIU Local 204 took on Ontario Premier Mike Harris and his union-bashing Tory government, which, after coming to power in 1995, had gutted the province's Pay Equity Act. An SEIU legal challenge to the Tories' action forced the government to resume pay equity payments that raised nursing home workers' wages by more than $1 an hour.[58]

Privatization, always popular among conservative politicians, posed a new threat to SEIU's public sector workers. With the Clinton Administration's new welfare program, Republicans in Congress and the state government in Texas wanted to privatize the administration of the Texas Medicaid and food stamp programs. Huge companies such as EDS, Arthur Andersen, and Martin Marietta had been jockeying to win lucrative contracts, even hiring former top Texas welfare officials to bolster their efforts.

"The principle of public accountability for public dollars would have been set back a hundred years," noted SEIU's Kirlin. A vigorous SEIU campaign, joining with other labor and progressive allies, convinced Clinton to reject the plan. SEIU activitated a second effort involving a nationwide phone-bank campaign to crush Republican efforts to override the President's decision.

With ample militancy and a willingness to take on management with innovative tactics, SEIU leadership also believed that a fresh look was needed at how workers could build more constructive relations with employers. That re-evaluation was rooted in Andy Stern's earlier experiences in the union.

Stern had been a local union leader in Pennsylvania, where steelworkers, mineworkers, and autoworkers often took on big companies and won rich contracts by their willingness to walk the picket lines when necessary. When state workers in Pennsylvania won organizing rights and became SEIU members, Stern had become assistant shop steward of the Vine District Welfare Office in Philadelphia. With the new state union about to settle a contract, Stern helped lead a wildcat strike.

"I didn't think they were fighting quite hard enough," he recalled. "And I had remembered from watching a movie the idea that was 'No Contract-No Work.' So when the contract ran out and the union wanted to take a couple of extra days, many of us in Philadelphia said that's not really what unions do, and we led a wildcat strike of our little chapter of this big statewide union."

As he rose through the ranks, Stern did not hesitate to get tough with employers. He said frequently he preferred the "power of persuasion," but when that didn't work, the alternative was the "persuasion of power." When reason failed, when innovative new pressure strategies didn't work, then "we also used effective old-school tactics," Stern said. "We demonstrated, picketed, and led strikes when necessary."[59]

Stern's later work organizing janitors had put him in rooms with union cleaning contractors who frequently complained that SEIU couldn't "protect the wage." Those employers were losing business to nonunion contractors who underbid them because they didn't have to pay SEIU wages and benefits and were free to exploit their nonunion workers. Only by organizing competitors' workers could wage differentials be taken off the table (see pages 22-23).

"Learning to appreciate employers' competitive reality and attempting to create or add value to their business models became a basic operating principle of SEIU's strategies," Stern said in his book *A Country That Works*. "But finding employers to meet us halfway or even part of the way was nearly impossible."[60]

Shortly after his election in 1996, Stern flew to Los Angeles to enter negotiations with Kaiser Permanente, the union's largest healthcare employer. Kaiser's corporate "re-engineering" effort, involving unilateral cost cutting, had poisoned relations with its unions and led to a series of strikes. This one was averted and afterward Stern called David Lawrence, Kaiser's CEO, with a simple message: We need to change our relationship.

Lawrence took the call (although he later said he had no idea who Stern was). The Stern-Lawrence discussions that ensued helped lead ultimately to the largest labor-management partnership in America's service sector. "It wasn't always easy for union members to hear that their elected leader—someone who they thought should be fighting for them tooth and nail—was

talking peaceably with the CEO of their company and promoting new relationships," Stern said.[61]

But they did at Kaiser. About 30,000 SEIU workers and another 25,000 in various other unions approved an unprecedented program in which those workers got an expanded voice in how their facilities were run. And the unions won a card-check recognition procedure at all of Kaiser's worksites, as well as a commitment that the company would push subcontractors to remain neutral in organizing campaigns at their sites.

Before the innovative Kaiser program, said Priscilla Kania, Local 535 chapter president and steward, Kaiser employees had been told how to do their jobs "by people who aren't even trained in the field. With this agreement, we have the opportunity to make decisions with management."

With support from the AFL-CIO's John Sweeney, most other unions with Kaiser contracts approved the new program, although the California Nurses Association did not.

"Our groundbreaking relationship improved the quality of patient care and enhanced revenue growth for Kaiser and produced some of the best contracts in the healthcare industry," Stern later noted. The Kaiser program definitely was not perfect, he said, but it opened up new, productive opportunities and got workers there off the track of responding to unilateral company decisions with ineffective strikes ending in concessionary contracts.[62]

Not many employers responded to SEIU's approach of seeking constructive relationships from the outset. "If the going gets rough with employers, SEIU is more than adept at holding its own and is viewed as a powerful force to defend workers' interests," Stern said. "Disappointingly, only a few employers have shifted from their 'unions are the problem' mentality. Their lack of creativity and courage is an impediment to building a new model of labor-management relationships and to confronting the challenges of globalization."

"We have reinvented ourselves, but it takes two to tango."[63]

Mount Sinai
WORKERS
CAN'T LIVE
ON $32 • A
WEEK
ON
STRIKE

City Welfare
LOWANCE
is
GER than a
Sina
RY

unt Sinai
ORKERS
T LIVE
A
• WEEK
IKE
ELP US WIN!
1199 AFL-CIO

A strike at New York City's Mount Sinai Hospital
in 1959 by 1199 helped widen support for the
unionization of healthcare workers there.

# CHAPTER 8

# 1199 Merger With SEIU

## Groundwork For A National Healthcare Union

SEIU's path to becoming the largest and strongest health-care union in North America started when the Cook County Hospital workers helped found the union in 1921. But perhaps the crucial moment in that long struggle came in January 1998 when the 130,000 members of New York City-based 1199, the National Health and Human Service Employees Union, voted to affiliate with SEIU.

The 1199 affiliation with SEIU united 600,000 healthcare workers in the United States and Canada. Two months later, the 30,000 members in SEIU Local 144, the dominant union force in New York's private nursing homes, voted by a 10 to 1 margin to merge into 1199/SEIU.

"This is a defining moment in our effort to build a full-fledged movement of healthcare workers across North America," SEIU President Andy Stern said at the time. "It gives a major boost to our campaign to rein in the corporate greed permeating our healthcare system."[64]

Dennis Rivera, the powerful New York labor leader and president of 1199, became a major figure in SEIU's healthcare division and, a decade later, took the reins of SEIU Healthcare—helping to launch the national union within SEIU for healthcare workers. At the time of the 1199 affiliation with SEIU, Rivera said: "With the merger, we will have more money for politics, more money for organizing, more money for collective bargaining."[65] The militancy and vibrancy of 1199 also reinvigorated a new unionwide effort to reach out to all healthcare workers.

As part of SEIU's drive for greater union density and the power to bargain gains for workers that it brings, the union im-mediately formed a broad New York State Health Care Alliance that sought to unite more than 200,000 SEIU healthcare workers statewide to fight for quality patient care and better wages and working conditions. And 1199/SEIU also launched an intensive organizing drive among New York healthcare workers.

One reason the affiliation of 1199 had such an impact was that it brought into SEIU a large number of highly skilled, experienced union organizers and political activists. SEIU's progressive politics and strong emphasis on growth, particularly in the union's core sectors, meant many 1199 members and staff felt at home with the new arrangement.

Pharmacist Leon Davis, a Russian immigrant, helped found 1199 in New York City in 1932 with a small group of drugstore workers, and it later became a local of the Retail, Wholesale, and Department Store Union (RWDSU). Although small, 1199 was driven by political radicals who were swept up in the upsurge of labor and the left in the 1930s.[66] The union pushed for many of the labor laws passed in the New Deal, but ultimately hospital workers were excluded from the collective bargaining rights won then by other workers.

The progressive politics of the union and its commitment to represent all drugstore employees—not only pharmacists, but also porters and clerks—regardless of race, gender, ethnicity, or professional standing helped it grow to 5,000 members. Then in 1958, they decided to try to organize the largely minority healthcare workers in New York's private, nonprofit hospitals.

The workforce at these voluntary hospitals had been considered by many to be impossible to organize, but 1199 won a

Pharmacist Leon Davis, a Russian immigrant, helped found 1199 with drugstore workers. His organizing skill and radical politics built the union among healthcare workers at the same time it backed civil rights and anti-war struggles. His dream was to unify all healthcare workers in one union.

628 to 31 election victory at Montefiore Hospital in the Bronx on December 30, 1958. The union then launched a citywide organizing campaign that met with staunch management opposition.

Most of the 3,000 healthcare workers at New York's seven nonprofit hospitals earned $32 or less a week,[67] which in many cases qualified them for public assistance. Under the law, they did not have a legal right to union representation, so bargaining leverage came mainly from a strike.[68]

But with right on their side, 1199 President Davis and Elliot Godoff, the union's organizing director, defied a court order and led a walkout that began on May 8, 1959.

For Gloria Arana, a laundry worker at Mount Sinai Hospital, a strike was a huge risk, and she wondered what to expect when she got there the first day. Arana found a solid wall of picketers on Madison Avenue who succeeded in convincing workers not to go inside. It was a moment that made her feel like "it was a beautiful day," she later said.[69]

Arana became one of the strike leaders, and her co-workers were joined each day by "crack-of-dawn brigades," made up primarily of Jewish pharmacists who walked the picket lines. The hospital strikers won widespread public support as newspapers editorialized about the union's "crusade on behalf of New York's forgotten workers." African American and Hispanic leaders gave the walkout their strong support, as did Harry Van Arsdale Jr., president of the New York City Central Labor Council and a major powerbroker.

The strike ended on June 22 and, while 1199 won a grievance procedure and some bread-and-butter gains including a minimum wage of $1 an hour, it had not gained union recognition. But 1199 treated the settlement as a major victory, and Moe Foner, the union's public relations officer at the time, said the workers "were prepared to go to hell and back for the union."[70] Soon chapters of 1199 had formed at most of the city's 81 voluntary hospitals with workers paying union dues, attending meetings, and feeling like they were part of a movement.

A second major strike by 1199 followed in 1962 and it had strong support from Dr. Martin Luther King Jr., Malcolm X, James Baldwin, and many other figures that the union had come to know through its support of the civil rights movement. A number of 1199 activists had raised money for the bus boycott led by Dr. King in Montgomery, Alabama, and supported other early civil rights crusades.

With the success of the 1962 strike, the union took on Beth El Hospital in Brooklyn, and 1199 President Davis spent 30 days in jail for refusing to halt the work stoppage. Then New York Governor Nelson Rockefeller intervened and, in the spring of 1963, signed into law legislation granting collective bargaining rights to New York City hospital workers.

With bargaining rights, 1199 grew to 40,000 members by 1968 and had a citywide hospital contract with a $100 weekly minimum wage—triple what it had been only nine years earlier. Members also had won healthcare and pension coverage.

Over time, 1199 had some success in its national organizing campaign, winning contracts from New England to Washington State. In New York, the union continued to make gains even in the hard economic times during the 1970s.

But following Leon Davis's retirement in 1981, 1199 faced some difficulties as internal divisions developed. Discussions had occurred between SEIU President George Hardy and 1199's Davis about a possible merger in the late 1970s.

Dennis Rivera (right) led 1199 when it merged with SEIU in 1998 to form a unified healthcare union. Rivera became chair of SEIU Healthcare, a national healthcare union with more than one million members, in 2007. George Gresham (left) replaced Rivera as president of 1199SEIU-United Healthcare Workers East and is the fifth president in 1199's 75-year history.

And more than 75 percent of healthcare members voting in a referendum conducted by 1199 wanted to hold talks with SEIU that could lead to a dual affiliation (1199 had won semi-autonomy from the RWDSU). But RWDSU leaders quashed that effort (see pages 27 and 30).

By 1984, 1199 districts outside New York City representing 75,000 members had split from RWDSU.

1199 New York, with about 100,000 members, remained in RWDSU. But a failed six-week strike and tampering in the union's district leadership election in 1984 made for more difficulties there.

Ultimately, in 1989 some 14 districts of 1199 representing 52,000 healthcare workers outside New York chose to join SEIU, becoming 1199NW, 1199NE, 1199PA, and 1199WV/OH/KY, etc. Others affiliated with AFSCME.

Dennis Rivera was elected president of 1199 New York and an era of reform began with the union winning a hefty 42 percent wage increase for its very low-paid home care members in 1989. The union's lead role in the election of David Dinkins, New York City's first African American mayor, helped build 1199's reputation for political clout. And soon 1199 had won its six-month effort to gain a 24 percent wage hike for 50,000 members in a new three-year hospital contract.

By 1991, 1199 New York had left RWDSU. Under Rivera, the union won historic job security language in 1994 as hospitals there experienced a period of massive restructuring. The union earned a reputation for militancy and good contracts that secured innovative Taft-Hartley funds for healthcare, pensions, training, and child care.

Stern met with Dennis Rivera in a restaurant at the Democratic Party's convention in Chicago in 1996 shortly after he became SEIU president. He told Rivera he believed what 1199's Leon Davis and SEIU's George Hardy had attempted to do in uniting was a powerful goal that should be tried once again. The 1199 leadership had seen SEIU affiliate nursing home workers in District 1115 as well as medical doctors in the Committee of Interns and Residents—moves that reinforced SEIU's growing reputation as a healthcare union. SEIU's home care organizing and gains at hospital chains also did not go unnoticed by 1199.

Rivera, a major figure in New York politics, had not felt particular empathy with old guard SEIU leaders there, such as Local 32BJ President Gus Bevona and Local 144 President Frank Russo (both of whom later left the SEIU in disgrace). But Rivera saw changes top SEIU leaders were making to take the union in a more activist, progressive direction and believed that 1199's political vision was compatible with SEIU's new overall direction.

"Dennis was probably the most important legislative and political player in New York and he had done it in a very bipartisan fashion, which validated what SEIU had been moving to—an issue-based politics," Stern later recalled. "And 1199 brought to SEIU a whole sense of campaigning around policy issues with their grassroots, high-tech comprehensive legislative campaigns that SEIU had not really done much of."

The 1199 merger with SEIU, negotiated by Stern and Anna Burger, also moved the union further toward its goal—institutionalized in 2000—that workers who do the same type of work belonged in the same union. A number of healthcare unions in New York that had been divided began to come together after the merger. That had been a goal of Davis and Hardy, but it foundered in the Sweeney era, only to be revived successfully by Stern, Rivera, Burger, and their colleagues.

By unifying many New York healthcare workers, big bargaining gains were won. Another major impact 1199 would have on SEIU would be to show the connection that a union's political action and legislative work can have on collective bargaining gains. Over time, members would see the close relationship between their wages and job security and SEIU's electoral and lobbying work.

"Dennis and the 1199 leadership and all those new members further directed the union towards a larger role in terms of our ability to change the society," Stern said. "And it gave SEIU a much bigger footprint in political action. Dennis was really wise about how to use political power to benefit members and how to play really big. He taught us a lot of good lessons in SEIU."

"This affiliation honors the legacy of George Hardy and Leon Davis," SEIU President Stern said when the 1199 affiliation was announced. "It is our duty to see that their dream of one big healthcare union is fulfilled." With the 1998 affiliation of 1199NY to SEIU, many of the locals involved when the national 1199 split apart were once again reunited. Since then, 1199NY has grown into United Healthcare Workers East, with more than 300,000 workers from New York to Washington, D.C., as well as Massachusetts.

# CHAPTER 9

# 'The Best Organizer Is A Rank-And-File Member'
## Columbia/HCA Workers Win Breakthrough

With important ballot box victories in 1998, SEIU also could celebrate a good year on the organizing front. The union gained 185,000 new members that year. Of that number, 63,000 were newly organized. At the same time, SEIU took big strides to build strength for members in its industries and to expand the organizing ability of local unions.

And the union's performance, which more than doubled the previous record in 1997 of 81,000 new members, showed gains in SEIU's core sectors: healthcare, public employees, and building services.

While the results of the Bold Action program adopted in 1996 began to add up, a union assessment found that "we still don't represent a large enough number of workers in our major industries to win the kind of wages and benefits our families need."

Yes, SEIU was the fastest-growing union in America, but that was a little like winning the "taller than Mickey Rooney award"—you could be very short and still win. Few other national unions had even focused on organizing, and most spent nearly all their resources on servicing existing members rather than organizing new ones.

Local unions remained the key to SEIU's growth program. "Just as the best organizer is a rank-and-file member, the best organizing force is a local union," Stern noted.[71]

By the end of 1998, local unions had more than 300 organizers on staff. And 77 locals had organizing plans and budgets committing a total of more than $30 million to organizing. In addition, 67 locals had full-time organizing directors.

A record 1,500 local union members volunteered to work as member organizers in 1998. For example, more than 50 SEIU nurses volunteered for the Nurse Alliance flight team that stood ready to fly into organizing drives of fellow nurses and assist by making house calls and worksite visits. They talked nurse to nurse about shared workplace issues.

Concerned about increased workloads, short-staffing, declining patient care, and lack of respect from employers, about 15,000 hospital workers joined SEIU in 1998—more than any year since hospital workers won bargaining rights under federal law in 1974.

Janet Bunnell, a licensed practical nurse at Mercy Hospital in Scranton, Pennsylvania, became one of those new members when she and 1,400 other workers there voted to join SEIU. She had worked at Mercy for 18 years and could remember when conditions were better.

"It wasn't nirvana, but you were treated fairly," she recalled. "And your patients got the care they deserved." Mercy/Scranton, like many hospitals, began to consolidate, however, and "patient care standards went out the window. We were told to think about the dollar signs." Managed care policies, often criticized for controlling costs by denying patients medically necessary services, also severed the closer ties many nurses once had with hospital managements. RNs soon saw that the union could provide a voice at work at a time when bottom-line managers turned a deaf ear to individual concerns.

Workers began to complain about the inability to provide quality patient care, as well as a wage freeze, a pension cut, and threats of subcontracting. Mercy hired an anti-union consultant and began delaying the union election process. "The hospital's strategy was to litigate, litigate, litigate, and tie everything up," said organizer Neal Bisno at the time.

SEIU's lawyers won each case before the National Labor Relations Board, but the union election kept being delayed by management's tactics. "It's an example of how an employer can use labor law to derail the very objective of the law: to allow workers to organize freely," Bisno said later.

Finally, when the vote did occur, workers chose overwhelmingly to join SEIU. For Bunnell, the LPN, the victory helped restore the climate there when she started at Mercy. "We're a family again," she said. "A union family."

Across the country, SEIU found similar anti-union tactics. When 2,100 RNs and other healthcare workers at the University of Iowa Hospital and Clinics organized to improve staffing and patient care, the employer hired union-busting consultants to fight unionization. RNs from SEIU locals around the country traveled to Iowa, and workers there voted to join SEIU Local 150.

A similar anti-union campaign occurred at Stanford University and Packard Children's Hospitals. Two dozen member-organizers helped the 1,500 workers there fight back and successfully become part of SEIU Local 715. Same for the 1,000 workers at Good Samaritan Hospital in Rockland County, New York, who organized for respect on the job in the face of a vicious anti-union campaign.

But perhaps the most crucial win of 1998 was at Columbia/HCA's Sunrise Hospital in Las Vegas, Nevada. Sandra Pickney, an LPN at Sunrise, once had a normal workload of six patients on her shift. After Columbia/HCA took over in 1993 under former CEO Rick Scott, her workload skyrocketed.

"I was assigned 11 patients," she remembers. "Even though I had done my best each day, I felt an enormous sense that I had cheated them." Columbia/HCA's new policies eroded patient care standards and working conditions at Sunrise.

Driving home from work, Pickney would pray. "I realized that doing my best wasn't good enough when patient care is suffering—and that it was my Christian responsibility to speak out."

She became a regular in the small trailer in a Las Vegas parking lot near the hospital, where SEIU ran its organizing effort at Columbia/HCA. The company had bought more than 460 healthcare facilities in the United States and Europe and had become the "Wal-Mart of healthcare" under then-CEO Scott—slashing operating budgets with quality-related results, such as supply shortages, inferior medical products, and cuts in services for the poor.

The firm's drive for profits included committing massive Medicare and Medicaid fraud and illegal kickbacks to doctors. At one point in 1998, 700 federal agents conducted investigations and raids on Columbia/HCA facilities. In response to the scandal, the company fired Rick Scott, who departed in disgrace. (Scott would reappear in 2009 as the money man who financed "Conservatives for Patients Rights"—a right-wing effort to derail President Obama's healthcare reform legislation.)

In addition to the massive fraud and the slashing of patient care at Columbia/HCA, Sunrise garnered even more unwanted attention when the hospital refused to treat an uninsured homeless man, who was found dead an hour later on the hospital lawn in Las Vegas.

Pickney, the LPN, took the union's case to the national media, where she appeared on the ABC-TV program "20-20" and described the reasons healthcare workers at Sunrise wanted to unionize. SEIU had developed a growing media profile, in part through a skillful sense of linking what newspapers and broadcast media viewed as big stories (in this case, Medicare fraud and patients getting substandard or no treatment) with the union's own goal of empowering workers.

SEIU won a breakthrough at Columbia/HCA when the union negotiated a commitment for a fast and fair election process so that the nearly 2,500 healthcare workers at Sunrise Medical Center could vote on unionization without employer interference. Mary Kay Henry, who played the leading role in achieving the breakthrough agreement, announced the terms of the settlement at a packed employee meeting held jointly with the employer.

In December 1998, the registered nurses, service workers, technicians, and office personnel at Sunrise voted overwhelmingly to join SEIU Local 1107. With the victory, the local came to represent a majority of hospital workers in Las Vegas.

"It is clear from the election results that when there is no employer interference, workers will choose a union to benefit their families and communities," SEIU President Stern said after the vote.

The Columbia/HCA Sunrise victory boosted SEIU's strategy of using an array of campaign tactics, including research and media, to hold employers accountable on the corporate social responsibility front. Companies willing to violate their employees' right to organize too often infringe upon the rights of patients, taxpayers, shareholders, and communities. The union's goal was to get fast and fair procedures for workers who want to unionize and to eliminate the full frontal assault from employers and their anti-union consultants and lawyers. Commitments for union representation elections without employer interference were one route. Another was a majority sign-up procedure ("card-check") in which a majority of workers sign cards authorizing the union to represent them and the employer accepts that outcome and then negotiates with SEIU for a contract for those workers.

SEIU also showed progress in nursing home organizing through its "Dignity, Rights & Respect" campaign. In 1997-98, more than 14,300 workers at nearly 200 nursing homes joined the union—almost double the number of homes organized in the previous two years.[72] SEIU also launched a coordinated multilocal campaign to organize corporationwide at Genesis Health Ventures, a large nursing home chain with patient care problems and an aggressive opposition to unions.

In the public sector, SEIU helped workers organize to oppose massive budget cuts and anti-worker political attacks that could mean lost jobs, wage freezes or cuts, work contracted out, and threats to pensions and other benefits. In California, SEIU locals used the strength of their membership base to launch two major coordinated organizing drives. That led to more than 8,000 public workers in San Joaquin and Riverside counties joining SEIU in 1998.

Michigan's Republican Governor John Engler sought to privatize hundreds of state employment service jobs, but Local 31M led a coalition effort that defeated the plan. SEIU won support from the U.S. Labor Department in the fight, causing anti-worker politicians in many other states to drop similar privatization measures.

In Puerto Rico, SEIU locals worked to win passage of a historic bill that gave collective bargaining rights to thousands of public employees (see Chapter 29).

Building services, another essential sector SEIU targeted for organizing to build density and bargaining strength, saw continued gains as well. SEIU Local 82, which had launched a Justice for Janitors campaign in Washington, D.C., a decade earlier, had 70 percent of commercial janitors in the city organized by the end of 1998. The union won a master contract covering some 4,000 members.

The rise of powerful multinational cleaning contractors in the late 1990s often meant more work and less pay for thousands of building services workers, but SEIU had been successfully rebuilding its strength in many cities where membership had declined.

In Denver, Colorado, for example, downtown commercial cleaners belonged to Local 105 and had a strong master contract. But their wage standards were threatened because of business growth in the suburbs, where contractors paid low wages because there was no union. Local 105 ran a vigorous campaign and succeeded in 1998 in unionizing 70 percent of Denver's suburban janitors and winning coverage for them under the downtown master contract.

SEIU had been organizing home care workers for years across the United States and Canada. In 1998, more than 4,000 home care workers in Contra Costa County in California joined SEIU Local 250. And in Ontario, Canada, the union launched a provincewide campaign to organize 30,000 home care workers. In Chicago, Local 880 home care workers led successful coalition efforts to win living-wage laws in Chicago and Cook County, Illinois.

It was in California where a huge breakthrough for SEIU loomed at the end of 1998. Longtime efforts by the union had positioned more than 74,000 home care workers in Los Angeles County to have a chance finally to choose whether or not to join SEIU.

# Nurse Alliance: Standing Up For Patients

Caught in the cross-fire of managed care, nurses in the 1990s were rethinking what it meant to be true to their patients and their profession. Historically, some had shunned organized labor (too "blue collar") in favor of the white-collar appeal of professional nurse associations.

But radical changes in the healthcare industry were causing them to put aside such stereotypes. In 1997, Diane Blaski, a registered nurse in Wilkes-Barre, Pennsylvania, was one of many nurses who were taking a look at the hard, cold reality: "Staffing has been reduced, more job responsibilities have been added. Plus, when patients come to the hospital nowadays, they're sicker. With less staff and less time to devote to them, it's a dangerous situation because you have so many things to do."

So when she and her nurse colleagues at Penn State Geisinger's Wyoming Valley Hospital decided they wanted a strong voice in patient care issues, they voted to join forces with SEIU District 1199P. "The hospital has a lot of power and a lot of money. We needed a union with knowledge and know-how," said Blaski.

They were part of a wave of tens of thousands of nurses who joined ranks with SEIU starting in the mid-1990s, swelling the union's total nurse membership to more than 100,000 in 2010. Uniting nurses from across the health care spectrum—HMOs, acute care hospitals, long-term care facilities, clinics, and home health agencies—the SEIU Nurse Alliance fights for contract language and state and federal legislation addressing a range of issues including short-staffing, patient acuity systems, healthcare restructuring, fair compensation, and career development.

SEIU nurses gathered in Washington, D.C., in 2001 to seek safe staffing legislation during the union's "Stand for Patients" rally. They laid out nursing shoes on Capitol Hill and demanded: "Fill These Shoes With Nurses."

The work has paid off. SEIU nurses helped win landmark legislation in California establishing minimum staffing levels in healthcare facilities and a 2009 law in Pennsylvania banning mandatory overtime. They also played a crucial role in the successful fight for federal legislation to prevent deadly accidental needlesticks.

One of the things sparking their momentum was the SEIU Nurse Alliance flight team—a corps of dozens of nurses who, for days and weeks at a time, pack up their bags, hop on planes, and travel across the country to add to ongoing organizing campaigns the invaluable ingredient of face-to-face, nurse-to-nurse discussion.

As one SEIU nurse, a member of Local 285, said of her work on a flight team visit to meet with nurses at Las Vegas Sunrise Hospital in 1998, "We phonebanked and home visited. We stood outside and leafleted. It was great to be able to talk with people about the strength of being organized."

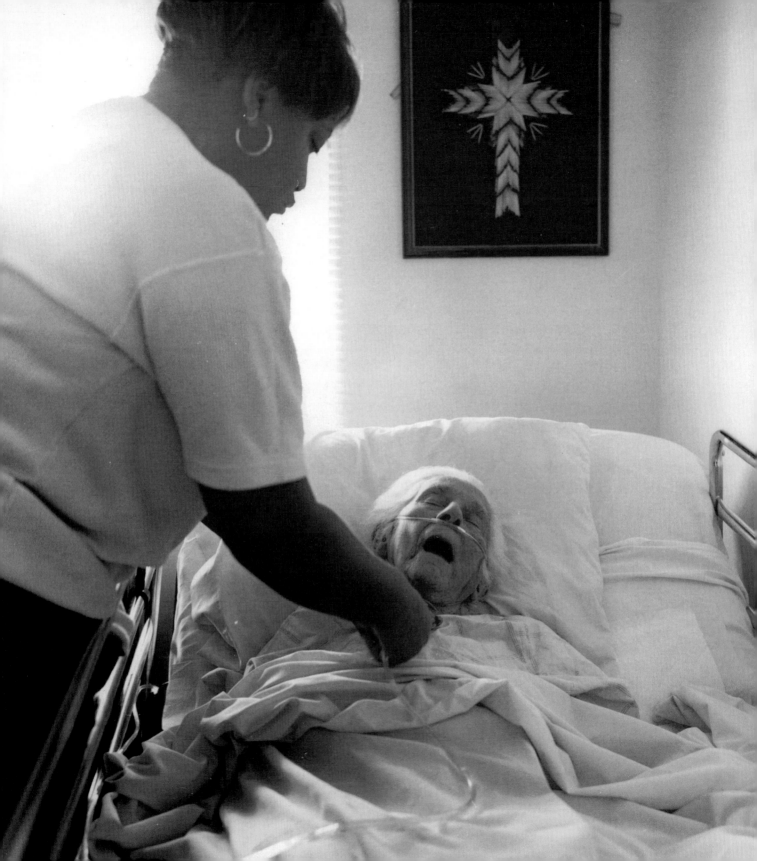

# CHAPTER 10

# Los Angeles Home Care: 74,000 Join SEIU
## Biggest Organizing Win Since 1941

For 25 years, Verdia Daniels spent each workday caring for the elderly, sick, and disabled in Los Angeles. As a home care worker, she sometimes had to take two or three buses to get to her clients, with whom she always felt a strong caregiver's bond.

"You don't just go in to dust or run the vacuum cleaner," said Daniels. "You have patients who are bedridden, but whose insurance doesn't allow hospital stays. Some of your job is giving them medication. Some of it is changing their diapers.

"Some patients have back injuries—you have to get them out of bed just the right way," she noted. "You lift the patients and you do their therapy. For the minimum wage."[73]

Daniels never met the legendary Walter Reuther of the United Auto Workers, who helped organize Ford's huge River Rouge complex outside Detroit back in 1941 when more than 100,000 workers won UAW representation. But she played a critical role in what remains the single biggest organizing success achieved since the UAW won recognition at the Rouge 58 years earlier.

As the ballots were counted on February 26, 1999, at the Westin Bonaventure hotel in Los Angeles, Daniels became one of 74,000 home care workers to choose SEIU to represent them. The vote for the union was overwhelming—only 1,925 votes were cast against unionization.

Nearly all the L.A. home care workers earned only the state minimum wage, which at that time was $5.75 an hour. Most were women of color and immigrant workers. They made up the backbone of the low-wage service economy that had grown in the 1990s, while the manufacturing sector, including the

Ford Rouge workers, had lost jobs as technology and free-trade globalization expanded.

"This is a home run for labor amidst a lot of strikeouts, in that it is a huge victory in a pivotal sector of the economy, the service sector," said Harley Shaiken, a labor expert and academic. "And it represents the new face of labor—women workers, minority workers, low-paid workers, people who have often been so hard to organize."[74]

Verdia Daniels helped launch the organizing effort in 1987 with SEIU Local 434B. "We wanted a union contract so we could win decent wages, some benefits, and some respect," she told *SEIU Action* after the victory.[75] Like her fellow home care workers, she had no idea what a long, difficult challenge loomed ahead.

Unlike the autoworkers at Ford, for example, the L.A. home care workers each went to a different location to perform their jobs, individually caring for a client in that person's home. Isolated from each other, the home care workers were united by a common concern as caregivers, but also by the low wages they received. Their pay did not even elevate the home care workers above the federal poverty standards at the time.

Nor were they entitled to health insurance, sick leave, pensions, or holiday pay. They did not receive overtime pay, though most L.A. home care workers had a hard time finding a full 40 hours of work each week anyway. "We were the invisible workforce," recalled Esperanza De Anda. "Nobody even knew we existed."[76]

SEIU had experience with home care workers. The community organizers in ACORN (Association of Community

Organizations for Reform Now) found some of its members were home care workers. They helped organize a nontraditional labor group called the United Labor Union and it won several home care organizing drives in Boston and Chicago. Those home care workers were part of a union affiliation in 1984, and their locals pioneered new strategies for winning collective bargaining rights at the state level.[77]

The home care sector expanded in the 1980s and '90s as government and the public increasingly opted to have long-term care for the elderly and disabled occur in a non-institutional setting. Care shifted to some extent from nursing homes to individuals' residences, but employment standards for the long-term caregivers often deteriorated.

"Working in consumers' homes, they are isolated from each other, and [home care workers] often lack a codified employment relationship that expresses the obligations of government and home care consumers to them," noted Jess Walsh, then an academic who studied the issue.[78]

SEIU researchers found there were 40,000 home care workers in Los Angeles County in 1988, but that number had jumped to 74,000 by 1999—an increase of 85 percent over the period. Of those workers in 1999, 83 percent were women. Two-thirds were 40 years of age or older. Two-thirds were people of color and half were immigrants. Some 79 percent of them lived below the federal poverty line. They averaged 25 hours a week in home care, with a third

Verdia Daniels, a home care worker in Los Angeles, helped 74,000 fellow workers join SEIU in the biggest U.S. organizing victory since 1941.

working a second job to make ends meet.[79]

As Daniels and others began to organize in 1987, they ran into an obvious difficulty: the absence of a common worksite where workers come and go. This isolation indeed remained a reason that many home care workers wanted to form a union to bring them together around common issues, such as low wages and lack of benefits. But at the same time the isolation made organizing difficult.

"Sometimes in this job, you feel like you're all alone," Mary Simmons told the *Los Angeles Times*. "You might be with your client eight hours a day, even longer. You lift them out of bed, put them on the potty, put on their clothes. You pray with them, and you try to keep them from getting too depressed. I don't think most people understand what that's like. At least here at the union, you get to meet other people who are going through the same thing."[80]

Isolation and the lack of a central worksite posed one problem, but another crucial issue was that there was no employer for bargaining purposes. The money that paid the home care workers came from federal, state, and county funds. But the workers were hired and fired by individual clients— the elderly and disabled consumers who needed the care.

Local 434B's initial organizing drive ran aground when a state court held that Los Angeles County was not the employer of the home care workers under the state's collective bargaining law despite setting their wages.

The union had signed up 22,000 workers in less than three months—a tremendous outpouring that showed how desperate home care workers were to organize. The court ruling was heartbreaking, but it didn't stop the momentum.

SEIU shifted to a new strategy based on passing state legislation that would enable counties to set up home care authorities with which the union could bargain. Vital to this process was to make allies of the consumers of home care—the elderly and disabled and the various groups that represented them.

Home care for low-income families in California ran under a consumer-driven model, known as Independent Provider (IP). It allowed consumers to hire, fire, and supervise their own attendants, although the funding came from the state and federal governments. A competing approach, called the contract model, had a company or agency hire and train a home care staff that was then deployed to various individual homes.

Disability activists generally supported the IP consumer-driven model, rather than the contract model, which they argued robs those under care of the ability to control their own bodies, homes, and lives.[81] SEIU sought the support of disability rights groups, but ran into some difficulties and misunderstandings as the union worked its way through complex issues.

There are many different viewpoints within the disability rights movement, but generally it advocates on behalf of "individual" rights. Labor generally works through a "collective" rights model. As SEIU activists met with those involved with Independent Living Centers and the California Senior Legislature, the challenge was to find a way to develop a common front that defended the rights of the clients and of the workers who cared for them.

Among the concerns of the disability community were:

> SEIU sought the support of disability rights groups.

- Would the clients' right to hire, supervise, and fire their home care providers be compromised if unionization occurred?
- Would there be strikes and grievances that affected clients?
- Would there be trade-offs, with higher wages meaning fewer hours of care?
- The union was powerful and well-resourced, while clients and the disability movement was not. Would clients get steamrolled by the union?[82]

After months of discussions and give-and-take, SEIU and the disability activists finally agreed to push the concept of a public authority with the state legislature. The public authority would be the employer of the workers under the state's collective bargaining law, but also the rights of consumers would be enshrined and their powers protected through a consumer-dominated board.

County and state officials involved in home care would only back this approach if the new public authority didn't mean new costs for them. They also wanted to ensure that home care workers would not show up directly as employees on the government payroll.

Finally, the Public Authority Act was passed in 1992, reflecting those concerns. Each county was free to accept or reject this model. The issue then shifted to coming up with the funding needed to both improve wages and working conditions for home care workers, while protecting and expanding quality care for clients. After an all-out lobbying effort, SEIU helped get California to adopt the Medicaid Personal Care Option—major federal funding through which the federal government began to provide 60 percent of the total program costs. This freed some funds to cover the start-up costs of the public authorities in the state.

Mary Kay Henry, who became SEIU president in 2010, led many of the union's organizing and contract victories in healthcare. Kirk Adams (left) played a crucial role in launching the successful L.A. home care campaign.

Soon, public authorities were created in San Francisco, San Mateo, and Alameda Counties. In 1994, SEIU Local 616 successfully organized 6,000 home care workers in Alameda County. Some progress also was made elsewhere. But in Los Angeles County, more work needed to be done to build coalitions with the disability rights and senior communities. A group opposed to creating a public authority emerged and started to lobby the L.A. Board of Supervisors.

But SEIU's ties to other disability activists led to formation of In-Home Support Services Recipients and Providers Sharing (IRAPS), a progressive coalition including both consumers and workers who backed creation of a public authority. Lillibeth Navarro, a disability rights leader, became a major supporter of the SEIU effort and the first president of IRAPS.

"We could not fight for our rights at the expense of those who are getting dirt poor wages," she said at the time. "They [L.A. home care workers] were there in the trenches with us. Now it is our turn to give them our support and respect."

The fight for home care workers in Los Angeles got a boost in 1995 when David Rolf, a skilled organizer fresh from some major victories for SEIU in Georgia, arrived as deputy general manager of the home care union. Rolf and other SEIU activists pushed the effort into the neighborhoods where the home care workers lived.[83] Chapters were established in 15 areas, including African American and Latino neighborhoods where SEIU home care workers met in libraries and community centers or homes.

"Workers found out for the first time that they weren't alone," Rolf later said. "They found out that other workers had similar problems: late paychecks, abusive clients, no benefits."[84] In that process, home care workers began to build a strong culture based on the dignity of their work and the fact that together they could achieve strength.

The union had won the right to voluntary dues deductions for members who signed up during house visits through an agreement with Gray Davis, then-Controller of California, back in 1989. Rolf and his allies further boosted SEIU's credibility by having the local play a lead role in the fight for Proposition 210, an initiative that raised the state's minimum wage. The local gathered more signatures than any other group[85] and the minimum wage hike passed.

"Planning and executing direct action, such as marches and rallies, occupations of government offices, street demonstrations and civil disobedience resulting in arrest were key to bringing home care workers together to experience power," wrote Jess Walsh in her excellent analysis of the home care workers' struggle.[86]

Rolf's strategy, boosted by new funding from top SEIU leadership, shifted to strengthening the union's political muscle in L.A. County and to building more support within the disability rights community there.

The approach was based on SEIU's new worker- and issue-centered political action strategy, as opposed to the old model of candidate- and party-centered efforts. The shift to political activism required investing in strategic, high-profile campaigns, such as that of Carl Washington, who ran for state Assembly (and was a close ally and staffer for L.A. Supervisor Yvonne Burke, whose vote SEIU needed in the fight for a public authority for home care).[87]

Home care workers walked the precincts door to door, campaigning for an array of candidates who had come to know the issues that mattered to Local 434B. Many of those for whom they campaigned actually would have the power, once elected, to change home care workers' lives directly. "By becoming a political force in the city and state, SEIU Local 434B developed a cohort of politicians who were accountable to the union and who supported publicly, and in the back rooms, its public authority agenda," Walsh said in her analysis.[88]

All that work paid off in September 1997 when the L.A. County Board of Supervisors passed an ordinance creating the public authority that gave SEIU an employer with which it could ultimately bargain once workers had voted for union representation.

Local 434B, with its 12,000 members, then set out to win the union election among the 74,000 L.A. County home care workers. David Rolf's early neighborhood organizing and later political strategy helped union organizers go house to house in state legislative districts. Within those, they targeted voting precincts. Spanish-speaking home care organizers worked in Latino neighborhoods, Armenian speakers targeted Armenian neighborhoods, and so forth.

Over about nine months, a team of member organizers made 70,000 home visits seeking support for SEIU in the union representation vote set for February 1999. The home care workers' campaign got a huge boost from other SEIU locals, including 99, 250, 399, 347, 535, 660, 1877, and 1957. Members and staff of those locals completed 64,000 phone calls to L.A. home care workers, many from Local 99's telecommunications center.[89]

Finally, late on February 26, 1999, Verdia Daniels had her moment. After 25 years of changing adult diapers and lifting patients to avoid bedsores—and after 12 years of organizing her fellow home care workers across 4,083 square miles of Los Angeles County—finally Verdia Daniels could smile and laugh and hug her fellow workers who had just won the largest union organizing victory in 58 years.

It felt good.

On election night in 1999, Los Angeles home care workers join SEIU's David Rolf in celebrating their victory. They went on to negotiate big wage and benefit gains in future contracts and gave a huge boost to SEIU home care organizing in other states.

# Home Care Workers Win Contract Gains

The inspirational victory of Los Angeles home care workers led the way to some 450,000 home caregivers uniting with SEIU since 1996. By 2010, SEIU had 500,000 home care members working in nine states: California, Illinois, Massachusetts, Michigan, Missouri, New York, Ohio, Oregon, and Washington.

Most worked as "independent providers" employed by the consumers themselves, rather than through private agencies. About 40 percent of all independent provider home care workers in the United States belonged to SEIU as of 2010.

In 2006 home care aides who had formed unions received wages at least 10 percent higher than those who had not and experts estimate that differential widened through 2009. Union home care aides were almost twice as likely to have health insurance as their non-union counterparts and more than twice as likely to have some type of pension or retirement plan.

In California, there were more than 270,000 home care workers in 31 counties in 2010, with 78 percent of all home care workers belonging to SEIU. Union home care workers in Santa Clara County received 50 percent more in wages than nonunion independent provider home care workers there.

## HOMECARE WORKERS ORGANIZED

| Year | Number Organized |
|------|------------------|
| 1996 | 8,826 |
| 1997 | 4,016 |
| 1998 | 7,872 |
| 1999 | 82,754 |
| 2000 | 17,222 |
| 2001 | 23,801 |
| 2002 | 67,528 |
| 2003 | 15,585 |
| 2004 | 10,111 |
| 2005 | 64,171 |
| 2006 | 5,852 |
| 2007 | 42,108 |
| 2008 | 8,385 |
| 2009 | 2,733 |

SEIU represented about 24,000 independent provider home care workers in Illinois in 2010 and another 11,675 agency home care workers—82 percent of all home care workers in the state. IP workers won a 33 percent increase in wages in their first contract and a 24 percent gain in their second, which brought wages to $11.55 per hour in 2010.

After a long campaign that involved outreach to build a robust coalition, about 42,000 Michigan home care aides united in SEIU in 2005. With a creative grassroots campaign, workers won wage increases of up to 55 percent.

It took home care workers in Massachusetts two years to secure state legislation allowing collective bargaining in their sector. Some 22,000 caregivers in the Bay State chose to unite in SEIU in 2007, and by 2010 about 68 percent of all home care workers in Massachusetts were represented by SEIU. Wages prior to bargaining had averaged $10.84 per hour, but rose to $12.48 in 2010 under the SEIU contract.

Home care workers in Ohio persuaded the governor there to issue an executive order that paved the way for 7,000 to unite in SEIU. They bargained directly with the state and are the highest-paid home care workers in the nation.

SEIU won big gains in the Northwest as well. The union represents about 13,000 home care aides in Oregon who won pay gains of 10 percent, health insurance with dental and vision coverage, workers' compensation, and paid time off in their first contract.

In Washington State, home caregivers advocated and passed a ballot initiative in 2001 that allowed them to form a union in 2002. By 2010, about 31,000 independent providers and 8,000 agency home care aides in Washington belonged to SEIU—73 percent of all home care workers in the state. Since they unionized, those workers have won a 40 percent increase in wages.[90]

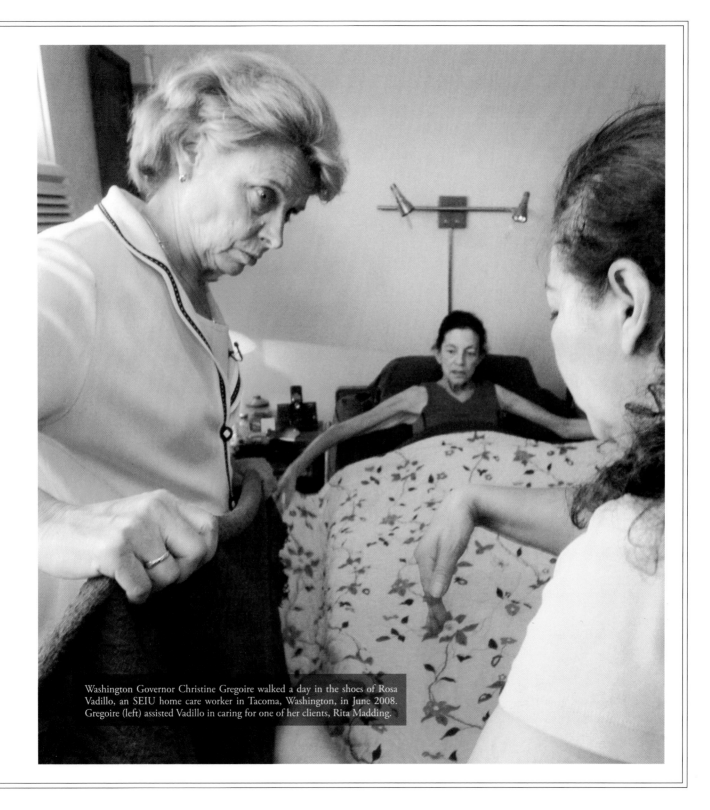

Washington Governor Christine Gregoire walked a day in the shoes of Rosa Vadillo, an SEIU home care worker in Tacoma, Washington, in June 2008. Gregoire (left) assisted Vadillo in caring for one of her clients, Rita Madding.

# CHAPTER 11

# Protection From Needlestick Injuries
## Healthcare Workers Win Safer-Needle Laws

To be a nurse is to know about death. And Peggy Ferro knew a lot about death. A member of SEIU Local 250, she had worked at Kaiser Hospital in San Francisco in the early 1980s as HIV/AIDS began its terrifying spread through a public deeply fearful of the disease and the unknowns then surrounding it.

At age 49, with everything to live for, Peggy Ferro died of AIDS from a needlestick injury on the job that could have been prevented.

She was cleaning up a patient's bedside table on which a doctor had left a blood-filled needle underneath a swatch of gauze. She reached to pick up the gauze and the needle embedded in her finger.[91]

On her 41st birthday two months later, Peggy Ferro was told she had tested positive for HIV. "It was devastating," she said later.[92]

She was not alone. When she suffered her injury, thousands of workers every year were contracting HIV and hepatitis from accidental needlesticks, and hundreds were dying, according to the *San Francisco Chronicle*. It reported that "syringes with safety features such as sliding plastic sheaths that covered needles were on the market, but few were being purchased by hospitals and healthcare facilities."[93]

Ferro years earlier had fought successfully to create the first AIDS ward at Kaiser at a time when fear of contracting the disease from patients had led some to shun them. "I was seeing these young people die, and I felt I had to do something," she said. "At some point, you have to take a stand."[94]

In those early days of the AIDS epidemic, scientists did not yet fully understand how HIV, the virus that causes AIDS, is spread by blood and other bodily fluids. Ferro, a licensed vocational nurse, helped create the first AIDS education program at her SEIU local union.

Like her colleagues in Local 790 at San Francisco General Hospital and elsewhere, Ferro and SEIU Kaiser workers agreed that prejudice and lack of education about HIV/AIDS could have no place in their wards, where providing patients the best care possible was the top priority. And they also argued healthcare workers should not be put at unnecessary risk of contracting the disease.

By the late 1980s, after the *New England Journal of Medicine* carried an article stating that up to 90 percent of all needlestick injuries could be prevented, SEIU escalated its efforts on the issue. The union knew that the primary way its members contracted blood-borne diseases—not only HIV/AIDS, but also hepatitis B and hepatitis C—was from medical devices, such as needles.

As needles and other medical devices with integrated safety features became available, SEIU activists began pressing employers to purchase the safer versions, but ran into strong resistance from management unwilling to pay more for the safer equipment.

Protected by SEIU contracts, Locals 790 and 250 became the first in the union to file needlestick safety grievances. They won, and San Francisco General began buying safer IV catheters. In Miami, Local 1991 nurses became the first to negotiate successful safer-needle contract language. And Local 535 filed a complaint with the California Occupational Safety and

Health Administration demanding safer needles.

With this local activity underway, SEIU joined with the American Public Health Association to sponsor the first national safer-needle meeting in 1990. The union worked to get Congressional hearings on the issue in 1992.

One of those who testified before a subcommittee chaired by then-U.S. Rep. Ron Wyden of Oregon was a "Jean Roe," a member of Local 250 who had contracted HIV/AIDS through a needlestick and spoke under the condition that her identity remained confidential.

Before her death, Peggy Ferro revealed that she was "Jean Roe," who had told the House panel that safer medical devices were available, but her hospital did not use them even as she was forced to carry a heavy patient load. "Let me give you a dose of reality about being a healthcare worker," she testified. "We are told by management to be more careful, to work slower, and to act safely. This is meaningless when you are working 12-to-16-hour shifts.

"The technology was available in 1990 to prevent my needlestick injury," she said. "Unsafe medical devices must be taken off the market and medical facilities instructed to choose the best available technology."

Ferro later said the hospital worried about the expense of safer needles. "They said that it was not cost effective," she told the *San Francisco Chronicle*. "They were saying to me that my life was not cost effective."

Gwyen Spruill, a medical laundry transport worker in Michigan where he belonged to Local 79, brought to the subcommittee hearing on Capitol Hill an array of contaminated needles he and co-workers had found in the medical laundry. "This is the real deal," he told the panel.[95]

Despite some progress at the local union level, such as Kaiser agreeing to pilot testing and buying safer needles in Southern California, the issue remained that safer needles and similar medical devices could save hundreds of lives each year, but were not being used by a medical industry unwilling to spend more for them.

In 1997, a nurse practitioner named Ellen Dayton was moonlighting at a city clinic for substance abusers and, after drawing blood from a patient, saw some glass blood collection tubes start to roll off the countertop. As she lunged over to catch the tubes, she got a needlestick from a contaminated needle that she was carrying in her other hand.

Had the needle been protected by a safety device, Dayton would have been fine. But instead she contracted AIDS and hepatitis C. SEIU activists, including fellow Local 790 member Lorraine Thiebaud, an RN and chief steward, took Dayton's story to the the *San Francisco Chronicle*. It carried an extensive series entitled "Deadly Needles" that got national attention highlighting administrative indifference and manufacturer culpability.

With more than 800,000 needlestick injuries to healthcare workers reported each year, the number contracting HIV/AIDS and hepatitis C grew, shattering thousands of lives. But Dayton's story and rallies, such as one in front of San Francisco General Hospital, showed growing political support for action on needlesticks. SEIU President Andy Stern gave the campaign a boost on May 9, 1998, when he appeared on the *NBC Nightly News* calling for government and industry to require the use of safer needles.

SEIU members in California escalated the push for a safer needle bill in the California Assembly, where state Assemblywoman Carol Migden had worked with the union on the legislation.

The bill eventually passed, but when it was sent to then-Gov. Pete Wilson, a Republican, he initially held off signing it. SEIU's Nurse Alliance faxed more than 1,200 letters to his office and held candlelight vigils and rallies in Los Angeles, San Francisco, and Sacramento. The bill also got the support of Kaiser, where SEIU had forged a new and more cooperative relationship.

Finally, Wilson signed the legislation in September 1998, making it the nation's first safer-needle law. Shortly before she died, Peggy Ferro—very weak and in pain—called Republican Gov. Wilson, who didn't take the call. She left a message congratulating him for signing the legislation.

With that victory in hand, SEIU launched a "Safe Needles Now!" campaign coordinated through the union's state councils, using common messages and strategies. Legislation was introduced in more than half the states, and soon Tennessee became the second state to enact a law, followed quickly by Maryland. SEIU 1199 pushed the issue hard in New York State. In Ohio, members of SEIU Locals 47, 627, and SEIU District 1199WKO joined forces to pass a safer-needle bill.[96]

Many SEIU healthcare workers fought hard for legislation requiring safer needles. Lorraine Thiebaud (above), an RN and chief steward at SEIU Local 790 in San Francisco, played a leading role as did Peggy Ferro of Local 250, Ellen Dayton and Janet Christensen of 790, Noreen Prill of District 1199P, Gwyen Spruill of Local 79, and many others.

"I've had to go through a series of tests, and I'm still going through them," Bev Miko, an LPN and member of Local 47, said during the Ohio fight. "Just try to imagine living your life not knowing whether or not you're going to contract a fatal disease. When you say you've been stuck with a needle, legislators immediately pay attention."[97]

But as gains occurred in other states, back in California SEIU leaders found that hospital managements too often continued to avoid introducing the safest needles and medical devices.

"It's not enough to just pass legislation," said Michael Morrissey, a respiratory therapist at St. Francis Memorial Hospital, a Catholic Healthcare West (CHW) facility in San Francisco. "We have to be vigilant in seeing that the law is enforced. In my facility people are still being stuck by dangerous needles."

SEIU Local 250 members at Seton Medical Center, another CHW facility, filed a CalOSHA complaint, and the hospital was fined more than $5,000 for nine violations of the needlestick law in 2000.

As more states passed SEIU-backed safer-needle laws, top SEIU leaders, including Betty Bednarczyk and Anna Burger, worked with the U.S. Congress and some in the healthcare industry to push for federal legislation. They argued that thousands of healthcare workers—many SEIU members—suffered unnecessarily when technology made safer needles possible. And they also said that 50 separate state laws with different standards and timetables made it needlessly complex for multi-state healthcare providers to establish systemwide purchasing of safer devices that would bring costs down.

By then SEIU had won passage of 17 state laws on safer needles, and the healthcare industry saw the writing on the wall. The union's success underscored the way member political action could improve directly the conditions experienced every day on the job.

The Needlestick Safety and Prevention Act of 2000 soon

SEIU members pushed for safer needle legislation in California. They won a state law in 1998 after years of struggle.

won unanimous support in both the U.S. House and Senate and President Clinton signed the bill into law at the White House. Clinton invited Stern to stand with him at the signing ceremony on November 6, 2000.

"This is a tremendous victory that builds on the incredible work of many people," Stern said just after the bill was signed into law.

One of those people he cited was Peggy Ferro, who didn't live to see the federal law enacted, but whose courage and drive helped create the momentum that brought the safer needle campaign to success. The words she spoke to Congress in 1992 live on:

"It is too late for safer needles to save my life now, but they will save people's lives who I cherish and feel are precious."

# 925: Raises, Rights, And Respect For Working Women

In the early 1970s, a young man walked into an office at Harvard University and uttered three words that sparked a national movement of working women. Looking directly at the clerk-typist, he lamented, "Isn't anyone here?"

For Karen Nussbaum, the clerk-typist behind the desk that day, his words summed up the frustrations of women office workers everywhere—the lack of respect, the low wages, the minimal chances for career advancement.

But Nussbaum didn't let the indignity simply simmer. She began meeting with other women in the Boston area, and, along with Ellen Cassedy, founded an organization called "Boston 9to5" to advocate for women office workers. In 1975, Boston 9to5 affiliated with SEIU to form Local 925, giving the emerging movement its first autonomous union with collective bargaining rights.

Six years later, SEIU and 9to5—by then operating nationwide and known as the National Association of Working Women—entered into a historic partnership linking the labor and women's movements. The new organization, SEIU District 925, was made up of chapters nationwide, with the mission of organizing office workers throughout the country.

And there was plenty at stake. Office workers were one of the largest, lowest-paid, and most-exploited groups of workers in the nation. The question was whether the predominantly female office workforce would think joining a union was too blue collar and too male.

That question was quickly answered by a pioneering group of women at the Equitable Life Assurance Company in Syracuse, New York. They voted in March 1982 to join SEIU District 925 and later that year launched a nationwide boycott of Equitable to force the company to bargain a first contract. After a long fight, they won an agreement in 1984.

District 925 members also were tackling issues such as pay inequity and family-medical leave, and were energetically organizing chapters of working women across the nation. Debbie Schneider, Kim Cook, and Bonnie Ladin, along with Nussbaum and Cassedy, helped thousands of office workers join District 925 between 1981 and 2001. The membership was concentrated primarily in Massachusetts, Ohio, and Washington State.

District 925 members also played a leading role in getting the federal Family and Medical Leave Act approved in 1993. The landmark legislation, which requires employers to give workers unpaid leave for pregnancy and family medical issues, was one of the first pieces of legislation signed into law by President Bill Clinton.

In 2001, the members of SEIU District 925 voted overwhelmingly to transform their union and merge with other SEIU locals in their respective states. They would no longer have the District 925 name and a unique identity within the union, but they said they would gain much more: strength in numbers.[98] They would continue their union's historic fight for raises, rights, and respect for women workers—but in a more strategic way.

# CHAPTER 12

# President's Committee 2000 Charts Strategy
## SEIU Needed Resources, Industry Focus

SEIU's successful organizing and political action programs had changed the union dramatically over the initial years of the new leadership elected in 1996, which had moved quickly to implement the recommendations of the Committee on the Future.

Seeking a fresh assessment of where SEIU was and where it should go, Stern in 1998 appointed 20 local union activists to serve on a "President's Committee 2000." The union's next convention was in 2000, so the work of the committee would provide the basis of a further and perhaps even more comprehensive agenda for change.

As the President's Committee 2000, or PC2K as it became known, began its work, the broader American society—indeed, the entire world—had started to buzz over what the new millennium would bring when the calendar rolled over to January 1, 2000.

Organizations have their own rhythms and methods for evolving to meet new circumstances. For SEIU, the convention every four years had become a moment when the union defined the agenda for the following four years and then set about to implement the changes mandated by delegates.

Because of the new and intensive member involvement spurred on by the leadership, the run-up to the convention became a period when rank-and-file members and local union leadership participated in rigorous debates over what SEIU should be doing. While the top leadership drove much of the process, they were intent on having ideas filter up from the union's grassroots, rather than selling their own agenda from the top down.

Between 1998 and 2000, the wide variety of SEIU structures and bodies—the local unions, state councils, caucuses, regional conferences, committees, and industry divisions—all debated in various ways where the union was and where it should go. But key to the process was the President's Committee 2000, which was co-chaired by Secretary-Treasurer Betty Bednarczyk and Executive Vice President Eliseo Medina. The 20 local union leaders included those from Chicago, Miami, Detroit, Los Angeles, San Francisco, New York City, San Jose, Boston, Denver, Everett (Washington), Columbus (Ohio) as well as Montreal and Windsor, Canada.

"Often, unions and organizations adopt broad strategies, form a blue-ribbon panel, hear testimony from experts and produce a fine document…that ends up collecting dust on a shelf," Stern said in his charge to PC2K. "But not SEIU. We've made great progress, but this is no time to rest on our laurels."

"We need to increase the unionization rate in our industries, build our political strength, and strengthen the bond between our members and the union," Stern noted. "If we are going to raise our members' wages, improve their benefits, and give them a real voice in their workplace and in their community, we have to respond to what's going on in their lives."

The PC2K began by seeking the views of SEIU members, leaders, and staff through questionnaires, polling, focus groups, and face-to-face discussion. Leaders and workers representing more than 80 percent of the union's membership were asked to evaluate the union's progress since 1996. This first stage led to a report titled *Evaluate* that described PC2K's findings. A second report, *Imagine*, sought out new ideas for SEIU's direction, and a third report, *Decide*, provided a set of recommendations for the 2000 convention to debate.

The committee found that the organizing and growth program of the union had been successful, but had far more potential.[99] The analysis showed, for example, that the Bold Action program's "Organizing Pledge" that more than 90 locals (representing about 600,000 members) had signed committing them to spend 10 percent of their total budget on organizing in 1996, 15 percent in 1997, and 20 percent in 1998, had paid off.

SEIU spent $20 million on organizing in 1995 and organized 22,200 new members. In 1996, Stern's first year as president, the union spent $31.7 million on organizing and won 38,500 new members. Organizing expenditures rose to $43.5 million in 1997 and yielded 58,700 more members. And in 1998, $62.8 million resulted in 63,900 new members. The union's overall membership gains were even higher, due to affiliations in which existing unions chose to join SEIU.

The political progress in 1998 also got good reviews from PC2K. The expanded member involvement and the new emphasis on an issue-driven politics brought results. Voluntary donations to the SEIU COPE political action fund rose from $535,000 in 1993 to $679,000 in 1996 and $890,000 in 1998.

In 1996, SEIU had only five state councils with year-round, full-time political and legislative staff and programs. By 1997, a strong state council system was in place in 18 states. And in 1999, SEIU had active political programs in 21 states representing 94 percent of SEIU members in the United States.

Polling showed members' attitudes about the union's performance had improved from surveys done in 1993 for the Committee on the Future. Some 65 percent of those polled in 1998 said the union was doing either an excellent or a good job, up from 57 percent in 1993. The polling showed strong support for SEIU's decision to focus on organizing, increased political action, and giving members more voice in the workplace.

Compared to earlier polls, more members reported they had "a lot of contact with the union steward or delegate on the job." And 58 percent said they believed that organizing new members in their sector would have a positive impact on what happened to them in their own workplaces.

When SEIU asked workers what they wanted in a union, they responded that they wanted a stronger union and a more united one.[100] And the members, according to then-Organizing Director Tom Woodruff, said they wanted to win. "Fighting and trying were OK, but they were tired of not winning at the end of it all," he later wrote.

The President's Committee 2000 looked in the mirror to assess SEIU's performance over the previous three years, but it also looked out the windows to the broader world and examined the economy, the state of the entire labor movement, and the political scenarios the union could find itself in going forward.

Among the elements of that analysis were:

• Wages, benefits, and working conditions had gotten worse in the midst of the economic boom of the late 1990s. American workers faced a 20-year pattern of stagnant and declining workers' wages. Union workers did fare better than those who were nonunion—earning 34 percent more, or $640 a week, compared to $478 a week for nonunion workers.

• Yet pay for corporate executives had skyrocketed. The average CEO in 1965 made 44 times the salary of the average worker, while in 1999 that CEO got 326 times the pay of the average worker.

• African-American workers earned only 76.5 percent as much as white workers, while Latino wages were 79 percent of white workers' wages—and declining.

• Women workers earned only 76.8 percent as much as men in 1999.

• The number of Americans without health insurance reached a then-record high of 41.7 million. Those still fortunate enough to have insurance were paying more for it.

- Only 43 percent of all full-time, private-sector workers were covered by a retirement plan at work.

- As wages, healthcare, and retirement benefits declined, the average married couple had to work longer hours to make ends meet. From 1989 through 1996, married workers worked additional hours amounting to an extra three weeks per year, making it tough on family life.

- Corporations continued to close operations in the U.S. and Canada and shift work overseas to countries with cheaper labor markets and often repressive practices toward unions and workers. Millions of jobs had been lost, despite the U.S. economy's strength in the late 1990s, and the trade deficit hit $248 billion as the impact of NAFTA and other free trade policies of President Clinton and Republican members of Congress took hold.

- The gap between the rich and everyone else continued to widen. The richest 10 percent of Americans owned half of all the wealth in 1976, but that figure rose to 70 percent by 1995.[101]

In addition, the President's Committee 2000 found that one reason for the huge wealth gap in the United States was the decline in union strength. The rate of unionization had been 35 percent in 1955, but dropped to only 13.9 percent by 1998. And despite SEIU's impressive organizing gains, the percentage of union membership actually declined in 10 of the 12 industries in which SEIU was the lead union or a major union.

PC2K in its second report—*Imagine*—outlined a number of obstacles SEIU faced:

1. SEIU lacked the union strength necessary to take wages and benefits out of competition. In the union's core industries—healthcare, building services, and public services—the vast majority of workers remained unorganized.

2. The level of membership involvement in union activities was too low.

3. Too often, the union tried to "go it alone" in campaigns, instead of working with alliances and coalitions that would provide more strength.

4. SEIU continued to compete, rather than coordinate, with other unions.

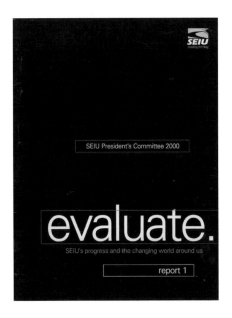

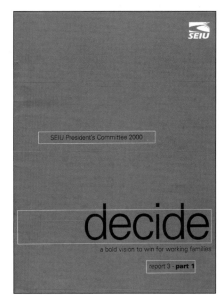

5. SEIU bargaining structures did not align with employer structures. Employers coordinated regionally or nationally, but SEIU locals took on fights by themselves.

6. The union did not always use the most effective, proven strategies.

7. SEIU still did not have sufficient resources, or adequate mechanisms built into the union's structure for sharing and pooling resources.

At meetings of SEIU members all around the United States and Canada, the issue of "industry strength" gained momentum throughout 1999 and early 2000. The committee began to compile common themes among workers' views about the strength of the union in their sectors. Among the topics were the overall unionization rate and SEIU density in a particular industry market; organizing of relevant workforces; union bargaining structure aligned with employer's; political strength; local leader involvement and active rank-and-file members; community/public support; employer's economic health and its relationship with the union; and union relationship with employer stakeholders, such as clients, tenants, and shareholders.

In the early days of SEIU, most members were janitors at apartments and office buildings, as described in the early chapters of this book. Bargaining then was done on a local basis, and if one local did poorly for its members, it seldom affected workers in other locals.

But PC2K found huge changes had occurred over time in core SEIU sectors. Building ownership by the 1990s had gone regional, national, and even international. Major owners included privately held real estate firms, large financial institutions, and publicly held corporations with properties in many cities, regions, and countries.

In healthcare, hospitals that were once independent in many cases had become part of giant healthcare conglomerates. Sixty percent of nursing homes, once primarily local operations, had become part of national, regional, or in-state chains. And in public services, state and local employers had organized into associations to advance national agendas.

The President's Committee 2000 established 11 principles for creating what it called "A 21st Century SEIU." As it tried to move to the decision recommendations phase, its *Imagine* report laid out a frame for the final debate leading to the 2000 convention with these broad strokes, starting with a Declaration of Unity:

"Our mission is to improve the lives of working people and their families and lead the way to a more just and humane society. We must have the courage to lead with this mission in the face of new and ever-changing challenges and obstacles. No matter how threatening our environment is, one thing is certain: When we are stronger and more united, we can make a difference for our members and all working people."

As the President's Committee 2000 approached its final recommendations for change, it expanded its outreach to members, through its own website, production of reports and materials (in a variety of languages), and videos and slide shows summarizing their work and the big questions facing SEIU.

With the debate and discussion surging through locals from San Jose to Sarasota, decision time approached.

# The Principles For A 21st Century SEIU

**Principle 1:** We are stronger and more united when we speak with one voice at the bargaining table, within our industries, at the worksite, in organizing, in federal, state, and local legislative arenas, in politics, in relations with other unions, and in the communities where our members work and live.

**Principle 2:** We are stronger and more united when our union's structure and decision-making processes fit the structures and decision-making processes that drive the industries and markets where our members earn their living.

**Principle 3:** We are stronger and more united when locals and the International Union have the capacity to carry out the most effective strategies and when we all carry out high-priority strategic program initiatives together.

**Principle 4:** We are stronger and more united when every SEIU and AFL-CIO structure has a consistent and effective role in serving workers' interests and when we can put significant resources and decision-making authority at the level where they will produce the best results for workers.

**Principle 5:** We are stronger and more united when all locals and intermediate bodies are known by "SEIU."

**Principle 6:** We are stronger and more united when we use the best available tools, including new technology to be developed in the future, to educate, organize, mobilize, and communicate with our members.

**Principle 7:** We are stronger and more united when local union leaders have greater decision-making responsibility within the International Union and there are opportunities for leaders at all levels to take more responsibility for developing and carrying out the union's program.

**Principle 8:** We are stronger and more united when the International Union and industry divisions establish those standards of accountability that have been proven, through the union's experience at all levels, to maximize our effectiveness.

**Principle 9:** We are stronger and more united when we have the courage to make changes that have the power to change workers' lives.

**Principle 10:** We are stronger and more united when union leaders, staff, and programs reflect the diversity of our current, future, and retired membership and the many languages they use to communicate.

**Principle 11:** We are stronger and more united when we ensure the best training of leaders, members, and staff.

ether
PFAFFENBICHLER 2002

CHAPTER 13

# Convention 2000

## New Strength Unity Plan

By the time thousands of rank-and-file SEIU members from the United States, Canada, and Puerto Rico filed into the David L. Lawrence Convention Center in Pittsburgh on May 21, 2000, SEIU had become the largest private sector union in North America.

The union had added 316,300 members in the four years since Andy Stern became president in 1996 and surpassed the 1.4 million-member mark, putting SEIU ahead of AFSCME, Teamsters, UFCW, and other labor powerhouses.[102]

"Four years ago we came to this convention as the fastest-growing union in North America," Stern said in his keynote address. "Today, we are the fasting-growing in the world."[103]

Indeed, more than 155,000 workers won a voice on the job in 1999 with SEIU—the largest gain in membership for any union in 82 years. The victory of 74,000 Los Angeles home care workers, of course, headlined the year's successes, but the union also gained another 8,000 home care workers in the United States and Canada.

Other healthcare workers also chose SEIU that year, such as the 1,500 nurses at Allegheny General Hospital who voted to join SEIU District 1199P, becoming the first group of registered nurses at a Pittsburgh hospital—near where the convention was held—to form a union. Other health aides, technicians, nurses, and doctors joined some 46 SEIU locals in 1999, pushing total healthcare gains above 100,000 new members.

In the public sector, convention delegates heard that nearly 46,000 federal, state, county, and municipal workers organized with 35 SEIU local unions to gain a voice to improve public services. Among them were 10,000 school workers in Puerto

Rico, such as Mayra Perez-Ruiz, a special education aide who voted to join Local 1996SPT because of the short-staffing, insufficient training, obsolete equipment, and chronic lack of supplies.

SEIU and other AFL-CIO affiliates had allied with public workers in Puerto Rico to win collective bargaining rights a year earlier. Janitors and security guards subsequently voted to join SEIU, as did nonteaching professionals and office workers—on election night shouting "¡GANAMOS!" (Spanish for "We Won") in celebration (see Chapter 29 on SEIU in Puerto Rico).

In California, nearly 30,000 public employees joined SEIU, including a number of county clerical and blue-collar workers, school playground aides, substitute teachers, and courthouse workers.

Convention delegates also heard reports that more than 5,000 janitors won recognition. Some did so in part through a Justice for Janitors campaign enlisting the aid of community allies to help win voluntary union recognition. At Fairfield University in Connecticut, for example, students went on a hunger strike to support 60 janitors who wanted to join Local 531. The result: janitors won union recognition.

In the months leading up to the 2000 convention, SEIU had launched a nationwide janitors' campaign to move to nationwide coordinated bargaining aimed at winning uniform contract goals, such as family medical insurance, full-time work, organizing rights, and significant pay raises. The union's building services division and locals had been successful in lining up year 2000 expiration dates for contracts covering 100,000 of the 185,000 members in that sector.

In Los Angeles, 5,000 janitors in Local 1877 struck 18 commercial building cleaning contractors in April 2000 seeking wage increases. Maria Santania, a janitor and single mother of two, wore a Justice for Janitors T-shirt as she joined others marching down L.A.'s Wilshire Boulevard. "I don't like to be

out on the picket line—I'd like to be working," she said. "But more than half my pay goes just to pay my rent. We all need a raise."

Janitors in Chicago's suburbs pushed for health insurance with the support of Local 1. All over the country, other janitors' locals lent support and staff to coordinated activity as part of the campaign. In Seattle, for example, Local 6 janitors sought and received sanction to honor the Los Angeles strike at Seattle worksites of the same employers.

On the stage with Stern during his convention keynote address were two janitors: Rodrigo Rodriguez and Roberta Hunter. Rodriguez was from Local 32BJ in New York, whose members were supporting the coordinated janitors' campaigns. His contract provided the best wages in the industry: $17.41 an hour with healthcare and pensions (in year 2000). Hunter, on the other hand, worked for Golden Mark, a nonunion cleaning contractor that paid her only $6.50 an hour with no benefits.

"Rodrigo and their entire bargaining team at 32BJ fought to include in their contract language provisions to make it easier for workers like Roberta Hunter to organize and get the same standards," Stern told the delegates. Organized workers knew their standard of living would be undercut if owners and contractors could operate nonunion in the same market, paying significantly substandard wages and benefits, he said.

"Building service workers have chosen to bargain together, to fight together, and to win together by uniting their strength from urban to suburban, and from sea to shining sea," Stern told the delegates. "It's simple and it's just been proven again. We are stronger together. We're stronger, when? Together!"

The convention delegates began to chant: "Stronger together, stronger together, stronger together." And that soon became SEIU's motto, not only for that convention, but for years into the future.

Stern also singled out Ruth Masacan and Evelyn Gaston, who were on the stage.

"Ruth was a temporary part-time worker with no union representation, no seniority rights, and low pay and benefits," the SEIU president said. "But the 8,000 members of Local 500 like Evelyn made the fight for union rights and benefits for those temp workers a central part of their contract campaign.

"And when they won, they made everyone's jobs and everybody's standards in Local 500 more secure. That's just one example of how SEIU public service employees have pooled resources to win tough fights."

Stern similarly introduced Lisa Taylor and Marilyn Hofsteder from Pennsylvania. Taylor was a nurse at Allegheny General Hospital who received help in the successful organizing drive there from Hofsteder and other members of Local 1199P from Hershey Medical Center.

The union nurses helped Taylor and those seeking to join SEIU "because they knew that the more healthcare workers in the state that are union, the more all workers will have more strength.

"So let me ask the leaders of North America's largest healthcare union," Stern questioned. "Are we stronger together?"

Members of SEIU Local 32BJ rallied in New York City to support residential building service workers seeking a contract from building owners in 2000. Anna Burger, then SEIU executive vice president for the Eastern region, joined 32BJ President Mike Fishman and 1199SEIU President Dennis Rivera at the rally.

Again, the delegates yelled back a hearty "Yes…stronger together!"

With that as a backdrop, SEIU delegates took up the recommendations of the President's Committee 2000, which were gathered under the rubric of the "**The New Strength Unity Plan**."

"It is time to decide if we are ready to take the risks necessary to build a union whose members can win every day—not just once in a while," Stern told the delegates. "Let's decide if we're content with eating the crumbs off the floor of this booming economy or whether we want a seat at the table.

"Let's decide whether we want a union that understands that trying is nice, and fighting is good, and mobilizing is important—but WINNING is the real deal for SEIU."

The outlines of the New Strength Unity Plan were:

1. **Build Strength Through Membership Unity.**
   - Help members solve problems in the workplace, win better contracts, hold politicians accountable, and help organize new members by creating a Member Involvement Program in each local union.
   - Improve communications with members by making sure every local union develops an effective communication plan and budget and by standardizing and upgrading membership lists for use by locals, state councils, and the International Union.
   - Help talented member activists gain the skills they need to become union leaders by creating a comprehensive leadership development program jointly supported by local unions and the International Union.
   - Ensure that all members have the opportunity to participate in their union by developing local union diversity plans.

   - Draw on the skills of retired members by involving them in union activities through state council-coordinated initiatives.

2. **Increase Coordination Among SEIU Local Unions.**
   - Pool some local union resources to support each other and pursue joint strategies by creating SEIU Unity Funds for healthcare workers, public employees, and building service, industrial, and allied workers.
   - Make the SEIU divisions a vehicle for local unions to coordinate regional, state, national, and industry bargaining, organizing, and action strategies to strengthen members' voices.
   - Negotiate better contracts by coordinating bargaining and organizing efforts when dealing with common employers and common markets.

3. **Greater Accountability to Each Other.**
   - Involve local unions in jointly establishing performance standards for winning better contracts, communicating with members, holding public officials accountable, and uniting all workers who do the same type of work.
   - Issue each member an annual report showing what has been achieved under the New Strength Unity Plan.

4. **Hold Politicians Accountable to Working Families.**
   - Train stewards, delegates, and member political organizers to lead a year-round program to involve members in making politicians respond to the needs of working families.
   - Create a strong political program in each local to raise funds and involve members in an unprecedented way to help candidates for office who demonstrate support for issues working families care about.
   - Make sure every state council has the financial resources to hold politicians accountable.
   - Ask every local to have a year-round, full-time political ac-

tion program, with locals of more than 6,000 members assigning staff to work full time on mobilizing members, and smaller locals sharing staff to build political action.

**5.   Keep Members Connected Using New Technology.**

*   Help members stay informed by ensuring that each local union has its own website.

*   Improve and speed up communications, expand member participation, and reduce costs by working to see that every local union and regional office has access to video-conferencing facilities.

*   Make sure local unions can keep members informed by acquiring or upgrading the technologies they need for maintaining member and email lists and contract databases.

*   Help new members get involved in the union by contacting and orienting them quickly using telecommunications technologies.

**6.   Increase Resources to Build New Strength.**

*   Adopt a special dues increase to ensure that local unions have the capacity to carry out the New Strength Unity Plan and win improvements and security for members.

*   Guarantee that every penny of new dues money will be used to strengthen the union.

The new Unity Funds were to be administered by SEIU's divisions—healthcare, building services, public employees—for industry- and sector-focused campaigns. Each local would pay $1 per member per month starting in 2001 and an additional dollar each year until it reached $5 per member per month in 2005.[104]

By 2005, the dues increase would yield $20 more a month per member, which meant a net increase of $360 million available at the local level.   Nearly 75 percent of the entire dues hike would stay with the local unions, even though the International Union grew its own resources.   One top union

officer said, "The idea was to keep the local union program strong and growing, while overlaying a national campaigns' breakthrough piece."[105]

Under the plan, SEIU raised per capita tax from $6.80 per member per month to $7.65 over five years—bringing the per capita to $12.65 (including the $5 Unity Fund contribution) that each local paid to the International.   It was a significant increase. But the leadership team did not seek any dues increases at the next two SEIU conventions, so the dues levels in 2010 remained the same as those adopted at the 2000 convention.

The new resources would allow local unions to fully fund the 20 percent organizing requirement, as well as to beef up all of their work: member representation, bargaining, and politics.[106]   Although most locals met the goal of devoting 10 percent of their budgets to organizing, only some had reached the 15 percent goal, and very few were spending the 20 percent. Given that the great majority of dues income remained at the local level, the big national breakthrough campaigns that required long-term commitments of resources often could not be funded.

SEIU NEW MEMBERS ORGANIZED
1997-2000

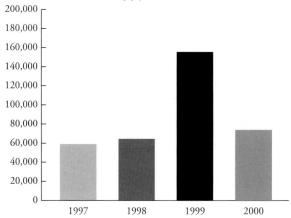

One SEIU official told researchers at Rutgers University that "through focus groups and polls, we learned that members would not be afraid of raising their dues, but there is going to be an evaluation of your job performance if you double the investment. . .[Members] were down for it—they don't just want to fight hard, they want to win."[107]

Under SEIU's democratic procedures, the union-wide dues increase required convention approval. Like tax hikes for the broader public, dues increases normally do not evoke cheers and euphoria among the local union leaders who regularly must stand for election.

But the New Strength Unity Plan ended up with broad and strong support on the convention floor (and later even in the local membership votes conducted by some locals). The two-year process of involving those at every level of SEIU in the debate over the President's Committee 2000 clearly helped local leaders and members to embrace the direction top officials advocated.

Cedric Crawford, a hospital worker in Baton Rouge, Louisiana, took a floor microphone at the Pittsburgh convention and told delegates: "No matter how fast we grow, there's still lots for us to do. Our members totally support this New Strength Unity Plan. It's the only way we can increase the resources we need, industry by industry, to truly make organizing a real priority."

Others noted the difficulties a significant dues increase posed, such as Cora Coleman, a home care worker from Illinois, who said support "was not an easy decision" for her local. "Our members are low-wage workers," she said. "We had some hard discussions, but we came to support this plan because we know it's what we need to do to win."

Ed Novak from Local 517M in Michigan noted that his local, which represents public employees, had more than doubled in size during the previous four years. "To do this, we've had to raise our dues," he said on the convention floor. "But as much as we've done, there's a lot of things we still can't do

SEIU members at the 2000 convention voted to be "Stronger Together" by adopting the New Strength Unity Plan that provided for expanded union resources to win gains for workers, organize effectively, and hold politicians accountable.

because we're too small and don't have the resources." The dues increase would enable them to seek collective bargaining rights for all public employees, he said.

In the end, only two delegates spoke against the proposal, both on the grounds they were opposed to the funding mechanisms.

The vote for the New Strength Unity Plan, and the new direction and resources for SEIU, was overwhelming.

"We came here to decide on our future," Stern told the cheering delegates after the vote. "And we just decided to fight like hell for our children—to fight against corporate greed and for human need."

Carmen Valcarcel of SEIU Local 32BJ is comforted by Lisa Barona (in pink), also of 32BJ, and others just after the south tower of the World Trade Center collapsed on September 11, 2001.

# CHAPTER 14

# The Tragedy Of 9/11
## SEIU Loses 61 Members In Terrorist Attacks

Every now and then after a long, humid summer, you get one of those days that dawns cool and bright with a sky so blue you just want to reach up and touch it. Roko Camaj of SEIU Local 32BJ often told his kids his work as a window cleaner put him so high he could do just that.

Camaj, a native of Albania, delighted in hanging at breathless heights over New York City. He even had been featured in a children's book about dangerous jobs called *Risky Business*. Camaj earned his hero status in 1993 when the World Trade Center was bombed in a terrorist attack. He had a sponge that he used to cover his mouth so he could breathe while helping a woman trapped in a stairwell to safety.[108]

But on this day, back at work after a vacation in Montenegro with his four brothers and hanging from the side of the 102nd floor of the North Tower washing windows, Camaj lost his life to terrorists who flew planes into the World Trade Center. He no doubt would have been a hero a second time, but he didn't have a chance.

Nor did 60 other SEIU members who died in the carnage on September 11, 2001. Nearly 2,000 SEIU members worked at the World Trade Center and adjacent structures. And about 700 were on-site when the first plane hit at 8:46 a.m. and the second at 9:02 a.m.

Local 32BJ had about 350 members on duty that morning—workers such as Roko Camaj who washed windows, operated elevators, and served as porters, tour guides, and security guards. Building engineers who belonged to SEIU Local 56FO also were at their posts. At three hotels in the shadows of the Twin Towers, 56 members of SEIU Local 758 were hard at

work when the attack occurred.

About 300 state employees who belonged to SEIU Local 4053/PEF were in their offices that morning—55 on the 82nd floor of the North Tower that was the first to be hit, and another 186 spread out over the 16th, 86th, and 87th floors of the South Tower, which was the first to fall.

Rose Riso, a state tax auditor and member of Local 4053, moved quickly when her tower took the hit. She served as the fire marshal on the 86th floor—a voluntary position that took on real importance after the 1993 attack on the World Trade Center. Riso ran to various workstations and insisted people evacuate the building after the other tower was hit.

But many chose initially to keep working, according to Dianne Fattah. "You think you're in an indestructible building," she recalled.[109] Many of those rounded up by Riso made it to the streets just moments before the second hijacked jetliner slammed into the South Tower. Riso, who had stayed behind to push stragglers to evacuate, didn't make it out in time.

Many of the first responders who rushed to Ground Zero to help also were SEIU members. David Marc Sullins, a member of 1199/SEIU, had almost finished his shift as an emergency medical technician at Cabrini Hospital. He and his partner rushed their ambulance to the scene and began immediately to stabilize the injured. Sullins was last seen entering Tower 2 to help rescue others. Then the building collapsed and Sullins, a father of two young sons, was killed.

New York City firefighter Christopher Blackwell, who worked a second job as a paramedic for an ambulance company in Danbury, Connecticut, had spearheaded the union organiz-

Rafael Escoto, a member of SEIU Local 32BJ and a PATH station janitor from New Jersey, reacts in shock to the towers of the World Trade Center burning after being hit by 9/11 terrorists.

ing drive there with SEIU District 1199NE. He died when the towers collapsed on 9/11. So did 32BJ member Esmerlin Salcedo, a security officer, who had rushed to his command center. An immigrant from the Dominican Republic, Salcedo was killed helping evacuate others when the tower he worked in collapsed from the terrorist attack.

With both towers down and smoke billowing as debris burned, hundreds of SEIU healthcare workers—nurses, paramedics, doctors, LPNs, and others—rushed to Ground Zero. They risked their own lives to help survivors who they treated for burns, broken bones, deep gashes, smoke inhalation, and other medical problems.

"I felt like crying," said Taufik Kassis, a physician and member of SEIU Local 1957, the Committee of Interns and Residents. But he kept treating victims in the midst of the carnage. Within hours, first responders like Kassis had help from other SEIU healthcare workers. Emergency medical technicians who belonged to SEIU Local 5000 in Massachusetts drove down to New York City immediately and went to work. Soon SEIU locals elsewhere had begun to assemble teams of psychologists, social workers, and psychiatrists—all members of the union—to go to New York to help with trauma and grief counseling.

The Pentagon, where 40 members of SEIU Local 82 worked as cleaners, got hit that morning as well, but all SEIU members survived because the attack occurred hours before their scheduled afternoon and evening work shifts. Local 82 members and staff—not knowing the status of their fellow workers as well as a group of disabled workers who often worked alongside them—went door to door until all were confirmed safe.

Christoffer Carstanjen, a member of Local 509 and a computer research specialist at the University of Massachusetts, had just begun his vacation, boarding United Airlines Flight

175.  His plane was highjacked by five al-Qaeda terrorists and crashed into the South Tower killing all 65 aboard.

SEIU President Andy Stern and Anna Burger, who had become the union's new secretary-treasurer in June 2001 upon Betty Bednarczyk's retirement, moved immediately with local union leaders in New York City and around the country to put a plan in place to help affected workers and their families.[110] A tax-deductible relief fund established by SEIU drew donations of $75,000 within the first hour after it was announced. SEIU's International Executive Board earmarked a $250,000 contribution, and money poured in from all over after the relief fund information was posted on the union's website. SEIU Local 32BJ President Mike Fishman helped lead the effort by the union to deal with the devastation to members and staff in the aftermath of the tragedy.

A 6-year-old in New York City sent in a $5 bill and a schoolgirl in Pennsylvania raised $230 for the fund. In the first two weeks alone, nearly $1 million was donated to help the victims' families. Becky and Gene Yates wrote to *SEIU Action* magazine, reporting that their 12-year-old son donated $50 from his savings account and helped to organize a rummage sale at his school.

Others volunteered to help, such as Diana Armstrong, an SEIU member in Michigan, who said that "as a mother and a grandmother, I can cook, clean, and baby-sit for some family who has been directly affected by this tragedy."

The huge outpouring of support underscored SEIU members' links to one another and a sense of a broad and diverse union family suffering an unthinkable, outrageous blow.

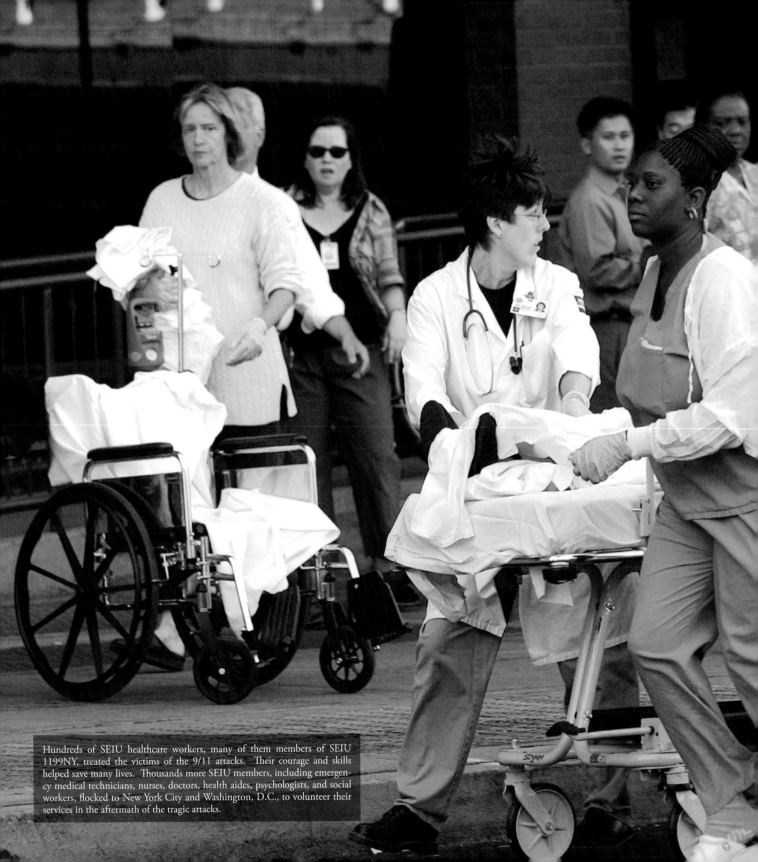

Hundreds of SEIU healthcare workers, many of them members of SEIU 1199NY, treated the victims of the 9/11 attacks. Their courage and skills helped save many lives. Thousands more SEIU members, including emergency medical technicians, nurses, doctors, health aides, psychologists, and social workers, flocked to New York City and Washington, D.C., to volunteer their services in the aftermath of the tragic attacks.

The initial shock soon gave way to anger among the broad American public. While much of that anger was justified, right-wing talk show hosts and extremists of the religious right soon sought to turn the shock and disgust over 9/11 into a vehicle to advance their own agenda of intolerance.

The sounds of sadness from St. Patrick's Cathedral still echoed from the memorial for the 24 members of Local 32BJ when the hatemongers around the country began their attacks on immigrants, even though so many of the 9/11 victims themselves had been immigrants.

SEIU President Stern, the other top officers, and local union activists quickly called for tolerance in the broader community.

In a statement issued September 14, Stern urged that action be taken to find those responsible for the attacks and ensure that they can never strike again.

"At the same time, we cannot condone attacks here at home on Arab Americans or other innocent people based on the color of their skin or the country they originally come from," Stern said. "Just as we are a nation of immigrants, we are a union of immigrants, with members from all countries of the Middle East as well as all continents."

Stern also blasted Jerry Falwell and Pat Robertson, calling them hatemongers who attacked American values when they said on national TV that "feminists, civil liberties organizations, Americans who believe in a woman's right to choose about abortion, and gays and lesbians invited the terrorist attacks on this country by making God mad."

SEIU confronted the backlash against Muslims and Arabs directly, with Secretary-Treasurer Burger convening a conference some weeks later devoted to strategies for not allowing the terrorist acts to pit workers against one another.

John Duengfelder of SEIU Local 4053/PEF drops a rose into waters near Niagara Falls, New York, in memory of 34 SEIU public workers who died in the 9/11 attacks.

# SEIU Window Cleaner Saved Six Lives On 9/11

Although 61 SEIU members died in the 9/11 attacks, the number would have been higher had it not been for the heroism of workers such as Jan Demczur, a window cleaner and Local 32BJ member.[111]

Demczur got on an express elevator in Tower 1 of the World Trade Center with the tools of his trade: a bucket, some rags, cleaning supplies, and his squeegee. In the elevator, he shared the ride up with five men employed by the New York Port Authority.

The elevator began shaking violently and came to a stop. The men pressed the emergency call button and were told there had been an accident. The intercom then went dead and smoke began filtering into the elevator.[112]

Window cleaner Jan Demczur, a member of SEIU Local 32BJ, found himself trapped in a World Trade Center elevator with five others on 9/11. He used his squeegee to cut through thick drywall, allowing all the elevator's occupants to escape before the tower collapsed.

After prying open the elevator door, they looked out on a wall painted with the number "50" on it, the 50th floor. They tried kicking the wall, but couldn't break through, as the smoke in the elevator grew thicker.

SEIU member Demczur took out his window squeegee and removed the handle so he could begin to pick away at what was three inches of sheetrock. He made some progress, then dropped the squeegee blade, but somehow managed to fish it back up from its landing point.

"It was like he had a willpower that we were going to get out of there," recalled Alfred Smith, one of those in the elevator. About 30 minutes later, still having no idea that terrorists had slammed an airplane into the building, which was soon to collapse, Demczur had made a grapefruit-size hole in the wall.

The others began to kick at it and broke through, only to be confronted by a second wall. But that wall was only one inch thick and Demczur and the five Port Authority workers soon broke through. They found themselves in the men's restroom on the 50th floor.

They became separated in the rush to get out of the building, but all made it out just before the tower collapsed.

Shivan Iyer, one of group that escaped, said, "I think of Demczur as a guardian angel."

Six months later, the SEIU member got a call from the Smithsonian Institution in Washington, D.C. It wanted Demczur to donate the squeegee used in the World Trade Center escape to the National Museum of American History.

David Shayt, a curator at the museum, told the Local 32BJ member that six million visitors each year would see the squeegee and reflect on the fight for survival in the midst of the terrorist 9/11 attack.[113]

Demczur agreed and also donated a soot-covered work uniform and boots.

The months leading up to September 11, 2001, saw immigration reform being hotly debated. President George W. Bush had called for an expanded "guest worker" program and SEIU, working with a coalition of religious and labor activists, had launched a national campaign called "Reward Work!" The goal: winning legal status for immigrants already working and paying taxes in the United States.

Sparked by Eliseo Medina, SEIU executive vice president, the union sought to fend off the wave of anti-immigration anger fueled by the far right, even as SEIU expanded its own work on behalf of the 9/11 victims. The families of those who lost their lives came first, but SEIU also ran extensive programs that sought to help the more than 100,000 workers in the New York City area who lost their jobs in the aftermath of the 9/11 attacks.

SEIU joined with hotel and restaurant unionists to form the Immigrant Worker Assistance Alliance (IWAA), which provided food, shelter, child care, and other needs of the workers who lost their jobs in the economic aftermath of the attacks.[114] With travel and tourism at a standstill, for example, workers in those sectors soon were laid off.

With the nation's focus on national security and retribution, combatting the backlash against immigrants remained a focus of SEIU political organizing. Union activists fanned out throughout the summer that followed 9/11 collecting signatures urging Bush and Congress to adopt a legalization process for immigrants already working, living, and paying taxes in the United States.

The coalition effort culminated in a huge rally near the

White House in October 2002 where Medina and other labor and church leaders called for reform of immigration laws (see Chapter 32).

"When immigrant workers don't have a voice in our society, when they're not paid a living wage, when they are forced to live in fear of deportation for simply going to work each day—that hurts all working people," Medina told the crowd.

And when Arlene Charles, an SEIU member who was working at the World Trade Center on the day of the terrorist attacks, rose to speak, the boisterous crowd quieted in respect as she addressed the rally:

"Hundreds of people I knew—workers from many different countries—were killed or injured. The terrorists didn't care about our nationalities or our immigration status. You didn't have to have a green card to be a victim."

Bruceville Terrace, Sacramento
Mark Twain St. Joeseph's, San Andreas
Mercy, Folsom
Mercy General, Sacramento
Mercy San Juan, Carmichael
Methodist, Sacramento

**SACRAMENTO**

St. Dominic's, Manteca
St. Joseph's, Stockton
St. Joseph's Behavioral, Stockton
Woodland Memorial, Woodland
Woodland Healthcare, Woodland

**SAN FRANCISCO**

O'Connor, San Jose
St. Louise, Gilroy
St. Mary's, San Francisco
St. Francis, San Francisco
Sequoia, Redwood City
Seton, Daly City
Seton Coastside, Moss Beach

**BAKERSFIELD**

Bakersfield Memorial, Bakersfield
Mercy Bakersfield, Bakersfield
Mercy Southwest, Bakersfield

**Organizing**

**Negotiating**

**Under Contract**

Marian, Santa Maria

St. John's Pleasant Valley, Camarillo
St. John's Regional, Oxnard

California, Los Angeles
Community, San Bernardino
St. Bernadine, San Bernardino

**LOS ANGELES**

Glendale Memorial, Glendale
Northridge, Northridge
Robert F. Kennedy, Hawthorne
St. Francis, Lynwood
San Gabriel Valley, San Gabriel
St. Mary, Long Beach

SEIU Gains At
Catholic Healthcare West
In 2001

# CHAPTER 15

# Breakthrough At Catholic Healthcare West
## SEIU Wins Huge Gains After Fair Elections Deal

Healthcare workers at St. Francis Medical Center in Lynwood, California, couldn't believe their ears.

Brother Richard Hirbe, who gave morning prayers at the hospital each day at 8 a.m., normally offered an inspiring spiritual message that comforted both patients and staff. But that day he had called for God to lead workers on the right path by opposing unionization.

Catholic Healthcare West (CHW), California's largest hospital chain at the time, owned St. Francis. Healthcare workers at a number of CHW facilities had been seeking to join SEIU, but faced harsh anti-union opposition. Indeed, Brother Hirbe didn't confine his attack on the organizing effort at St. Francis to his public address system prayers.

The director of spiritual healthcare services sent a letter to St. Francis employees noting that the hospital is dedicated to "building up the kingdom of God." Hirbe, a member of Brothers for Christian Community, wrote: "No union can make claim to building God's kingdom as its mission, just as no union can make you a guarantee, only a shallow promise of a 'better life'."[115]

SEIU Executive Vice President Eliseo Medina called Catholic Healthcare West to account, saying it argued that employees "have to make a choice between being good Catholics and being in the union."

"I'm a Catholic," Medina said. "And I've always listened to what priests, nuns, and brothers tell me. But I don't think this is what Catholic social teaching is all about."

CHW's anti-union campaign did not stay confined to PA-system homilies. In Sacramento, Mary Hillman began to notice security guards following her as she went about her tasks as a respiratory therapist at Mercy San Juan Medical Center. "Security would constantly follow union activists," she recalled.

CHW managers intensified their anti-union activity from 1998 through 2000. "Some of us were threatened by supervisors who said that voting for the union would mean we'd lose all our benefits," recalled Teresa Schwager, a clerk at a CHW facility in Sacramento. "I was one of several union supporters put under surveillance by security guards."

CHW retained the services of Management Science Associates, a firm with a reputation for "union busting." The healthcare chain, a nonprofit owned by a number of Catholic orders and run by lay management, spent at least $2.6 million on its anti-SEIU campaign.[116]

"A union—an outside third party whose values greatly differ from ours—would drive a wedge in the relationship," wrote three Daughters of Charity in a "Dear Team Members" letter to employees of CHW's Robert F. Kennedy Medical Center in Hawthorne, California.[117] Another Daughters of Charity letter at St. Vincent Medical Center in Los Angeles stated: "A union sets up an adversarial relationship within the hospital. It breaks down, even eliminates, direct communication with employees." Such ills emanate from unions "by their very nature."[118]

Workers at seven Catholic Healthcare West facilities didn't buy it. They united with SEIU between October 1999 and May 2000, bringing more than 1,600 caregivers into SEIU Locals 250 and 399. Importantly, those workers gave a boost to others at nonunion CHW hospitals.

But in Sacramento the relentless and harsh anti-union

campaign, including surveillance of SEIU supporters by private security forces, resulted in the workers at five facilities losing their bid to join the union.

"For us, forming a union was about patient care and the future of our hospitals," respiratory therapist Mary Hillman told *SEIU Action* magazine at the time. "By not respecting our freedom to choose a voice without interference, CHW management has done a great disservice to our community."[119]

The anti-union tactics of the former management of Catholic Healthcare West, while not that different from those often used in other sectors such as manufacturing, nevertheless crossed a line. Political leaders normally not disposed to take on orders of nuns such as the Daughters of Charity began to look hard at CHW's conduct. Antonio Villaraigosa, then the Speaker of the California Assembly, appointed a Fair Elections Oversight Commission to examine the hospital chain's conduct.

The findings of the commission, made up of prominent community and religious leaders and chaired by Speaker Villaraigosa, were devastating to CHW:

- CHW managers abused their power by taking employees away from their patient care responsibilities to attend mandatory anti-union meetings;
- Management was placing union supporters under surveillance and disciplining them for speaking about the union; and
- Management provided false and distorted information about the union.

M any CHW workers chose to work at its hospitals over the years in part because of the attraction of working in a nonprofit setting run by people with a mission or higher calling to care for the sick and those in need. CHW was founded in 1986 with eight hospitals and grew to have 37 by the time the conflict worsened in 1998. It then was the seventh largest hospital network in the nation.

As healthcare costs escalated in the late 1990s, CHW struggled to adapt to a more competitive and cost-cutting environment.[120] It escalated its merger and acquisition thrust and increasingly became obsessed with the bottom line under managed care.

For the healthcare workers at CHW, this translated into huge concerns over the declining quality of patient care, just as it did for other SEIU caregivers throughout the country who confronted similar problems. The short-staffing and broader deterioration of care spurred CHW workers to turn to SEIU locals as they sought a voice at work. Local 399 in southern California heard from workers there, while Local 250, which already represented about 3,000 CHW employees, received requests for support in northern California. Local 535 did as well.

The common thread in the CHW workers' complaints involved the chain's lay management not understanding how to prioritize patient care and to involve its employees to achieve that mission.

"They took a corporate approach to cost pressures," recalled Eliseo Medina. "They believed in order to survive the [healthcare] crisis, they could not allow workers to unite. We believed just the opposite is true."

SEIU's new and quite positive relationship with Kaiser Permanente provided a sharp contrast to the hostility CHW showed toward dealing with its workers. SEIU had tried to engage CHW leaders in a dialogue about cooperative labor-management possibilities. With tough struggles facing the healthcare industry, a unified and committed workforce could be an important ally for CHW, Medina argued privately to management, which remained uninterested.

Local 250, which already represented about 800 CHW workers, had bargained for the West Bay Area of San Francisco contract language that called for a speedy election—without employer interference—for CHW employees who wanted to join the union. In October 1999, about 255 CHW technicians voted for SEIU representation by a 3-to-1 margin after a campaign in which management honored its contractual commitment not to interfere with the workers' right to decide on unionization.

The Fair Elections Oversight Commission established by Villaraigosa took note of the difference in CHW's conduct in the West Bay and the massive abuses that occurred in the Sacramento organizing campaign. "By agreeing in advance to avoid such practices [used in Sacramento], the CHW hospitals in San Francisco made it possible for the election process to be carried out smoothly and without serious problems," found Monsignor George Higgins, a prominent Catholic cleric who had been a consultant to the commission.

The CHW workers' efforts to organize with SEIU won further support as prominent Catholic leaders, including the Cardinal in Los Angeles, publicly reaffirmed the many clear teachings of the Catholic Church that workers have the right to organize into unions.

In 1999, as workers at CHW sought to unite with SEIU, the United States Conference of Catholic Bishops convened a high-level group to develop principles and practices on labor issues for Catholic healthcare facilities. Chaired by Spokane Bishop William Skylstad, the committee included prominent

Workers at Seton Medical Center in California joined SEIU in 2001 after the union won the right to speedy elections without management interference.

Catholic leaders as well as Mary Kay Henry, SEIU organizing director, and Tom Balanoff, a top SEIU leader in Chicago.

The report the Bishops' committee issued, *A Fair and Just Workplace*, laid the groundwork for CHW workers to press the Catholic-owned hospital chain to provide a fair process for determining union representation.

Several years later, the Cardinal in Los Angeles put additional pressure on CHW when he stated: "Catholic teaching upholds the rights of workers—not bishops, managers, union business agents, or management consultants—to decide through a fair and free process how they will be represented in the workplace."

Along with the Cardinal, Archbishop William Levada, Sister Mary Roch Rocklage of the Sisters of Mercy, and then-California Attorney General Bill Lockyer all began to expand discussions with SEIU and Catholic Healthcare West, including a new problem-solving CEO named Lloyd Dean.

In April 2001, a landmark agreement was forged between the union and CHW that gave more than 10,000 healthcare workers the right to freely decide on whether or not to form a union without the interference of management. The deal laid groundwork for a new and positive relationship.

Monsignor Higgins called it "a historic document" that "goes far beyond" any previous labor-management agreement in the healthcare field.

"This is a tremendously important step forward," he told Catholic News Service at the time. "If anybody had told me a year ago that they [CHW] would agree to a card-check election, I wouldn't have believed it."

The agreement provided for representation elections within 35 days after authorization cards were presented by at least 30 percent of the employees in a potential bargaining unit. A similar arrangement was made between CHW and the California Nurses Association covering RNs. The SEIU deal committed both sides to expedited mediation and arbitration to

Mary Kay Henry led the successful organizing drive at Catholic Healthcare West in 2001. More than 10,000 workers at 45 facilities chose SEIU to represent them in a huge victory for the union.

resolve disagreements—thus forgoing many of the legal moves and countermoves that can delay a union election for months or years under National Labor Relations Board procedures.[121]

The deal also established a set of guidelines enabling workers at 45 facilities in California and Nevada to prohibit the use of pressure or intimidation to interfere with the workers' choice.

One-on-one meetings with supervisors and other mandatory meetings often used by anti-union employers were prohibited. The guidelines also established procedures for speedy union elections and provided for mediation and arbitration of disputes. Union staff and member organizers were granted access to CHW facilities to discuss employee issues.

Labor and management agreed under the pact to work together to address issues such as affordable healthcare, coverage for children, education and training for healthcare workers, and expanded rights for immigrant workers, including access to healthcare.

On the eve of signing the agreement, SEIU Locals 250 and 399 won breakthrough contracts at CHW hospitals already organized by SEIU that signaled what was to come. The two contracts separately empowered healthcare workers at CHW facilities to expand greatly their voice on patient care issues through a labor-management committee to set staffing levels, with disputes presented to a neutral arbitrator for a binding decision. The contracts also provided substantial pay increases.[122]

"We stood together and won a contract to improve nursing jobs in our hospital so we can deliver the best possible care to our patients," said Elaine Thomas, an RN at Local 399, which won its first contract at the time.

In the broader SEIU-CHW deal, the hospital chain did make clear that it still preferred to remain nonunion, and a letter to employees said CHW "prefers a direct relationship between employer and employee" but CHW will "fully support our employees' choice.

"If our employees choose SEIU, we will enter into good faith negotiations to reach a collective bargaining agreement in an expeditious manner and will work together with the union to develop a constructive ongoing relationship."

Between April and the end of 2001, SEIU organizers, led by Mary Kay Henry, fanned out across California. The result: more than 10,000 Catholic Healthcare West workers at 45 facilities chose SEIU to represent them, bringing the total number of CHW employees united within SEIU to 14,000. It was a victory of huge proportions for the union.

Today at St. Francis Medical Center near Los Angeles, the 8 a.m. morning prayers over the public address system provide spiritual comfort without any anti-union references.

# SEIU Unites 500,000 Hospital Workers By 2010

SEIU in 2010 represented about 500,000 hospital workers, including some 150,000 who united with the union since 1996.

Much of this growth came about in response to the cost-cutting and restructuring that occurred beginning in the late 1990s under managed care programs. Large health-care chains fought unionization efforts with intimidating one-on-one meetings with employees, mandatory "captive audience" sessions with larger groups, and an onslaught of literature that sought to mislead workers about the union.

SEIU began to engage hospital workers in corporate social responsibility campaigns to win fair organizing rules at large hospital systems.

In 2010, workers at all of HCA's hospitals in California were unionized and 100 percent of those in Nevada were as well.[123] California and Nevada SEIU members at HCA won across-the-board raises totaling 29.6 percent between 2007 and 2011, as well as step increases based on experience. Workers at 23 HCA hospitals also won a fair and just process for recognition through April 2011.

The successful struggle at Catholic Healthcare West described in these pages helped SEIU members there, over the six years that followed, to win raises of 30 percent to 90 percent depending on job classifications. SEIU also bargained family health insurance with CHW paying the total cost, pension gains that increased retirement checks by 30-40 percent, first-ever retiree health benefits, and staffing levels agreed to by both employees and managers.

SEIU also squared off at Tenet Healthcare Corporation, a large for-profit chain that had pursued vigorous anti-union policies. At its Garfield Medical Center in Monterey Park, California, for example, 450 registered nurses had to overcome aggressive opposition in 2001. They voted to join SEIU, but months later still had not been able to achieve a contract with Tenet.

SEIU launched a nationwide corporate social responsibility campaign that drew attention to Tenet's staffing policies and joined with community allies seeking to prevent hospital closings. By May 2003, the workers' efforts paid off with Tenet agreeing not only to respect workers' rights to form a union without management interference, but also agreeing to a first contract at Garfield and other newly organized hospitals.

SEIU members won unprecedented raises of up to 29 percent over four years, a real voice in staffing decisions, a ban on mandatory overtime, and strong job security language. Further gains followed in subsequent years with the most recent Tenet agreement at the end of 2007 providing wage increases averaging 28 percent, a ban on subcontracting in California, and fully employer-paid healthcare in Florida.[124]

## WAGE RATE FOR A PATIENT CARE TECH AT CHW'S NORTHRIDGE HOSPITAL MEDICAL CENTER

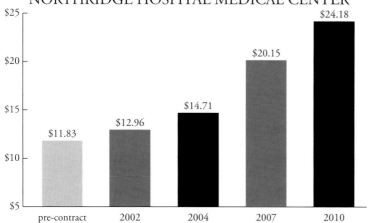

| pre-contract | 2002 | 2004 | 2007 | 2010 |
|---|---|---|---|---|
| $11.83 | $12.96 | $14.71 | $20.15 | $24.18 |

# CHAPTER 16

# SEIU's Political Clout Grows Despite Bush Wins
## Campaigns In 2000, 2004 Build 'Purple Army'

If SEIU members weren't so busy fighting for a better future, they could look back to the 2004 presidential election and say a well-deserved "I told you so."

The American people re-elected George W. Bush as President, despite a massive and sophisticated effort by SEIU and many others to defeat him. By the end of the second Bush term, just about everyone—Republican and Democrat—wished there could be a do-over.

Bush ended his presidency with the lowest poll numbers of any President in history. After eight disastrous years, Bush left behind the worst economic collapse since the Great Depression, as well as a nation enmeshed in two U.S. wars costing thousands of lives.

He damaged America's global reputation with his approval of torture and defiance of the Geneva Conventions. He inherited a budget surplus and, through huge tax cuts for the wealthiest Americans during wartime, managed to run up the biggest deficits in history. He eroded precious civil liberties, using the "war on terror" to excuse his assault on the Bill of Rights.

A poll in 2008 by the History News Network asked professional historians to rate the Bush presidency. The survey found that 98 percent of the historians concluded it was a failure. More than 61 percent of the historians said that George W. Bush was the worst President in the nation's history. Less than four percent ranked Bush in the top two-thirds of American Presidents.[125]

As SEIU geared up for the 2004 general election, the country had lost three million jobs from the time Bush took office and the number of Americans without healthcare had risen by four million. Bush also tried to slash overtime pay for millions

of workers. His tax cuts for the richest Americans caused budget problems that threatened many valuable public programs, such as Head Start and health clinics. And he sought to further weaken workers' right to unite together to form unions.

Massachusetts Senator John Kerry had won the Democratic nomination earlier in 2004 and picked North Carolina Senator John Edwards as his running mate. The Kerry-Edwards ticket had very strong SEIU support in the general election. In the earlier campaign for the Democratic nomination, the union's International Executive Board had backed former Vermont Governor Howard Dean in November 2003.

Dean won SEIU's early endorsement in large part because he embraced the importance of healthcare reform legislation. He also positioned himself as a progressive from "the Democratic wing of the Democratic Party" at a time when many activists viewed the party as too dominated by corporate interests. Dean also had opposed the Bush invasion of Iraq, a position shared by SEIU. Grassroots anti-war views within SEIU locals galvanized the union to send a letter to President Bush two months before the invasion urging him not to go to war with Iraq.

Thousands of SEIU members geared up to become involved in the early primaries and caucuses behind Dean. The union's money plus its skilled nut-and-bolts member political organizers boosted the former Vermont governor's campaign. Gina Glantz, a top assistant to Stern and one of the country's most highly respected political operatives, signed on as political director of the Dean campaign.

But missteps by Dean led to defeat in the Iowa caucuses and the news media seized on Dean's "scream" at the end of his

Vice President Al Gore won the popular vote in 2000, but lost the Presidency to George W. Bush. About 20,000 member political organizers worked on the Gore campaign and SEIU spent $20 million in that election aimed at defeating Bush.

concession speech in Iowa—repeatedly airing it in a portrayal of Dean most voters found to be strange. In fact, Dean's shouting in a loud and noisy room of campaign supporters came across quite differently on TV because the media had outfitted him with a special microphone that greatly diminished room noise. The incident helped bring an early end to his campaign after he lost New Hampshire, where he had been frontrunner before the "scream."

SEIU moved to support Senator Kerry quickly and by Labor Day 2004 had geared up for an all-out effort to defeat George W. Bush.

Just as the new leadership of the union had begun quickly to ramp up organizing efforts back in 1996, SEIU also had devoted more resources to political action. The union had mobilized thousands of members that year who had pledged to spend five days on political work, such as voter registration and get-out-the-vote efforts, and they had helped President Clinton easily win re-election over Republican Senator Robert Dole.

In 2000, SEIU built upon not only the 1996 experience, but also the union's huge victories in California in 1998, including the defeat of Proposition 226—that would have weakened labor there—and the election of pro-worker Gray Davis as governor.

In the 2000 New Hampshire primary, SEIU leaders there mobilized "Barney," a large purple tractor-trailer that served as a mobile, high-tech phonebank operated by union volunteers. The union proved crucial to Vice President Al Gore's campaign there with 24 percent of all New Hampshire voters coming from union households. Those union voters favored Gore by a 62 percent to 37 percent margin over former Senator Bill Bradley, Gore's main opponent.[126]

SEIU played a major role in Gore's nomination victory and in the 2000 general election. It spent more than $20 million and deployed thousands of skilled volunteers.

Gore strongly backed pro-worker positions on most key SEIU issues, such as healthcare, increasing the minimum wage, and protecting Social Security from privatization (as George W. Bush had proposed). But Gore also suffered from having had to embrace President Clinton's strong free-trade agenda, just as workers were hard hit from job losses due to NAFTA, WTO, and new trade arrangements with China.

SEIU activists such as Artie B. Hill, a Pennsylvania nursing home worker and member of District 1199P, worked hard for Gore in 2000—talking one on one with more than half of her 50-member chapter in Aliquippa. "I'm not telling people how to vote, but to look at the comparisons between the candidates that the union has prepared based on issues like healthcare," she said before the election. "A lot of people don't realize that Bush's proposals on healthcare are as weak as they are, and Gore comes out much better."[127]

Alice Cochenour, a member political organizer with SEIU District 1199WV/KY/OH in Columbus, Ohio, saw a threat in pledges by Bush to privatize Social Security and to privatize many public services. A similar fear that Bush would slash America's safety net motivated Doug Johnson, a housekeeping and maintenance worker at Northview Nursing Home in St. Louis and a member of Local 1001. In his work for Gore and other SEIU-backed candidates, Johnson said: "I've talked with the majority of my co-workers—I tell them that each of their votes counts."

The 2000 election remains a good example that every vote truly does matter. Gore won 544,000 more votes nationwide than Bush, but the U.S. presidency is decided by the electoral votes of the individual states. To win the electoral vote, Bush needed to win Florida. TV networks had called Florida for Gore as the polls closed, but by the end of the evening Bush appeared to have won there by several hundred votes—a margin so close it triggered mandatory recount requirements in Florida state law.

The Florida election had been marred by numerous reports of ballot irregularities. Among the problems were the design of the ballot in some counties where so-called "butterfly ballots" confused some voters. Other problems included so-called "hanging chads" in which punch-card voting failed to accurately and clearly reflect voter choices due to various mechanical failures of the voting machinery.

George W. Bush prevailed in the end after the U.S. Supreme Court issued an extraordinary ruling that halted Florida's recount process and effectively declared Bush the winner. Harvard Law Professor Alan Dershowitz found the Supreme Court's decision in favor of Bush to be "the single most corrupt decision in Supreme Court history, because it is the only one...where the majority justices decided as they did because of the personal identity and political affiliation of the litigants. This was cheating, and a violation of the judicial oath."[128]

Despite Gore's defeat, SEIU helped elect eight new U.S. Senators in 2000 and many pro-worker members of the U.S. House, including Hilda Solis (who went on to become Secretary of Labor in the Obama Administration). SEIU's "purple army" handed out more than 2.1 million flyers to co-workers at worksites. Members conducted more than 1.5 million phone calls to help turn out more than 750,000 voters from SEIU households. About 20,000 member political organizers worked throughout the long campaign.

The work in 2000 helped those activists gain valuable experience for the 2002 election in which SEIU helped elect 29 of the 55 supported congressional and gubernatorial candidates. More than 15,000 member political organizers mobilized in that election cycle.

SEIU members in Detroit, Michigan campaigned in the 2004 general election for Democratic presidential nominee John Kerry, who lost to George W. Bush.

By 2004, SEIU was able to take the lessons learned in the previous campaigns and shape the presidential election and other races that year in three important ways:

- SEIU fielded more than 2,000 "Heroes"—members who took leaves of absence and worked full time on the campaign for months in battleground states, along with some 50,000 part-time member volunteers.
- The union applied its organizing know-how to help set up the strategy and structure for a whole range of progressive coalitions active in 2004.
- SEIU made the largest investment by any single organization in the history of American politics through 2004—a total of $65 million.

The "Heroes" effort began early with about 1,000 SEIU activists packing their bags and moving to 16 strategic states to begin grassroots political work on behalf of union-backed candidates and issues. By late October 2004, that number had surpassed 2,000 and they had been joined by another 50,000 "weekend warriors"—SEIU members volunteering on their days off to canvass, work phone banks, and get out the vote.

Francois St. Phar, an SEIU member from Flushing, Queens (New York), was part of the "Heroes" program in 2004. He went to Duval County, Florida, where in the 2000 election nearly 27,000 ballots had been rejected, including many in predominantly black precincts where Al Gore captured about 90 percent of the vote.

"I'm here for my children and grandchildren and to make sure that what happened in 2000 never happens here again," he said in 2004. "This time the world will be watching Florida." St. Phar joined 13 other Heroes in working for Americans Coming Together (ACT) in Jacksonville.

ACT was a major player in the 2004 campaign. SEIU provided about $26 million to ACT, which was a national coalition of some 30 unions and progressive groups that did voter education and get-out-the-vote activities in battleground states. Led by Steve Rosenthal, former AFL-CIO political director and a close ally of SEIU, ACT had nearly 90 offices, 50,000 political canvassers, and a staff of 4,000.

SEIU also provided funding to America Votes, which helped to coordinate independent electoral activity and particularly grassroots initiatives by progressive interest groups. Cecile Richards directed America Votes, which worked with SEIU and other unions on voter registration and mobilization and provided electoral research and data to expand the impact of labor and progressives.

The union also supported Mi Familia Vota, American Families United, New American Opportunity Campaign, Voting Is Power, Caribbean Power Vote, Rock the Vote, and the New Democratic Network.

The SEIU-led Americans for Health Care helped make healthcare reform a top campaign issue throughout the 2004 primary season with billboards and TV spots featuring Iowa and New Hampshire nurses calling on the candidates to offer comprehensive healthcare reform plans.

SEIU spent more than $3 million on independent expen-

SEIU's "Heroes" program put about 2,000 members into the 2004 presidential campaign full time in battleground states. Another 50,000 "weekend warriors" used days off to canvass and work phone banks. The union put $65 million into the 2004 campaign and helped win crucial Senate and House elections.

diture TV and radio ads in 2004. And it sent out more than 4 million pieces of campaign mail. Heroes and volunteers from SEIU made about 19 million phone calls to voters and knocked on more than 10 million doors. About 355,000 new voters were registered by SEIU in battleground states during the 2004 election campaign.

Despite Kerry's defeat in the presidential race, SEIU's Fight for the Future campaign in 2004 helped win many significant contests at the state and local level:

- In Washington State, SEIU members played a vital role in Christine Gregoire's come-from-behind victory in the governor's race (Gregoire went on to implement her pro-worker policies, including executive actions supporting child care and education that also made it possible for child care workers to organize);

- In Oregon, SEIU helped Democrats win control of the state Senate, as well as gaining seats in the state House, and defeating a ballot measure that would have dismantled workers' compensation;

- In Nevada and Florida, SEIU helped win minimum wage initiatives;

- In Colorado, Democrats won control of both the state Senate and House and also elected Ken Salazar to be U.S. Senator;

- In Pennsylvania, SEIU supported Senator Arlen Specter's successful re-election campaign and helped win the state treasurer and state auditor races;

- In Maine, SEIU helped defeat a tax proposal that would have hurt vital public services by reducing state revenues;

- In New Hampshire, SEIU backed Democrat John Lynch in his successful campaign to oust the incumbent Republican governor;

- In Minnesota, SEIU member Patti Fritz of Local 113 won election to the state legislature, defeating a 10-year incumbent by fewer than 300 votes; and

Despite Senator John Kerry's loss to President Bush in 2004, SEIU's huge effort helped build a large group of member political organizers whose experience would be key to big pro-worker election victories in 2006 and in 2008.

- In Puerto Rico, the SEIU-backed candidate won the governor's race.

As Bush settled into his new term in the White House, SEIU Secretary-Treasurer Anna Burger, who directed the union's political operations, noted: "The second Bush Administration has wasted no time in launching attacks on working families' paychecks, healthcare, retirement security, and the right to form unions. To build the strength we need to overcome those challenges, we are going to take the political program we built in 2004 and expand it even further."

The union did just that. The valuable campaign expertise gained at all levels in 2004 would prove crucial in huge victories in 2006 and 2008 for pro-worker candidates. In 2006, SEIU helped Democrats regain control of the U.S. Senate and widen their majority in the House. And in 2008, the union played a major role in electing Senator Barack Obama as President (see Chapter 27) and electing large Democratic majorities in the Senate and House.

# SEIU's Fight For LGBT Rights

The March 2004 headline in New York's *Gay City News*—"Labor Cautious On Marriage"—hardly seemed like breaking news. As the article noted, the labor movement, despite its long history of supporting progressive causes, was slow to sign on to support marriage equality.

But SEIU and a handful of other unions had broken out of the pack and were standing up for the right to choose same-sex marriage. In Massachusetts, the SEIU State Council, representing 85,000 workers, had endorsed a court ruling allowing same-sex marriage in that state.

And just a few months later, in June 2004, delegates to the SEIU convention in San Francisco pushed support of gay marriage to an even more visible level. They adopted a groundbreaking "Equal Rights for All SEIU Members" resolution, with the vote concluding one of the most emotional and respectful floor debates ever seen at the union's conventions.

In 2008, SEIU and its locals across California opposed Proposition 8, which called for a ban on same-sex marriage, but it passed by a 52.3 percent margin. SEIU then joined others in urging the California Supreme Court to overturn Prop. 8.

"If a simple majority of voters can take away one fundamental right, it can take away another," read the unions' legal filing. "If it can deprive one class of citizens of their rights, it can deprive another class, too. Today it is gays and lesbians who are singled out. Tomorrow it could be trade unionists."

After the court upheld Proposition 8, SEIU joined with allies in California in a long-term effort to repeal the ban on marriage equality.

Paul Gonzales-Coke, a member of Local 1000 and a leader in SEIU's Lavender Caucus, evoked purple—the union's signature color—in summing up the union's history in support of gay and lesbian workers. "Purple," Gonzales-Coke said, "is just a deeper shade of lavender."

The path leading to SEIU's historic gay marriage debate—and to the union's continuing stand against discrimination on the basis of sexual orientation, whether in the workplace or in society at large—began decades earlier, when the labor movement was anything but an outspoken proponent of gay rights.

In his book *Laboring for Rights: Unions and Sexual Diversity Across Nations*, Gerald Hunt quotes a California gay rights activist as recalling that in 1976 Tim Twomey, then secretary-treasurer of SEIU Local 250 in California, "put out word to all his staff that people needed education on gay and lesbian issues and should not use derogatory language."[129]

It's notable because 1976 was only a few short years after the Stonewall protests that sparked the American gay rights movement and it also was a time when unions too often dismissed gay rights as a social, religious, or cultural issue—anything but a *union* issue.

In 1978, the link between gay and union rights was made clear by the proposed "Briggs Amendment" to the California state constitution. It would have banned gays and lesbians from teaching in California public schools. Teachers' unions—whose gay and lesbian members would have lost their jobs—worked successfully to defeat Briggs, with support from a coalition of progressive groups including SEIU local unions.

In the 1980s, the HIV/AIDS crisis raised consciousness of gay and lesbian rights even further, with SEIU healthcare workers witnessing the need for compassionate care for all patients—regardless of sexual orientation—and the need for all workers to have a safe and nondiscriminatory workplace. Local 250's AIDS Committee grew out of the crisis and did much to advance gay and lesbian rights as a unionwide priority.

In 1984, another turning point came when John Mehring, a young healthcare worker and member of Local 250, stood at a microphone on the floor of the SEIU convention in Dearborn, Michigan. He declared himself a gay man and urged the union to stand up for the rights of gay and lesbian workers. As Gerald Hunt's *Laboring for Rights* records, one delegate recalled later that "you could have heard a pin drop" during Mehring's speech.

Over the next few years, gay and lesbian members and staff began forming caucuses and committees at the local and regional level. These groups, such as Oregon Local 503's Gay and Lesbian Concerns Committee, networked with each other and were the forerunners of SEIU's national lesbian, gay, bisexual, and transgender (LGBT) group, the Lavender Caucus.

They fought to include domestic partner benefits in union contracts, for contract clauses and legislation to prohibit LGBT workers from being fired because of their sexual orientation, and for programs to train and educate SEIU members and staff on ways to fight homophobia in the workplace. Alameda County (California) workers in SEIU Local 616 were among the first in the nation to win domestic partner ben

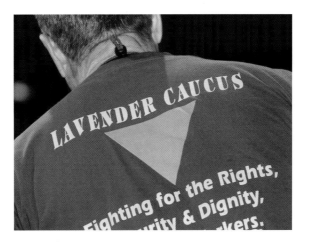

efits. Members and staff including Becky Capoferri and Ann Montague of Local 503, Ginny Cutting and Tom Barbera of Massachusetts Local 509, Bob Lewis of Local 250, and then-International organizer Mary Kay Henry were among the leaders in these early battles.

In 2004, Henry made SEIU history as the first openly gay woman to be elected to the union's top leadership. Her election as an executive vice president also made her one of the highest-ranking LGBT leaders in the national labor movement. Henry has been an outspoken advocate for marriage equality. She became SEIU president in 2010.

By 2009, with President Barack Obama and a progressive coalition including SEIU waging an epic battle to win quality, affordable healthcare for all in the midst of the worst economic recession in decades, the union's LGBT activists were doing what they had done for years: linking their fight for equality to the larger fight for healthcare reform and nondiscrimination in the workplace.

They were working to make sure that healthcare for "all" would include lesbian, gay, bisexual, and transgender Americans.

And they were making it clear that, as workers struggled to keep their jobs and provide for their families, it was more important than ever to fight for federal legislation to ensure union organizing rights through the Employee Free Choice Act and to protect LGBT workers through the Employment Non-Discrimination Act.

Dignity
Rights & Respect
All Pennsylvannia Nursing Home Workers
85·Local 668·District 1199P·Service Employees International Union AFL-CIO,CL

# CHAPTER 17

# Dignity, Rights, And Respect
## SEIU Unites 160,000 Nursing Home Workers

In 2004, thousands of SEIU members in Pennsylvania celebrated a victory that stood as dramatic testimony to the ability of low-wage nursing home workers to win improvements for themselves—and to improve the quality of care for their residents—by standing together in their union.

They won a master contract providing not only wage and benefit improvements, but an agreement by their employer to respect workers' freedom to choose a union without employer interference. What made the victory so remarkable was that the employer in question was Beverly Enterprises, known throughout the United States for its fiercely anti-union stance.

The roots of that amazing victory were in a three-day strike the workers launched in 1996. In the spring of that year, the long-simmering tensions between Beverly, then the nation's largest for-profit nursing home chain, and SEIU members at more than a dozen Beverly homes in Pennsylvania hit the boiling point. After futile attempts to bargain a new contract and tired of constant labor-law violations by the company, the workers went out on strike. Beverly's response was to "permanently replace" 500 of the striking workers.

It was the unlikely beginning of a dramatic and positive turnaround in relations between the company (now known as Golden Living) and its SEIU employees across Pennsylvania, which in 2010 included 34 facilities.

In the immediate wake of the strike, however, relations were close to the breaking point. SEIU members—at the time represented by SEIU Locals 585 and 686, and District 1199P, which later consolidated to become SEIU Healthcare Pennsylvania—set out to get their "permanently replaced" co-workers

reinstated, and they continued fighting for a new contract that would expand organizing rights at Beverly facilities. The year-long battle that followed included lawsuits filed by the union and public protests organized by SEIU to draw attention to the company's blatant labor law violations. When the dust settled, a federal court ordered the reinstatement of the "permanently replaced" workers and Beverly agreed to a new, four-year contract. "We not only preserved our union, we made it stronger," said Thomas DeBruin, then president of District 1199P.

But the new contract did not provide expanded organizing rights at Beverly facilities. And from the company's perspective, its goal of breaking the union had not been achieved.

"It had been a year of enormous resources being expended on both sides," said Neal Bisno, an 1199P staffer in the mid-1990s who went on to become president of the consolidated SEIU Healthcare Pennsylvania. "In the end, it seemed we had battled to a stalemate."

At that point, Beverly's SEIU members resumed their quest to reach out to the state's unorganized Beverly workers. They kept organizing more Beverly facilities, one at a time, through the traditional NLRB process. The breakthrough came when both the union and the company realized their long battles against each other were not, in the end, leading to better care for nursing home residents, sustainable wages for workers, or decent labor-management relations.

Beverly, by then under new leadership, and its SEIU members entered into a remarkable new partnership that ushered in a new era for SEIU nursing home workers at Pennsylvania Beverly facilities. As a result of the 2004 master contract provision guaranteeing workers the freedom to choose a union without employer interference, some 600 additional workers at 11 new Golden Living facilities were able to unite in SEIU, bringing the total number of SEIU-represented Golden Living facilities in Pennsylvania to 34.

The master contract also led to the creation of "Pennsylvanians United for Quality Care," a joint training and education fund that has provided enhanced training for more than 200 certified nursing assistants. The nursing homes that participated in that program saw worker turnover rates drop from 75 percent to 40 percent. And compared to 20 years earlier, when workers had been paid at or barely above the minimum wage, by 2010 they had some of the best nursing home wages and benefits in the nation.

Nationwide, SEIU represented about 160,000 nursing home workers in 2010 in 22 states. Some 56,000 of those had joined SEIU since 1996.

The nursing home sector changed when private equity firms entered the industry, with purchases of nursing home chains such as ManorCare by the Carlyle Group, a large buyout firm. But SEIU redoubled its efforts to bring gains to nursing home workers, who have a long and proud history as SEIU members and leaders.

Wages and benefits for nursing home employees are driven primarily by Medicare and Medicaid reimbursement rates. An example of SEIU's political strength: nursing home workers in

six states have won more than $850 million in rate increases during an era of strong pressures on states to cut Medicaid funding. In addition, SEIU nursing home workers in New York won more than $375 million in temporary and grant Medicaid funding.

In 2010, SEIU nursing home workers won wages that averaged $1.34 more per hour than those of nonunion nursing home workers. Typical SEIU contracts would include paid healthcare coverage, pensions, prescription drug coverage, paid time off, and a voice in decisions affecting nursing home residents.

### AVERAGE WAGES FOR CERTIFIED NURSE ASSISTANTS AT FORMER BEVERLY FACILITIES

| Year | Average Wage |
|------|--------------|
| 1997 | $7.66 |
| 2004 | $10.25 |
| 2010 | $13.54 |

As is true in other industries, nursing home elections supervised by the National Labor Relations Board (NLRB) often have been marked by strong employer opposition to unions and interference in workers' decisions about forming a union. SEIU frequently sought majority sign-up commitments at nursing home providers that agree to respect workers' freedom to choose a union. The union then would work to improve public funding levels, staffing, and quality of care under "alliance agreements." SEIU also backed legislative and political efforts to restructure state nursing home funding systems so that they encouraged, rather than discouraged, improvements in standards for nursing home workers and resident care.

More than 10,000 nursing home workers have united with SEIU as a result of successful corporate social responsibility campaigns in the nursing home industry. At Extendicare, for example, workers at 20 locations filed for NLRB representation elections in 2004, but intense employer opposition resulted in only a handful of workers joining SEIU. But Extendicare workers then launched a campaign to call public attention to poor conditions for workers and residents at the company's nursing homes. SEIU utilized billboards, newspaper ads, direct mail, and public events to educate the public. Two days after Extendicare workers began signing cards to unite in SEIU, the company agreed to majority sign-up at nearly 70 facilities in four states.

One of the union's toughest fights came in Connecticut in 2001, when 4,500 nursing home workers in SEIU 1199 New England conducted a four-week strike at 39 nursing homes. Republican Governor John Rowland deployed National Guard troops to escort strikebreakers to work and spent $20 million of taxpayer dollars to help owners pay replacement workers.

SEIU sued the governor, and the federal court found in 2002 that he had violated the nursing home workers' right to strike. Governor Rowland resigned in disgrace two years later and went to federal prison in 2005 for corruption.

Horizon nursing home workers in Ohio in 2002 had brought public attention to the need for higher quality patient care standards and a voice on the job for caregivers. As a result of the campaign, workers at 12 Horizon homes in Ohio joined SEIU.

In California, SEIU members in some 140 nursing homes voted to approve a strategy that involved an alliance agreement between the local unions and nursing home employers. Nursing home workers agreed to work constructively with employers to improve funding, staffing, and quality of care for nursing home residents. The employers agreed in return to respect their workers' right to choose a union without company interference or intimidation.

Through a neutrality framework, 3,400 nursing home workers in 48 facilities chose SEIU over the 2003-2005 period—nearly 90 percent more than had been able to join SEIU in the previous five years. In Los Angeles County, for example, the proportion of nursing home workers belonging to SEIU doubled.

In 2005-2006, for the first time, nursing home workers in California coordinated their bargaining with 16 of the 18 largest providers in the state. They won raises for most workers of 19-28 percent over 30 months as well as improvements in employer-paid health coverage. By 2008, the average wage for SEIU nursing home members at companies that had participated in the alliance agreement in California was $13.33 per hour.

SEIU organized nursing home workers at 69 facilities in Florida between 1996 and 2010—almost all through NLRB-supervised elections that involved strong employer opposition. Workers there fought hard for a rigorous state nursing home staffing standard and succeeded by 2007 in achieving rules requiring 2.9 hours of care per patient per 24-hour day. SEIU members in Florida also won a statewide law in 2002 banning employers from using public Medicaid funds to oppose union organizing by workers.

Gains achieved by SEIU home care workers in Washington and Oregon spurred nursing home workers in those two states to pursue arrangements with employers including protections for workers to organize in return for support for improving public funding levels. With SEIU's support, a $70 million increase in nursing home funding occurred in Washington from 2005 to 2008. And workers in Oregon helped achieve $51.8 million in increased funding for nursing home care.

The 2004 convention adopted the "Seven Strengths" program and elected top officers (from left) Tom Woodruff, Gerry Hudson, Andy Stern, Anna Burger, Mary Kay Henry, and Eliseo Medina. They joined in a march across the Golden Gate Bridge in San Francisco demanding passage of healthcare reform.

# CHAPTER 18

# The 'Seven Strengths' Program
## 2004 Convention Revamps SEIU's Focus

SEIU's 2004 convention, held in San Francisco, adopted a strategy for the following four years that came to be known as the **"Seven Strengths."**

The union had developed an institutional practice noted earlier of using the four-year convention cycle as a way to drive institutional change. Members and leadership would:

- study and debate the challenges and opportunities facing SEIU and what has and hasn't worked since the previous convention;
- seek to reach a broad consensus on what needed to be done over the following four years, through ad hoc committees of elected leaders as well as research and discussion;
- submit the program to convention delegates and adopt it there with refinements; and
- take necessary steps after the convention to implement the new program at all levels of the union. [130]

At the 1996 convention, delegates adopted the **"Bold Action"** program that set the new leadership off to reinvigorate the union. In 2000, SEIU's convention launched the **"New Strength Unity Program."** And, in 2004, convention delegates adopted the "Uniting Our Strength to Win Big" program—which soon became known within the union as the **"Seven Strengths."**

Top SEIU leaders believed the union had far more to do in aligning its structures to combat more effectively the way employers' corporate structures had changed. And the increasing globalization of the economy demanded that SEIU expand efforts to unite with other workers around the world that do the same kinds of work.

Seven Strengths became the blueprint for the work of SEIU local unions and industry divisions and called for shifting the union's focus from local autonomy to a new interdependence by building strength in seven interconnected ways:

1. **Industry Strength.**

SEIU decided that over the 2004-2008 period, all of the major organizing and bargaining work of the union would be driven by the union's industry divisions made up of the locals with members in each industry or sector. Members of each local union would develop a specific plan to do their part in carrying out the strategies of the four divisions: Public Services, Health Systems, Long Term Care, and Building Services.

2. **National Strength.**

To build the strength members needed to win big, SEIU delegates decided the union must transform from a "bookend" union with most of the members on the East and West coasts into a strong, nationwide union. Employment standards won in states such as California and New York—where SEIU had its greatest strength and more than 60 percent of its membership—were dangerously threatened by low standards in the majority of the country. Members in California and New York pledged to send member volunteers and experienced staff to reach out to unorganized workers in the South and Southwest.

**4. Global Strength.**

Huge global service sector companies routinely cross national borders and industry lines as they search for places where they can shift operations to exploit workers with the lowest possible pay and benefits. To confront this challenge, SEIU committed to step up its mutual support alliances with unions in other nations. The goal: unite workers who do the same type of work around the world.

**5. Political Strength.**

SEIU vowed to expand its political action programs at the local, state, and national level. The union established a new accountability fund dedicated to supporting public officials who show unusual courage in standing up for working people. That fund also would support efforts to unseat those politicians who betray workers.

**6. Community Strength.**

The union pledged to expand collaboration with community-based and constituency groups to win campaigns for healthcare reform, immigration reform, fair taxes to fund public services, and other major initiatives. SEIU sought to unite allies via the Internet who want to support campaigns through a type of virtual union to be called "Purple Ocean."

**7. Local Union Strength.**

SEIU launched new efforts to identify and develop the next and most diverse generation of leadership in the union's history, including the establishment of a new SEIU Institute for Change. The goal: to help local unions transform to meet the challenges of the 21st century. The institute introduced an innovative and comprehensive approach to developing leaders while helping them bring needed changes to local unions. The institute's premise was that leadership development and organizational change need to happen simultaneously.

**3. Labor Strength.**

Delegates chose to work to transform the AFL-CIO from its outdated structure to one that could confront the issues and challenges posed by 21st century employer giants such as Wal-Mart. SEIU acknowledged it alone couldn't muster the strength needed to win major gains for working families. And the union vowed to build new partnerships with other national unions on campaigns in particular industries and states.

"We have a chance to make changes that will help working people win big—not just in SEIU, but around the world," Andy Stern told the 2004 convention delegates. "We can create a union that transforms the powerless into the powerful."

The union had organized 351,000 new workers from 2000 through 2003, as the New Strength Unity Program was implemented. SEIU had strengthened its division structure, and local leaders comprised a steering committee within each division that, along with staff, made a plan to organize their industry.

Going into the 2004 convention, the revamping of local unions had meant that 80 percent of SEIU members were in differently configured locals than they were in 1996. The shift resulted in locals being organized along industry/sector lines, rather than geographic lines. Locals continued to operate in a geography, but only in one industry in most cases and their connection to the national union ran through their division

SEIU Executive Vice President Tom Woodruff played a leading role in many of the union's organizing successes. He began as an organizer in 1974 for 1199 and became SEIU's organizing director in 1996. Woodruff went on to run Change to Win's Strategic Organizing Center.

(i.e., Health Systems, Long Term Care, Public Services, and Building Services).

Locals had to have an annual organizing plan; had to spend 20 percent of their budgets on real organizing costs; and had to have an organizing director, full-time organizers, and a member organizer program.[131]

The local union organizing plans were coordinated in the industry divisions. This yielded a national plan for each SEIU industry that incorporated the plans of each local and added national projects. The SEIU divisions at the national level also had begun by this time to plan and carry out major "breakthrough" organizing campaigns made possible by the dues/per capita tax actions in 2000, including the creation of the special Unity Fund for that purpose.

Stern had appointed a committee of top union organizers and officials to analyze the union's performance since 2000. Executive Vice President Tom Woodruff recalls: "We were disturbed by the organizing results. We'd thought that by doubling the resources, we could double the results. That had not happened."

Many of the major breakthrough campaigns were multiyear efforts that had not resulted yet in victory. And the day-to-day organizing done by local unions had slackened as they devoted resources to the bigger campaigns.

"SEIU was not taking employers by surprise anymore," Woodruff noted. "Management was ready and waiting—having hired their union-busting consultants well in advance of our campaigns."[132]

This analysis led to the Seven Strengths program adopted at the San Francisco convention.

After the 2004 convention, the union shifted the responsibilities of its top national officers to meet the demands of the new mandate. Until then, executive vice presidents were assigned to oversee geographic regions of the country and worked with the locals in their region to carry out the work of

At SEIU's 2004 convention, President Stern welcomed Local 668 activist Roni Green to the podium.

the union. The new approach shifted to giving those officers supervision over the union's industry divisions, eliminating the regional approach.

There were two exceptions. First, the delegates had prioritized major new organizing and political efforts in the heavily nonunion South and Southwest, so Executive Vice President Eliseo Medina took on that responsibility. And the convention had voted to launch a major new global effort to join with foreign unions to organize multinational employers. Executive Vice President Tom Woodruff got that assignment.

The convention also elected two new executive vice presidents: Mary Kay Henry and Gerry Hudson.

Hudson came to SEIU in 1978 from the Hebrew Home for the Aged in Riverdale, New York, where he was a member of SEIU Local 144. Elected as executive vice president for the former District 1199 in 1989, Hudson spent more than a dozen years supervising 1199 New York's political action, education, publications, and cultural affairs departments.

A seasoned veteran of social justice movements and a skilled political strategist, Hudson earlier had served as political director of the New York State Democratic Party. He also helped lead the New York campaign in support of Jesse Jackson's presidential efforts and the successful New York City mayoral campaign of David Dinkins. Working with progressive groups and causes such as the environmental movement established Hudson as a labor leader who could fight in both the workplace and the broader community on behalf of SEIU goals.

Henry began working with SEIU in 1979 and rose to become organizing director and chief healthcare strategist and was elected to the International Executive Board in 1996. Her vision and leadership helped pave the way for groundbreaking agreements between SEIU and hospital chains such as Catholic Healthcare West, Tenet, and HCA. She played a leading role with the national Labor-Management Partnership at Kaiser Permanente. In the Midwest, Henry helped build a strategic alliance between SEIU and Allina Hospitals and Clinics in Minnesota that is centered on improving the quality of patient care, with caregivers working side by side with management to solve problems. Henry went on to lead the union's health division and, on May 8, 2010, became SEIU president following Andy Stern's retirement.

She was a founding member of SEIU's Lavender Caucus and spoke for equal rights for lesbian, gay, bisexual, and transgender workers at the 2004 convention. Henry took the floor on the importance of marriage equality. Noting that she and her life partner of 16 years (in 2004) were practicing Catholics who built their lives together, Henry said that because "we don't have a marriage license, my pension plan, her pension plan, and our home are not safely in the hands of the other should one of us die."

The equal rights resolution adopted by the delegates committed the union to support the right of same-sex couples to access the full and equal rights, responsibilities, and commitment of civil marriage and oppose laws and constitutional amendments that deny that right.

SEIU also committed to making equal rights, regardless of sexual orientation, a collective bargaining and legislative goal.

In addition, the 2004 convention delegates strongly condemned the Bush Administration's war in Iraq. The convention resolution noted that the Bush Administration had weakened rather than strengthened security in the United States, creating enemies around the world and alienating long-time allies.

It called for "an end to the U.S. occupation of Iraq" and urged support for troops and their families by bringing them home safely. "SEIU calls for full trade union rights in Iraq, including the right to organize, bargain collectively, strike, and oppose job loss through privatization schemes," the resolution stated.

The adoption of the Seven Strengths Program by the 2004 convention delegates charted the union's course for the next four years. But perhaps the biggest reverberation in the convention's aftermath was signaled in Andy Stern's keynote address when he warned that the AFL-CIO, as it stood, had "no hope of uniting the 90 percent of workers who have no union at all in America."

Stern said that in SEIU, when its own policies, traditions or even individual leaders slowed workers from uniting their strength, "we changed them.

"And sisters and brothers, it is time. It is so long overdue that we join with our union allies and either change the AFL-CIO or build something stronger."

SEIU Secretary-Treasurer Anna Burger became the first woman in the nation to be elected to lead a national labor federation when she was elected to chair Change to Win in 2005.

FOUNDING CONVENTION
Change to Wi

# CHAPTER 19

# Reform AFL-CIO, Or Build Something Stronger
## SEIU Helps Launch Change To Win Federation

The eight words spoken by SEIU President Andy Stern at the union's 2004 convention in San Francisco—*"either change the AFL-CIO or build something stronger"*—set off an intense public debate about the failure of the labor movement to structure itself to truly serve working families.

Those words served up a clear ultimatum and a challenge to the AFL-CIO and its member unions to either change or confront the prospect that SEIU would withdraw to build a new federation that would.

Stern, Secretary-Treasurer Anna Burger, and the top SEIU leadership had gone through a tough and often painful process over eight years of restructuring their own union so that it could better grow and enable its then-1.7 million members to win gains that gave them a better life. But they also knew that the broader economic, social, and political justice SEIU sought could not be achieved absent a labor movement that also revitalized itself.

At that time, only 1 in 12 workers in the private sector belonged to a union and fewer than 1 in 7 workers overall (private and public sectors) were union members. And nonunion wages paid by major employers such as Wal-Mart put downward pressure on the broader American and Canadian workforces.

Most U.S. workers, if they had health insurance, now were paying more for it in co-pays and deductibles, and employers faced higher premiums that pushed some to abandon their benefit programs. Employers now operated in a global economy that saw increasingly cutthroat competition, expanded utilization of new technologies requiring fewer workers, and increased imports into the United States from China and other low-wage producers. Many employers were dropping pensions, once commonly provided to workers when they retired after years of work.

"Our employers have changed, our industries have changed, but the labor movement's structure and culture have sadly stayed the same," Stern told the convention delegates.[133]

The union had spent several years analyzing the elements of SEIU's gains since 1996 and determined that similar changes and reforms would yield success for the broader labor movement.[134] "Within SEIU, when our own policies, traditions, or the interests of individual leaders kept workers from uniting their strength, we changed them," Stern said as he made the case for change in the AFL-CIO.

Three deep-seated failures of the AFL-CIO pointed to the need for it to change in order to better serve workers in a new era. First, it had failed to confront its own underlying structural impediments and those of its affiliates. Second, it needed to refocus on membership growth through reinvigorated organizing of nonunion workers. And it needed to modernize its strategic approaches to employers in the new, competitive global environment.

While the AFL-CIO had millions of hardworking, dedicated trade unionists in its ranks, it remained a loose association of 65 separate and autonomous unions, instead of a strong, united organization with internal discipline to carry out strategic plans to organize workers into strong unions.

"It's a structure that divides workers' strength by allowing each union to organize in any industry, then bargain on their own—even when workers share common employers," Stern told the delegates in 2004. "It has no enforceable standards to stop a union from conspiring with employers to keep another stronger union out…or from negotiating contracts with lower pay and standards than members of another union have spent a lifetime establishing.

"One more reason that the labor movement needs an overhaul is that it was not set up to deal with today's global economy or growing global companies," the SEIU president noted. "Today's global corporations have no permanent home, recognize no national borders, salute no flag but their own corporate logo, and move their money to anywhere where they can make the most and pay the least."

## AFL-CIO Consensus = Inaction Or Worse.

SEIU's 2004 challenge to the AFL-CIO highlighted the difference in the union's strength and reach in the 50 years since the labor federation was founded. In 1955, one in three workers belonged to a union. AFL-CIO membership was 16.8 million, while SEIU's was 215,000—just 1.3 percent of the federation's total. SEIU then did little political fundraising and did not play prominently on the national political scene.

John Sweeney's SEIU presidency saw the union grow both in membership and in its role within the AFL-CIO. His skill and personal relationships brought increased stature to SEIU. And the union's affiliations and expanded organizing yielded more members for the federation. When Sweeney became SEIU president in 1980, one in four workers belonged to a union and AFL-CIO membership had risen to 20 million workers (of whom about 3 percent were SEIU members).

SEIU also had begun to be a factor in the progressive movement. It was a founder and major funder of Citizens for Tax Justice, the Economic Policy Institute, Jobs with Justice, and other groups that sought to shape policy and political debates in Washington, D.C., and around the country. On the electoral front, SEIU by the early 1990s was raising more than $1 million in voluntary member contributions in an election cycle.

By the time Sweeney won the AFL-CIO presidency in 1995, SEIU had been playing a major role in the federation's debates and initiatives and on its committees and other structures. And the union had become a major initiator of a broad range of progressive alliances. SEIU contributed organizing experience, funding, staff, and volunteers for campaigns as well as strategic thinking about the major issues of the day, such as the need for healthcare reform and expanded job creation.

By 2004, Sweeney's ninth year as AFL-CIO president, the decline in national union membership worsened, with only 1 in 7 workers belonging to a union; more significantly, only 1 in 12 in the private sector were in a union, as noted earlier. This represented a drop of some seven million members from 1980.

SEIU's clout within the federation had grown as it reached 1.7 million members under Stern. The union made up 10.6 percent of the federation's membership. SEIU had two members on the Executive Council, was represented on the smaller and more powerful Executive Committee, and sat on all the main sub-committees.

In the broader community, SEIU's influence had grown as well, increasing its central role in defining the American labor movement to the outside world. The union recognized it alone could not change the country and needed to be a catalyst to help create and expand the impact of progressive partners. SEIU had founded and funded Americans for Health Care. It was a founding member of electoral groups such as America Coming Together, America Votes, America's Families United, Mi Familia Vota, and Caribbean Power. It held two seats on the Democratic National Committee, contributed more than $1 million annually to allied community and religious organizations seeking social justice, and spent more than $65 million on politics, including sponsoring more than 2,000 members working full time on get-out-the-vote efforts in its "Heroes" program during the 2004 Presidential campaign.[135]

Stern and Burger met with John Sweeney in September 2004 and outlined SEIU's broad concerns about the need for reforming the AFL-CIO. SEIU and four other unions had come together in a New Unity Partnership in 2003 that had no formal structure, but provided a vehicle to discuss the need for more coordinated industry-based organizing and other reform ideas.

"John was no stranger to our proposals, since most mirrored the changes and resultant successes within SEIU that he had instigated and watched blossom over the past 10 years," Stern later recalled. "I had approached John out of both personal respect and an understanding that if the change process was led by the president of the organization, its odds of success would be exponentially increased." Stern said he was prepared to be flexible in modifying SEIU's plans if Sweeney would accept the leadership of the reform process.

Sweeney suggested a small working group to consider the reforms, and his representatives mainly agreed with the merits of SEIU's suggestions. But they argued about their practicality, repeatedly saying that many unions within the AFL-CIO would oppose SEIU's proposals.

That resistance went to the heart of the problem. Often, Sweeney and federation staff had good ideas for combating labor's decline, as did individual union affiliates. However, the AFL-CIO's culture and history had made it an organization that operated by consensus—a constant balancing act trying to keep all the member unions happy.[136] That frequently meant that strategies that required tough choices and

discipline among affiliates were watered down to the lowest common denominator.

With 65 unions belonging to the federation, keeping them "unified" repeatedly meant either inaction or worse. The AFL-CIO constitution specifically states that the federation shall be composed of unions that "are affiliated with, but are not subordinate to, or subject to the general direction and control of, the Federation" (Article III, Section 1).

As SEIU continued to press the case for reform in 2004, no concrete proposal for change was forthcoming from the AFL-CIO. SEIU decided to defer issuing its own set of proposals publicly until after the November 2004 election because Stern and Burger wanted the union, and the entire labor movement, to focus all possible energy on defeating President Bush and electing a Democratic Congress.

AFL-CIO President John Sweeney

Members of SEIU, United Food and Commercial Workers, Teamsters, UNITE HERE, Laborers, Carpenters, and United Farm Workers sought the reform of the AFL-CIO. When that failed, they formed Change to Win, a new labor federation, in 2005.

The re-election of George W. Bush as President in November 2004 was a depressing development for the labor movement and the broader progressive community. The outcome reinforced SEIU's determination to push for meaningful change within the AFL-CIO—or, if that could not be achieved, to "build something stronger."

Months of discussions among SEIU workers and leaders in local unions across America and with allies for reform within other AFL-CIO-affiliated unions had led to a broad set of principles that SEIU and other allies in the labor movement believed could lead to change.

The "Unite to Win" program contained 10 elements urging new strategies by the AFL-CIO. The document, released in 2004, called for the following actions:

### 1) Build New Strength By Stopping The "Wal-Marting" of Jobs.

Good jobs are the foundation of strong and healthy families and communities. But the Wal-Mart business model of providing low wages and few benefits, shifting jobs overseas to exploit workers under poverty conditions, and viciously opposing workers' freedom to form unions is setting a pattern that undermines good jobs for all working people at home and abroad.

**Action Needed:** A key function of the AFL-CIO should be to support a strategy to win good jobs in America that is larger than the members of any one union could accomplish on their own. The AFL-CIO should establish a center to support such projects and should allocate to the center all of its $25 million royalties from Union Plus (affinity) credit card purchases. Challenging Wal-Mart should be its first project.

### 2) Build New Strength By Leading A National Campaign For Quality Healthcare For All.

Out-of-control healthcare costs and declining quality have become one of the leading threats to every family in America. At any given time, 45 million people have no coverage at all, and even those who do see needed improvements in wages and other benefits undermined by the rising costs of healthcare. Healthcare costs are now a leading issue in virtually every strike or lockout.

**Action Needed:** The AFL-CIO and its affiliated unions and allies should unite behind an all-out national strategy to win access to quality healthcare for all. The AFL-CIO should lead a grassroots campaign for this purpose with dedicated funding, campaign staff, and other necessary resources.

### 3) Build New Strength By Protecting Workers' Free Choice.

Independent polls show that between 40 million and 50 million workers would choose to have a union if they could do so without employer intimidation, pressure from their supervisor, and the threat of firing. The laws protecting worker choice were created more than 70 years ago and need to be modernized for the 21st century.

**Action Needed:** The AFL-CIO and its affiliated unions and allies must make it a top priority at both the national and local level to re-establish the right of workers to freely choose to form a union without employer interference. Far more resources and focus must be dedicated to that goal, and no elected official should receive labor support, including an AFL-CIO endorsement, unless they actively support free choice for workers.

### 4) Build New Strength In National Unions That Matches 21st Century Employers'.

Today's employers are more regional, national, and international in scope. While they pursue united strategies, workers' strength is divided in two basic ways. First, workers who do the same work and are in the same industry, market, or craft often are divided into multiple unions and have their strength divided in dealing with employers and public officials. Second, many union members are divided into national unions that do not have the size, strength, resources, and focus to win for workers against today's ever larger employers.

Transportation union members are divided into 15 different unions, and the same is true in construction. There are 13 unions with significant numbers of public employees and nine major unions in manufacturing. Healthcare union members are divided into more than 30 unions. In 13 of the 15 major sectors of the economy, there are at least four significant unions, and in nine of those sectors there are at least six unions. Meanwhile, only 15 of the 65 AFL-CIO national unions have more than 250,000 members and 40 have fewer than 100,000. Many of these unions, even with good leadership, do not have the strength to unite more workers in their industry and change workers' lives.

Most of the 15 largest unions that now represent more than 10 million of the 13 million union members in the AFL-CIO are increasingly becoming "general unions"—organizing pockets of workers in a wide variety of industries and further dividing workers' strength...True union democracy is impossible when workers who do the same type of work and deal with the same employers don't have the opportunity to decide how to pool their strength behind common strategies.

**Action Needed:** The unions of the AFL-CIO should involve union members in a process to develop and implement a plan by 2006 to: 1) unite the strength of workers who do the same type of work, or are in the same industry, sector, or craft, to take on their employers, and 2) ensure that workers are in national unions that have the strength, resources, focus, and strategy to help nonunion workers in that union's primary area of strength to join together and improve workers' pay, benefits, and working conditions.

To achieve these goals, the AFL-CIO Executive Council should have the authority to recognize up to three lead national unions that have the membership, resources, focus, and strategy to win in a defined industry or craft, or with an employer, and should require that lead unions produce a plan to win for workers in their area of strength. In consultation with the affected workers, the AFL-CIO should have the authority to require coordinated bargaining and to merge or revoke union charters, transfer responsibilities to unions for whom that industry or craft is their primary area of strength, and prevent any merger that would further divide workers' strength.

The unions of the AFL-CIO should work together to raise pay and benefit standards in each industry. Where the members of a union have clearly established contract standards in an industry or market or with a particular employer, no other union should be permitted to sign contracts that undermine these standards.

SEIU and its allies continued to press for reform in 2004.

## 5) Build New Strength Where Unions Already Have Some Strength.

One urgent need is to unite all workers in each industry, sector, or craft where union members already have some strength. In the early 1930s, few American workers had unions. A group, including the United Mine Workers, Amalgamated Clothing Workers, and the Ladies Garment Workers, made a commitment to change that. They formed the Congress of Industrial Organizations (CIO) to carry out a strategy of uniting workers in new unions in each industry.

The United Mine Workers alone provided $17 million (in 2004 dollars) just in the first year to help the United Auto Workers organize, and the Steelworkers and others received UMWA support as well. The result: By 1937, the CIO unions had united 3,419,600 members and had more than doubled the number of unionized workers in the United States.

**Action Needed:** Lead unions whose members have built strength in an industry or craft should be required to develop a strategic plan to help more workers organize and build new

Change to Win's founding convention met in St. Louis, Missouri, in September 2005.

strength and unity in that sector. To concentrate resources to help carry out those strategic plans, the AFL-CIO should return to those unions half of what they now pay in AFL-CIO dues ("per capita") each year. Those unions' plans must include using at least 10 percent of their national union revenue for organizing and uniting more workers in their particular industry, sector, or craft by 2006; 15 percent in 2008; and at least 20 percent beginning in 2010. Their local unions would have to use at least 10 percent of their income for this purpose by 2008 and at least 15 percent by 2010.

These changes will build new strength for workers by reallocating from union members' current dues at least $2 billion over the next five years for uniting more workers in each industry, sector, or craft.

## 6) Build New Strength Where Unions Have Little Strength Now.

The economy changed substantially in the 50 years since the founding of the AFL-CIO. Globalization and new technologies have reshaped work. In whole sectors of the economy, such as finance, insurance, and nonfood retail, workers are in unions in other countries, but have less union history in the United States.

In addition, few workers have unions in certain regions of the country, especially in the South, Southwest, and Rocky Mountain states. That undermines standards won in more unionized parts of the nation, produces more anti-worker politicians who dominate national policy, and makes it difficult to elect pro-worker candidates in national elections.

**Action Needed:** Key unions that have seen massive changes in their own industries that have left them with few opportunities for uniting more workers with the labor movement should have the option of being provided additional, matching resources to focus on uniting workers and building strength in new and growing sectors. The AFL-CIO should

Bruce Raynor supported the formation of Change to Win and was joined by United Food and Commercial Workers President Joe Hansen (left), Anna Burger (behind), and Laborers' Union President Terence O'Sullivan. Raynor went on to become an SEIU executive vice president and to lead Workers United, an SEIU-affiliated union representing workers in the garment, textile, laundry, distribution, property services, and hospitality industries.

help workers create new unions in sectors where they are needed and experiment with nontraditional forms of organizing in industries with little history of unions. The unions of the AFL-CIO jointly should develop a strategy to help workers in highly nonunion regions to join strong national unions for their industry or craft.

### 7) Build New Strength In Politics.

The members and unions of the AFL-CIO in the last decade have become more active and effective in political action. Using political action to create opportunities for more workers to unite with us and then using that new strength to change workers' lives through legislation and bargaining is a proven and essential strategy.

**Action Needed:** Member involvement and alliances with other organizations that share workers' goals should be the engines of our political action efforts. The AFL-CIO should allocate at least 10 percent more resources to its political member-mobilization fund and involve members in achieving: 1) public policies that help more workers unite with unions; and 2) other

major national legislative goals, such as healthcare and good American jobs, that improve the lives of all workers.

### 8) Build New Strength At The Local Level.

National strategies to change workers' lives cannot succeed without vibrant, democratic, and accountable local labor movements. Uniting the strength of members in each local union, in each community, and in alliances with other community organizations is crucial to growing stronger and winning changes on issues that affect everyone.

**Action Needed:** Leaders of the AFL-CIO's community-based organizations, the Central Labor Councils, have proposed that every local labor council be required to have a strategic plan for political action, for supporting organizing campaigns by unions that are uniting workers in their industry or craft, and for developing deep and ongoing community alliances. Their proposal calls for all unions in a metropolitan area to be required to participate in and support the local labor council, and for the councils to be accountable to the affiliated unions and the AFL-CIO for carrying out their strategic plans.

Their proposal also calls for the AFL-CIO to ensure that each council is provided with training to help carry out its plan and develop the next generation of leaders. This proposal should serve as a starting point for a renewed discussion about how to build strong local labor movements and community alliances. Consideration should also be given to new ways of bringing together stewards and other activists from all unions in a local area to help develop and carry out their council's strategic plan.

### 9) Build New Strength By Drawing On Our Diversity.

In today's America, no labor organization can be strong and united unless it draws on the diversity of our workforce and our communities. The AFL-CIO and its affiliated unions must be leaders in demonstrating that regardless of the color of your skin, the language that you speak, or your age, gender, ethnicity, sexual orientation, disability, or immigration status, you are empowered to play an active role as a member or leader.

**Action Needed:** The AFL-CIO and each of its affiliated unions should have concrete goals and training programs to ensure that the diversity of their membership is reflected in membership participation, elected leadership, staff, and conventions and other decision-making bodies.

## 10) Build New Strength By Uniting A Global Labor Movement.

The big corporations that dominate today's economy have gone global, moving from country to country, without national loyalties, to find and exploit the cheapest labor. "American" companies now do much of their production in countries such as China, Mexico, and India, while corporations originally from Europe and Japan are shifting operations to the United States, where the rate of unionization and standards for pay, healthcare benefits, and pensions are lower.

Global corporations have won trade agreements that make it easier for them to move production from place to place, while providing no rights to help workers improve pay, working conditions, and job security. The result of globalization is that workers in any one country cannot set and maintain high labor standards without uniting to raise standards everywhere.

**Action Needed:** U.S. unions must join with others around the world to form a global labor movement that unites workers by industry, sector, and craft to have the strength to win for workers with common employers. Friendly relationships between national labor federations, along with occasional international expressions of support during particular union crises, are not enough.

Unions in each country that have the focus and the capacity to effectively use resources to build strength in their industry or craft must jointly carry out international strategies to unite all the workers in their area of strength to win higher stan-

dards and stop the corporations' global race to the bottom. In addition, a new global labor movement must fight for trade agreements that raise labor and environmental standards to the highest level, instead of bringing them down to the lowest.

The "Unite to Win" proposal that drew the most sustained hostile opposition involved reducing the number of unions in each industry or sector. There were 40 unions that belonged to the AFL-CIO that had fewer than 100,000 members, and the average membership of the smallest 50 affiliates was 58,000.

SEIU wanted to see the consolidation of union membership into a core group of unions each focused on a specific industry or sector where it could build density and "market share." Stern strongly believed that density (the percentage of the workforce in an economy, industry, or sector that is unionized) held the key to labor's ability to bargain good contracts and to organize new members. Workers want unions to represent them when they see that organizing yields improved wages and working conditions.

The SEIU proposal for consolidation held out hope for such gains, but each union that would be merged had elected officers and paid staff that faced uncertainty about their own futures, no matter what good the plan would do ultimately for their members.

Indeed, throughout the American labor movement there had been a long history of tension over how to structure itself. The early days saw skilled workers organize along craft lines. Employers faced a workforce with workers in a number of different craft unions seeking their own separate agendas. The advent of mass production saw industrial workers form the Congress of Industrial Organizations (CIO) that wanted one union for each industry or employer.

The rise of the United Auto Workers, United Steelworkers, and other CIO unions increased labor's power by concentrating on building strength in particular industries. But the conflict between craft and industrial unionism continued on as the CIO merged with the AFL in 1955—a merger that did little to actually resolve that conflict.

With SEIU's consolidation proposal, the battle once again was joined. In the intervening years after the AFL-CIO merger, unions tended to service their existing members, who voted in union elections, and they put more rhetorical energy into organizing new members than they did on actually growing their base. Many unions let their core jurisdictions become more nonunion, while they organized the so-called "low-hanging fruit" in the public sector and in other industries where the employer resistance shaped up to be less brutal.

SEIU took heat as various AFL-CIO union leaders blasted the "Unite to Win" proposals. But in December 2004 a game-changer occurred.

Teamsters President James P. Hoffa, who had been at odds with SEIU on some issues, sent a tremor through the 16th Street AFL-CIO headquarters when he announced that his union agreed with a number of SEIU proposals, particularly the 50 percent per capita rebate plan. The Teamsters believed that per capita funds paid by affiliates to the AFL-CIO could be better utilized if half of the money was returned to the unions to grow through strategic organizing plans in their assigned industry or sector.

Suddenly, the SEIU no longer was isolated. And opponents of reform found in tatters their carefully constructed story line about an ambitious Andy Stern seeking to overthrow the man for whom he once worked as a protégé. Soon other major unions joined SEIU by offering their own reform proposals, such as the United Food and Commercial Workers (UFCW), the Firefighters, Laborers, and even the AFL-CIO's Building Trades Department.

With some 28 different reform proposals on the table,

Sweeney still offered no plan of his own—only appeals to unity and consensus. That continued until the March 2005 meeting of the Executive Council, where the Sweeney forces unexpectedly demanded a surprise vote on the Teamster proposal for the 50 percent per capita rebate.

"This was politics at its most savvy," Stern recalled later. "If you know you've got the votes, roll your opposition; put a motion on the floor, call for the end of debate, and take the vote to show who is in control." Sweeney did just that and the reform proposal went down 15 to 7.

Instead of routing the reformers, however, Sweeney's tactic ended up unifying unions that earlier had been mainly backing change individually, rather than as a group.

Anna Burger and Stern joined other union leaders who had supported the rebate proposal at a press conference after the vote. The reform group decided to form an informal alliance and begin to merge all of the proposals to modernize the AFL-CIO into one set of recommendations they could unify behind.

The Sweeney forces launched a public relations effort to frame the reformers as primarily seeking a shift of the federation's resources and emphasis away from political action and toward organizing. By misrepresenting the issue and framing it as a question of whether or not the federation would diminish its political activities, the AFL-CIO hoped to gain allies in the broader world of the Democratic Party and the progressive community.

With SEIU having just spent $65 million on the 2004 elections, Sweeney's public relations effort gained little traction. Stern and the other reform unions, such as UFCW, Teamsters, and UNITE HERE, clearly saw the need for *both* organizing and political action and reaffirmed their commitment to both.

Relationships worsened when AFSCME, whose president, Gerald McEntee, was a staunch Sweeney supporter, filed a lawsuit seeking to overturn an executive order in Illinois that had put SEIU on the verge of unionizing 49,000 family child care workers. SEIU's Illinois locals had been building support for 10 years among those workers, who were primarily low-wage workers, mainly women and people of color (see Chapter 21).

AFSCME had made little progress among those particular workers. But with the governor authorizing bargaining with the state government over child care reimbursement rates, AFSCME suddenly sought to take advantage of SEIU's long period laying the groundwork for unionizing those workers.

Stern called upon Sweeney to convince AFSCME to withdraw its lawsuit that would have nullified the organizing rights executive order, but the AFL-CIO leader promised only to look into it. SEIU lawyers prevailed in court and AFSCME's lawsuit was dismissed in the weeks that followed, but the gambit by McEntee further worsened the broader debate.

On June 15, 2005, Stern and Burger joined the presidents of the UFCW, Teamsters, Laborers, and UNITE HERE to announce the formation of the Change to Win coalition. They detailed a program that followed the outlines of reform that SEIU had been advocating. The unions in the coalition had 40 percent of the AFL-CIO's membership, but under AFL-CIO convention rules, the reformers had only 9 percent of the voting delegates. This raised the crucial issue of whether or not Change to Win unions would participate in the federation's convention.

As unionists gathered in Chicago for the convention on July 25, 2005, word came that Sweeney had offered to resign if the unions would remain in the AFL-CIO.

"It was a noble gesture," Stern said. "But his resignation would not have solved the underlying problems." While AFL-CIO convention resolutions incorporated some elements of reforms advocated by SEIU, Stern believed that the federation lacked the will to change its culture substantially enough to yield real progress.

One year after Stern had issued his challenge to either change the AFL-CIO or build something stronger, he stood together with allies in four other unions representing nearly six million workers and announced that SEIU would not attend the federation's convention. The following morning, SEIU and the Teamsters delivered letters to Sweeney and held a press conference to announce they would leave the AFL-CIO.

"It was a bittersweet moment, but after 84 years of SEIU's membership in the AFL-CIO, 10 years of discussion, and eight months of concerted but failed efforts to make change—it was time," Stern said.

The Carpenters and United Farm Workers soon joined SEIU, Teamsters, UFCW, Laborers, and UNITE HERE to create the first new labor federation in America in 50 years: Change to Win. The new federation had its founding convention in September 2005 in St. Louis and SEIU's Anna Burger was elected as chair—the first woman ever to lead an American labor federation.

Soon some 2,000 organizers and researchers from the Change to Win unions were meeting to develop strategies and campaigns. Adopting the mantra "Make Work Pay," the new federation established a Strategic Organizing Center under SEIU Executive Vice President Tom Woodruff that would be funded by 75 percent of Change to Win's income from dues. And the new federation began the exceedingly difficult task of expanding union growth at a time when the forces allied among employers and conservative politicians had seldom been stronger.

News media coverage of the withdrawal of SEIU and the other unions as well as analysis by some academics focused on the conflict between Stern and his former mentor Sweeney and the issue of relative funding for organizing and politics. That view remained prevalent even five years later, but as sociologist Ruth Milkman noted at the time, "These issues, however, were not at the heart of the split."[137]

SEIU, then and now, saw the need to fight to reform and energize the AFL-CIO so it could reverse the labor movement's decline as both a moral campaign and a practical one about survival. The union believed that not to act would condemn labor to continue to diminish in size and clout.

After the founding of Change to Win, Stern felt excited about the potential of the new movement, but he publicly and repeatedly noted that leaving the AFL-CIO and forming Change to Win were not accomplishments, but only opportunities.

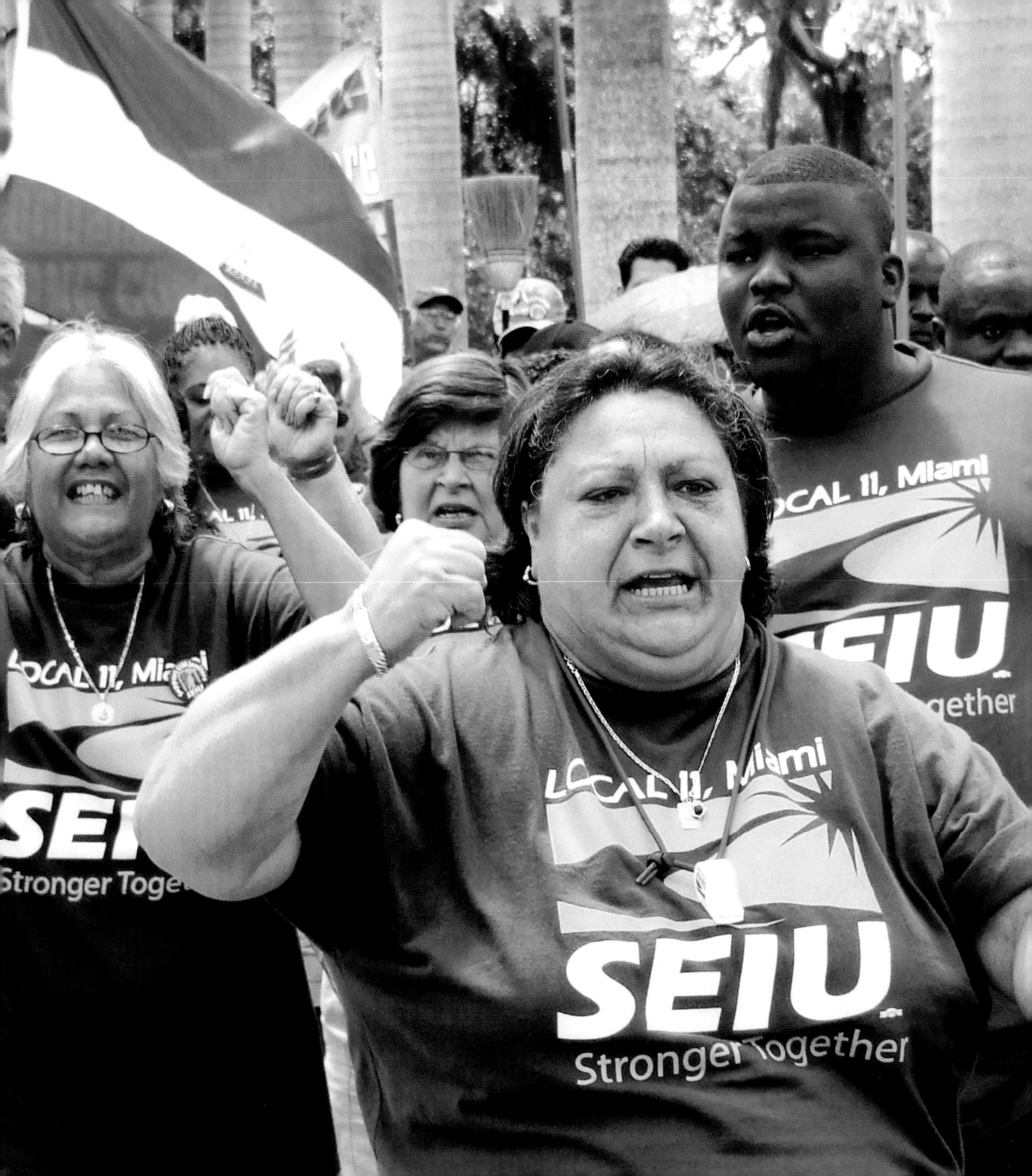
LOCAL 11, Miami
SEIU
Stronger Together

# CHAPTER 20

# SEIU's Moral Campaign At University of Miami
## Low-Wage Workers Say "Yes, We 'Cane'"

Zoila Garcia, a janitor at the University of Miami, could not be counted among the regular readers of *The New York Times Magazine*. But the 51-year-old immigrant from Cuba sat in her 24-by-57 foot mobile home on Southwest 8th Street after a 10 p.m. to 6 a.m. cleaning shift in 2006[138] clutching the publication with her blood boiling.

After five years of efforts to organize a union to improve their conditions, Garcia and other janitors working at the University of Miami had only been rebuffed, despite *Chronicle of Higher Education* rankings that revealed the school's average janitorial wages ranked 194th out of 195 universities surveyed.

Janitors there sought the support of Donna Shalala, UM's president and a former member of President Clinton's cabinet with a reputation as a liberal. Shalala had repeatedly rejected the janitors' pleas for her intervention—even after the National Labor Relations Board (NLRB) issued a complaint against UNICCO, the contractor providing custodial and landscaping services for the university.

Now Zoila Garcia, who earned $6.70 an hour, leafed through the glossy pages of the *Times Magazine* featuring Donna Shalala's 9,000-square-foot mansion in Coral Gables with its dining table for 24, collection of fine antiques, dock with a fancy powerboat, and luxurious gardens where she grew mangoes and grapefruit.[139] Shalala, who earned $516,904 a year, confessed that she couldn't get by without the hired help making her bed each morning.

Garcia's anger only grew as she discovered from the *Times* profile that Shalala's dog "Sweetie" had four dog beds. On and on it went. . .the luxury Japanese SUV, the Lenox china, and the

1790 French country cabinet. Shalala's perfect day ends with three sets of tennis.

Facing bankruptcy herself, Garcia wondered why Shalala's dog needed four beds. None of her fellow cleaners had an answer to that question, but they did have a response to Shalala's intransigence in the face of their organizing efforts: an unfair labor practice strike that would pressure the University of Miami's janitorial subcontractor for a majority sign-up process that could lead to unionization and, ultimately, to a contract.

Like the other 400 janitors and landscape workers, Garcia had no health insurance. Yet Shalala made her name in Washington, D.C., with her advocacy of healthcare reform during her tenure as Secretary of Health and Human Services (HHS). Garcia saw the irony of Shalala's disinterest in her workforce without health insurance, even as the janitor rubbed her leg blackened from knee to foot from a blood clot. A doctor had told her it would cost $4,000 to treat.

Ana Menendez, a *Miami Herald* columnist who reported with great insight on the janitors' plight, admonished Shalala: "No one is going to begrudge you your 29-foot motorboat or Sweetie's four beds. But for God's sake, get these people health insurance and a dignified wage. The bare minimum, that's all they're asking." The columnist contrasted Shalala's interview (favorite vacation spot: Kingdom of Bhutan) with similar questions for Garcia. Favorite vacation spot: "I'd like to take my grandchildren to Parrot Jungle, but we can't afford it." Shalala's ride was a new Lexus, but Garcia drove "a 1995 Ford Aerostar—when it rains outside, it rains inside."[140]

Two weeks after the *Times Magazine* featured Shalala's lifestyle of the rich and famous, Garcia and her fellow workers went on strike.

Technically, the UM janitors and landscape workers struck the Boston-based national cleaning subcontractor called UNICCO the university had hired. Much like office building owners in other major cities, universities had shifted to contracting out janitorial work and groundskeeping instead of employing workers directly. College presidents and administrators sought the same cost-cutting that outsourcing brought to commercial building services.

Within the academic community, with students and faculty often sensitive to wages and working conditions of university employees, school administrations found an added benefit to contracting out. It allowed them to evade responsibility for the very workers who served them. When workers complained about their pay or lack of healthcare and other benefits, college presidents shrugged their shoulders and said: "We don't employ those workers, so talk to the cleaning companies that do."

For companies such as UNICCO, winning the work almost always involved being low bidder. With labor costs the crucial factor, the cleaning conglomerates faced tough pressure to keep wages low or face losing their contracts to firms that could undercut them with nonunion wage levels.

With the 400 campus janitors on strike, Shalala kept to a script SEIU had seen before. She sought to maintain the fiction that the university was "neutral" in a dispute between janitors seeking SEIU representation and their employer, UNICCO. This fiction, of course, ignored what workers, students, faculty, alumni, and the community knew: that UM controlled UNICCO's strategy and ability to reach a settlement.

In Miami, a city marked by stark gaps between the rich and poor, there was a particular sensitivity at UM where professors, administrators, and researchers employed directly by the school enjoyed good pay and traditional benefits. By contrast, the primarily immigrant cleaning and groundskeeping work-

force—mainly people of color, including Cuban Americans and Haitians—worked extremely hard for poverty wages. And those workers had no health insurance and few other benefits enjoyed by the school's direct employees. A core group of faculty members—known humorously as "the comitato"—won a UM faculty senate endorsement of the idea that a "living wage" should be paid by UNICCO. But administrators ignored that call and did nothing on the health insurance issue other than to suggest a "health referral service" that would have done little to address janitors' real insurance needs.

A number of the workers wanted to join SEIU for years before the pressure began to build in 2006. One major motivating factor: word had spread that their fellow janitors who worked for UNICCO at Harvard University saw their wages rise to as much as $14 an hour after they joined SEIU. This had been the result of a worker-student alliance that led to a Harvard student sit-in in 2002 that helped win a living wage victory for SEIU workers. At UM, where they earned an average of $7.50 an hour, conditions for the Harvard workers sounded quite attractive.

So, too, did Harvard appeal to others, particularly the beleaguered Donna Shalala, who—in the midst of the SEIU strike—began to eye the presidency at Harvard, which had a sudden opening when the Ivy League school forced out Larry Summers.[141] Fresh from a damaging public relations debacle over Summers' sexist pronouncement on the alleged inability of women to do well in the sciences, the Harvard search committee sought a woman president to repair some of that damage.

On paper, Shalala fit the bill, but word soon spread in Cambridge, Massachusetts, about the Miami janitors' strike. The Harvard Student Labor Action Movement and the union janitors there took out an ad in the *Harvard Crimson*, the campus newspaper, that asked: "Will Harvard's Next President Respect Workers' Rights?" It described how UNICCO had been forced to pay more than $1 million to settle charges around the country involving sexual harassment and retaliation against female employees. After detailing the University of Miami conflict, the *Crimson* stated: "Until she's willing to make companies like UNICCO respect workers' rights, Donna Shalala should not measure up to our standards at Harvard."

The Harvard leaders, gathered in the wood-paneled enclaves where such decisions are made, wasted no time in rejecting Shalala's candidacy.

The Miami janitors began to win support as more people learned about their plight. Low wages and lack of health insurance brought some sympathy, but even more came from the compelling personal stories that the campaign highlighted. Clara Vargas was a good example. Like millions of other immigrants, she came to the United States seeking a better life for herself and her family and got a job cleaning six-story buildings with her fellow workers.

Vargas earned $7.10 an hour at UM with no health ben-

efits. "Workers like Clara don't have stock options or golden parachutes," an SEIU newspaper ad stated. "They don't own vacation homes or fly in company jets. What they do have is the heart and soul to keep our economy going. Don't let the middle class vanish—it's time to make work pay."

It was hard for Shalala to claim poverty. The university reported $1.38 billion in assets and had an endowment of close to $500 million. An additional $1 billion had been raised in the period before the dispute for the UM Momentum Fund. The university was the largest employer in Miami-Dade County, where the median annual household income was $35,966, far less than the national average. And UM janitors' wages of $13,104 a year put them below that county median.

The janitors' desire for a union was fueled when they learned that Harvard was not alone in paying its janitors fair wages negotiated with the union. St. John's University, for example, used UNICCO for cleaning services and workers there had united with SEIU. St. John's janitors received $18.40 an hour and enjoyed full family healthcare. SEIU janitors employed by UNIC-

Janitors and groundskeepers went on strike in 2006 at the University of Miami seeking SEIU representation and a fair contract. The strikers, mainly low-wage immigrant workers, had the support of students and faculty as well as local religious leaders. After a hunger strike, the Justice for Janitors campaign ended with an SEIU contract that gave workers big economic gains and affordable healthcare.

CO at Simmons College in Boston earned $11.85 to $17.29 an hour, depending on their jobs, and they received full individual health insurance.[142]

Students were an important constituency at UM, just as they had been at Harvard, Stanford, Georgetown, and other campuses where service workers had sought to unite with SEIU.

Organizers were pleasantly surprised to find a decent base of support among the students who believed the janitors and maintenance workers deserved better wages and health insurance. The union developed good ties with a student group called Students Toward a New Democracy (STAND) seeking its help in the struggle. A minority of students who backed the strikers included Amy Salmanson, a sophomore who lived in a dorm no longer being cleaned once the work stoppage began.

"I live on a floor with 17 football players," Salmanson told the *Orlando Sentinel*. "It's going to be a mess."

Organizers put together a kick-off rally for the campaign in September 2005 at which the janitors, groundskeepers, and other workers described their low wages, lack of healthcare, and desire to be represented by SEIU. Forums also were held in dormitories and some not only provided for janitors to tell their stories, but also included representatives of UNICCO, the cleaning contractor. In that informal setting, a UNICCO official had conceded that the university really controlled wage rates and the

firm would accommodate whatever wages and working conditions UM would accept.

This was a pivotal issue throughout the UM struggle. After janitors and students had marched on Shalala's office, a spokesperson had announced that UM would "remain neutral." As one UM grad described the situation to the *Miami Herald*, "UNICCO kind of puts the blame on UM and UM puts the blame on UNICCO, and neither of them has to take responsibility."[143]

As Shalala and UNICCO played the blame game, SEIU organizers, campus activists, and UM workers focused on widening their alliances. In addition to targeting students as one key to building support for the janitors' struggle, union organizers had begun outreach to Miami's faith communities shortly after SEIU decided at its 2004 convention that an expanded commitment would be made to organize workers in the South and Southwest.

SEIU asked for assistance from Kim Bobo, who led Interfaith Worker Justice and had extensive ties to progressive religious organizations. Bobo had worked with coal miners during a difficult strike at Pittston Coal in 1989. She and the Reverend C. J. Hawking, a United Methodist pastor from Bloomington, Indiana, initially had been enlisted by SEIU to help South Florida condominium workers unite with the union. Rev. Hawking developed union ties while assisting workers at A. E. Staley Manufacturing Company who were locked out in 1994. Bobo and Hawking soon shifted attention from the condo organizing efforts to the UM janitors as their campaign heated up.

SEIU President Andy Stern emphasized the importance the union placed on support from the religious community when he joined a Martin Luther King Day prayer rally attended by more than 400 people in January 2006. Father Frank Corbishley, the university chaplain, became a crucial supporter of the janitors, as did Miami Bishop Felipe Estevez, Father Richard Mullen, and the Reverend Dr. Joaquin Willis.

Striking janitors at University of Miami got strong support from activist students there, as well as faculty.

Striking janitors employed by UNICCO, a subcontractor at University of Miami, marched April 25, 2006, with their mops and buckets.

One major concern of the clergy and many others was UNICCO's poor record at UM on worker health and safety issues. That issue also hurt the university administration, because it seemed to be tolerating OSHA violations on its campus, even as it proclaimed neutrality in the labor dispute.

SEIU ran an ad in the *Miami Herald* headlined: "Why is the University of Miami Ignoring Its Cleaning Company's Dirt?" The ad said UNICCO had been cited for 40 violations of federal health and safety standards, including three incidents nationwide in which workers died as a result of on-the-job injuries. It also noted that the company had been hit with more than 300 workers' compensation claims in Florida related to hazards, including exposure to dangerous chemicals, burns from steam or hot fluids, and falls from unsafe ladders and scaffolding.[144]

Maria Isabel Galindo, a janitor, reported nosebleeds and headaches from chemical exposure from cleaning at the UM Jackson Memorial Medical Center complex, but without a union she could do little to fight back. "I am expected to clean the medical facilities at Jackson without safety equipment, without gloves, without training, and without health insurance—all for $6.40 an hour," she said. "I want to work hard, but I also want to build a life for my family that has a future."

The National Council on Occupational Safety and Health issued a report during the Miami campaign based on a detailed study of employers' workplace health and safety records. The independent report found that UNICCO ranked among the "Dirty Dozen" companies with the worst nationwide records for workplace fatalities, injuries, and hazards.[145]

UNICCO ignored the criticism and suspended six union supporters after they refused to carry a heavy machine up a flight of stairs out of fear it might fall and crush them. "We were summoned to the head supervisor's office and accused of refusing to work," said Feliciano Hernandez. SEIU filed unfair labor practices charges on behalf of Hernandez and his fellow workers and ultimately won not only reinstatement, but also back pay for the time lost due to their suspension.

Eight workers and six University of Miami students conducted a hunger fast to raise the moral pressure for a settlement. Several collapsed and were hospitalized after days without food.

The National Labor Relations Board earlier had issued a complaint against UNICCO for interrogating and threatening workers who supported the union and for promising better treatment to workers who did not back SEIU. As the campaign continued, additional unfair labor practices charges in the dispute included surveillance of workers by photographing and videotaping those on strike; threatening to fire workers if they did not end the strike; increasing the workloads of workers who supported the union; revoking vacation for an employee planning to visit her home country, in retaliation for union activities; and many others.

The workers voted on February 26, 2006, to authorize an unfair labor practice strike, which began on February 28, the evening before Ash Wednesday.

With crucial support from both student groups and the clergy, the strikers conducted a massive protest march three days after the strike began. Some members of the university faculty moved to support the janitors in yet another blow to Shalala. Law Professor Michael Fischl estimated about 100 faculty members backed the strike and even more sympathized. That led to about 200 courses being taught off-campus to avoid picket lines

and to allow professors and students to show overt support for the strike. Updates on the dispute appeared on a "Faculty for Workplace Justice" blog.

Shalala, a skilled maneuverer in the Clinton cabinet, knew she was presiding over a disaster as students, faculty, the religious community, Cuban-American activists in Miami, and the media all questioned her stance. Seeking to shift the climate, the university suddenly proclaimed in mid-March that it would provide 25 percent raises to the strikers (and all its contract workers). Predictably, much of the media praised Shalala for acting to resolve the crisis and some effectively declared the dispute all but over.

The striking workers didn't see it that way, nor did their supporters. The janitors still were denied an effective path to gain union recognition through majority sign-up procedures. They wanted a permanent voice at work, not just a one-time management gift.

For a brief moment it appeared Shalala had the upper hand. But then came word that same day that janitors employed by UNICCO in other states had put muscle behind their earlier expressions of support for their Miami sisters and brothers. SEIU Local 32BJ, led by Mike Fishman, conducted strikes in Pearl River, New York; Piscataway, New Jersey; and Hartford and Stamford, Connecticut.

"We are standing up for our fellow janitors in Miami, who are trying to win a better life for their families and are being mistreated by UNICCO," said Luis Vega, a UNICCO janitor in Hartford after his fellow workers walked off the job. "Until workers in every city have the right to organize and good jobs with healthcare, their fight is our fight."

Shalala traveled to Haiti in the midst of the labor dispute, but found she couldn't escape the conflict. She gave a talk on health policy there, but an organization of Haitian workers called Batay Ouvriye strongly criticized her for not providing UM janitors with decent wages and health insurance. "President Shalala knows that the Haitian community is upset with her inaction on the [labor] issue, and is conscious of the hypocrisy of giving a talk on health insurance while in Haiti," Batay Ouvriye said. "We exhort Mrs. Shalala to positively respond to the janitors' demands at the University of Miami, including those concerning healthcare."[146]

Back at home, Shalala had a new problem to deal with. Striking janitors had gone to Legends Field in Tampa, where the New York Yankees baseball team holds spring training, to appeal to Alex Rodriguez, the star third-baseman, for his support. "A-Rod," as he is known to fans, served on the board of trustees at University of Miami. The janitors delivered a letter to Rodriguez that said: "You are a hero in sports, a hero in the community, and a hero in many of our hearts." It appealed to him to intervene and tell UNICCO "to stop threatening, firing, and intimidating workers who want to form a union." The union had sought support from pop singer Gloria Estefan, who served on the UM board of trustees as well.

With the strikers holding strong, students and faculty still backing the work stoppage, and the clergy continuing to argue the moral case, activists stepped up the pressure. While some

SEIU leaders Andy Stern and Eliseo Medina assist weakened hunger fasters Leonor Ramirez (left) and Victoria Carbajal at the University of Miami. SEIU leaders took up the fast after urging the strikers and students to begin eating again to rebuild their health.

blocked traffic on U.S. Route 1 near the campus on March 28, others occupied the administration building until 1:30 a.m.—during which time they were denied access to bathrooms, water, and food. The students were threatened with arrest, forced removal, and possible expulsion.[147]

As the strike dragged on with Shalala remaining intransigent despite the pressure, some of the janitors' student supporters began to talk about a hunger strike. They felt UM had shown it would continue to reject majority sign-up as the vehicle for workers to express their desire to unionize and argued Shalala and UNICCO remained unwilling to deal with the unfair labor practices, such as the suspension of pro-union janitors.

The UM students knew that activists in Stanford's Labor Action Coalition (SLAC) had conducted a nine-day hunger strike in 2003 seeking a code of conduct aimed at better wages for workers there. And in 2005 Georgetown student activists seeking a living wage for school employees fasted for nine days and won many of their demands.

The hunger strike idea appealed to some of the strikers in their discussions with the student activists. They knew it would increase the sense of crisis and could help force a settlement. Some janitors had seen hunger strikes used in Cuba, before they had come to Miami.

But the idea worried SEIU organizers, who had concerns about the health risks for the workers and students who would participate. Nevertheless, the union respected their decision to employ tactics that would raise the stakes.

Hoping to force the stubborn Shalala to reach an agreement, eight workers and six students began the hunger strike on April 5, 2006. The son of one of the striking janitors joined them. They and supporters set up a tent venue called "Freedom City" outside the university entrance that soon hosted a 24-hour-a-day series of rallies, prayer services, and other strike-support events.

Ramon Saul Sanchez, a Cuban democracy activist, helped launch the fast and agreed to work with the Cuban American groups to build support for the janitors' struggle. "Civil rights are universal and no company has the right to violate them," he said. "Immigrants have made an incredibly positive contribution to our society and their rights should be respected here in Miami, just as in any other part of the country," he said.

Isabel Montalvo, a janitor, was the first to collapse. After the nurse SEIU had onsite determined on April 8 that Montalvo needed immediate medical treatment, she was taken to a nearby hospital. A day later, Odalys Rodriguez also collapsed and was hospitalized.[148]

The pressure mounted five days after the hunger strike began when janitors at Nova Southeastern University went on strike against UNICCO, seeking SEIU representation and wage and benefit increases. They had learned of the 25 percent pay hikes the UM strike had already yielded. Soon, the Nova janitors joined the fasters and other activists in a march to Shalala's office, but the Ashe administration building was padlocked shut.[149]

Feliciano Hernandez, a leader of the strike, became the next to fall. SEIU medical personnel had him rushed to the hospital.

Janitors joined students, faculty, and clergy in blocking traffic on U.S. Route 1 outside the University of Miami campus to protest unfair labor practices there.

SEIU President Andy Stern told reporters on April 13 that Shalala held the fate of the hunger strikers in her hands and could decide to end the conflict at any time she chose. Stern expressed concern that the situation "appears to only have a tragic end in sight."[150]

On the 13th day of her fast, student Tanya Aquino collapsed. Taken to the hospital, she rejected treatment and demanded that Shalala order UNICCO back to the bargaining table. But the university president refused to budge. Indeed, UM had filed unfair labor practice charges against SEIU for the earlier march on the administration building that had been joined by the Nova janitors.

Gail Rohner, the SEIU nurse at Freedom City, reported on day 14 of the hunger strike that Pablo Rodriguez had begun to shake after his blood pressure dropped to dangerous levels. He was taken by ambulance to Doctors Hospital. "I am concerned that we will see metabolic deterioration that can cause serious complications in the remaining janitors on the fast," Rohner said.

Civil rights leaders met with Shalala to urge a settlement of the dispute, but she rebuffed them. Instead, she issued yet another statement attempting to claim the university was an innocent party caught between an outside contractor and that firm's employees. Shalala seemed not to realize that the neutrality claim had no traction among those who had followed the dispute.

With the fasters' health difficulties escalating, Stern went to Miami on April 21 with Eliseo Medina, executive vice president of the union and a skilled veteran of such protests going back to his days as a leader of the United Farm Workers union. Medina had helped gain union recognition for 5,000 Houston janitors just six months earlier.

Stern and Medina said SEIU leaders would continue the fast on a rolling basis, freeing the strikers and students who had not eaten solid food for 17 days to break their fast with bread and water and begin the process of rebuilding their health. The rolling fast, with Medina living in Freedom City, sparked a flow of other national union leaders and political figures who came to Miami to show their support for the janitors' struggle.[151] International labor support came via visits of foreign trade unionists and solidarity messages from around the globe.

With top leadership having taken the reins of the strike and the fast, SEIU's staff at all levels in Washington, D.C., were fully engaged in support of the effort. Political staff and others throughout the union with ties to old Clinton Administration officials who knew Shalala used their contacts to pass the message that SEIU would expend any resources necessary and fight however long it took.

Justice for Janitors activists established a campaign website, yeswecane.org (combining the union's "Yes, We Can" motto with the "Canes," as the Miami Hurricanes sports teams were called). They posted daily video podcasts from the hunger fasters. This generated thousands of emails supporting the strikers and sent a further signal to Shalala that the janitors were gaining strength as time passed.

The university administrators also realized that graduation was approaching. They did not relish the possibility of massive disruption of such an important campus event involving families and the outside world. And Shalala's friend Madeline Albright, former secretary of state, was scheduled to speak.

UNICCO, too, faced new pressures as a few major building owners in other cities privately began to question the firm's ability to deal with its workforce.

Fittingly, Shalala yielded to the janitors on May 1, 2006. Workers throughout the world celebrate May Day as the workers' holiday, but also there were huge demonstrations of Latinos and others that day in the United States in support of immigrant rights.

The UM janitors won the right to unionize by card-check—if 60 percent of them submitted cards stating they wanted to join SEIU, then the union would be their bargaining representative.

Medina ended his 11-day fast by sharing bread with striking workers and leading a jubilant rally on campus that evening. "It's a great day for Miami's workers because it shows that if you persevere, you can win," he told the media. "It was very clear that we were not going to go away—that this was an issue that needed to be resolved."[152]

With the university de facto acknowledging it determined the outcome, not UNICCO, Medina now spoke positively of Shalala's role, since she would be the key to winning a first contract for the workers with decent wages and benefits. Many of the striking workers, too, voiced their excitement at the victory. "I'm going to return with my head held high, protected by the name of the union, which is rare in the state of Florida," janitor Maritza Paz told the *Miami Herald*, soon after casting her vote to accept the agreement.[153]

Contract negotiations quickly followed the card-check recognition and a new contract running through August 2010 gave the workers substantial wage increases. Housekeepers—about 80 percent of the workforce—won a starting rate of $8.55 an hour; landscapers a minimum $9.30 an hour; and food service workers $8 an hour. The rates jumped 25 cents an hour the first year, 40 cents the second, and 50 cents in each of the third and fourth years of the deal. SEIU also won a guaranteed affordable healthcare plan, at least one week of paid vacation, three paid personal days, and three additional paid holidays.[154]

Back at work with her fellow cleaners, Zoila Garcia finally could make arrangements under the new health benefit for the operation she needed on her leg. And, yes, she pledged to take her grandkids to Parrot Jungle when the first new paycheck arrived.

**Kids Come First**

**Kids Come First!**

I199 **Family Child Care Providers Union**
District 1199, SEIU

SEIU

# CHAPTER 21

# Family Child Care Workers Organize
## SEIU Wins Public Sector Gains With Kids First

Martina Casey, a child care provider in Illinois, had no health insurance in 2004 when doctors discovered she had fluid on her brain and a rare tumor. She went from one overcrowded hospital to the next. Finally, when she found one that would take her, Casey ended up with emergency surgery and a $30,000 debt.

But today, if Casey had similar medical problems, she would get high-quality care under health insurance she enjoys as one of about 49,000 SEIU family child care providers in Illinois covered under a union contract that includes good benefits.

Since 2005, nearly 100,000 family child care providers in Washington, Oregon, Illinois, Maryland, and Maine have won SEIU contracts. SEIU Kids First—the country's largest child care and early childhood education union—has sought to unite providers, parents, children's advocates, business, community leaders, and public officials in a new movement to improve child care and early learning.

For a child care provider such as Martina Casey, an SEIU contract meant not only affordable healthcare, but also training incentives, and a 35 percent average reimbursement rate increase. In Illinois and Washington State, SEIU's agreements focused on ensuring a well-trained workforce by creating tiered reimbursements for licensed family providers that are based on a quality rating system. Workers who meet quality standards for the child care they provide and who get extra training are eligible for increases on top of their base pay.

SEIU's success in organizing child care workers has been tied closely to the union's advocacy of high standards for pro-

viders aimed at improving early care and education for children. That has linked SEIU with working parents, who need child care for their kids, as well as educators and family advocates who increasingly have helped the public recognize that investment in quality child care pays long-term dividends for the economy and broader society.

"For every $1 the government spends on quality child care, the government saves $7 on welfare, incarceration, etc.," said Dan Lesser, an expert on child care policy at the Sargent Shriver National Center on Poverty Law.

"And the Federal Reserve Bank of Minneapolis found that there is a 17 percent annual rate of return on investment in quality early learning programs—and that this is the best investment of public dollars that we can make," Lesser told the founding convention of the Early Learning Division of SEIU Local 925 in Tacoma, Washington, in 2007.

SEIU's growth in the child care/early education sector evolved in part out of the union's successful strategies that enabled thousands of home care workers to win union contracts. Family child care providers who worked in their homes lacked the rights to organize and to bargain collectively, much like the home care workers in Los Angeles when they began their struggle (see Chapter 10). In order to successfully unionize home care workers, SEIU had to win state legislation in California for counties to create public entities with authority to bargain with the union representatives of home care workers.

SEIU pursued a similar model for child care and won a breakthrough in Illinois in February 2005 when the governor there issued an executive order permitting family child care

SEIU's child care organizing breakthrough came in Illinois in 2005 when 49,000 workers joined the union and won wage gains and healthcare.

providers receiving state subsidies to organize into unions. The order required the state to engage in "collective negotiations" with the representatives chosen by the child care workers.

SEIU under then-Local 880's chief organizer, Keith Kelleher, had been working for years in Illinois to build a base of support among child care providers at the same time SEIU leaders had been developing the framework that would allow those workers to win union protections. But once the executive order was issued, another union—AFSCME—filed a lawsuit seeking to overturn the order.

In the end, SEIU lawyers prevailed and AFSCME lost its lawsuit. In short order, more than 49,000 Illinois child care providers voted for SEIU to represent them.

Soon the union and the state of Illinois began bargaining and eventually reached a three-year contract worth an estimated $250 million. It provided:

- **Subsidy Rate Increases.** SEIU members received four increases in subsidy base rates totaling 35 percent over three years (which began in April 2006).
- **Training/Quality Incentives.** Providers who met certain training and/or quality standards received an additional 5 percent increase on top of the base rate.
- **Health Insurance.** Illinois contributed $27 million toward premiums for health insurance.
- **Grievance Procedures.** Payments to SEIU child care providers had to be made in a timely fashion and grievances could be settled by binding arbitration.

In addition to the contract gains in Illinois, SEIU pushed the governor and the state legislature to expand funding of child care centers providing subsidized care, even though the workers at those centers were not members of the union and the centers were not covered by the SEIU contract. Outside experts saw SEIU using its political power to advocate for quality child care in Illinois—even in programs where it didn't have members.

The National Women's Law Center, in an in-depth study entitled *Getting Organized*, found the work SEIU and child care advocates did at the centers was "a model for how advocates can use unionization of [child care providers] to help lift all boats."[155]

SEIU also produced white papers and other documentation of the very positive impact of expanding child care and education. The union played a major role in convincing governors and other top officials that education and care of children from birth to school would pay great dividends to society.

The successful organizing of the 49,000 family child care workers in Illinois and the achievement of a first contract with big pay increases and healthcare coverage predictably set off strong interest among similar workers in other states. SEIU had brought major gains to a workforce made up mainly of women and people of color. They worked in their homes for low wages so that other low-wage parents could have their children cared for while they went to work themselves.

In Washington State, SEIU members turned out in large numbers to back Christine Gregoire for governor in 2004. A strong advocate for working families, she defeated a conservative Republican in that race. The governor went on to issue an "executive directive" permitting home-based providers to organize and directing the Department of Social and Health Services to "meet and confer" with union representatives. By March 2006, SEIU won legislation giving stronger collective bargaining rights to family child care providers who receive subsidies.[156]

Two bargaining units developed in Washington: one for those providers who receive subsidies and the other for those who do not. Those without subsidies had "meet and confer" authority only for the purpose of shaping the regulatory requirements that apply to them.[157]

Child care providers in both bargaining units chose SEIU Local 925, led by Kim Cook, to represent them by huge mar-

SEIU Local 880 leaders and members who worked in family child care celebrated a three-year, $250 million contract that gave 49,000 workers training and quality incentives, a grievance procedure, and other gains.

gins and began bargaining in July 2006. In November, SEIU and the state reached an agreement giving members who participated in the subsidy program:

- a 10 percent increase over the existing pay rates for licensed providers and a 7 percent increase for license-exempt providers;
- state-provided health insurance beginning in 2008 for licensed providers with a health plan that provides no deductible, no screening for pre-existing conditions, vision, and 90 percent to 100 percent in-hospitalization;
- a training fund for license-exempt providers—they were given paid training and a $250 bonus if they become licensed and get a $600 bonus upon completion of 10 hours of approved training each contract year;
- a grievance procedure that holds the state accountable to all terms of the contract; and
- contract language that required that child care providers get accurate and timely payments from the state.

To help meet the needs of working parents, SEIU negotiated provisions that gave licensed providers a bonus for caring for children during nonstandard hours. And the contract also increased the state reimbursement rate for infant care in response to the shortage of such care.

One of the major problems facing families with children who need care is that nearly one-third of child care center workers leave the early education field each year. SEIU partnered with child care centers and schools in an effort to help keep experienced staff doing the jobs they love. SEIU teachers at 10 child care centers in King County, for example, worked with child care providers, state legislators, and child advocates to establish the state's first Child Care Wage-Career Ladder, which established job titles and wages based on teacher experience and education.

The union won a second contract running through 2011 in Washington, which was suffering from the severe economic downturn. SEIU members, putting meaning behind the commitment to place Kids First, agreed to give back their raises to the state in return for keeping parent co-pays stable. The raises, which would have amounted to an estimated $8 million, went instead to maintain affordable care for families in Washington State.

Sue Winn, who has been a child care provider for more than 27 years, works in La Conner, Washington, and gave up the raises in the second contract. "Parents can only afford so much," she noted. "We need to invest more funds into early learning so that our children can go to school ready to learn. Family home child care is one of the best investments we can make."

In Oregon, SEIU helped win executive orders from Governor Ted Kulongoski in 2005 and 2006. The union reached a contract with the state for license-exempt family child care providers. It provided an average rate increase of 18 percent and established a training program to help them improve their skills, with a 7 percent increase for completing the training. More than 500 SEIU members took advantage of the training and received the bonus for improving their skills.

SEIU Kids First providers in Oregon also won an agreement that gives thousands more families access to affordable child care by reducing parent co-payments by 20 percent, as well as widening the eligibility ceiling so more parents can participate in the subsidized care programs.

Elsewhere, inadequate federal funding has driven cash-strapped states to raise eligibility requirements for child care assistance, increase parent co-pays, institute waiting lists, and freeze or even cut reimbursement rates.

As in Illinois and Washington, SEIU Kids First contracts have given child care providers access to low-cost health insurance plans—either from the state or from SEIU's own insurance plan.

SEIU's public services division won another big organizing victory in the Kids First child care/Head Start campaign when some 5,000 family child care providers in Maryland won a first contract in July 2009.

Licensed and license-exempt providers in SEIU received an average 2.9 percent increase over existing subsidy rates, but

Leaders and workers in Kids First Maryland/SEIU Local 500 won a breakthrough contract in 2009 covering some 5,000 family child care providers. SEIU has other child care workers in Washington State, Oregon, Illinois, Maine, and elsewhere.

without a corresponding increase in parent co-pays. There was a grievance procedure in the deal, as well as requirements that SEIU members be paid on time, accurately, and through direct deposit.

The majority of parents receiving state subsidies in Maryland for child care were single mothers entering the workforce or gaining an education through welfare-to-work programs. They were concentrated in Maryland's most underserved communities.

The Kids First Maryland/SEIU Local 500 contract with Maryland Governor Martin O'Malley's office and the state's Department of Education also provided SEIU members with access to decision-making committees and the creation of a new training committee of state officials and child care providers to recommend future improvements.

Workers ratified the Maryland contract by a 30-to-1 margin, but the union noted that "much remains to be done to mend a system that for too long has pushed quality in-home child care providers out of business." The number of family child care homes in Maryland dropped by 26 percent between 1997 and 2007 due in part to the low subsidy rates and lack of provider access to affordable health insurance and other benefits. The 2009 contract provided vehicles to address those problems, SEIU Local 500 leaders said.

After winning the first contract, Crystal Barksdale, a child care provider in Baltimore County, said: "We hung in there; it's been more than four years. We're really teaching a great lesson to the children in our care: you work hard and stick with it, and you can accomplish anything."

# CHAPTER 22

# Fighting Wal-Mart's Low-Wage America
## SEIU Campaigns To Reform Anti-Union Retailer

Without much fanfare, the huge power of Wal-Mart began to remake the American economy in the first years of the 21st century.

Wal-Mart's below-poverty wages drove down wages all around its stores. Wal-Mart's predatory business practices pushed thousands of small businesses into bankruptcy. Wal-Mart's purchasing practices resulted in huge American job losses as factories moved work to China. Wal-Mart's fierce anti-unionism made a mockery of the right to organize.

SEIU had begun focusing on the "Wal-Martization" of America shortly after a major strike by members of the United Food and Commercial Workers at grocery stores in southern California. Supermarket chains there claimed they had to lower their wages and benefits to compete with the nonunion, low-wage Wal-Mart stores.

Fairly quickly, the Wal-Mart business model was spreading and, while it meant big profits for shareholders and executives, workers faced the very real threat of being pushed into poverty as the giant Arkansas-based employer rapidly expanded. In fact, Wal-Mart had become the world's largest private-sector employer.

At the 2004 convention, SEIU President Stern asked for and received approval to launch a new coalition of allies to combat Wal-Mart's negative impact on communities and workers and its broad corporate irresponsibility. While Wal-Mart workers were not in SEIU's jurisdiction, the Wal-Mart model of low-wage jobs set an employment standard that hurt workers across the United States and Canada and worldwide.

"Wal-Mart is leading the way for corporations that seek to lower pay and benefits everywhere," Stern told the delegates. "I will ask you to make a $1 million investment of your money to start up a new network of workers and communities to bring Wal-Mart's standards up, instead of having Wal-Mart bring our standards down."

In the months that followed, SEIU convened small groups of experts and activists to discuss how best to bring reform to Wal-Mart's worst corporate practices. SEIU staff and outside consultants sought to develop a campaign that would defend the broad interest American and Canadian workers had in forcing Wal-Mart to clean up its act.

With the debate occurring over the need to modernize the AFL-CIO, SEIU also made Wal-Mart an issue with a call for the labor federation to do more to go after the company. Indeed, the first plank of the "Unite to Win" program pushed by AFL-CIO reformers talked about building new strength by stopping the "Wal-Marting" of jobs.

"The Wal-Mart business model of providing low wages and few benefits, shifting jobs overseas to exploit workers under poverty conditions, and viciously opposing workers' freedom to form unions is setting a pattern that undermines good jobs for all working people at home and abroad," stated the document urging AFL-CIO reform. It called on the federation to establish a center that would target Wal-Mart and fund it with all of the roughly $25 million in royalties the AFL-CIO received from its affinity credit card arrangement then in effect.

Although the federation began to step up its anti-Wal-Mart activity, the real action shifted to the organization SEIU created: Wal-Mart Watch.

The goal was to spark a broader alliance of progressive forces around the need to transform the way Wal-Mart operated and, in doing so, at least build some speed bumps that would slow down corporate followers on the road to making the Wal-Mart model the American norm.

Playing off the old line about what was good for GM was good for the country, Stern said: "What's good for Wal-Mart ends up being good for five families—the heirs to the Walton fortune."[158] The five heirs of Wal-Mart founder Sam Walton controlled about 39 percent of Wal-Mart stock and had a net worth of more than $90 billion. They earned nearly $1 billion a year in dividends then and were richer than Bill Gates and Warren Buffett combined.

Wal-Mart executives did quite well, too. Then-CEO Lee Scott reported compensation in 2004 of $17.5 million—871 times more than the average U.S. Wal-Mart worker. He received pay amounting to $8,434 an hour, while the official figure given by the company for its average worker was $9.68 an hour.

The top five executives at Wal-Mart received $219 million over the five years prior to SEIU launching Wal-Mart Watch. Tom Coughlin, second in command at Wal-Mart, got more than $12 million a year, until he was caught stealing company funds. Coughlin's initial defense: he didn't steal the money but siphoned it off to create a secret slush fund to finance anti-union activity.

The Walton family and Wal-Mart itself had given large grants to the anti-union National Right to Work Legal Defense Foundation. And the company maintained an elaborate anti-union "hit squad" ready to be dispatched to any store in the United States and Canada at the first sign of worker discontent.

The only successful organizing effort in a U.S. Wal-Mart was in the butcher department of a store in Jacksonville, Texas. Within two weeks, Wal-Mart made a "strategic decision" to close its butcher departments nationwide. In Canada, workers formed a union in 2004 at a store in Quebec, which Wal-Mart then closed down citing "low profitability."

The message to Wal-Mart workers became very clear: attempt to exercise your legal right to join a union and you'll end up in the unemployment line.[159]

SEIU repeatedly made it crystal clear that it had no intention of organizing Wal-Mart workers, who it said rightly belong in the United Food and Commercial Workers (UFCW) union. Both SEIU and UFCW were in discussion during this time on the need to reform the AFL-CIO and both joined in withdrawing from the federation. UFCW had its own anti-Wal-Mart group called "Wake-Up Wal-Mart" that added effective pressure on the company to reform.

The SEIU-funded Wal-Mart Watch scored a publicity coup in 2005 when it got its hands on an internal memo from a top Wal-Mart executive to the company's board of directors outlining new steps to reduce healthcare costs of its workforce. It proposed hiring even more part-time workers and recruiting younger (presumably healthier) workers. The memo acknowledged that "our critics are correct" that the health coverage provided Wal-Mart workers was very expensive for its low-income

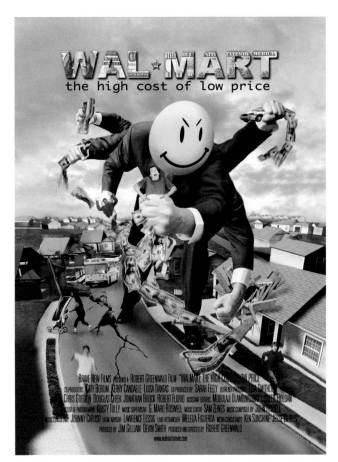

SEIU helped fund the documentary *Wal-Mart: The High Cost of Low Price* in 2005. Produced by Robert Greenwald's Brave New Films, it detailed Wal-Mart's assault on its own workers and communities.

workforce and that Wal-Mart had a significant percentage of its workers and their families on Medicaid.

A firestorm ensued, as Wal-Mart had to admit that, as the world's largest corporation with more than $288 billion in annual sales and 1.2 million workers at the time in the United States, it did not pay for health insurance for more than half of its employees.

Instead, Wal-Mart cost taxpayers more than $1.5 billion annually by forcing hundreds of thousands of employees to rely on government programs from children's health insurance to school lunches.

"The obvious question: why should taxpayers subsidize the healthcare costs for a corporation that reported more than $10 billion in profits in 2004 alone," Wal-Mart Watch said in a counter annual report it issued shortly before the company's shareholders' meeting.

With Wal-Mart paying sales clerks about $14,000 per year—a wage below the government-defined poverty level for a family of three—a clerk would have to pay the first $1,000 of healthcare costs out-of-pocket, if that worker was covered under the Wal-Mart health plan.

Politicians—both Democrats and Republicans—soon felt the heat from voters angered over the news that taxpayers had to pick up much of the tab for workers' healthcare that Wal-Mart, as a matter of corporate policy, sought to shift to the public.

The controversy over Wal-Mart and healthcare sparked by the SEIU-funded Wal-Mart Watch laid the groundwork for two later developments. First, the company had to offer better, more comprehensive (although still inadequate) health plans to many of its workers.

And second, it ultimately shaped a climate in which SEIU pressed Wal-Mart to give President Obama's healthcare reform a boost when the company joined SEIU in a letter calling for legislation to require all large employers to offer health insurance to their workers. "We are for an employer mandate which is fair and broad in its coverage," the letter said.

While this helped create a climate in which some members of Congress, particularly conservative Democrats, could embrace an employer mandate for healthcare in 2009, some SEIU critics decried any initiative that had the union and Wal-Mart on the same page. In 2007, many of the same critics had become apoplectic when SEIU reacted positively about Wal-Mart after it joined the Better Health Care Together partnership to push for universal healthcare. But SEIU knew that on the one issue of healthcare reform, little hope for progress would exist if some of corporate America could not be cajoled and maneuvered into publicly accepting concepts such as universal healthcare and an employer mandate.

At the same time, Stern continued to blast Wal-Mart on a wide variety of fronts: its anti-union behavior, its discrimination against women, its low-wage business model, its sweatshop production sourcing from China, and so on. And SEIU continued to spend $2 million to $3 million a year funding Wal-Mart Watch's activities to hold the company accountable to higher standards of corporate social responsibility and fight for the rights of Wal-Mart employees.

# Women And People Of Color Energize SEIU

When Andy Stern and his leadership team began their push in 1996 to diversify the union's leadership, they often would tell audiences that, for too long, the labor movement had been "too male, too pale, and too stale." It would draw a knowing laugh from the audience, but everyone knew it was no laughing matter.

As the new global economy was taking hold, the service-sector workers joining SEIU included tens of thousands of women and people of color working in sectors such as building maintenance, security, home healthcare, and family child care. Between 1996 and 2004, for example, 900,000 new workers joined SEIU, and a majority of them were women and workers of color.

By uniting with SEIU, these workers—often the "last hired, first fired" in the workforce—were able to make gains for themselves and their families and communities. The African American, and mostly male, security officers who joined SEIU in Los Angeles and other cities won better wages and benefits, as did home care and janitorial workers in communities of color in Los Angeles, Chicago, and New York City. It was estimated, for instance, that SEIU's Justice for Janitors campaign, by raising wages and standards for that workforce, had pumped more than $100 million into L.A.'s Latino community.

The challenge was to make sure that the union's leadership reflected this fast-growing and ever-diverse membership. One way was to recruit and hire organizers of color. As Cornell University's Kate Bronfenbrenner noted in her 2005 *New Labor Forum* article "Labor's True Purpose,"

SEIU had been successful in organizing workers in the historically anti-union South in part because "of a willingness to hire organizers of color and develop rank-and-file leaders of color...and to build relationships with community groups and clergy in the African American, Haitian, and Hispanic community."

By 2004, when delegates met for the union's International Convention in San Francisco, the union's Committee on Social and Economic Justice could report that SEIU "has the most diverse leadership team and staff in the labor movement." But, the committee said, more work was needed, including training and education programs that would ensure diversity at all levels of the union and help to create a new pool of leadership talent.

SEIU Executive Vice President Gerry Hudson, writing in 2005 on the subject of "Rebuilding the Union Movement to Empower Communities of Color," said SEIU had adopted "a conscious policy" to include women and people of color in its top leadership positions. As a result, he said, "SEIU's International Executive Board today is 40 percent female and 33 percent people of color." And, he said, it was "no accident" that the union's ability to connect with women and workers of color was coming at a time when the union had strengthened its commitment to developing a diverse leadership team.

In the following years, that work continued. As Hudson noted, SEIU had made significant progress in moving away from the "too male, too pale, and too stale" labor movement of the past, but there was work still to be done.

# CHAPTER 23

# Houston Janitors' Big Victory
## SEIU Workers Gain In South/Southwest

Big smiles adorned the faces of janitors who cleaned Houston's huge office buildings as they gathered at the Texas Medical Center on December 17, 2008, to launch a new clinic to offer accessible and affordable healthcare for service workers there.

The clinic had been created as a joint project resulting from a groundbreaking labor-business partnership between SEIU janitors in Houston and local business and community leaders. The Houston Service Workers Clinic costs the janitors just $20 a month, with employers paying $185 a month per worker to cover 100 percent of the workers' treatment.[160]

Staffed by doctors and other health service professionals from Baylor College of Medicine, the clinic serves more than 5,300 commercial office janitors, who also have insurance coverage from Cigna Healthcare for medical care beyond what the clinic can offer.[161]

"Houston janitors called attention to the crisis faced by hardworking people…people who don't have access to quality, affordable healthcare" including the one in three in Harris County, Texas, where Houston is located, said one SEIU leader as the clinic opened.

The Houston Service Workers Clinic was launched on the two-year anniversary of a huge victory for SEIU when janitors won a tough strike involving wealthy employers in the energy capital of America.

The Houston janitors organized through SEIU's "trigger" strategy in which employers respond to a corporate social responsibility campaign by agreeing to a neutrality/card-check agreement with the understanding that bargaining won't be triggered until a large percentage of the market is unionized.

The successful campaign for union recognition for 5,000 janitors in 2005 was the biggest organizing success in the South in more than 50 years, but the workers still needed to win a first contract.

One year later, the SEIU janitors, who earned about $5.25 an hour for mainly four-hour shifts and had no healthcare, halted work for a month to achieve an agreement.

Against a backdrop of police violence, harsh Texas-style court rulings, and staunch employer hostility, the Houston janitors won their historic strike. The contract bargained by the union doubled wages, ensured more hours of paid work, achieved new holidays and vacation, and won healthcare provisions that led, two years later, to the opening of the clinic.

To understand how the Houston janitors won their struggle, it's useful to consider the story of Ercilia Sandoval, then a 42-year-old from San Miguel, El Salvador, who worked a four-hour shift in the Aon building in Houston's fancy Galleria district. She came north in 1996 under temporary protected status,[162] working first at a tortilla factory, then at an Episcopal church, and eventually for GCA Services, a cleaning contractor where she scrubbed bathrooms, vacuumed, and mopped floors.

A hard worker, Sandoval began to tire much quicker on the job in the fall of 2005. She frequently felt ill, but without health insurance a visit to the doctor meant spending money she needed to put food on the table for her children. Her pay amounted to a mere $22 a night, or $106 a week—less than $6,000 a year.

Nearly a year after first feeling like she needed to see a doctor, Sandoval went to the emergency room for pain in her chest. Doctors ultimately diagnosed her as suffering from advanced breast cancer. Without health insurance, Sandoval waited four months to be approved for state disability coverage and finally—and belatedly—began to receive chemotherapy treatments she needed.

While her cancer was spreading, Sandoval had met an SEIU organizer at her church who was seeking out janitors em-

Ercilia Sandoval, a leader of SEIU's Houston janitors' strike in 2006, helped win huge wage gains and new benefits. She had developed breast cancer that went undiagnosed and untreated before the janitors organized and won an SEIU contract that provided affordable health insurance.

ployed at Houston's high-rise buildings. "Some of the workers were afraid," she said. "But often I said, 'Afraid of what? We are not going to lose a good job. We are not going to lose a good salary—we don't have benefits, we don't have anything.'"[163]

"I am supporting the union for all the other Ercilias who are out there or who might have already died because of no health insurance," she told *The Washington Post*.[164]

In the mid-1980s, janitors in Houston had sought to form a union and win wage and benefit gains, but their efforts were crushed by the Texas establishment of big energy conglomerates, right-wing politicians anxious to keep the state's anti-labor reputation, and police and courts known for their hostility to unions.

In 2005, the union pursued the call to expand organizing in the South and Southwest. Home to some of the wealthiest companies in America, such as Chevron and Shell, Houston had only become richer and more anti-union when SEIU succeeded in organizing the 5,000 primarily immigrant janitors.

With SEIU Executive Vice President Eliseo Medina mobilizing multiple campaigns in the region, the union faced an environment in which the gap between the rich and the poor had widened, the social safety net had been shredded under President George W. Bush, and corporate power seemed unstoppable.

After a year of trying to bargain a contract from the five unionized cleaning contractors, the SEIU janitors voted to go on strike—a strike that became the biggest in Texas in 50 years. Careful coalition building and outreach by SEIU organizers, part of the Justice for Janitors program, garnered strong support from important elements of the Houston community, such as religious leaders, civil rights activists, and progressive politicians.

The workers' demands hardly qualified as radical. They sought a wage hike to $8.50 an hour plus health insurance, some paid days off, and full-time work (rather than the four-hour shifts). SEIU janitors' contracts in other cities, some of which were with the same cleaning employers, paid far higher wages, provided health benefits, and gave full-time employment. SEIU janitors in Chicago, for example, then had a top wage of $13.40 an hour, family health insurance paid for by the employer, and full-time work.[165]

Although the strike was against the cleaning contractors, the Houston janitors believed the building owners and tenants held the key to a settlement—something SEIU knew from its janitor bargaining elsewhere in the United States.

Hines Interests, Brookfield Properties, P.M. Realty, and Transwestern owned the 58 buildings that were struck. Hines, one of the largest private owners of real estate in the world, held properties in 15 other countries and could afford to have its cleaners receive better wages and benefits without much impact on the bottom line.

The Houston strike was coordinated by Tom Balanoff, SEIU's skilled leader of Chicago Local 1 and a top member of the national union leadership. When bargaining stalled on October 18, 2006, Balanoff told the media that the union had made a proposal and three weeks later the five cleaning companies still had failed to respond. He also announced that SEIU locals from throughout the United States and Canada had pledged more than $1 million in strike support to the Houston janitors, if needed.

With no progress by October 23, the janitors walked off the job at the 58 buildings across Houston. Most of them Latinas, the strikers soon were demonstrating in front of the buildings they usually mopped and vacuumed. They marched to the beat of drums and makeshift maracas made from soda cans filled with dried beans.[166]

The strikers soon were joined by unionized janitors from around the country. They picketed at Chicago, Los Angeles, and New York City operations of the Houston cleaning contractors, and other unions such as the Teamsters honored their

picket lines. In addition, SEIU janitors from other cities came to Houston on what were called "Freedom Flights" to support the struggle there. Medina referred to the tactic as "multiplying organizing" and said it was the heart of the strategy of the recently formed Change to Win labor federation.

SEIU lawyers had to go to court to block enforcement by Houston authorities of unconstitutional restrictions in the city's parade and sound ordinances.

A thousand janitors and supporters marched on a police station during the second week of the strike demanding freedom for two strikers who had been arrested. They chanted *"Arriba La Union"* as Houston and the world saw via the media the once invisible faces of the poor, immigrant janitors, who were nearly always hidden from the rich and powerful who employed them to clean their offices at night.

The moral power of their story came through even as they and their Freedom Flier supporters were arrested for chaining themselves to buildings, blocking streets, and engaging in other forms of nonviolent civil disobedience. The campaign starkly highlighted much of what the gap between rich and poor really meant for America, with Chevron reporting some $14 billion in profits and paying the janitors who clean its offices only $20 a day with no health insurance.

SEIU President Andy Stern put the entire resources of the union behind the strike of mainly low-wage immigrant women who worked as janitors in Houston. The victory was part of the union's commitment to expand organizing and contract gains in the South and Southwest mandated by the 2004 convention.

"We learned over many years that these fights can't be just about unions," SEIU President Stern told *The Washington Post.* Instead, these fights "are symbolic of what's wrong in our country. The voters in the [2006] election said loud and clear that we're growing apart, not growing together in this economy and they want it to change."

On November 17, as demonstrators including both strikers and unionized janitors from other U.S. cities nonviolently sat down to block the intersection of Capitol and Travis streets in downtown Houston, they were attacked by mounted police who violently charged into the group, injuring a number of protesters.

Mateo Portillo, who worked for GCA at the CenterPoint Energy building, described what occurred:

"The horses came all of a sudden. They started jumping on top of people. I heard the women screaming. A horse stomped on top of me. I fell to the ground and hurt my arm. The horses just kept coming. I never thought the police would do something so aggressive, so violent."[167]

Hazel Ingram, an 83-year-old strike supporter from New York City, had to be rushed to the hospital. She was at the time a 52-year-member of SEIU Local 32BJ where she worked for the cleaning firm called Pritchard. Ingram told the strikers she earned $19 an hour in her job doing much the same work they were doing in Houston for $5.25 an hour.

Balanoff, the union's chief negotiator, condemned the police behavior as "a reprehensible and unnecessary act of violence by the police" against protestors who "engaged in the American tradition of nonviolent civil disobedience—janitors who make $20 a day with no health insurance were risking arrest in order to better provide for their families and to make a peaceful stand for a better future for all working people."

Onlookers reported that Houston police seized one of the janitors' signs reading "Stand Up For The American Dream," threw it to the ground, and stomped on it. Police officers were seen giving each other high fives after the attack.

Late that night, SEIU lawyers scrambled to help arrange bail for the 40 demonstrators who remained jailed. Told that bail was $800,000, SEIU counsel began to arrange to put someone on a plane with an $800,000 money order so bond could be posted quickly and the strike supporters could be freed.

"Our people at the courthouse said, "You don't understand—it's $800,000 bail *per person*—we need over $32 million for bond," the union lawyer later recalled. "The Republican district attorney and the Houston police were letting us know that peaceful civil protests over worker rights were not welcome in their town."[168]

The mounted police attack and the outrageous bail drew criticism and attention to the strike as Houston's elite power structure became more and more uncomfortable with the focus on the janitors' low pay and the contrast with an energy establishment then flush with huge profits.

At the same time, the big real estate and energy executives involved were seeing a new front open in the janitor wars. SEIU's global staff had engaged unions and federations in a number of foreign countries, and they were targeting buildings owned by the same multinationals that owned the Houston towers where the striking janitors had worked.[169]

The low wages shocked the European trade unions particularly, as did the idea that the predominantly female and immigrant workforce would have no health insurance whatsoever. Echoing the well-known line from the Apollo 13 astronaut, one unionist picketing a building in Germany carried a sign in German that translated: "Houston, we have a problem."[170] Demonstrations supporting the Houston janitors occurred as far away as Moscow—the strike had developed strong international support.

The national and global solidarity highlighted a major shift that empowered the workers' struggle in Houston and elsewhere. Where the cleaning contractors were once local, they had now become national and international as the globalizing of the economy expanded. The five companies in Houston that cleaned more than 70 percent of that city also operated throughout the United States. And the real estate companies that owned the buildings were mainly global companies, as were their tenants such as Chevron.

Support actions in Mexico, London, Berlin, and Moscow could be launched against them because they were global firms. And, because they needed capital for their international expan-

Houston, home of some of the wealthiest companies in America, saw the SEIU janitors' strike as highlighting the gap between rich and poor. The elite there wanted and got a tough police crackdown that included many arrests of SEIU strikers and union supporters who took "Freedom Flights" to join the struggle. Violent attacks, some by officers mounted on horseback, put a number of demonstrators in the hospital and others in jail with injuries.

sion from pension funds and other national and international investors, SEIU and its allies could open an additional front with entities such as the California Public Employees' Retirement System and others concerned about the negative impact the dispute would have on the value of their investments.

As negotiations with the union continued, employers looked across the bargaining table and saw an unfamiliar face: that of Ercilia Sandoval, who had joined the SEIU negotiating team. She was there to raise the issue of the lack of health insurance that, in her case, had led to her breast cancer remaining undiagnosed and untreated so long that her life had been jeopardized.

Before she spoke, Sandoval had gone into a nearby bathroom to steady herself. She came back into the conference room where the negotiators for both sides sat and asked the employers if they were looking at her.

"And I looked them all in their eyes," she later recalled. "I assured myself that they were all looking at me. And I took off my wig."

The companies' negotiators stared at her head—totally bald from the chemotherapy treatments she had belatedly begun. They were in shock, sitting there with their mouths open, not blinking. "And that," Sandoval said, "is what I wanted."[170a]

Her story of not having health insurance and not getting the care she needed for her breast cancer put new pressure on the five cleaning contractors. At Sandoval's request, savvy SEIU organizers skilled in the social media communicated her situation widely. She soon had her own MySpace page, for example, and people around the world could download podcasts and hear her story.

After a month that saw a new demonstration or march nearly every day, after picketing at a number of their buildings in other countries, after disruptions by unionized janitors with the same employer in other U.S. cities, after strong support for the strike from the faith, political, and community groups

in Houston, finally the business community decided it had had enough.

The Houston janitors achieved their first citywide contract that began their rise out of poverty. The settlement doubled the janitors' compensation over the life of the agreement. It also guaranteed affordable quality health insurance, more hours of work, and new paid holidays and vacation time.

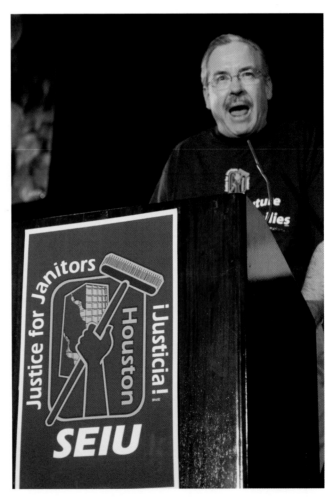

Tom Balanoff, one of SEIU's top leaders of Chicago property services workers, headed a bargaining team of Houston janitors that won contract breakthroughs for the low-wage, mostly female immigrant workers.

Tom Balanoff announced what the strikers had accomplished in the new contract:

- **Higher Wages.** Janitors would see their wages rise by 35 percent over the course of the contract—with an immediate 9 percent increase. Janitors' pay rose to $6.25 an hour on January 1, 2007, $7.25 an hour on January 1, 2008, and $7.75 on January 1, 2009.

- **More Hours.** The new contract increased work hours for janitors who had only four hours of work a night to six hours a shift in two years. The additional hours and the wage increase meant that janitors who made $5.25 an hour saw their income more than double by the end of 2009.

- **Quality, Affordable Health Insurance.** At a time when many employers were shifting healthcare costs onto workers, Houston janitors won individual health insurance at a cost of only $20 per month. Family insurance became available for a cost of $175 a month.

- **Paid Holidays and Vacation Time.** The contract provided workers—many for the first time in their lives—paid time off from work. Janitors got six paid holidays per year and began to accrue paid vacation time beginning the first year of the contract.

Outside observers hailed the contract as a major breakthrough for low-wage, mostly female immigrant workers. "Houston janitors have shown that organized labor still has the power to inspire and improve the lives of workers," said Julius Getman, a labor law expert and a professor at the University of Texas Law School. "If low-wage janitors in Houston can win a victory of this magnitude, the message to workers throughout the South should be clear—in solidarity lies strength."

For Ercilia Sandoval, it was "an incredible victory for our families and for all families. When I go back to work, I will go back proud of what we have accomplished—not just for us and our families but for all of the workers in this city who work very hard, but are paid very little.

"We showed what can be done, what must be done, to make America a better place."

# SEIU Janitors Achieve Big Wage, Benefit Gains

The victory of the Houston janitors was one piece in a mosaic of success for their movement. Some 40,000 janitors have chosen to unite in SEIU since 1996. As of 2010, about 44 percent of all janitors in 25 of the 30 largest commercial office markets in the United States were SEIU members.

Critics of SEIU, including right-wing talk show hosts and even some on the left, argue that the union's strong focus on organizing comes at the expense of members who are shortchanged at the bargaining table. The actual record easily refutes such claims.

Most of the 151,000 janitors in SEIU have won wages that are far above the national average for janitorial employees. In 2008, a nonunion janitor was paid about $412 per week. By contrast, SEIU janitors earned as much as $920 per week in New York City, $592 per week in Chicago, $519 in Minneapolis, and $527 in Los Angeles.

And 21 of SEIU's collective bargaining agreements covering janitors include family healthcare coverage and another 10 include individual healthcare coverage.

Key to winning good contracts for janitors has been SEIU's effort to engage the real decision-makers—the building owners—in discussions about using responsible contractors that respect workers' right to form unions and negotiate good contracts. The union has won recognition often from employers through majority sign-up, rather than via elections that unfairly favor companies that delay the process; foment high turnover; and harass, intimidate, and fire union supporters.

In many cases, the union has won agreements from contractors to take part in marketwide master contract negotiations once a critical mass (often between 50 percent and 60 percent) of all similar contractors in the market agreed to do the same. Such "trigger agreements" mean that contractors

that "go first" in respecting workers' right to form unions aren't underbid and driven out of business before their competitors agree to recognize the union.

The SEIU strategy has brought big wins for janitors. Local 32BJ, led by Mike Fishman, began in 2001 to reach out to unite thousands of nonunion janitors in the markets between New York City and Washington, D.C. The union used the hallmark tactics of SEIU janitorial organizing—multiday strikes, outreach to the religious community, rallies at worksites and corporate headquarters, and leafleting. By 2003, 47 contractors in New Jersey signed the master collective bargaining agreement. Two years later, nearly 5,000 New Jersey janitors had joined SEIU and won a 24 percent wage increase as well as improved healthcare coverage.

Similar successes occurred in the Philadelphia suburbs where workers who were paid as little as $6.50 an hour got strong support from SEIU janitors in central Philadelphia who worked for many of the same contractors. The suburban janitors won wage gains of up to 60 percent and employer-sponsored health coverage for the first time after gaining union recognition in 2006.

Gains also occurred in the Washington, D.C., suburbs and Baltimore where primarily Latino and African-American office cleaners used many of the same tactics downtown D.C. janitors had used years earlier to win a first contract. By the end of 2009, nearly 3,000 commercial office janitors in northern Virginia united in SEIU. The union built on the successes of the rekindled immigrant rights movement to engage poverty-wage cleaners in a series of strikes in late 2007. Under the resulting master contract, northern Virginia cleaners won nearly 30 percent more in wages, guaranteed paid sick leave and vacations, and employer-paid health benefits.

The success of Local 32BJ in organizing and winning good contracts on the East Coast had parallels elsewhere. In Boston, 2,000 janitors at 97 buildings went on strike for three weeks in 2002 to win better wages for all 11,000 Boston-area janitors. The settlement resulted in 30 percent wage increases, extension of health insurance, equal pay for 1,000 part-time workers, and the addition of two paid sick days.

In Chicago, SEIU's Tom Balanoff and other leaders helped win a strike of suburban Chicago janitors who gained full, employer-paid health insurance. That success spurred a wave of organizing by nonunion janitors in the Chicago suburbs to unite with their fellow cleaners in SEIU Local 1. Within two years of the strike, the proportion of all Chicago suburban janitors who belong to SEIU had increased to more than 80 percent from less than 60 percent.

SEIU's Chicago janitors who worked at a firm called Lakeside used their leverage to back janitors in Columbus, Ohio, who worked for the same company. The Chicago janitors honored picket lines set up by the Columbus janitors and management responded by firing two dozen of the Chicago workers. An intensive three-week campaign resulted in Lakeside agreeing to both a majority sign-up process for the Columbus janitors to join SEIU and also to return the fired Chicago workers to their jobs.

By early 2008, commercial janitors in Columbus, Cincinnati, and Indianapolis had become SEIU members and won master contracts that raised wages, provided affordable health insurance, began the transition to full-time work, and extended the freedom to choose a union through majority sign-up to cleaners at other sites in the three cities.

"I'm proud of what we have accomplished," said Cincinnati janitor Lauressie "Dee Dee" Tillman of the first city-wide union contract won by workers like her. "Not just for us and our families, but for all of the workers in this city who are paid so little."

Chapter 3 describes the struggle of Los Angeles-area janitors to regain strength lost during a decline in the late 1980s. Another major strike occurred in Los Angeles in 2000 when the janitors there—largely immigrants and women—won a historic victory after massive marches and civil disobedience aimed at contractors that refused to pay livable wages. Workers at Local 1877 gained wage increases of more than 25 percent along with provisions requiring employers to absorb all health insurance cost increases.

Gains for L.A. janitors led later to nearly 3,000 Orange County janitors—many working for the same contractors SEIU members had struck in Los Angeles—joining SEIU and, within a year, winning wage increases of $1.20 an hour as well as family healthcare coverage.[171]

*Barbara Shulman of the SEIU Research Department provided organizing and bargaining data for this and other boxes in this book.*

JANITORS' WEEKLY WAGES, 2008

| | | | | |
|---|---|---|---|---|
| Average nonunion | Minneapolis union | Los Angeles union | Chicago union | New York City union |
| $412 | $519 | $527 | $592 | $920 |

# SEIU Security Officers Win Good Contracts

SEIU in 2010 had more than 50,000 members who worked in private security, law enforcement, and other public safety jobs in Boston, Chicago, Los Angeles, Minneapolis-St. Paul, New York City, Sacramento, the San Francisco Bay Area, Seattle, and Washington, D.C. About 32,000 SEIU members worked in private contracted security and most had joined the union since 2000. Their successes almost always came with strong support from local clergy and community groups.

The union negotiated hourly start rates that range from $10 to $13 an hour for security officers. Most enjoy affordable family healthcare coverage. In every city where security workers have united with SEIU, they have won additional paid leave through a combination of improved sick days, vacation, and holidays. Gains in the security sector also include contract and other arrangements that provide increased training and licensing standards.

When security officers who worked for the multinational Securitas began organizing in Minneapolis, many pro-SEIU workers were Somali immigrants who faced harsh threats from management. Some were suspended and others fired. After the terror attack on 9/11 in New York City and at the Pentagon, one Securitas supervisor told a pro-union Somali worker that he had "gotten a call from the FBI which said I should kill all Muslims."

The security officers filed unfair labor charges and mobilized labor, religious, and Somali communities in a campaign called "Hate Has No Home Here." The federal government ultimately issued a complaint against Securitas for interfering with and coercing employees who were active in the effort to join SEIU. After a long struggle involving Securitas workers that included help from the Swedish Transport Workers Union, Securitas signed an agreement to respect workers' freedom to form a union.

SEIU also took on other giants in the private security industry, such as G4S/Wackenhut, Allied Barton, and Guardsmark.

By 2010, security officers protecting more than 80 percent of commercial office space in Los Angeles and Century City had become SEIU members. Before organizing, average wages for security officers in L.A. were about $8 an hour. There were few benefits, no sick days, no holidays, no vacation days, and no pension for security officers, the majority of whom were African American with many residing in low-income communities in South Central L.A. After tough struggles lasting more than five years, SEIU security officers in Los Angeles won a first contract in 2007 that raised wages and benefits by nearly 40 percent.

Security workers in Boston launched their effort to form a union in 2006. After two years of organizing and coalition-building, they won majority sign-up agreements and first contracts from Northeast Security, Apollo Security, USI Security, Palladion Services, and Aeropoint Security.

By 2010, 88 percent of commercial office space in Boston was protected by SEIU members. The lowest-paid workers there won wage increases of 47 percent over a four-year agreement that will put them at $14.75 per hour by 2013. SEIU workers there won paid holidays, sick days, and vacations for the first time, as well as more affordable health insurance and overtime pay.

SEIU security officers in Seattle and Washington, D.C., also organized and won big contract gains. And in New York City, where 53 percent of commercial office space is protected by SEIU workers, the union organized FJC, Guardsmark, and Summit. In 2009, security officers at city buildings in the five boroughs won 26 percent pay raises over three years, employer-paid family health coverage, paid days off, a 401k plan, and advanced security training.

Union public employees partnered with Colorado's Department of Transportation to solve problems involving getting snowplows and asphalt where they were needed.

# CHAPTER 24

# Public Workers Wage A Quiet Revolution
## SEIU Represents One Million Public Employees

Employees of state and local governments work hard each day to make sure that water in their communities is drinkable, that libraries and roads stay open, that schools get cleaned, and so much more.

Polls show, however, that citizens often are frustrated with the inefficiency and bureaucracy they experience. And few are more fed up than public employees themselves.

Full of ideas for containing costs and improving public services, public employees are frequently held back by the very bureaucracies the public finds so challenging to navigate. With state and local governments facing massive budget crises, public employees nationwide demand to be part of the solution, but too often struggle to make their voices heard amid waves of furloughs, cutbacks, and layoffs.

SEIU's Public Services Division reshaped itself in the past decade and led a quiet revolution in public employee unionism, winning major organizing victories using a new model for solution-oriented partnerships between labor and management in the public sector. While SEIU's big wins in the property services sector, such as those in Miami and Houston, deservedly captured headlines, the union's public employees quietly scored unprecedented gains as well.

At the 2004 convention, SEIU made a commitment to organizing in the South and Southwest. The union followed through on that commitment with important victories in Colorado, Arizona, and Texas. Led by SEIU Executive Vice President Eliseo Medina, a dedicated group of organizers in 2004 devoted themselves to figuring out how to build strength for public workers in the fastest-growing parts of the country.

Public employees throughout the South and Southwest then largely still lacked the legal rights to organize unions that their counterparts in most parts of the Northeast, Midwest, and Pacific Coast states had won decades earlier.

Sunbelt states (except California) historically were dedicated to small government and many had minimal experience with unions. SEIU believed that confrontational tactics were not going to win over skeptical publics, politicians, and potential members. At the same time, many of these states faced real challenges delivering public services effectively, resulting in dissatisfied communities and employees alike.

Turning to a new approach for public employee unionism, SEIU asserted that challenges facing state and local governments and their employees were less likely to be solved in an environment of confrontation. Instead, the new model focused on a simple idea: that front-line employees often have the best ideas for how to make improvements to the services they deliver, and should be able to have their voices heard.

Public workers in Colorado responded enthusiastically to this vision of having a real voice in how their work could better serve their communities. Under the leadership of Mitch Ackerman, a longtime SEIU activist in Colorado who went on to become an executive vice president of the International Union in 2009, the union began organizing among public employees and formed an alliance with the Colorado Association of Public Employees (CAPE).

In 2006, state employees presented newly elected Governor Bill Ritter with 1,000 new ideas on how to improve state government. Shortly afterward, Ritter issued an executive or-

der allowing the state's 32,000 employees to vote for an organization to represent them—not only to negotiate job standards, but also to facilitate service improvements in partnership with the state.

Colorado's public employees at every state agency in 2008 chose to join Colorado Workers for Innovations and New Solutions (Colorado WINS), a joint local that SEIU formed with AFSCME and the American Federation of Teachers. Workers voted overwhelmingly in favor of the new organization, in defiance of a coordinated right-wing attack on the idea of public employees having a voice at work.

Colorado proved the effectiveness of the partnership model. For example, Colorado's Department of Transportation (CDOT) had been plagued with problems following a computer system upgrade. The department was struggling to get asphalt and snowplows to the places they were needed, and employees were not getting paid. Newly organized public employees went to Russell George, head of CDOT, with ideas for solutions and he agreed to try working together. The partnership was so successful that George, a former Republican member of the state legislature, became one of the strongest voices

testifying to the positive role the Colorado public employees union had in improving state services.

At the same time that Colorado public workers were winning improvements, public workers in Arizona had embraced the same idea and organized with SEIU. Workers in Arizona decided in 2004 that they wanted to be a different kind of public employee union—one with a strong focus on fostering innovation and quality, which they dubbed the "IQ Process." Potential members were told explicitly that "if you're here because you're a bad employee and you think the union will help you, you're in the wrong room—we're not that kind of union." Instead, the union focused on helping workers do more for the public, do better for themselves, and save money for taxpayers.

The message resonated with employees and elected officials alike, even in places like Gilbert, Arizona, recognized as one of the most conservative cities in the United States. In Pima County, after a county ordinance passed, public employees voted to form a union and got a first "contract"[172] for 5,000 workers. In Tempe and Chandler, where workers won raises of up to five percent, the union set up an innovative conflict resolution process to resolve workplace and disciplinary issues efficiently. Rather than have union staff process grievances "for" members, members were trained to be resolution specialists themselves, and won the right to deal with labor issues during work time.

Texas workers scored impressive breakthroughs through organizing with SEIU as well. More than 25,000 public sector workers there won the right to a voice at work by joining SEIU in 2005 and 2006.[173] Houston city employees successfully convinced the Republican-controlled Texas state legislature in 2005 to pass first-ever legislation allowing civilian public sector workers in the state to form a union and negotiate a "meet and confer" agreement with their employer.

In June 2006, members of SEIU and AFSCME came together and formed HOPE, the Houston Organization of Public Employees. After filing thousands of petition signatures, city employees won recognition of their organization by the Houston City Council in December 2006.

However, Houston public workers found their employer to be a less-willing partner for change than their counterparts elsewhere. They soon got to work organizing to hold their management accountable. A bargaining committee comprising 40 city workers led thousands of their colleagues during a year-and-a-half struggle for a first agreement.

Workers testified before the City Council, held rallies and a candlelight vigil at City Hall, and made appearances on billboards and in radio advertisements to highlight problems with city services that city workers could address with a good first agreement. One example Houston workers highlighted through outreach to local news media was the problem of the city's 911 emergency call center using high school interns to take calls.

In March 2008, Houston's 13,200 civilian city workers' orga-

Mitch Ackerman, who went on to become an SEIU executive vice president, played a strategic role in uniting some 32,000 Colorado public employees in "Colorado WINS," a joint local union with AFSCME and the American Federation of Teachers. After serving as president of Local 105 and leading SEIU's Colorado State Council, he became head of the union's 225,000-member Property Services Division in 2009.

nizing efforts paid off, winning a historic first agreement that provided an immediate 45 percent wage increase for the lowest-paid workers. The deal also created a community action leave pool through which city workers have donated vacation time to be used for volunteering on important community projects. The union also won worker-management consultation committees to promote idea-sharing and better communication on the job in order to strengthen city services.

Public workers in other parts of Texas scored victories as well. More than 6,300 San Antonio city employees won a step pay plan that raised the average worker's wages 6.5 percent a year from 2007 to 2011. And city workers in Dallas won badly needed pay increases in 2009, despite tough economic times.

In the Rio Grande Valley, where several hundred county employees have united with SEIU since 2004, Hidalgo County employees partnered with the county to expand hurricane preparedness and health promotion efforts. They also successfully advocated for lower health insurance rates for county employees.

Much as SEIU members in New York and Illinois had come to the support of janitors seeking to join with the union in Miami and Houston, so too did SEIU members and leaders from other state employees associations who traveled to North Carolina in 2007 and 2008.

They did so to support members of the State Employees Association of North Carolina (SEANC) in their deliberations over whether or not to affiliate with SEIU.

They told SEANC workers about how being part of SEIU strengthened their ability to maintain quality public services and protect worker benefits. The union also arranged for SEANC members and leaders to travel to Oregon and Connecticut to learn more about SEIU state employee locals' experiences.

In the largest labor victory ever for working people across

the South, the 55,000 state employees in North Carolina voted in 2008 to affiliate with SEIU and soon after signed up a record number of new members.

"We did a lot of praying about whether we should join with SEIU, because we wanted to do what was right for our members," said Linda Rouse Sutton, a training coordinator from Kingston, North Carolina, and then president of SE-ANC. "We were so impressed by Andy Stern's vision, and how he talked about how unions could be a vehicle to help working people all across the nation and all across the world," Sutton later stated. "I truly believe the Lord has led us in this direction…and this is just the beginning—we made history in North Carolina."[174]

In February 2010, North Carolina Governor Beverly Perdue issued an executive order enabling SEANC to "meet and confer" with the state on matters involving workplace issues. The move expanded SEIU's ability to seek gains for public employees in a state that prohibits them from collective bargaining.[175] Overall, a record 110,000 public service workers united together in SEIU in 2008, pushing the union's number of public employees well past the one million mark.

Building on these organizing victories and on the partnership model, SEIU's public employee members expanded the vision of taking initiative to improve services in their communities.

Members of SEIU Local 503 in Oregon undertook a major effort with the state's Department of Human Services to revamp the speed and quality of the delivery of critical services to the community. Building on member ideas, the department eliminated red tape and reduced the waiting period to receive food stamps from 30 days to same-day or next-day service in

SEIU public employees in San Antonio, Texas—city and county together—marched in 2005. The union won gains in Dallas, Houston, and Hidalgo County, Texas, as well.

most of the state. With that increased efficiency and the exact same staff, these members tripled the number of cases they saw each day.

Pat Perry, a Department of Transportation traffic officer and member of SEIU Local 721 in Los Angeles, took the initiative to solve a problem plaguing the neighborhoods she served: stolen cars that sat for weeks on city streets. Working with her union representative, she crafted a proposal for traffic officers to take over the duties of removing stolen cars and, when possible, returning them to their owners.

These quality and innovation efforts not only helped improve conditions for the communities SEIU public employee members serve; they also helped fight the privatization of what should be public services. "We all need to pitch in and do this [work]," said Perry to her co-workers as she persuaded them to take part in her stolen-car return initiative. "If we do this, that will mean we'll have job security, and it will be hard for them to privatize us."

Workers in other parts of the country won crucial organizing victories with SEIU as well, overcoming legal barriers to organizing through their dedicated political efforts. In New Hampshire, for example, SEIU Local 1984 helped pass a law guaranteeing public employees the freedom to form a union by majority sign-up, without interference from their employers. New Hampshire thus became one of a growing list of states where public workers could choose to join a union through card-check, demonstrating that majority sign-up can work to give employees a voice at work. Members in New Hampshire also helped defeat an anti-worker "right-to-work" bill by the largest margin ever.[176]

Another profound challenge facing communities and the public employees who serve them was the increasing trend of governments toward contracting out public services rather than providing them directly. Child care services, school transportation, mental health services, and so many more community

A huge victory for working people across the South came in 2008 when the 55,000 members of SEANC, the State Employees Association of North Carolina, voted to unite with SEIU. Linda Rouse Sutton was SEANC president at the time.

needs were shifted from governments to nonprofit and for-profit companies. As this work left the public sector, SEIU made gains in organizing workers in these new privately owned but publicly funded industries. Nonprofit contractors in particular often lacked the political voice necessary to secure the funding required to provide services at high standards for communities and employees.

To build member strength in these private, publicly funded industries, SEIU and its locals forged alliances with people who rely on vital public services in the community. Working parents, for example, need high-quality yet affordable child care and expect their school-age children to be able to board a safe school bus to get to public school. People with mental illness and developmental disabilities need access to community-based services and support so they can live and work independently. These constituencies have often found common cause with SEIU as they work together to improve standards for these critical community services.

For example, SEIU's successful efforts to organize 49,000 Illinois family child care providers in 2005 led nonprofits pro-

SEIU grew to represent one million public employees in part by aggressively pushing to deliver better services for the public. Public employees united in SEIU to have a voice at work.

viding child care services there to ally with SEIU, agreeing to work together politically and to allow a free and fair process for their employees to join the union. (See Chapter 21 for more on this and other SEIU Kids First victories.)

Mental health workers at the Brien Center in western Massachusetts voted overwhelmingly in 2009 to unite with thousands of other mental health workers in SEIU Local 509, overcoming management intimidation as they organized to address client care and staff turnover issues.

In Connecticut, SEIU members partnered with families and people with autism in 2006 to convince legislators to set up a $1 million, two-year pilot program to provide 50 adults and their families with support services such as job coaching, life skills, and case management.

At Northern California's La Clinica de la Raza, SEIU members partnered with families of people with developmental disabilities in 2008 to advocate for a streamlined respite care program so that families could take a break from caregiving with confidence that their loved ones would be supported with quality services. Jim Burton, president of the Regional Center of the East Bay, hailed the program, saying: "This has truly been a great partnership for our community, and the families are going to be the ones who benefit most in the end."

In 2004, SEIU members in California helped lead the campaign for Proposition 63, a ballot initiative which used a new one percent tax on millionaires to fund more than $1 billion in sorely needed community mental health services.

In 2007, SEIU members in King County, Washington, worked with employers and advocates to help pass an increase in the local sales tax to fund $50 million in additional mental health services.

SEIU's partnership with the Teamsters and the United Kingdom's Transport and General Workers Union led to the successful "Driving Up Standards" campaign for outsourced school bus drivers. The effort held the for-profit First Student Inc. accountable for necessary improvements to safety, service, and employment standards in the private school bus industry in both the United States and the United Kingdom.

SEIU locals have also been at the forefront of fights to ensure that their communities have a greater say in decisions about whether or not to privatize essential government functions. SEIU Local 73 members, for example, won a law covering all Illinois public schools that gave the community a stronger voice on privatization. The law requires private contractors to provide wages and benefits comparable to those set by the state. And Connecticut public workers in Local 2001 got a law passed for "clean contracting" that set a new standard for protecting health, safety, and public funds when state services are contracted out to private firms.

In California, workers in both Los Angeles County and San Francisco campaigned for quality public services in 2006 while winning agreements providing salary increases of 8.25 percent to 15.5 percent. They also won unprecedented requirements for safe staffing levels at Local 790 and limits on contracting out at Local 660. Members of California's public sector locals reached out in 2007 to unite 17,000 more state, county, and city workers there and were a major force behind progress toward securing health insurance for more Californians.

While SEIU members and their allies fought to maintain and improve public service quality nationwide, the union faced political campaigns from corporations and the wealthy who backed draconian ballot initiatives seeking to force cuts in vital public services and severely restrict government budgets (often known as the so-called Taxpayer Bill of Rights, or TABOR). SEIU and its allies helped defeat such measures in Maine (twice), Montana, Nebraska, and Oregon.

SEIU represented a total of one million public service workers in 2010, with 330,000 of them uniting in SEIU since 1996.

## PUBLIC SERVICE MEMBERS ORGANIZED
### 1996-2008

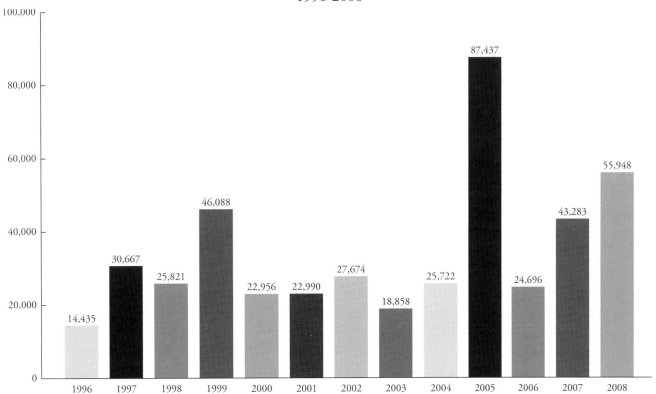

PROUD OF OUR PAST

Local 1

SEIU

RETIREES CELEBRATING LABOUR DAY

Stronger Together

Service Employees International Union

STOP PENSION CUTS

STOP PENSION CUTS

Budget

Members of SEIU Local 1 Canada celebrate Labour Day 2009 in Ontario.

# CHAPTER 25

# SEIU In Canada Charts Course To Growth
## Stronger Than Ever After CAW Raid

No matter how hard or how long he worked, the wage and benefit stars just weren't aligning for Canadian janitor Steven Singer.

In 2003, he took a 40-hour-a-week, $13-an-hour job as a cleaner at the Whitby Mall, employed by Impact, one of the many janitorial firms jockeying for business in the cutthroat, competitive bidding world of the Ontario cleaning industry. A year later, the company cut Singer's wages to $12 an hour. So he took a second, part-time job at another mall, also with Impact, that paid only $9 an hour.

By 2007, Singer was working 68 hours a week, with no days off. His average hourly pay had progressively gone down, not up. In search of relief, he called the Ontario labor board with a question about holiday pay. He found something much more important—that he was entitled to overtime pay for time worked beyond 44 hours a week. He did the math and realized that Impact owed him thousands of dollars.

Singer contacted the company with a request for the back pay owed to him, and was quickly rebuffed. As he recalled, Impact "basically refused to even talk about it." He then contacted a lawyer, who wanted $10,000 to handle the case. To Singer, it just didn't seem right to have to spend that much money to get what he was legally entitled to receive.

His star-crossed story might have ended there, but during the years he had been working for Impact, a new movement of property services workers was growing in Ontario, based out of SEIU Local 2.

In 2005, the small local union had embarked on some big changes. Like other SEIU workers and leaders across Canada, members in Ontario were taking on the challenges presented by the union's program adopted by delegates to the 2004 SEIU convention in San Francisco. The goal was to pool resources, coordinate organizing and bargaining strategies, and build membership on a bigger, faster scale so that workers would have the ability to take on intransigent companies such as Impact and win real improvements in wages and benefits.

From the U.S. perspective, it might have seemed that SEIU locals in Canada could simply be content with the status quo. After all, one out of every three workers in Canada was a union member, and every man, woman, and child in the country benefited from publicly funded healthcare. But holding on to those health and labor rights was always a challenge. Beyond that, Canada certainly was not immune to the ravages the global economy was wreaking on service-sector workers everywhere at the turn of the 21st century.

For property services workers in Canada, an important first step was the 2005 merger of the Brewery, General, & Professional Workers Union with SEIU. Over the next three years, through a series of other mergers and organizing campaigns, membership of the resulting SEIU Local 2 grew from 2,500 to nearly 12,000 workers in Ontario and British Columbia. A big part of the growth was the result of the Justice for Janitors organizing program Local 2 launched with a founding convention in Toronto in 2007.

Justice for Janitors had begun with SEIU janitors in the United States in the mid-1980s. Through a mix of civil rights-style street protests and demonstrations, outreach to religious and community allies, and support from pro-worker elected officials, the Justice for Janitors movement had helped many thousands of U.S. janitors win better wages and benefits.

It was time for Canadian janitors, some of the most impoverished and exploited workers in the country, to claim the same measure of respect and recognition as their U.S. counterparts—and Steven Singer was one of them.

In 2008, Local 2 assisted him with filing a lawsuit against Impact for back overtime wages—resulting in a $6,000 judgment in his favor—as part of its broader campaign to help Impact workers unite with SEIU to win better wages and working conditions. By 2009, more than 2,000 janitors in Toronto, Ottawa, and Vancouver had united with SEIU, and campaigns reaching out to thousands more were under way.

The changes at Local 2 were part of a broader, overall shift in SEIU's Canadian local unions. In 2004, members of

five local unions across Ontario—at Thunder Bay, Belleville, London, Hamilton, and places in between—had voted to build a stronger, more unified presence by merging into a single, provincewide local union called SEIU Local 1 Canada.

In Saskatchewan, three SEIU locals also merged in 2008, forming the new Local SEIU West. That same year, the leaders of the union's Atlantic, Central, and Western Canadian Conference—the ACWCC—adopted an ambitious, long-term national strategic plan aimed at giving tens of thousands more Canadian workers the ability to unite with SEIU to win a better life for themselves and their families.

Speaking to members in 2007, Sharleen Stewart, president of Local 1 Ontario, called SEIU "a new union ready to tackle the new problems, the new realities of today's workplaces." In the case of SEIU Local 1 Canada, she said the merger of many locals into one had put workers in a far better position to

Activists in Canada's Local 268 demonstrated for pay equity during a Dignity Rally on April 5, 1995. Local 268 joined with Locals 204, 519a, 183, and 532 to unite into a single local, known as SEIU Local 1 Canada, in 2004.

Delegates from Canada's Local 299 in Moose Jaw, Saskatchewan, participated in the parade of locals at SEIU's 2000 convention. In 2008, Local 299 joined with Locals 333 in Saskatoon and 336 in Swift Current to form SEIU West, which now represents about 12,000 healthcare, education, and community-based workers in western Canada.

stand up for their rights—and win—as they dealt with employers that, in the global economy, increasingly were bigger and more powerful.

Stewart, who virtually grew up in the labor movement, had made SEIU history in 2000 by becoming the first woman elected as a Canadian international vice president. She also won a seat on the executive committee of the Canadian Labour Congress (CLC), a sign of SEIU's rising prominence within the Canadian labor movement. She had begun her life in the labor movement in Saskatchewan, organizing private-sector workers there when she was only 18 years old. By the age of 20, she had been elected to the executive board of then-Local 333 in Saskatchewan.

In many ways, SEIU's roots in Canada mirrored the union's early days in the United States. As in the United States, the first SEIU local union in Canada was established by workers that unions in the traditional manufacturing sector had no interest in representing—office building custodians and window cleaners, many of them women, who earned as little as 35 cents

an hour. A small band of custodians and window cleaners in Vancouver was granted the first charter in Canada, forming Local 244 in 1943.

Two years later, the first group of hospital workers to form a union in Canada, workers at Toronto General Hospital, joined together to establish SEIU Local 204. Later that year, workers at four hospitals in the Thunder Bay area joined the new and growing healthcare union. In the 1960s, workers in the nursing home industry began uniting with SEIU, the first group joining the union in 1966.

By the 1990s, SEIU's membership in Canada had grown to 80,000, with local unions in Ontario, Quebec, British Columbia, Saskatchewan, Manitoba, and Nova Scotia. Most members worked in healthcare, but others worked as janitors, cooks, clerical workers, and in other professions. Like their fellow SEIU members in the United States, they were a diverse group, speaking languages including French, Italian, Portuguese, English, Chinese, and Korean.

While members in the United States were fighting to rebuild a declining labor movement, SEIU's Canadian members were living and working in a country where, as noted, one-third of the workforce was union. But cost-cutting government policies and massive changes in the Canadian workplace posed a threat to the wage and benefit standards that workers had enjoyed for years.

SEIU local unions in Canada were determined to prevent the kind of dangerous slide in union membership that had occurred in the United States. So when the new SEIU leadership team called for "Bold Action" by the union in 1996, Canadian local unions responded to the challenge. They began by stepping up the pace of new organizing, particularly in the healthcare sector. Then-Locals 204, 210, and 268 united more than 1,000 home care workers into SEIU, as did then-Locals 333, 336, and 299 in Saskatchewan.

In Ontario, then-Local 204 launched a court challenge

# SEIU Is Major Force In Quebec

SEIU is a growing force in Quebec, Canada's French-speaking and most densely unionized province.

SEIU's roots in Quebec go back to 1946, when a group of 12 elevator operators in Montreal were chartered as Local 298 and were soon joined by a unit of hospital workers. By 1986, the local had grown large enough that it split into two locals, roughly along public-private sector lines. Public-sector members mainly remained in Local 298, with private-sector workers transferring to the new Local 800.

By 2010, membership of the two locals had grown to nearly 40,000. About 25,000 healthcare and social services workers are represented by Local 298. Local 800 has about 15,000 members working in property services, schools and universities, hotels and restaurants, and service, financial, and commercial services.

In recent years, SEIU members in Quebec have dedicated energy and resources to organizing thousands of new healthcare and property services workers. Local 298 is now the largest home care workers union in Quebec and the main union of healthcare workers; Local 800 is the largest cleaning-sector union in the province.

The Quebec delegation to the 2008 SEIU convention in Puerto Rico included SEIU International Vice President Danielle Legault of Local 298 and International Executive Board member Raymond Larcher, president of Local 800.

After listening to reports of the troubled U.S. healthcare system, with its millions of uninsured citizens, Legault and Larcher reported on SEIU's work in Quebec to maintain the public healthcare system and to protect workers' rights.

As Legault noted later, "In the past four years, the Quebec government has passed laws that infringe upon our members' rights. But we have fought back and had victories...the Quebec union movement is more active than ever."

when the provincial government attempted to gut pay equity laws. The local ended up winning a historic court ruling that translated into more than $418 million for SEIU members. The pay equity adjustments directed by the court boosted wages for thousands of women working in nursing homes, home care agencies, child care, and other predominantly female workplaces.

SEIU local unions also were fighting through the union's "Dignity" campaign in Ontario to preserve minimum standards of nursing and personal care for residents in long term care facilities. Action by several SEIU locals prompted the government to release an additional $100 million in long term care funding.

In the 18 months leading up to the 2000 SEIU convention, a working group of SEIU's U.S. and Canadian leaders and staff known as the November Group (the month of their first meeting) began a series of meetings to hammer out a structure that would offer Canada's local unions more independence. The thinking was that the different set of political and economic realities faced by SEIU members in Canada called for a different structure than that governing the International Union; the goal was to develop a Canadian self-determination plan that could be voted on by delegates to the 2000 convention.

Just three months before that convention, however, a bruising, high-profile jurisdictional dispute broke out between SEIU and the Canadian Auto Workers (CAW)—threatening not only the strength of SEIU in Canada, but the unity of the Canadian Labour Congress.

The dispute began abruptly in February 2000, when Ken Brown, president of then-SEIU Local 210 in Ontario and a Canadian International vice president (and a member of the November Group), announced that representatives of eight SEIU local unions across Ontario with a total of 30,000 members had voted for a resolution to leave SEIU and join the Canadian Auto Workers. Moving to fend off what they saw as a brazen attempt by the CAW to raid nearly one-third of SEIU's membership in Canada, SEIU's leadership placed the eight Ontario local unions into temporary trusteeship.

The CLC eventually imposed sanctions on the CAW for raiding the SEIU locals. Though Brown and the CAW initially had claimed that 30,000 SEIU members would gladly leave the union, the loss of membership to SEIU was far short of that when the dust finally settled. In the end, SEIU emerged from the fracas with fewer members, but with a sharper focus on its mission and the meaning of unity.

At SEIU's 2000 convention in Pittsburgh, the Canadian self-determination resolution was adopted, as drafted by the November Group. A new, more autonomous governing structure was put into place in Canada, one that united Quebec with the rest of Canada in a loose governing structure. Though SEIU undoubtedly was bruised by the experience, it was Sharleen Stewart, then newly chosen as a Canadian vice president, who voiced what many in the labor movement were seeing as the intangible loss: the time and money expended in the fight over the already-organized 30,000 members of SEIU that could have been spent on reaching out to the hundreds of thousands of unorganized Canadian workers who desperately needed the better pay and benefits a union could bring.

The handwriting was on the wall for workers everywhere by the time SEIU held its 2004 convention—an increasingly global economy was empowering big multinational employers more intent on increasing their profits than on respecting the wages and working conditions of their employees. Speakers drove home this theme, saying it called for the "Seven Strengths" program within SEIU—one intended to give SEIU members the strength to take on global employers by developing organizing, bargaining, and political action campaigns that harnessed workers' power by cities or regions, not simply worksite by worksite.

SEIU Local 902 members gathered in Halifax, Nova Scotia, for the union's Canadian Council Convention in 2008.

SEIU Local 1 Canada Red Cross members won a new contract in 2009 that provides pay covering a portion of their travel time between clients, which often is a third of their long workdays.

SEIU members in Ontario, where Local 204 had been the dominant healthcare local union for decades, moved quickly to meet the challenge to focus and consolidate their resources and energies. In 1999, members of Locals 468 and 663 had already voted to merge with Local 204. In 2004, members of Locals 204, 519a, 268, 183, and 532 took the historic step of merging into a single local, known as SEIU Local 1 Canada.

It was a move that created a more unified, powerful presence for SEIU members in Ontario. By 2010, Local 1 Canada had 46,000 healthcare and community services members working in hospitals, home care, nursing, and retirement homes across the province. The local had emerged as Canada's major home care union with contracts covering home care workers employed by Red Cross Canada and other providers.

In June 2009, after engaging in a contract battle that included rolling one-day work stoppages, Local 1 Canada Red Cross members ratified a new contract that provided, for the first time, pay covering a portion of their travel time between clients. It was a crucial issue because home care workers spend as much as a third of their day traveling between clients—meaning they had effectively been working 12 hours a day, but were paid for only eight. As home care worker Louise Leeworthy said, "I'm not asking for a six-figure salary. All we want is to be able to do our job."

In the wake of their contract victory, SEIU home care workers made it clear that their concerns extended far beyond pay and travel time. They were calling on the Ontario government to make sweeping changes to what they called a broken and dysfunctional home care system—one based on competitive bidding between home care agencies that drove down standards for workers and clients alike.

Members of other local unions were taking action, as well, to consolidate their resources and power by merging into provincewide local unions. As noted, the 2005 merger of the Brewery Workers created the opportunity for property services workers in Ontario and other provinces to consolidate their strength into a single local union, SEIU Local 2. The 2,500 brewery, general, and professional workers were joined by about 3,500 SEIU property services workers who had been members of Local 1 Canada.

Other mergers, including the 2009 merger of Local 902 with Local 2, and the local's energetic Justice for Janitors organizing program resulted in the local more than quadrupling in size—to approximately 12,000 members in 2010. The outreach to unorganized workers included janitorial campaigns in Ontario and British Columbia. In just two years between 2007 and 2009, more than 2,000 janitors who were making poverty wages and receiving no benefits had joined with Local 2 to win major improvements.

In Halifax, two groups of casino and food services workers joined the growing movement of low-wage, multi-service sector workers uniting with SEIU.

In Saskatchewan, meanwhile, members of three local unions also decided to consolidate their strength to win gains and improvements in their industry. Barbara Cape, president of the new local called SEIU West, said at the time that the members had their sights not only on winning new and improved contracts, but also on tackling such crucial issues as safe staffing levels at healthcare worksites.

SEIU's two locals in Quebec, Locals 298 and 800, responded by working to expand their memberships (see page 188).

SEIU's members were gaining political clout as well. In 2005, SEIU members, working together with the assistance of the union's health and safety staff, formed coalitions with other union members and lobbied provincial governments across Canada for the mandatory use of safety-engineered needles. This important legislation was won in several provinces across Canada. The first victories were achieved with support from the New Democratic Party in Saskatchewan and Manitoba.

Despite the gains SEIU's Canadian members and local unions had achieved since 1996, they knew that still more change was needed to meet the challenges of the 21st century global economy. "We know our old ways of doing business have a limit," is how leaders expressed the situation in November 2008, when the Council of Presidents of the Atlantic, Central, and Western Canada Conference met to develop a long-term, strategic vision and plan for the union.

Their goal was ambitious, indeed: to make SEIU the fastest-growing union in Canada and to build power for work-

ing people from coast to coast. Similar to the situation in the United States, where SEIU's membership and strength was concentrated on the "bookends" of the East and West coasts, SEIU's membership in Canada was concentrated in Ontario, Quebec, and a few other areas. The leaders wanted to develop a plan and structure that would give workers across the country a better chance to unite with SEIU so they could share in the gains of the global economy.

Looking forward to 2012 and beyond, they developed a plan to:

- focus resources on national campaigns in two national divisions: Property Services and Healthcare, with a longer-range goal of establishing a new Public Services division;

- develop an army of trained member organizers at the national and local level that can carry out the SEIU organizing plan all across Canada;

- dramatically increase the resources devoted to reaching out to unorganized workers, with 50 percent of national resources devoted to organizing; and

- establish industry coordinating councils for the Healthcare and Property Services sectors, so the national union and local unions can coordinate organizing, political, and bargaining goals in a cohesive manner.

With this plan, the union set its sights on doubling its membership in the coming years.

And the point of it all? They coined a new word to sum it up: "win-ability," which meant building the strength to really make good on what has always been SEIU's driving mission in Canada: to make a real difference in the lives of working people.

Justicia para todos. Pásalo

Justice pour toutes et tous. Disons-le

Justice for all. Pass it on

**SEIU** Convention 08

# CHAPTER 26

# 2008 Convention Seeks 'Justice For All'
## Stern Reports SEIU Passes Two Million Members

With a calculator in his hand that linked to a super-sized video screen on stage, Andy Stern clearly had something important to say and the delegates to SEIU's 2008 convention in Puerto Rico knew it.

The SEIU president began by admitting a mistake: the delegates' packets showed the union's membership had risen to 1,896,000. "But now I have an apology," Stern said. "That membership figure is wrong."

With the calculator flashing new numbers on the screen, he told the delegates they needed to add 55,000 more members from the newly affiliated State Employees Association of North Carolina. And 7,000 more security guards from Minnesota. And 22,000 new personal care assistants in Massachusetts. And another 23,000 child care providers in Pennsylvania.

Each time a new and higher calculator total flashed overhead.

"And if you add the other 20,000 new members who recently joined the SEIU, I think we are about to turn another page of labor history," Stern told the delegates. "From this day forward, we can recognize SEIU—two million members strong."

It was a huge accomplishment and one that local union activists in the hall that day had helped achieve. They reacted with great enthusiasm.

For SEIU to hit the two-million-member mark meant the union had added one million new members since new leadership took over the union in 1996. In the decade from 1997 through 2007, the average number of workers joining SEIU each year was 96,000—more than triple the average of 30,000 new members each year from 1988 through 1996. Each increase in numbers was another building block that helped create a powerful movement for workers. And that new strength translated directly into SEIU's ability to win wage and benefit gains at the bargaining table and a better life for members and their families.

The new growth came under some difficult conditions as well. The 2004 convention had committed the union to expand organizing in the South and Southwest—regions of the United States that include many states historically hostile to organized labor. With the huge victories of Houston janitors and University of Miami cleaners and staff, SEIU had broken through in property services—in part because of the support from the union's New York City and Chicago janitors. Stern could report in 2008 that the union had grown to represent 100,000 workers in the South and Southwest.

Building on SEIU members' combined political strength in California, the union expanded its home care workers base there and, in turn, used that strength to reach out to 345,000 other home care workers in the rest of California, Oregon, Washington, Michigan, Illinois, Massachusetts, Ohio, and parts of Wisconsin. Home care workers, with each new contract, were "Invisible No More," gaining more pay, health coverage, and other improvements.[177]

By pooling the financial and political strength of locals throughout the country, the union had helped 49,000 child care providers in Illinois win union representation in 2005. That model then was used to unite more than 75,000 family child care providers to win pay and benefit increases.

Using strength gained from SEIU's global relationships, the union won an agreement with Securitas, the largest security company in the world (based in Sweden), and then worked to organize thousands of mostly African American security officers to raise wages and gain healthcare.

Pooling resources and coordinating strategies across the union successfully reduced employer interference in scores of hospital organizing campaigns in California, Colorado, Connecticut, Florida, Iowa, Illinois, Maine, Michigan, Minnesota, Ohio, Oregon, Pennsylvania, Nevada, New York, Tennessee, Washington, and Wisconsin—as well as in Puerto Rico and Canada. More than 33,000 nurses and other hospital workers had joined SEIU since the previous convention in 2004.

In the multiservices sector, SEIU had worked with another national union, UNITE HERE, to expand unionization in a sector dominated by three huge global corporations (Sodexo, Compass, and Aramark) that contract to provide a wide range of support services to governments, businesses, hospitals, local school systems, universities, and other institutions. Together, the two unions won agreements with two of the three multi-services firms to respect workers' right to form a union through majority sign-up. By the time of the 2008 convention, more than 14,000 workers in multiservices had unionized. (The merger of UNITE HERE collapsed in 2009. About 100,000 members, largely from the former UNITE, then joined SEIU as "Workers United." The breakup of UNITE HERE came about because of difficulties within that union. The move of Workers United to SEIU proved very contentious and led to attacks on SEIU by other unions. SEIU repeatedly sought a negotiated settlement with UNITE HERE in 2009–2010, but no agreement had been reached as this book went to press.)

Gains in Puerto Rico, including public sector collective bargaining, led to new contracts there. And SEIU grew by more than 13,000 workers in Canada, making it the fastest-growing

SEIU President Andy Stern told delegates to the 2008 convention that the union had grown to more than two million members. That represented a gain of more than 1 million members since Stern and his new leadership team took office in 1996. He emphasized that the point of organizing was not numbers, but building the strength to win economic, political, and social justice gains for SEIU workers.

Convention delegates including Laphonza Butler adopted a program calling for "Justice for All." They urged further resources for organizing and political accountability and demanded that Congress pass healthcare reform, the Employee Free Choice Act, and comprehensive immigration reform.

union there. Coordinated campaigns with global labor federations and about 20 individual unions around the world helped SEIU win new members and improved workplace standards for about 60,000 workers in multinational corporations in SEIU industries in other countries.

Each convention under Stern had a theme and program. It had been Bold Action in 1996, New Strength Unity in 2000, and Seven Strengths in 2004. For 2008, SEIU's program was called "**Justice for All**."

SEIU could achieve its goals only "if we stand for 'justice for all,' and not for 'just us,'" the primary convention resolution stated. The message was that SEIU had a mission to unite workers and win a better life for all working people.

"Today's union members cannot expect to maintain and improve our living standards and working conditions if the percentage of union members in our industries and our society continues to decline," the resolution warned.

By moving to pool its strength, SEIU had been able to grow and to win major economic and workplace gains for its members. Its bargaining, political, membership, and financial strength had created new possibilities for organizing.

Implicit in the contrast of "justice for all" instead of "just us" was a rebuke of a strategy solely focused on leaders negotiating contracts that only address certain members' goals rather than improving conditions for all members. Members can't win at the bargaining table without a parallel strategy to organize nonunion workers at the same employer or in the same type of work. For a long period, the union had concentrated its resources in California to build density and workers' strength. But with national healthcare employers, such as HCA and Tenet, it was time to employ more SEIU resources throughout the country. While some leaders balked, workers understood that if their employers were nonunion elsewhere in the United States, their own strength ultimately would be weakened.

Another area of disagreement was over how the union should proceed on its restructuring plans in California to align members effectively. A small but vocal segment of delegates, led by Sal Rosselli from United Healthcare Workers West, strongly opposed uniting the strength of home care and nursing home workers from his local into a statewide SEIU long term care local that would include workers from two other local unions doing the same type of work. This was designed in part to strengthen long term care workers' voice in the state legislature, which controlled the funding for these services. The restructuring also sought to focus UHW on organizing the 100,000 nonunion hospital workers in California.

Rosselli and his forces made little headway at the convention, perhaps because the rank-and-file delegates saw them positioned as the "Just Us" element of the debate—at odds with the solidarity implicit in SEIU's theme of "Justice for All."

The convention delegates, the highest governing authority of the union, resolved the issues overwhelmingly in favor of the leadership, but the rift would go on for many months after the convention. Rosselli resigned from SEIU membership in January 2009 after the local was placed in trusteeship for financial malpractice and refusal to abide by SEIU's jurisdiction ruling. He had formed his own union secretly while at SEIU and later announced he would compete for UHW members. A year later, the rival union had no members under contract (see Chapter 31).

SEIU remained united around the idea that future challenges would require continuation of its ability to change and adapt. Polling data revealed that about 50 percent of U.S. workers would choose to have a union if they didn't face employer opposition—an unorganized body of some 40 million workers to be organized.

But union leaders laid out what they termed "stark realities" standing in the way:

- The organizing process established by the National Labor Relations Board could no longer be counted on to protect workers' freedom to form a union. In most cases, NLRB procedures took too long, left too much room for employer interference and intimidation, and imposed little or no penalty for violations of the law.

- Most employers refused to respect workers' right to form a union without management intimidation. Too often, SEIU had to conduct corporate social responsibility campaigns that held the employer accountable for the full range of ways its policies and practices affected the larger community. That takes money, political strength, and the ability to campaign effectively throughout the nation or worldwide.

- SEIU industries and employers increasingly operated on a regional, national, or global basis. They moved capital from one place to another with growing ease and drove down pay and benefit standards in one location, which in turn helps drive them down everywhere. Employers' increased size allowed them to exercise far more political pressure than a purely local employer could.

- Capital had blurred the lines across industries and between

the public and private sectors. In 2008, more than five million people worked for companies controlled by corporate buyout firms that had no industry focus. Those firms instead have as their goal taking steps to maximize profits for a limited group of executives.

- In SEIU's core sectors, corporate buyout firms had taken ownership of the nation's largest office building landlord, Equity Office Properties; the largest for-profit hospital chain, HCA; the nation's largest nursing home chains, Beverly Enterprises (since renamed Golden Living Centers) and Mariner Health Group; and the largest U.S.-based provider of cleaning and food services, Aramark.

- The percentage of overall unionization in the private sector had dropped below 8 percent, and two-thirds of public employees in 2008 had no union either. In the other core SEIU sectors of healthcare and property services, 90 percent of all workers had no union.

- Virtually all population growth in the United States in the next 20 years would be in southern and western states where unionization is lowest. Those states increasingly would have an economic impact on pay and benefit standards for the nation, so if SEIU failed to help workers there unite to win gains, the pressure would be greater to reduce standards in the rest of the country.

- Industries growing the fastest generally had been those with the least unionization.
- The experiences of some of the major U.S. industrial, construction, and transportation unions remained a stark reminder that SEIU could not expect to win or maintain high union standards for "just us," as an island in an increasingly nonunion economic sea.[178]

SEIU leaders told the delegates that "while we have doubled spending on organizing in four years, we have not doubled our results. Our spending to help each new worker join us has increased greatly, which jeopardizes our ability to unite more workers faster."

Spending per member on representation and other non-organizing activity had increased substantially from 1999 through 2007, but without significant enough increases in member satisfaction, according to polls and other research.

While many SEIU local unions were spending at least 20 percent of their budget on organizing, figures showed that at least $37 million that should be spent on organizing by locals was not being spent—money badly needed to help pay for larger-scale strategies.

"SEIU members and our allies have shown that we can overcome all obstacles if we choose to unite our strength behind a bold common strategy," the leadership recommendation to the convention delegates stated. "We have the *chance* of a lifetime if we make the *choice* of a lifetime."

After much debate, the program that was adopted and that charted SEIU's course through to 2012, included the following:

1. **Involve all local unions jointly to develop one national strategy for uniting more workers with SEIU to win gains for working people on a much larger scale.**

SEIU will have one strategy for uniting more workers and raising standards for all workers in our industries. It will be based on the integrated plans of each division, their locals, and the South/Southwest, and also will include opportunities and challenges that cross industries and regions. Local unions will continue to have organizing programs as part of an overall division plan. The overall SEIU strategy will include a numerical goal for the whole union, each division, the South/Southwest, cross-division opportunities, and each local union—and will be approved by the International Executive Board.

By 2012, SEIU will have united more than 500,000 more workers, the largest four-year increase in strength by any union in modern history.

That will make SEIU the largest and strongest union that includes private sector workers that North America has ever seen, with more than 2.5 million members.

It also is expected that, if we are able to enact the Employee Free Choice Act (EFCA) with a new U.S. Congress and President, SEIU will unite a total of at least one million more workers by 2012.

Local union leaders will collaborate as national leaders for their industry to make a united national strategy for their division based on a long-term vision for members and an initial four-year action program.

Through the divisions, local unions will collectively decide—instead of deciding individually—where to prioritize efforts for the best chance of large-scale gains for workers.

Every local union will set aside 20 percent of its post-per capita budget to organizing in a separate fund.

The International Union's resources will be used to implement the one national strategy.

All levels of the union will be accountable for their contribution to the strategy.

There will be regular unionwide review and evaluation of progress.

**2. Involve current members in helping more workers to unite with us for everyone's benefit.**

SEIU members have been very effective at reaching out to not-yet-union counterparts who do similar work and are or-

A delegate from Local 6434 heard speakers call for unifying California home care workers in one local to build greater bargaining and political leverage.

ganizing to unite with us. A new program—MOR (Member Organizing Reserves)—will expand member involvement in organizing campaigns and will work with the divisions to help staff large campaigns. And another program—SEIU Organizing Corps—will be modeled after the Peace Corps or Teach for America. It will involve temporary organizers who are interested in doing social justice work for a portion of their life, but who are unsure of what work they want to do in the long term.

The union will give high priority to providing members with the opportunity to go to nonunion locations and meet with not-yet-union workers.

SEIU will use its bargaining and political strength to unite more workers with us for everyone's benefit. Mechanisms for involving current members to use their strength to help more workers at national employers to unite with us should be developed nationally through the divisions. Divisions may designate strategic global/national/regional employers or sectors/subsectors where a comprehensive unionwide strategy offers the potential for breakthroughs in uniting more workers and raising standards.

**3. Help build a stronger union movement, as we are all stronger together.**

SEIU will help other unions in Change to Win to unite more workers in their industries. We will increase our capacity to conduct campaigns involving multinational corporations in other countries on behalf of members in SEIU and Change to Win industries.

We will work with union allies in other countries to increase the capacity to unite workers to improve living standards and working conditions in common industries and multinational corporations.

We will deepen the involvement of SEIU local union activists in SEIU's global work and will track employer globalization trends in all SEIU divisions.

SEIU's 2008 convention was held in San Juan, Puerto Rico.

The "Justice for All" program also called for new efforts to build a permanent pro-worker political majority; win affordable, quality healthcare for all; create an economy that rewards work, including the freedom to form a union without employer interference; win comprehensive immigration reform; and improve quality services in the community with fair, reliable funding.

To get there, the union proposed involving 200,000 members—10 percent of the total membership—in leadership roles and one million members in member action.

"Member action and participation on a whole new scale also will further expand democracy in our union," the recommendations approved by the 2008 convention delegates noted. "Real worker democracy includes majority participation in the actual activities of the union that aim to improve workers' lives."

In addition, the program called for providing every member with not only increased opportunities for involvement and leadership, but also an increased level of responsiveness and member satisfaction through Member Resource Centers. Those centers would use trained staff that could provide members with information in their own language, help solve job-related problems using new technologies, and be available 24 hours a day/7 days a week. Every local would be offered the opportunity to participate.

The new initiatives grew out of years of work by SEIU's Local Union Strength Committee made up of a team of local leaders from across North America who identified innovations that were aimed at making the union more responsive and involving rank-and-file members in building a better future. The committee, as part of its work, examined a number of creative approaches utilized by unions in other countries, such as Australia.

Out of the discussions came recommendations for pilot projects following the convention for the new member centers. In addition, the Local Union Strength Committee proposed freeing up of local union leaders by programs that would pool administrative functions, such as accounting, dues processing, and list management, so more time could be spent on core union priorities.

By 2010, SEIU had implemented a number of the Local Union Strength Committee's proposals. The union launched a new state-of-the-art Member Action Service Center near Detroit, Michigan. It offered members instant access to trained, multilingual staff who sought to respond promptly to individual member questions and issues. Members, for example, could get answers to benefit questions and help with filing grievances. The program reported 80 percent of members had their questions answered or problems solved with just one phone call.

Convention delegates also reaffirmed the importance of expanding diversity at all levels of the union.

In 1996, prior to the major leadership change in SEIU, 68 percent of the 50 largest locals were run by white men. But with the change agenda that SEIU implemented in the following 12 years, the leadership became more diverse, with only 38 percent of those big locals being run by white males. Of the 10 largest locals, four were led by African Americans and five by women. African Americans, Latinos, and women had assumed leadership positions over that time on the union's International Executive Board and Executive Committee as well.[179]

On the political front, SEIU's endorsed candidate for President, Barack Obama, was on the verge of achieving sufficient delegates to ensure he would be the Democratic Party nominee for President. But SEIU convention delegates called for an even broader effort to build a permanent pro-worker political majority in the United States.

"As the leading advocacy organization for working people in North America, SEIU has both the opportunity and the responsibility to play a leadership role in building that majority coalition based on issues important to working people, rather than the interests of particular political parties or candidates," the adopted resolution stated.

Delegates called for "even more emphasis on holding public officials accountable after they are elected and not just hoping that they will stand up for working people."

Top federal priorities singled out by the 2008 convention were:

- passage of **universal healthcare reform**;
- passage of the **Employee Free Choice Act**;
- passage of **comprehensive immigration reform**; and
- securing fair and reliable funding to support **quality public services** in communities.

In addition, delegates endorsed adoption of pension reform and a commitment for a specific Iraq War exit strategy in 2008 or 2009 that would bring troops home and allow redirecting war spending to vital needs at home.

To carry out the SEIU political and legislative program, all locals were to continue to dedicate at least 10 percent of their resources to political work in 2008-2010, at least 11 percent in 2011, and at least 12 percent in 2012. SEIU divisions may choose to set those standards higher, delegates said.

SEIU's state councils gained new powers to ensure that "ev-

eryone around the decision-making table is on the same page." The councils were directed to establish and coordinate a candidate endorsement process for all of the locals within a state.

With money being the mother's milk of politics, the 2008 convention approved plans urging that 20 percent of every local union's members contribute an average of at least $7 per month to the SEIU COPE program (the union's political action committee), with higher goals to follow. Locals would be expected to increase the number of member volunteers and member political organizers as well.

The delegates backed expanded civic participation and new work with communities of color and immigrant members and families, as well as setting the goal for local unions to register at least 80 percent of their eligible members to vote by 2010 and 90 percent by 2012. SEIU also committed to expand the broad electorate by providing leadership to America Votes' state-based and national bodies.

Delegates voted to help build a progressive political and policy infrastructure and develop expertise in framing issues for the public. SEIU committed to supporting technology and information-based organizations that can strengthen the progressive movement.

With political accountability a theme, the union voted to commit at least $10 million to 2008-2009 post-election political accountability work and also to build a multilevel grassroots rapid response system to hold members of Congress and local elected officials accountable. Included were additional resources in issue-based and electoral accountability campaigns that SEIU leads or helps with, such as They Work for Us and Working for Us PAC.

The delegates also voted to expand political communications systems, voter information tracking systems, and the SEIU GOP Advisory Committee as well as encouraging more SEIU members to run for office and increasing the involvement of SEIU retirees in political action. And the convention called for increasing SEIU strength in the community through developing annual plans and expanding training.

The convention agenda had been shaped in part by a wide range of SEIU caucuses that provided forums for the vast and rich diversity of the union. The caucuses helped to identify and develop leaders, served as a bridge with groups outside the union, and broadened member participation.

At times over the years, the caucuses challenged the union to rethink its programs, policies, and practices. Among the active caucuses at the 2008 convention were the African American Caucus, Asian Pacific Islander Caucus, First American Caucus, Lavender Caucus, Latino Caucus, People with Disabilities Caucus, Retiree Caucus, and Women's Caucus.

The convention delegates also re-elected SEIU President Andy Stern and Secretary-Treasurer Anna Burger and chose six executive vice presidents: Eliseo Medina, Tom Woodruff, Mary Kay Henry, Gerry Hudson, Annelle Grajeda,[180] and Dave Regan. They were joined by a diverse International Executive Board of 65 additional union leaders, including nine rank-and-file members.

Dave Regan, who led SEIU District 1199 in West Virginia, Kentucky, and Ohio from 2000 to 2008, won election as an executive vice president at SEIU's 2008 convention.

As the Justice for All program was debated on the convention floor, Monica Russo from SEIU Healthcare Florida took the floor to speak in favor of the proposals.

"We are going to have to step up like never before to elect the next President of the United States," she said. "And that is only where it begins, because President Barack Obama will need us. He needs an army, a grassroots army of activist members—healthcare workers, public employees, property services janitors—an army of members in the streets.

"Because Barack Obama is not going to win healthcare by himself; it is healthcare workers who are going to transform the healthcare system," Russo said. "It is public employees who are going to fight for money put into education. It is property service workers that are going to fight to make sure that global corporations are accountable."

As the delegates flew home from Puerto Rico, they faced not only the challenges of expanding SEIU membership by 500,000, but also electing Barack Obama and a pro-worker Congress that would create the real possibility of healthcare, labor law, and immigration reform.

A daunting agenda loomed ahead—one that would start with nuts-and-bolts political work at the grassroots—something SEIU members have proved they do with great skill.

During the 2008 presidential campaign, Barack Obama spent a day walking in the shoes of SEIU home care worker Pauline Beck. From dawn to dusk, Obama experienced firsthand what it's like for American workers. Here Obama and Beck assist John Thornton, an 86-year-old former cement mason.

CHAPTER 27

# SEIU Proves Vital To Obama Victory
## Early Endorsement, Skilled Volunteers Help Bring 2008 Win

You can make a good argument that Barack Obama might not have made it to the White House were it not for the effective grassroots political efforts of thousands of SEIU members, including Pauline Beck, a home care worker in Oakland, California.

As Obama faced off in the early days of his presidential campaign against the big Democratic names such as Hillary Clinton, Joe Biden, John Edwards, Chris Dodd, and Bill Richardson, he was a first-term Senator whom many Americans frankly had never heard of.

But Obama spent a day walking in the shoes of Pauline Beck, going through her workday from dawn to dusk and experiencing what it's like to be a home care worker, like many thousands of SEIU members.

The empathy and understanding Obama showed that day for America's working families played a vital role later in winning him an early endorsement from SEIU members. And that support—skilled volunteers and funding—throughout the hard-fought primary and caucus season helped Obama win the Democratic nomination…and ultimately the presidency of the United States.

"Walk a Day in My Shoes" is a program of SEIU that puts politicians to a test. Candidates for political office from the local level all the way to the White House now are told: "Before you ask for my support, Walk a Day in My Shoes."

The program was part of SEIU's new approach to politics under Secretary-Treasurer Anna Burger, who coordinated the union's 2008 political effort. It was an attempt to force politicians to confront what it's like to work and raise a family in America. Those candidates had to earn their SEIU endorsement in part by spending time at home and on the job with the union's members.

"We juggle work, child care, bills, PTA meetings, second jobs, caring for aging parents, soccer practice, and everything else we try to cram in from the time our alarm clock goes off in the morning to when we hit our pillows at night," one SEIU member said. "If politicians experience firsthand what it's like to work and raise a family today, then maybe they can go back to the mayor's office, or the Senate floor, or even the White House and help enact real change for working families."

On August 8, 2007, Senator Barack Obama arrived at Pauline Beck's home before dawn and had breakfast with her daughter—an Oakland school worker—and her grandnephew and two foster children.

Obama and Beck then drove to the home of Beck's 86-year-old client, John Thornton, a former cement mason. Together, they got him out of bed, prepared his breakfast, and helped him get ready to start his day. Thornton, for whom Beck had cared for four years, was completely dependent on Beck and another home care worker for 24-hour care. He had a broken hip, a prosthetic leg, and nerve damage to his fingers and could not get out of bed, bathe, or dress himself on his own.

The man who is now the most powerful person in the world set about the work of an SEIU home care worker: he mopped the floors, he did some sweeping, and he did the laundry. Thornton listened to Beck describing the next set of tasks to Obama and said: "She's working the hell out of him."

Afterward, Obama said that "walking just one day in Pau-

Gerry Hudson (left), SEIU executive vice president, said of the union's early endorsement of Barack Obama: "Neutrality or Hillary might have been a safer bet, but we're not folks who play it safe." Hudson and Eliseo Medina (right) had joined with SEIU members to make healthcare and immigration reform into major campaign issues.

line's shoes was probably the best experience I've had on this campaign so far.

"I think it makes all the difference to have a union represent someone like Pauline," he said. "She described what it was like before SEIU reached out to her. She was getting paid a minimum wage. She didn't have healthcare benefits. Now, as a consequence of the work SEIU has done, she's got a wage that pays $10 and change an hour…she's got healthcare, but there's still more work to be done."

Other Democratic presidential candidates also walked a day in an SEIU member's shoes. Then-Senator Hillary Clinton, for example, went through a shift with a registered nurse, Michelle Estrada; Joe Biden, now the Vice President, walked in the shoes of school custodian Marshall Clemons; New Mexico Governor Bill Richardson spent a workday with family services worker Mark Fitzgerald; and John Edwards joined nursing home worker Elaine Ellis. Senator Chris Dodd walked in the shoes of Head Start teacher Colleen Mehaffey.

Senator John McCain and other Republican presidential hopefuls all declined to participate in the "Walk a Day in My Shoes" program.

The other priority SEIU initiative of the 2008 primary and caucus season was a challenge to the candidates to release a detailed healthcare plan.

*Time* magazine reporter Karen Tumulty, who participated in an SEIU issues forum, described the politics of the healthcare issue: "By 2008, healthcare had become practically radioactive to politicians. Yes, the problem was out there…but politicians—having seen what this cost the Clinton White House—had pretty much decided that healthcare reform was something they just didn't want to go near."[181]

SEIU had other ideas. Gerry Hudson, an executive vice president, said: "We didn't want to make this election about candidates. We wanted to make it about issues, and healthcare was one of the key issues."

SEIU President Stern described SEIU members' desire to "throw down the gauntlet and say, 'Don't come to our Member Political Action Conference without a healthcare plan that's comprehensive and universal and has a way to pay for it.'"

When the Democratic presidential candidates appeared at a forum sponsored by the University of Nevada–Las Vegas (UNLV) and organized by SEIU in March 2007, workers pressed them with tough questioning about how their healthcare reform plans would work. Jon Alter, a *Newsweek* reporter, later reflected: "I think it was smart of SEIU to put most of its chips on healthcare. By making it clear that this was a priority, it did have an effect on the Democratic primary campaign."

SEIU members also demanded to know where the candidates of both parties were on the Employee Free Choice Act to help workers exercise their right to choose a union without employer interference. Comprehensive immigration reform was another important issue that union members in the primary and caucus states raised with candidates.

"We went into our Member Political Action Conference with three favorites [John Edwards, Barack Obama, and Hillary Clinton] and we came out of that conference still with three strong candidates who our members all liked," Secretary-Treasurer Anna Burger noted after the meeting in September 2007 of more than 1,500 SEIU members who heard directly from the candidates.

In late fall 2007, as primary and caucus season approached, *The New York Times* carried a news story about SEIU's growing political power headlined "A Union With Clout Stakes Its Claim on Politics." It said Stern "has made his union the nation's fastest-growing over the past decade, and his focus on politics has led Democratic presidential candidates to court the SEIU endorsement aggressively."[182]

SEIU leaders strongly believed the union's endorsement had to flow up from the union's members, rather than from the top down. With some strong early support for John Edwards, as well as Obama and Clinton, the union went into the Iowa caucuses without a nationally endorsed candidate. SEIU state councils were free to back their own choices in their home-state primary or caucus.

Barack Obama found a "purple army" of SEIU supporters wherever he campaigned in 2008.

Obama's victory in Iowa surprised the political pundits and much of America. SEIU members, particularly those from Obama's home state of Illinois, quickly seized the initiative and pressed for an all-out endorsement of his candidacy.

"Our members and our leaders were passionate about making change and when John Edwards dropped out, they saw Barack Obama as the change candidate," Stern said later. "People just moved there quickly."

On February 15, 2008, SEIU endorsed Obama and geared up to put all of the union's people power and grassroots organizing skills behind his campaign.

"Their endorsing Obama at this point was not a safe bet," said *Time* magazine's Karen Tumulty. "This was right after Super Tuesday when Hillary Clinton essentially fought Barack Obama to a draw. And her big stronghold states were still ahead."

Change to Win (CTW) endorsed Obama as well and the labor federation, of which SEIU was an essential part, put a skilled field operation in place that the campaign relied on heavily.

Many other unions strongly backed Senator Clinton and put their political operations up against SEIU's. And the battle got very tough very fast.

In state after state, SEIU's purple army of member political organizers went knocking on doors, operating phonebanks, reaching out to voters, passing out campaign literature, and pressing voters to support Barack Obama.

Rank-and-file workers responded to SEIU appeals, campaigners said, for several reasons. Personally, they seemed reassured about his early efforts as an organizer in Chicago working with SEIU members to improve neighborhoods there. They also liked that he had met one-on-one with SEIU child care providers to talk about their issues. And they were impressed by his participation with home care worker Pauline Beck in the "Walk a Day in My Shoes" program.

But driving Obama's support among working families was his commitment to provide affordable healthcare coverage to all Americans and his support of the Employee Free Choice Act protecting workers' right to organize into unions. SEIU members also clearly prioritized the importance of an economic program to create good-paying jobs at home in America and reduce the widening gap between the ultra-rich and everyone else.

Obama also won support because of his call for comprehensive immigration reform and his commitment to end the war in Iraq and bring troops home safely.

The race for the nomination proved far closer than many anticipated with both Obama and Clinton fighting tooth-and-nail for every single delegate. By the time SEIU delegates to the union's 2008 convention began to meet in San Juan, Puerto Rico, it appeared Obama had won enough delegates to wrap up the Democratic nomination.

Obama himself confirmed he would be the nominee in his remarks to the SEIU convention via satellite link. "This is our moment, SEIU, this is our time," Obama told the delegates.

SEIU insisted the Democratic candidates for President tell voters what their plan would be for reforming America's healthcare system. From the New Hampshire primary through to the general election on Nov. 4, 2008, the union made healthcare reform a top campaign issue.

"If you keep knocking on those doors and making those phone calls and registering voters, if I keep seeing purple everywhere I go, then I promise you this: We will win this general election and then you and I, together, we are going to change this country and we are going to change the world."

And in his own SEIU convention speech, Andy Stern told delegates: "You are going to say, 'I was there, when we joined forces with Obama and wrote the new chapter of history'…you are going to say to your kids and grandkids, 'Because I made that choice, the world has never been the same.'"

SEIU Secretary-Treasurer Anna Burger addressed the Democratic Party convention in Denver in August 2008 and set the theme for the fall campaign.

"Our unions helped us pass on to our kids a better life than our own—and we call this legacy the American Dream," she said. "But today, that dream is fading.

"After eight years of George W. Bush, work hours are up, but wages are down. And John McCain is offering more of the same. The gap between the rich and the rest of America—it's staggering and growing. And John McCain is offering more of the same."[183]

The general election campaign did not have George W. Bush, whose popularity was at a record low, on the ballot. But his staunch anti-worker economic policies had cost many Americans their jobs, and many felt misled by his early and untrue claims about weapons of mass destruction that rationalized his taking the United States to war in Iraq. Still, the Obama-McCain race looked to be a toss-up early on.

Then, with some suddenness, the U.S. economy collapsed. Years of deregulation on Wall Street and predatory lending policies on Main Street led to a serious economic crisis, as Lehman Brothers went bankrupt. The prospect of another, perhaps worse, Great Depression loomed. Republican candidate John McCain shocked many Americans when he said "the fundamentals of our economy are strong."[184]

Andy Stern noted that McCain "completely got it wrong" with the comments about the "strong" economy. "For SEIU, you know this crisis meant the focus on the economy that we had been looking for was incredibly sharp," Stern said.[185]

From that point on, the Obama-Biden ticket really gained momentum, particularly among working families that, even before the collapse, had struggled to deal with median family income that had been falling for seven years under Bush.[186]

More than 3,000 SEIU members and staff worked full-time campaigning for Obama, pounding the pavement and talking with voters.

SEIU's "Road to American Health Care" bus tour spent four months on the road, traveling 8,500 miles. It held events in 17 states that featured real people struggling to keep up with rising healthcare costs (see Chapter 34). The union issued a report, *Making a Bad Problem Worse,* that detailed how McCain's healthcare proposal would have made it harder for average families to get quality, affordable health coverage. And the union distributed more than 250,000 copies of a DVD to senior citizens in swing states about McCain's problematic record on senior issues, particularly healthcare. Earlier in the campaign, on the same day McCain issued his healthcare program, SEIU launched the first independent TV ad of the general election. It featured nurses and other healthcare workers expressing concern about the McCain healthcare plan.

Working with other Change to Win unions and progressive groups, SEIU members held media events, such as "McCain Care: Putting Moms Last" and "McCain Care: Leaving Veterans Behind."

SEIU also issued a report, *Putting the Burden on Working Families,* that detailed Senator McCain's anti-working family record in the Senate. And the union ran a TV ad in six crucial states in September 2008 detailing the stark differences between Obama and McCain on jobs and the economy.

SEIU convention delegates meeting in Puerto Rico gave Barack Obama a standing ovation as he told them the Democratic nomination would be his.

Loretta Reddy, a nursing assistant and SEIU member, was typical of the union's campaign volunteers. "This last eight years I've seen a lot of changes in my community for the worse," she said. "I've seen my neighbors lose their homes. I've seen my son's friends have to move out overnight, because their home was foreclosed on." Her husband lost his job and "we took a huge financial blow...we feel it.

"To stand there and to watch it happen, and then to have the opportunity to be a part of making change, I just couldn't ignore that, and neither could my family," Reddy said.

Another good example of the SEIU ground effort was Teresa Butler, a nurse assistant and member of SEIU Local 1199WKO in Ohio. "I am a full-time student...I'm a full-time mother, and I am a nurse's aide," Butler said. "I'm a member political organizer for SEIU and I'm a registered Republican in the state of Ohio. I really started looking at things. I really started reading things. And I decided that Barack Obama was the better person for this job."

While SEIU ran a campaign with massive grassroots activity, its political sophistication had grown substantially from the 2000 and 2004 presidential elections. Working with the Voter Activation Network (VAN) and Catalist, and using new political technology, SEIU political experts did microtargeting to ensure that, in each targeted state, the union was canvassing, calling, and mailing to the most persuadable voters on the specific issues they cared about.

SEIU's modeling programs allowed it to identify the pivotal undecided voters who could tip the balance in a state. In Pennsylvania, they focused on swing voters younger than 55 years old residing in Pittsburgh and Philadelphia suburbs; in Virginia, swing voters in the 2nd and 11th Congressional districts; in New Mexico, infrequent-voting Hispanic registered voters and independent Caucasian women between 35 and 60 years old in Dona Ana and Bernillo counties; and so on.

Republicans historically had excelled at this type of microtargeting, but they met their match and more with the SEIU effort in 2008.

Finally, election day arrived and, as one SEIU volunteer put it, "There is no tired on the day of victory...on election day, when Barack Obama is elected, we're not going to be tired... we're going to be jumping and cheering tears of joy. Then we're going to sleep for a few days."

Election evening 2008 brought those cheers and the tears of joy to SEIU families across America. Stern and Burger were in Chicago's Grant Park with other leaders for Obama's victory address after all the major news organizations had called him the winner. Later, Stern looked back: "What struck me about Obama's victory speech was that there's a difference between winning an election and making change. Winning is only an opportunity to make change. Now the real work begins.

"It's fair to say that when we look back at this victory, we're going to think about Pauline Beck cleaning floors with Barack Obama and talking about what it was like to work in America and how she needed his help."

In a report issued by the union after the election, the numbers showed SEIU made a critical difference in political races with its work under Political Director Jon Youngdahl:

- SEIU members and staff knocked on 3,571,955 doors seeking support for those candidates, including Obama;
- SEIU made 16,539,038 phone calls during the 2008 election cycle;
- The union sent out 5,125,378 pieces of campaign mail; and
- SEIU registered more than 227,000 new voters in battleground states and California.

Other data compiled by the union showed that it helped 10,992 voters to vote early or by absentee ballot and it held 658 media events to spread SEIU's political message.

SEIU deployed more than 3,000 members as well as local and national staff to 19 states to work fulltime during the 2008 campaign. More than 100,000 SEIU nurses, janitors, home care and child care providers, and other members volunteered after work and on weekends to win for working families.

The union commissioned a nationwide survey in Novem-

SEIU Executive Vice President Mary Kay Henry played a major role in building the union's strong political action program. In 2008, she canvassed door-to-door in Ohio with SEIU activists for the Obama-Biden ticket.

ber 2008 of its own members to determine how they voted overall. The survey found that 77 percent voted for the SEIU-endorsed candidates Barack Obama and Joe Biden. The Republican ticket of John McCain and Sarah Palin won the support of 21 percent of SEIU members.

The SEIU performance in battleground states had 71 percent of SEIU members backing Obama and 28 percent McCain. The poll had a margin of error of plus or minus 3.4 percent.

Of the 19 states that SEIU targeted, Barack Obama and Joe Biden won 17 of them. The targeted states included Arizona, Colorado, Florida, Indiana, Iowa, Maine, Michigan, Minnesota, Missouri, Nevada, New Hampshire, New Mexico, North Carolina, Ohio, Oregon, Pennsylvania, Virginia, Washington, and Wisconsin.

SEIU members also helped win 8 of the 11 Senate races targeted by the union and 22 of 29 of targeted races for House of Representatives seats. Particularly impressive were wins in 8 of 9 Senate races in which the SEIU-backed candidates had been opposed by corporate interests that spent more than $20 million against them because they publicly supported the Employee Free Choice Act. Their wins sent a clear message that support for the major labor law reform legislation would not cost candidates their seats.

In the 2008 gubernatorial races, SEIU members helped win three of the union's four targeted races. And they aided in achieving new majorities in statehouses across the country, including the Delaware House, Ohio House, Wisconsin Assembly, New York Senate, and the Nevada Senate. In Oregon, they helped elect a super-majority in the Oregon House.

In addition, SEIU activists helped pass or defeat eight of the main ballot measures that were targeted in the states, including anti-union initiatives in Colorado and Oregon.

Critical wins for the union occurred in Missouri, where a proposition won that made it easier for elderly and disabled people who need care to remain in their homes, and in Washington State, where an initiative improved training standards for long-term care workers. In Massachusetts, SEIU members helped block a measure that would have denied the state funds necessary to provide vital services and investments in infrastructure by eliminating the income tax.

They say all politics is local. And SEIU's effort in communities stood out in 2008 where many local candidates committed to pro-working family positions won election. Mark Ridley-Thomas, who won his board of supervisors race in Los Angeles County, was just one example.

Another crucial SEIU election activity was voter protection—ensuring that those who vote get their ballots fairly and accurately counted, as well as more broadly working to remove barriers to participation in the electoral process. With the vote-count debacle in the Bush/Gore election in 2000 and questionable ballot practices in Ohio in 2004, SEIU and its coalition allies worked hard in 2008 to be sure voters got to cast their ballots and have them counted.

In Indiana, SEIU worked with several organizations during weeks of court battles that ended with union-backed groups and their allies winning a complete victory in keeping early voting sites open in Lake County, Indiana. Republicans had sought to challenge access to early voting sites for thousands of residents of Gary, Hammond, and East Chicago—many of them African Americans.

SEIU lawyers also helped win a case in the Ohio Supreme Court after McCain-Palin backers sought to disqualify more than 200,000 potential voters from casting ballots because of technical disparities involving their voter registrations not exactly matching other government data, such as Social Security records.

Many months after the 2008 election, data services firm Catalist issued an analysis of the 2008 election utilizing its detailed database of all voting-age individuals in the United States. Catalist provided data services to SEIU and a substantial majority of the progressive and political communities active in 2008 campaigning. Because Catalist users uploaded IDs from much of their own voter contact work to the database, the company was able to compile an increasingly accurate picture of the American electorate.

Among Catalist's major findings on the 2008 election:

- SEIU members turned out to vote at higher rates than nonmembers did, with 77 percent voting for Obama-Biden.
- SEIU made more than 5.2 million direct contacts to about 4.5 million voters during the 2008 presidential election cycle.
- SEIU's work—or "footprint"—was the largest in 10 key battleground states. All of those states saw critical progressive victories on Election Day, some by very narrow margins.
- Areas that received contact from SEIU correlated with a strong pattern of increased Democratic performance compared with 2004.
- 88 percent of SEIU activities were done person to person, through live phone calls (64 percent) or in-person interaction (24 percent). That was about 50 percent more than the average (as a percent) of all progressive organizations active in the 2008 elections.
- The union targeted independent voters likely to turn out for its persuasion campaign more than all other progressive groups.
- SEIU did a significant portion of all voter contact in Virginia (20 percent), New Mexico (13 percent), and Colorado (8.5 percent)—exceeding even that of the campaigns and party committees.
- In Indiana, after subtracting the work of the Obama campaign, more than 40 percent of all voter contact was done by SEIU. The union also had large shares of unique contacts in other highly contested states.

SEIU Secretary-Treasurer Anna Burger joined President Obama at a top-level discussion on jobs and the economy after the election. In February 2009, she was named to the President's Economic Recovery Advisory Board. The President regularly consults SEIU on important issues such as healthcare, labor law reform, immigration, and the economy.

Looking more closely at Indiana as an example, SEIU members knocked on 118,765 doors; made 186,145 phone calls to voters; and registered 14,003 new voters, according to the Catalist report. Obama won the state by only 25,000 votes, so SEIU's impact was very clear in Indiana.

Back in California, Pauline Beck continued to go about her day as an SEIU home care worker, helping the elderly and infirm to stay in their homes and live better, more independent lives. She knew the time Obama spent walking in her shoes helped shape the new President's understanding of the lives of America's working people.

Beck stood up in 2009 against California Governor Arnold Schwarzenegger's proposed budget that would have cut her pay and that of other home care workers by nearly 20 percent—dropping Beck back down to $8 an hour. She wrote to President Obama urging him to intervene to help home care workers facing cuts (which were blocked by the courts). And she was out there backing Obama's healthcare reform effort as well as the President's job-creation initiatives aimed at coping with the economic collapse that continued into 2010.

SEIU members certainly will invite more political candidates to walk a day in their shoes in future election campaigns. Holding leaders accountable remained a top union priority—home care workers such as Pauline Beck wouldn't have it any other way.

# CHAPTER 28

# SEIU Widens Global Union Effort
## G4S Victory Spurs Gains At Home, Abroad

Leon Maulana, like the security guards at Wackenhut in the United States, just wanted a union to fight for his interests.

Maulana worked for G4S, the giant multinational security firm, in the African country of Malawi. Trying to support his family, including three children, on $45 per month proved nearly impossible. So he jumped at the chance to become a union member in 2007 when UNI Global Union launched an organizing drive there with support from SEIU.

A fact-finding team of union leaders, including SEIU Executive Vice President Gerry Hudson, visited Malawi in 2007 and found that G4S security guards earned so little that "their families frequently don't have enough to eat and their children's school fees go unpaid." Many of them lived in mud homes without electricity or running water.

Maulana and other G4S workers put in long hours—often 12 hours a day, 7 days a week. In North America, most workers receive a premium for overtime work, but G4S in Malawi paid only 50 percent of the normal rate for overtime. So workers received two hours' pay for working an extra four hours on their shifts. For Maulana, all the overtime brought him only an additional $9 per month.

With the solidarity assistance of SEIU, an organizing campaign in Malawi by UNI Global Union sought to help security workers achieve a union to lift them out of poverty. Maulana joined with his co-workers in that campaign, which succeeded in July 2007.

Following the global agreement signed by G4S in 2008—and a round of successful negotiations between UNI and G4S in Malawi—Maulana and his co-workers enjoyed a marked improvement in their earnings and working conditions.

In 2010, his pay rose to $89 per month—double what he earned just three years earlier without a union. And Maulana received 100 percent of his overtime wages, instead of the 50 percent he got before workers organized with help from SEIU and its global allies.

G4S had a well-earned reputation as a harsh anti-union employer. It ranked as the second-largest employer in the world after Wal-Mart among private sector multinationals. Often, G4S workers were among the lowest paid within their countries.

Today, G4S owns Wackenhut, a security firm SEIU began to organize in the United States in 2003, when the company was owned by a Danish-based company called Group 4 Falck. That firm merged with Securicor in the United Kingdom to become G4S. SEIU sought support for its American organizing efforts of Wackenhut from UNI, the global union federation based just outside of Geneva, Switzerland, with which SEIU is affiliated.

Progress for SEIU and UNI Global Union came in a signed global agreement with G4S that goes beyond general assurances to respect international norms. The deal provides a specific set of commitments on labor rights by G4S, as well as a system to manage disputes. It also includes a specific guarantee of workers' right to organize and allows unions access to the G4S workforce.

In the United States, SEIU reached a separate neutrality agreement with Wackenhut aimed at enabling workers to freely join the union without employer interference. Valarie Long, who served as SEIU Property Services Division chief negotiator in the settlement discussions, said the deal was a "positive step forward for security officers and their families all over the country." In 2010, SEIU had efforts underway at Wackenhut in Minneapolis and Chicago, with Los Angeles expected to follow as part of an overall campaign involving nine cities where the firm does security work in commercial offices and local and state government facilities.

The G4S victory grew out of SEIU's decision at the 2004 convention to expand the union's global work. SEIU was responding to the fact that a global economy meant the service sector increasingly was dominated by multinational companies, rather than local or national firms. The union needed to step up its international work and form strategic global alliances with workers in other countries.

For janitors and other property services members, SEIU had seen real estate interests and cleaning contractors become major players in the world economy. That was true in the security sector in North America, where the two largest employ-ers at the time of the 2004 convention were Group 4 based in Denmark and Securitas headquartered in Sweden.

"To our union allies who are here [at SEIU's 2004 convention] from around the world, I ask that we join forces, to learn from each other, and replace old, outdated, weak, international relationships with real strategies and real unity," SEIU President Stern said in his keynote address. "I want to send this message to every emerging global corporation in this world: Justice, family, community, and union are the same in every language. And wherever you go, and whatever you do, a new labor movement is coming after you."[187]

The growth of multinational companies and the expansion of globalization weakened labor even in the historically unionized workforce in Europe. Union density declined in countries such as Britain, France, and Germany, although organizing often was not seen as a top priority there. And unions regularly faced huge difficulties in Asia, Africa, and many South American countries.

SEIU's global efforts won an agreement with Wackenhut, the security company, at the end of 2008 that is aimed at letting workers choose to join a union without employer interference.

SEIU soon had a staff of 15 working on global organizing partnerships, and the union worked with the Swedish transport workers to get a neutrality and card-check agreement covering the U.S. operations of Securitas. But a similar approach through the Danish union did little to move Group 4 (later G4S) to alter its staunchly anti-union posture regarding Wackenhut in the United States.

It was clear that a broader effort would be required. "We needed these companies to be organized worldwide and needed to work with unions in these countries to organize to raise standards together and force these companies to deal with unions and set up frameworks for doing their own national bargaining," said one staff member in SEIU's global effort.[188]

In a way, this was a logical extension of SEIU's efforts on a national level to organize to build density within companies and industrial sectors so that workers had greater leverage with

Trade union activists from many countries visit SEIU headquarters in Washington, D.C., to discuss global worker issues. Lee Keun Weon of the Korean Public Service Union exchanged ideas with SEIU in 2008.

which to win gains at the bargaining table. But doing it internationally, with different national labor laws and corporate cultures, posed tough challenges.

SEIU's focus on security workers led it to help those in Poland who worked for Securitas and G4S. American workers from SEIU Local 32BJ and Local 1—a number of whom were Polish speakers—traveled to Warsaw and helped security officers sign up their co-workers to join the union, *Solidarnosc*, which had started with shipyard workers organized by Lech Walesa years earlier.[189]

SEIU often partnered with the global union federation UNI Global Union, as well as counterpart unions in other countries. In India, SEIU helped develop joint security worker campaigns with UNI and two of India's national union centers. More than 22,000 members were organized at various security employers in four Indian cities. The global agreement with G4S helped make possible negotiations that led to gains for security workers in India, such as greater protections in case of injury or death on the job, guard uniform benefits, and greater job mobility with workers no longer bound to work for the same agency.

In Uruguay, some 7,000 building cleaners signed up as union members in the first year of the effort there working with FUECI, the Uruguayan services union. SEIU sent in members highly skilled in organizing, with the Uruguay effort spearheaded by Spanish-speaking organizers from SEIU's Puerto Rico locals.

In the United Kingdom, SEIU developed close ties to the Transport and General Workers Union and worked together with TGWU on campaigns for cleaners who maintained London's banks, financial houses, and multinational corporations. Efforts in Britain resulted in organizing campaigns that won new deals with cleaning contractors.

Unite—formed from a merger of the Transport and General Workers with another union called Amicus—ultimately won six agreements establishing the London living wage across Canary Wharf and the City (financial district) that united 2,500 new members, 80 percent of whom were immigrants.

In the Netherlands, where SEIU had been active, janitors won a major victory in 2008 when they negotiated pay of €10

Tom Woodruff, SEIU executive vice president, coordinated much of the union's global work after the 2004 convention.

($13.50) an hour and access rights for organizing new workers in the future.

SEIU also expanded its solidarity to Australia and New Zealand, where the "Clean Start" campaign aimed to organize cleaners in 10 cities. Working with the Liquor, Hospitality and Miscellaneous Union (LHMU), SEIU helped train new organizers and developed fresh approaches to community and political organizing there. The Clean Start effort during this period was equally financed by SEIU and LHMU and was the biggest organizing campaign in Australia since the 1890s.[190] By the end of 2008, cleaners in Australia had won contracts in eight cities that resulted in improvements in pay and working conditions.[191]

SEIU and the Change to Win labor federation formed a European organizing center in Amsterdam in September 2008. Three SEIU organizers, who had spent several years working with global unions on developing effective organizing strategies, helped staff the Amsterdam office, which served as the base for SEIU's European partnerships and strengthened work on behalf of U.S. workers employed by European multinationals.

At the SEIU convention in 2008, UNI Global Union signed a global organizing agreement with leading worldwide facility services provider ISS. The agreement was the most comprehensive and advanced of its kind, and guaranteed organizing

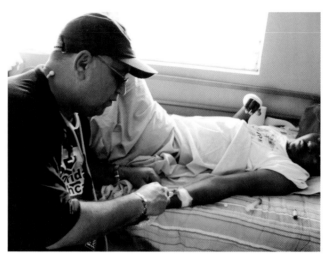

SEIU mobilized teams of healthcare professionals who were airlifted into Haiti after the devastating earthquake that killed thousands in 2010. A member of SEIU Healthcare Florida provided emergency care to a patient at St. Damien Hospital in Port Au Prince, Haiti, as part of SEIU's relief effort.

rights for almost 500,000 workers in 50 countries. SEIU leaders and staff played an important role in UNI's campaigns for the rights of workers at ISS.

The union also had plans underway in 2010 for a project with healthcare unions in Brazil.

Workers around the world, such as Leon Maulana in Malawi, have benefited from SEIU's global work that seeks to broaden the "stronger together" commitment to workers in other nations.

# SEIU Multiservice Workers Fight For Justice

If you've visited Paris, you don't forget it. As the writer Ernest Hemingway once said, "Wherever you go for the rest of your life, it stays with you—for Paris is a moveable feast."

The 13 SEIU supporters from Sodexo who traveled to France in January 2010 may have found the City of Light memorable, but it was Paris and the top executives of Sodexo who won't forget them or the message they brought to the huge, anti-union food services multinational.

Genevieve Repsher, a Sodexo worker from Pennsylvania, spoke out about the day-to-day struggles of working for a company that doesn't allow her time off to care for her sick child and that fights her efforts to join a union.

She was part of the SEIU delegation led by Mitch Ackerman, SEIU executive vice president, that conducted a major march on Sodexo's annual shareholder meeting in Paris along with French and British trade unionists who worked at Sodexo.

Sodexo's top executives basked in self-praise for several hours, but when it came time to open the meeting to questions, the firm's chairman cut off Ackerman and refused to allow Zella Dase, an SEIU member, to present petitions signed by more than 1,000 Sodexo workers across the United States who sought the SEIU to represent them.

"It is sad that—in a company that I have given so much to—I would be treated like I didn't matter and I wasn't worth listening to," Dase said. "This was a real reminder of what we are up against in forming a union, but I won't back down."

SEIU has targeted multiservice companies, such as Sodexo, that provide food services, housekeeping, laundry, and facilities management, often on an outsourced basis. The union took the fight to Paris because Sodexo is foreign based, as is another giant multiservice company known as Compass. The union also has focused on a third multiservice company, Aramark.

SEIU and other unions have organized about 18,000 workers in this sector in the United States and Canada through an understanding reached in 2005 that provided broader organizing rights, such as card-check and employer commitments to refrain from anti-union campaigns in return for agreements on target locations.

Since those agreements took effect, workers organized with SEIU have taken action to hold the multiservice companies accountable to higher standards of corporate social responsibility, both to their employees and to the public.

In 2008, as part of a nationwide organizing campaign, Aramark workers publicized details about their low pay and lack of access to affordable healthcare, as well as Aramark's health code violations and the company's shortchanging of cash-strapped school districts.

Workers staged multiple protests against these practices and the company's retaliation against workers who voiced their concerns, including raising issues at Goldman Sachs' (owner of 20 percent of Aramark) annual meeting in 2008.

Vernita Murdock, a former Aramark worker from Houston, who was fired after speaking out for good jobs and services, said: "I'm asking Goldman Sachs executives if they could live on $6.30 an hour—because I'm pretty sure I could figure out a way to live on $67.5 million a year."

SEIU workers joined French and British unionists in a protest at Sodexo's annual meeting in Paris in January 2010.

SEIU workers in Puerto Rico join a general strike in 2009 to protest the Republican governor's decision to lay off 17,000 public workers.

# CHAPTER 29

# SEIU Builds Strength In Puerto Rico
## Passes Bargaining Law, Protests Layoffs

Luis Fortuño, the Republican governor of Puerto Rico, had sat at the feet of George W. Bush for years when he represented the island commonwealth in the U.S. Congress. Fortuño learned one big lesson: when confronted with angry citizens who don't like what you're doing, cry "terrorism."

So when SEIU joined with civil society organizations and other unions to announce a one-day national strike scheduled for October 15, 2009, Gov. Fortuño threatened to charge Puerto Rican citizens with terrorism if they took part in the protest.

The Republican played the terrorism card in response to SEIU's opposition to massive cuts in essential public services. On September 25, 2009, the Fortuño administration announced it was cutting the jobs of 17,000 healthcare workers, schoolteachers, social workers, and other government employees. The layoffs were to come even after Fortuño laid off 7,800 workers in the spring of 2009.

With Puerto Rico's unemployment rate at 16 percent and the island's credit rating near junk status under the Republican governor, SEIU fought back.

Roberto Pagán, president of SEIU Local 1996SPT, chained himself to the gates of Governor Fortuño's home in an act of civil disobedience to protest the plan to dismiss thousands of SEIU public workers. Joined by three other Puerto Rican union leaders, Pagán said: "This is Camp Dignity and we will not move from here."

"*Es el momento de lucha en la calle, de transformar la indignación que todo el pueblo está sintiendo en acción,*" said Pagán. ["It's time to fight in the street, to transform the indignation that all people are feeling into action."]

The threat of being jailed as terrorists fell on deaf ears for between 200,000 and 300,000 Puerto Ricans gathered in the Plaza Las Americas in Hato Rey on the day of the general strike.

"If SEIU cannot help members in their time of need, what good would this organization be?" asked Dennis Rivera, who chairs SEIU Healthcare and was in San Juan for the general strike. "It is critical—7,500 members of SEIU are going to lose their jobs."[192]

Rivera, who was born in Puerto Rico, compared the massive crowd to the one he saw in Cape Town, South Africa, on the day in 1990 when Nelson Mandela was released.

SEIU and its labor and civil allies had called the Fortuño administration's bluff. "They stepped back for today," Rivera told the media. "What they basically have said is, 'If you come to the protests, you are a terrorist and we can jail you.'"[193] SEIU made a formal request to the U.S. attorney general to examine the matter.

The final outcome of the proposed layoffs had not been resolved by the deadline for this book, but what was clear was the strength and commitment of SEIU's 31,000 members in Puerto Rico.

The union's membership there had more than tripled from 1996 when new leadership took over the International Union. One of SEIU President Andy Stern's early acts was to invite members and leaders from Puerto Rico to the Washington, D.C., headquarters, where they held discussions about the fight to win full collective bargaining rights for the island's more than 200,000 public sector workers.

SEIU held a ceremony after the talks at which the Puerto

Rican flag was raised outside the union's D.C. headquarters—the first time the flag flew from its own staff. "This recognition of our flag fills us with pride," said Jose Rodriguez-Baez, then president of SEIU District 1199UNTS in Puerto Rico. He and Roberto Pagán both noted the strong ties Puerto Rican members felt with their SEIU counterparts in the United States and Canada.

Symbolism? Yes, but SEIU immediately set about to devote new energy and resources to Puerto Rico in 1997. The UNTS and SPT unions there soon became the shock troops behind the push to win a collective bargaining bill for public employees.

UNTS, founded in 1973, represented public sector healthcare workers and had become the largest healthcare union on the island. SPT began as a sugar cane workers union in the 1940s, but changed with the local economy over time and came to represent school workers, as well as those in food processing, transportation, and other industries. It affiliated with SEIU in 1996.

A partnership developed between the International Union and the two locals, which kicked off with the opening of a San Juan office in 1997 that provided a base for a large organizing staff. UNTS initiated campaigns among 20,000 hospital, clinic, and mental health facility workers, while at the same time leading political efforts to oppose the commonwealth government's plan for massive privatization of public healthcare facilities. SPT launched campaigns to reach out to 25,000 education workers during this period, including school cafeteria workers, janitors, clerical workers, and security guards.

In 1998, both SEIU Local 1996SPT and SEIU District 1199UNTS played an important role in a broad labor movement victory in Puerto Rico. Public workers fought for and won a new law giving them the right to collective bargaining.

Roberto Pagán, president of SEIU Local 1996SPT, protested proposed layoffs by chaining himself to the gates of the home of Puerto Rico's Republican governor.

Then-Governor Pedro Rosselló signed the Labor Relations Law for the Public Service of Puerto Rico after bitter opposition from business groups, such as the Puerto Rico Chamber of Commerce.[194]

However, the Chamber of Commerce won some anti-union concessions. Under that law, the workers had to vote in two separate elections. First, a majority of the total number of workers in a bargaining unit had to vote to affirm their right to union representation. Then they had to vote a second time—often months later—to determine which union they wanted to represent them.[195]

Even with these anti-union provisions, by the end of the following year, Local 1996SPT won more than 10,000 new members: classroom aides, nonteaching professionals, office workers, janitors, maintenance workers, security officers, and other school support workers.

Israel Marrero-Calderón was one of those who voted to

join SEIU. "We are the forgotten ones, the marginalized, the orphans of the school system," he said at the time. A school janitor who was active in the campaign, Marrero-Calderón noted that school officials "expect everything to be perfect even if we don't have supplies."

Mayra Perez-Ruiz, a special education aide and union activist, put it this way:

"I get frustrated with the shortage of classroom materials for my students—they need special-size pencils and scissors so they can hold them." The short-staffing, insufficient training, obsolete equipment, and chronic lack of supplies all were organizing issues that led to the overwhelming support for SEIU in December 1997.

Crucial to the organizing victory in Puerto Rico was that SEIU members from U.S. locals made numerous trips there to support the workers. SEIU Locals 285, 668, 82, and 32BJ,

as well as District 1199 New York, all sent members, leaders, and staff to assist the organizing drive. And the other SEIU local in Puerto Rico, 1199UNTS, loaned 10 staff organizers to the effort.

But the key to success, according to Roberto Pagán, who led Local 1996SPT, was the workers themselves. "Almost 1,000 workers helped mobilize people in the facilities and schools," he recalled after the win. The election process was spread over 10 days and teams of rank-and-file and staff organizers moved from district to district working phonebanks, preparing voter lists, and mobilizing on voting days.

In the end, 5,693 school janitors and security guards voted for a voice on the job, as did a unit of 4,179 nonteaching professionals, para-professionals, and office workers.

SEIU went on to affiliate the Unión General de Trabajadores—the UGT—in August 2001. At the time, it had more

than 6,000 private and public sector healthcare and construction workers on the island.

"At a time of growing pressure on healthcare workers throughout North America, we are proud to announce this agreement," said SEIU Secretary-Treasurer Anna Burger, who negotiated the UGT affiliation along with Dennis Rivera, who then led 1199 New York. UGT was the principal union at the Centro Médico de Puerto Rico, a major hospital.

The new Puerto Rican affiliate soon began to add new members, including 1,100 nurses, aides, technicians, and other support staff who were concerned about short-staffing and other patient care issues at the island's premier teaching hospital.

SEIU's successful organizing won more on-the-ground support in Puerto Rico when the entire union put its muscle behind the effort to win a halt to bombing and war games conducted by U.S. military forces on the Puerto Rican island of Vieques. The U.S. Navy had a 900-acre testing range there,

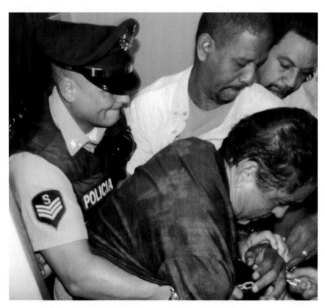

Police try to break up an SEIU sit-in to demand Puerto Rico's Resident Commissioner Pedro Pierluisi reject the anti-worker policies of the commonwealth's Republican governor in 2009.

and a bombing accident in 1999 caused the death of David Sanes Rodríguez, a security guard.

SEIU supported a permanent end to war exercises on Vieques and demanded that the U.S. government clean up and decontaminate the island, which had been the site of bombing with napalm and other toxic weaponry.

Dennis Rivera joined with Robert Kennedy Jr., an environmental lawyer, and actor Edward James Olmos in a peaceful protest in which they outmaneuvered a Coast Guard blockade seeking to reach the Navy test site. Rivera later served a 30-day jail sentence for trespassing. SEIU won broad support among Puerto Rican workers for its stand on Vieques.

In the United States, however, the union took heat for its position from some, particularly because it occurred around the time of the 9/11 terrorist attacks. "I cannot and will not support a union that does not support our U.S. military in its efforts to be prepared to defend our country and its allies," wrote Sharon Phelps of Henderson, Nevada, to the union magazine *SEIU Action*.

The response came from Andy Stern himself: "In the wake of the Sept. 11 attacks, the honor in which I and the other officers of SEIU hold the thousands of Americans who serve in the armed forces and reserves has deepened…SEIU's officers share your patriotism. However, there are good reasons why thousands of SEIU members and leaders—including many military veterans—oppose the bombing of Vieques.

"Vieques has more than 9,000 residents. Many have suffered long-term health problems as a result of the bombing and one resident has been killed," Stern said. "The residents of Vieques have repeatedly made clear they want the bombing to stop, including a landslide 'no' vote in a referendum this past July [2001]."

The SEIU position held, and George W. Bush ordered an end to the Vieques bombing in 2003.

SEIU membership in Puerto Rico in 2010 had more than tripled from 1996 when the union's new leadership assumed office.

SEIU workers marched on Wall Street in April 2010 demanding tougher regulation of banks and financial institutions.

# CHAPTER 30

# SEIU Demands Economic Reforms
## Need More Jobs, Fewer Bonuses In Aftermath Of 2008 Collapse

Lloyd Blankfein, the CEO of Goldman Sachs, pocketed his bonus of $9 million for 2009 with the typical arrogance of a Wall Street "Master of the Universe."

The Goldman Sachs bonus pool of more than $16 billion meant the "average" employee would get a bonus of $500,000 and many top execs would get seven- and eight-figure bonuses (much of it in stock).

All this for a company that would have gone bankrupt had the hardworking taxpayers not bailed them out when the economy collapsed at the end of 2008.

Further proof of Wall Street's insensitivity came when Blankfein told the press that he's just a banker "doing God's work."

Few Americans, and particularly the millions who were jobless, believed the titans of finance whose greed helped bring on the economic collapse deserved their bonuses and self-righteousness. Instead, the overpaid Wall Street bankers symbolized how wide the gap between the very rich and regular working families had become at the end of the 21st century's first decade. Incredibly, the top six banks paid their executives and staff $140.5 billion in bonuses and compensation in 2009—an amount that was almost enough to cover every state government deficit for fiscal year 2010.

SEIU ramped up its role as a progressive advocate for working families long before the financial meltdown that nearly collapsed the economy at the end of 2008. The union warned against the dangers posed by Wall Street greed, including private equity firms piling huge debts on companies they had acquired. And following the onset of the financial crisis, the union emerged as a powerful voice on global economic issues. SEIU members frequently took to the streets in a wide range of protests and demonstrations—in front of Goldman Sachs offices in Washington, D.C., at the American Bankers Association convention in Chicago, at Bank of America locations in Charlotte, North Carolina, and elsewhere.

The union's broad opposition to Goldman Sachs and Bank of America was rooted in the inequities inherent in those businesses (and many others) paying their executives huge bonuses and stock options after their own recklessness had plunged the economy into the worst downturn since the Great Depression. At the same time, firms such as Goldman Sachs and Bank of America had survived by benefiting from huge taxpayer bailouts and then launched vigorous lobbying campaigns against financial reforms aimed at preventing future collapses.

And the Wall Street banks and hedge funds also began lobbying hard against other SEIU-backed legislation, such as healthcare reform and labor law improvements through the Employee Free Choice Act.

At a taxpayer mobilization against Goldman Sachs in November 2009, SEIU President Andy Stern told the crowd the financial behemoth, which had just set aside billions to pay bonuses for its executives, was "out to lunch and out of touch."

With one American losing a home to foreclosure every 13 seconds at that point in time, Stern called upon Goldman Sachs to place its bonus money in a fund to help undo some of the damage its financial practices had caused. The bonuses "could prevent every single foreclosure in America in 2010," he told workers at the protest.

In 2008, when the economy faltered, Goldman Sachs received $64.6 billion in bailout funds from U.S. taxpayers and, despite its problems, turned a $2.3 billion profit. But the Wall Street firm paid executives $4.8 billion in bonuses. CEO Lloyd Blankfein got $42.9 million that year, far more than the $6.93 an hour received by workers at Burger King (partially owned by Goldman Sachs).

"America is not living up to its promise when one of the architects of the economic crisis gets paid millions in bonuses for his failures, while workers take home wages barely above the poverty level," Stern said. He called for passage of the Employee Free Choice Act as an important step toward restraining the huge disparity between those at the top and working Americans.

Anger at Wall Street's excesses remained very high in this period among diverse elements of the public and crossed many of the normal fault lines of Democrats and Republicans, blue-collar and white-collar Americans, rural and urban, young and old. With official unemployment surging above 10 percent and the real jobless rate more like 17 percent, SEIU gave voice to the concerns of those who felt a rising populist anger over huge financial institutions that were "too big to fail" and that seemed to know no shame in heaping rewards upon themselves.

SEIU members during this period participated in pension funds with more than $1 trillion in assets, some of that lost to the greed and speculation of the real estate bubble with its predatory loans and to the broader collapse of 2008-2009. Stern, who chaired the SEIU Master Trust, which had about $1.3 billion in assets, wrote to the boards of directors of 29 major companies in the Trust's investment portfolio demanding a stop to unmerited executive payouts. He also called for an overhaul of executive compensation practices to better align them with corporate performance.

"It's as if these guys got a windfall payoff for betting the family's savings on the wrong horse," Stern said in April 2009. "A fundamental duty to shareholders has been violated, and we expect immediate action…to put a stop to these unmerited executive payouts." From 2005 through 2008, the top five most highly paid executives at the 29 financial services firms targeted by SEIU received a total of more than $3.5 billion in cash and equity pay, and more than $1.5 billion in stock options. Those companies included Goldman Sachs, American Express, AIG, JPMorgan Chase & Co., and Citigroup.

At the time, AIG—the American International Group— had received a huge taxpayer bailout: more than $173 billion. More than $90 billion of that went toward paying banks, including Bank of America and Citigroup, that were part of the huge lobbying effort against legislation that would benefit working families, such as the Employee Free Choice Act.

Citigroup, which got $341.1 billion in taxpayer bailouts, hosted a conference call to build opposition to employee free choice and invited a top official of the anti-worker U.S. Chamber of Commerce to lead the call on March 11, 2009.

When Citigroup bankers and others in the American Banking Association held their convention in Chicago in late 2009, SEIU Secretary-Treasurer Anna Burger led thousands of workers and taxpayers in protest. Writing on *The Huffington Post* blog, Burger called the bankers' meeting "a four-day celebration of wealth and opulence.

"The financial section of the newspaper is starting to read like the script for a far-fetched crime movie," Burger said. "A group of villains hatch a plot to steal trillions of dollars from unsuspecting Americans. They drive the country into econom-

SEIU workers demanded that Congress pass financial reforms that would stop big banks, hedge funds, mortgage companies, and credit card firms among others from greedy and dangerous financial practices like those that led to economic collapse in 2008-2009.

ic chaos, funnel money from families and small businesses into their own pockets, then leave all of us to clean up their mess.

"And not only do they get away with it, they pay themselves billion-dollar bonuses and throw lavish parties to celebrate their conquest," Burger continued. "But this isn't a movie. It's really happening. Wall Street bankers have taken $17.8 trillion of our tax dollars through bailouts and turned them into massive pay and bonuses for themselves."[196]

The Chicago protest led by Burger and Tom Balanoff, an SEIU vice president and long-time leader of Local 1, called upon the big banks to stop lobbying against financial reform legislation that was pending in Congress.

President Obama recognized SEIU's important role in advocating for pro-worker economic policies by naming Burger to the President's Economic Recovery Advisory Board.

SEIU's prominent and outspoken role on behalf of economic fairness during the collapse of 2008-2009 grew in part out of work the union had been doing to urge reforms to halt abuses engineered by the multibillion-dollar "private equity" buyout financiers. Those firms invest in industrial and service companies whose common stock then ceases to trade on public stock exchanges.

The private equity buyout firms operate virtually free of oversight and accountability, yet their decisions affect large numbers of American workers and communities. Unlike publicly traded companies that are subject to federal securities laws and regulations, private equity firms often legally can keep their practices and profits largely hidden from public view. In addition, private equity firms, which get substantial capital from public employee pension funds, often pay very little in taxes. Their business model thus undercuts government's ability to finance public services.

Major brand names in the United States, such as Burger King, Dunkin' Donuts, Hertz, Hilton Hotels, and Toys"R"Us,

Change to Win Chair Anna Burger, SEIU President Andy Stern, and AFL-CIO President Richard Trumka joined the Rev. Jesse Jackson at a protest during the American Bankers Association meeting in Chicago in 2009.

have been taken over by corporate buyout firms. SEIU's concerns heightened when one of the nation's hospital chains was involved in a private equity buyout. And a leading multiservice company SEIU had been organizing, Aramark, was acquired by private equity, as was the nation's largest office building landlord, Equity Office Properties.

The union estimated that, of the $1 trillion in assets held in trust by pension funds of SEIU members, about 5 percent to 10 percent of those assets are invested in private equity.

Often, union experts say, corporate buyout deals end up costing workers their jobs as the new ownership borrows to the hilt and then cuts costs in order to manage the payments on the debt and maximize its profits. *Business Week* noted, for example, that "buyout shops have always been associated with job losses."[197]

If workers suffer from the decisions made by private equity executives, the firms engaging in the deals do extremely well. Consider these facts:

- The five biggest private equity deals together are larger than the annual budgets of all but 16 of the world's largest nations.

- The annual revenue of the largest private equity firms and their portfolio companies would give private equity four of the top 25 spots in the Fortune 500. These private equity firms have more annual revenue than companies such as Bank of America, JPMorgan Chase, and Berkshire Hathaway.

- The top 20 private equity firms alone control companies that employ nearly 4 million workers.

Even in a slow economy, the private equity partnerships receive hefty fees and the top executives get lavish salaries, perks, and other riches. Many leading partners at private equity firms are billionaires at a time when inequality has widened to historic levels.

Stern, Burger, Mary Kay Henry, and other SEIU leaders repeatedly raised the wealth gap issue in the debate over the need for much tighter regulation of the financial sector generally and private equity in particular. They found a strange bedfellow seeming to agree with them in Alan Greenspan, the former Federal Reserve chairman, who warned that growing inequality "is not the type of thing which a democratic society can really accept without addressing."[198]

While millions of Americans are unemployed or working harder for less money and eroding benefits, the top 300,000 Americans enjoyed almost as much income as the bottom 150 million Americans combined.[199] SEIU, in a publication titled *Behind the Buyouts*, argued in 2007 that "there is no doubt the income being accumulated in the buyout business is a major contributor to the concentration of wealth among the top one percent of Americans."

Stern widened the debate over the economic unfairness of current policy when he joined union leaders from UNI Global Union; Unite, the British union; and the Trade Union Advisory Committee to the Organization for Economic Cooperation and Development (OECD) in a global teleconference in early 2009.

"Financial manipulation, greed, and deregulation have led to economic havoc," Stern said. "For our global economy to thrive and grow again, corporations, governments, and non-state actors, like labor unions, must work together toward a system where competition is based on the quality and sustainability of goods and services provided—rather than a race to lower costs at the expense of workers, the environment, and product quality."

# SEIU's Principles For The Private Equity Industry

As the threat of private equity buyouts expanded, SEIU's private equity campaign, coordinated by Stephen Lerner, developed a set of principles for the industry:

1. **The buyout industry should play by the same set of rules as everyone else.**
   - The industry should provide transparency and disclosure about their businesses, their deals, their income, their plans for the companies they buy and sell, and the risks of the debt they load onto portfolio companies.
   - The industry should invest in the health, security, and long-term prosperity of America by supporting equitable tax rates and the elimination of loopholes that increase the tax burden on working Americans.
   - The industry should work to build confidence in the securities markets by eliminating conflicts of interest and other potential abuses in their deals.

2. **Workers should have a voice in the deals and benefit from their outcomes.**
   - Workers should have a seat at the table when deals are being made.
   - Private equity deals should create economic op-

portunities that align the long-term interests of everyone who builds the value of a company—from direct employees and contract workers to senior management.
   - Workers should have paychecks that can support a family.
   - Workers should have quality, affordable healthcare coverage.
   - Workers should have secure retirement benefits.
   - Workers should have a voice at work—meaning the freedom to join a union using majority sign-up without interference from any party.

3. **Community stakeholders should have a voice in the deals and benefit from their outcomes.**
   - Buyout firms should play a proactive and constructive role in the communities affected by their deals.
   - Community stakeholders should be involved as deals are being made.
   - The private equity buyout industry and community stakeholders should use wealth generated by deals to improve the quality of life, the environment, the health, the safety, and the long-term stability of communities.

SEIU demanded a range of reforms:

- Debt disclosure by private equity for every leveraged buy-out portfolio company.
- Engagement with unions on jobs and solutions to unstable portfolio companies.[200]
- Tighter regulations and reforms from governments to prevent future leverage-fueled crises from undermining the global economy.
- No bailouts for private equity firms without adequate reforms, oversight, and protections.
- End tax breaks for high-risk leveraging strategies.
- Accountability and enforcement of principles promised by private equity.
- Regulation of private equity to be on the agenda of the G20 countries, the major industrial nations of the world.

One example highlighted by SEIU in its broad public campaign for regulation of private equity and the financial sector was the case of Hertz, the rental car company. A consortium headed by the Carlyle Group bought Hertz from Ford Motor Company in the fall of 2006. They argued that since private equity firms are not under public scrutiny, they can focus on long-term business growth.

But Carlyle and its partners borrowed against the Hertz rental fleet, jeopardizing the company's credit rating and causing a downgrade of Hertz bonds to junk status. The private equity owners also had Hertz take out $1 billion in loans just six months after the purchase of Hertz was finalized in order to pay Carlyle and its partners a special dividend.[201]

Then they took the company public again and used that money to pay off the loan and, with the money left over, they had Hertz pay them yet another special dividend: this time of $200 million. All the increased debt piled on by Carlyle and its partners meant that even though Hertz increased revenues by 8 percent in 2006, the firm suffered a decline in net income of two-thirds due to an 80 percent increase in total interest payments.

The Hertz workers suffered from the deal when the private equity owners launched a new "productivity and efficiency" initiative in early 2007. Hertz announced the elimination of 1,550 jobs and later said that only one of every two departing workers would be replaced.

With Carlyle entering the nursing home business via its purchase of ManorCare, SEIU raised questions about the private equity firm's record in its earlier deals.

"Big buyout firms like the Carlyle Group and others should be held accountable for the impact of their actions on seniors, taxpayers, and workers," said Gerry Hudson, SEIU executive vice president. "When Carlyle and other private equity giants buy out nursing homes, they become the owners and, as such, are directly responsible for what happens to patients."

Large private investment groups had bought out 6 of the nation's 10 largest nursing home chains, containing more than 141,000 beds, or 9 percent of the total number of nursing homes in the nation, according to *The New York Times*. Private investment groups owned at least another 60,000 beds at smaller chains and were expected to acquire many more companies.[202]

"The first thing owners do is lay off nurses and other staff that are essential to keeping patients safe," said Charlene Harrington, a professor at the University of California in San Francisco, who studies nursing homes. She told Charles Duhigg of *The New York Times*: "Chains have made a lot of money by cutting nurses, but it's at the cost of human lives."[203]

SEIU's work on private equity in 2007 and 2008 situated the union to deal with buyouts that could impact members, such as those at ManorCare, Aramark, and Allied Security. It also empowered the union to speak for a far broader group of American workers when the economic collapse occurred in late 2008.

As Bank of America and Goldman Sachs and other su-per-wealthy financial firms expanded their gluttony during troubled times and lobbied hard against healthcare and labor law reform, SEIU workers were in the streets week after week. And they also campaigned on Twitter, Facebook, and Flickr as well as in mainstream media such as *The Wall Street Journal* and on television.

From a small union of flat janitors in Chicago had come more than two million members fighting for a more fair economy with great spirit at a time of bleak recession.

# CHAPTER 31

# SEIU Tightens Tough Ethics Rules
## Trusteeships, Independent Commission Expand Accountability

Business pages of the daily newspaper often read like a crime blotter as the economy boomed then crashed in the first decade of the 21st century.

Bernard Madoff, former chair of the NASDAQ stock exchange, traded in his yachts and his homes in Palm Beach and France for a prison cell in Butner, North Carolina, where he became inmate number 61727-054 after pleading guilty to 11 felonies in the biggest financial fraud in history.

Thomas Coughlin, Wal-Mart's executive vice president, pleaded guilty to five counts of fraud involving stealing money, merchandise, and gift cards from the retailer (his defense: he used the money for anti-union activities).

Enron CEO Ken Lay and protégé Jeffrey Skilling, who plunged the Houston-based energy company into bankruptcy, came to symbolize corporate greed, fraud, and conspiracy—leaving thousands of workers jobless in the aftermath.

Day after day, one could see YouTube and TV footage of insider traders doing the perp walk on their way to the slammer. Another popular feature was the "rich people gone wild" video of Tyco CEO Dennis Kozlowski's $2.1 million birthday bash for his wife that he fraudently billed to the company. Martha Stewart summered at Alderson federal penitentiary, while Halliburton faced scandal involving charges of everything from bribery to contract fraud in Iraq.

By contrast, the labor movement in the United States, Canada, and Puerto Rico had few comparable problems of misconduct during that same period. SEIU over time had remained remarkably clear of scandal, in part because of a culture of accountability that began under William McFetridge, president of the Building Service Employees International Union (BSEIU) from which SEIU evolved.

McFetridge and his secretary-treasurer, Bill Cooper from Milwaukee's Local 150, implemented a program of financial and record-keeping crackdowns in the early 1940s. They took over after George Scalise, the former BSEIU president, was arrested and later convicted of embezzlement and forgery.

More than half a century later, SEIU continued to make high ethical standards a basic element of the union's culture. In 2008, following several problems in local unions that forced the International Union to trustee them, SEIU announced a comprehensive ethics reform initiative.

"We represent some of the hardest-working men and women in America, and they have an absolute right to expect that their interests are protected and that their leaders are held accountable to the highest standards of honesty and integrity," SEIU President Andy Stern said in announcing the creation of a Commission on Ethics and Standards.

SEIU named outside authorities in ethics, labor, and law to the Commission and charged it with reviewing the union's existing rules and recommending tougher requirements to ensure the union served "as the ethics benchmark for organized labor everywhere."[204]

The Ethics Commission had a majority of members from outside the union. It was chaired by Justice James Zazzali, who had been Chief Justice of the New Jersey Supreme Court and Attorney General of New Jersey. Judge Abner Mikva, former Chief Judge of the U.S. Court of Appeals for the District of Columbia, served as vice chair.

Other members included James Brudney, professor of law at Ohio State University; Catherine Fisk, professor of law at University of California–Irvine; Linda Trevino, professor of ethics at Pennsylvania State University; the Rev. Nelson Johnson, pastor of Faith Community Church; Russell Pearce, professor of law at Fordham; and Benjamin Sachs, associate professor at Harvard Law School.

Eliseo Medina, SEIU executive vice president, served as a vice chair, and six other SEIU members joined the outside members of the Commission.

In June 2009, the union's International Executive Board adopted policies on ethics and standards that included a tough new Code of Ethical Practices and a Conflict of Interest Policy based on the Ethics Commission's recommendations.

"SEIU has made a serious and comprehensive move toward greater transparency and accountability at a critical time for the union and the larger progressive movement," said UC Irvine School of Law Professor Catherine Fisk. "From setting broadsweeping ethics guidelines, to developing new mechanisms for financial reporting, and to implementing a robust, unionwide training program, SEIU has created a landmark program to help locals be the best possible stewards of member dues."

The union then named Justice Zazzali as the SEIU's first ethics officer, an outside position charged with reviewing ethics complaints and issues. And another new position called ethics ombudsperson was created. Martha Walfoort, who accepted that role, led comprehensive training on ethics policies.

In addition, SEIU created an ethics review board, an independent body made up of three outside experts on law and ethics that reviews appeals of internal union cases on violations of the ethics code.

"Over the last 12 years, we have taken on corruption and the old political fiefdoms to build a modern organization to meet the needs of 21st century workers and families," Stern observed when he announced the tough new ethics approach. "As

our union has rapidly grown, so has the need to establish stronger accountability mechanisms."

Justice James Zazzali chaired the SEIU's Commission on Ethics and Standards after a distinguished legal career that included serving as Chief Justice of the New Jersey Supreme Court and Attorney General of New Jersey.

Indeed, shortly after his election in 1996, Stern responded to allegations made at the union convention by delegates from Local 25 in Chicago by investigating the conduct of Eugene Moats, the local president. Stern appointed an independent monitor to examine Local 25's affairs, and she found a wide range of misuse of funds and nepotism. Moats had four members of his family on the payroll of Local 25 and another five family members employed at its health and welfare fund and union health service program. She also found a major breakdown of democratic procedures in the local's day-to-day practices.[205]

In August 1996, Stern imposed an emergency trusteeship of Local 25, a procedure authorized under law and the SEIU constitution that involves a takeover of a local union's affairs for a period of time to correct corruption or other problems. A hearing officer who examined the evidence agreed Stern had acted within his constitutional authority. Moats and the local's secretary-treasurer resigned the day before the trusteeship was instituted.

SEIU also was forced to act in another high-profile case involving the president of Local 32BJ, Gus Bevona, in New York City. Following the International Union's intervention,

Bevona retired on February 1, 1999, and the local was placed in trusteeship. Records revealed that Bevona had been receiving about $530,000 in salary—more than all but a handful of top union officials in the entire labor movement.

Bevona's 23rd-floor penthouse was a 3,000-square-foot suite with marble everywhere from floors and walls to the two bathroom steam rooms. He virtually never allowed rank-and-file janitors and doormen to visit his union-provided office/apartment, which had two large terraces with beautiful views of lower Manhattan.[206]

"It's reprehensible," said a member of Local 32BJ and a doorman in New York City who saw the penthouse after Stern had forced Bevona out and trusteed the local. "This guy representing doormen and janitors was living like a king on our sweat."

Bevona's kitchen had top-of-the-line appliances, including seven Traulsen stainless-steel refrigerators, a Gaggenau double oven, and a Miele "super electronic" dishwasher from Germany. The Local 32BJ leader, known as a recluse, had a bank of 12 television monitors behind his U-shaped desk that allowed him to spy on subordinates elsewhere in the building.[207]

The lavish digs enjoyed by Bevona were built from 1990 through 1992 by two developers. Bevona signed a 99-year lease and obligated SEIU janitors and doormen to pay $197 million in rent over 20 years "at a rate significantly higher than rents in the neighborhood," according to *The New York Times*.[208]

Stern had blasted Bevona's pay and penthouse as "excessive" and faulted him for stifling democracy within the local, where Bevona's squad of business agents ran a political machine guaranteeing his re-election.[209] Under Bevona, Local 32BJ's membership had fallen in the 1990s from about 70,000 to 55,000 and the local did virtually no organizing.

SEIU also stepped in to trustee another New York City affiliate, Local 144, after officials found that its president, Frank Russo, had run up tens of thousands of dollars in improper expenses. The local, which represented about 30,000 healthcare workers including many nursing home workers, later voted to merge into the new healthcare union created when 1199, the National Health and Human Service Employees Union in New York, affiliated with SEIU.

In Boston, SEIU imposed a trusteeship in 2001 at Local 5000, the National Association of Government Employees, a nationwide local of federal, state, and local public sector workers. SEIU members had alleged wrongdoing involving personal expenses and destruction of union records by the Local 5000 president, Ken Lyons. Counsel for the ousted local president argued the trusteeship was "nothing more than an attempt by SEIU to take over NAGE."[210] The hearing officer ruled, however, that Lyons "offers no testimony whatsoever to substantiate the allegation…and what the whole record shows is a course of gross financial irregularities" by the local president.

More recent cases also show SEIU willing to act decisively to protect union members in the face of undemocratic actions or financial wrongdoing by local officials. Stern, for example, trusteed Local 6434 in Los Angeles, the large long term care local, and in August 2008 forced out Tyrone Freeman, a member of the International Executive Board who had been a close ally of the SEIU president and other top leaders.

Stern then permanently banned Freeman from holding a membership, a staff position, or office in the union following evidence the Los Angeles leader misused member funds. Stern took the action after adopting the findings and recommendations of former California Supreme Court Justice Joseph Grodin, who served as the hearing officer charged with examining the allegations against Freeman. Grodin found a pattern of financial malpractice and self-dealing that violated the SEIU constitution and local bylaws.

SEIU had filed seven separate charges against Freeman involving improper payments to a company owned by Freeman's wife, improper expenses relating to his 2006 wedding, the misuse of nonprofit funds to benefit Freeman and his family members, the improper expenditure of union funds on a private cigar club membership, and violations of procedural and democratic safeguards.

Stern had chosen Freeman to be one of those who seconded his nomination for president at the 1996 convention. But years later, Stern not only banned Freeman from the union, but ordered him to make full restitution to members of Local 6434—a sum of more than $1.1 million.[211]

"Today's decision sends a clear message across our union," Stern said at the time he banned Freeman. "We are all accountable. Our members do some of the toughest jobs anywhere, and we will not tolerate any actions violating their trust or putting their interests at risk."

## Stern forced out a close ally, Tyrone Freeman.

Another trusteeship involved United Healthcare Workers West (UHW), an Oakland-based SEIU local then headed by Sal Rosselli. UHW leaders then in power had defied decisions reached by the 2008 SEIU convention—the union's highest authority—and the International Executive Board (IEB) involving plans in California to unite all long term care workers in a new local union.

Unification of long term care members was part of SEIU's effort to strengthen the bargaining power of workers by bringing them together in locals organized around the type of work they performed. It was consistent with numerous mergers across the United States and Canada that had occurred since the New Strength Unity Plan was adopted by convention delegates in 2000.

An outside hearing officer, former National Labor Relations Board (NLRB) General Counsel Leonard Page, held hearings and then issued an extensive decision explaining why the proposed unification of long term care workers would strengthen their situation and why Rosselli's position should be rejected based on the prevailing circumstances.

Based on that ruling, the long term care members from the affected local unions voted together to support creation of the new statewide long-term care local. Rosselli and his allies boycotted that pooled vote—arguing instead that each local should vote in a procedure that would have permitted an individual local to block the policy set by the 2008 convention delegates and SEIU's International Executive Board.

SEIU's board then ordered the transfer of long-term care members from Locals 6434, 521, and UHW into a newly chartered local.

Rosselli had initially supported reorganization of SEIU locals in California after having been appointed by SEIU President Stern to lead UHW—a local created itself by an IEB-approved merger of two other locals, 250 and 399. But the UHW president shifted his position when it became clear his local would not absorb all the other California healthcare locals and might lose its long term care members to the new statewide long term care local.

Separate hearings were held on whether or not the local should be trusteed based on charges of financial wrongdoing by Rosselli and other UHW leaders. Those hearings were conducted by former U.S. Secretary of Labor Ray Marshall, a prominent labor relations expert. He took formal testimony from Rosselli and other members of UHW as well as representatives of the International Union.

The Marshall hearings were held in public with more than 1,300 local union members attending several day-long sessions and being allowed to give their views from the floor at the San Mateo Events Center. A hearing record of more than 1,911 pages was produced.

In January 2009, Secretary Marshall issued a ruling that found that Rosselli and other leaders of UHW "did engage in financial malpractice" and had undermined SEIU's democratic practices.

Noting the connection between the financial malpractice and UHW's interest in evading the jurisdiction decision, he recommended that Rosselli be given a final chance to abide by the SEIU's decision on long term care jurisdiction within five days. If UHW did not, Marshall recommended that a trusteeship be imposed on the local.

At the core of the ruling that Rosselli and UHW officers had engaged in financial malpractice was a scheme in May 2007 by Rosselli and other UHW officials to move up to $6 million of union dues money from the UHW treasury to what one UHW board member called a secret "war chest" to finance potential intra-union battles with the top SEIU leadership over matters including the jurisdiction issue.

Testimony and evidence revealed that Rosselli asked for and was given the unfettered discretion to transfer—at times of his choosing and in amounts of his choosing—up to $6 million of the local members' funds to a so-called "Patients Education Fund" (PEF) designed to appear to be a genuine nonprofit focused on healthcare issues. By the time this scheme was uncovered by the International Union, $3 million already had been transferred.

By moving money out of the SEIU local and into a private entity, Rosselli placed the funds outside the democratic governance structure of the local and its members and beyond the reach of the SEIU constitution's auditing and oversight powers. The move also would allow Rosselli to avoid legal reporting requirements of federal law under the Labor-Management Reporting and Disclosure Act (LMRDA).

And, perhaps most important, the shift of union dues money to an off-the-books entity would allow Rosselli and his allies to control millions of dollars even in the event they lost their union

positions, whether through a vote, a trusteeship, or a merger or other reorganization.

The former Labor Secretary ruled that SEIU was justified in initiating the trusteeship hearing and the union leadership's actions "were not initiated to retaliate against the UHW for its aggressive criticisms of International [Union] leaders' policies and strategies."

"No democratic labor organization can permit local unions to nullify International [Union] decisions reached through the democratic processes specified in their constitution and bylaws," Secretary Marshall wrote in his decision.

Instead of complying with the Marshall ruling, Rosselli and other leaders of UHW defied it—refusing to accept the decision. SEIU then trusteed UHW for the financial malpractice and refusal to abide by the union's democratic processes as outlined in the Marshall ruling.

Rosselli and other allies resigned from the SEIU after their ouster from the local, having already formed what they said would be a new union to compete with SEIU for members. Given the detailed factual record established by former NLRB General Counsel Page and, separately, by Secretary Marshall, Rosselli and his supporters chose not to challenge either the long-term care merger or the trusteeship in court.

With the Marshall decision and Rosselli's refusal to comply, the subsequent trusteeship of UHW led to SEIU Executive Vice Presidents Dave Regan and Eliseo Medina being asked to step in as trustees and sort out UHW affairs in the aftermath of Rosselli's resignation. Immediate audits of UHW books turned up a wide range of additional issues, involving destruction of union records and financial wrongdoing.

The records showed Rosselli and other officials spent more than $11.5 million in members' dues money in 2008 on their attempts to remain in power—that represented more than half of the local's net assets going not to support members, process grievances, negotiate contracts, or provide basic services, according to a report issued by the new UHW leadership.

The expenditures by Rosselli included more than $2.5 million on public relations agencies and more than $1.7 million to a management law firm hired by Rosselli to litigate against the International Union.

Rosselli and his allies formed a new union, the National Union of Healthcare Workers (NUHW), even as they still held positions as SEIU leaders. They planned to target SEIU workers and try to bring them into the NUHW. Nearly a year later, Rosselli's new union represented no members under contract.

The new leadership of UHW gained access to some of the local's records and emails that had not been destroyed. In a report issued in August 2009, they found that Rosselli and others canceled contract extensions involving at least 25 labor agreements covering nursing home workers and deliberately failed to negotiate numerous contracts in order to prevent workers from reaching agreements. Those actions left thousands of workers with no union protection and forced tens of thousands of others to negotiate new agreements in a deteriorating bargaining climate as the economy worsened.

The new leadership of UHW found those failures to be part of Rosselli's strategy, plotted while he led the local, so those members would be vulnerable to raiding by his new union.

SEIU-UHW Trustee Dave Regan, Debbie Schneider, and others who took over after Rosselli also found records that revealed that a top official of Rosselli's new union "plotted with a public relations consultant on how to bolster California Governor Arnold Schwarzenegger's attempt to cut the wages of home care workers by $2 an hour, from $11.50 to $9.50.

"A cut in wages gave NUHW an opening to criticize SEIU-UHW and perhaps win a few extra votes in an election to represent Fresno home care workers," the report said. "They wanted to win the election at all costs, even if home care workers—the people they sought to represent—lost $2 an hour in wages." Rosselli's new union lost the Fresno election, but filed charges seeking to overturn it. NUHW did win representation rights at several locations in early 2010.

SEIU also found, according to the report, that theft and destruction of local records, particularly bargaining and grievance documents, made it impossible to address management contract violations and defend members' rights on the job in a timely way.

Rosselli denied it, but U.S. District Court Judge William Alsup in San Francisco found otherwise and issued a temporary restraining order requiring Rosselli to return union records and property.

That order was reinforced in a preliminary injunction issued by the federal district court on July 27, 2009. Judge Alsup found that Rosselli and his allies "filched" and "sabotaged" UHW files, records, and union property as part of their plan to form a new union.

"Upon leaving UHW, the individual defendants took and reproduced UHW property for use at NUHW (Rosselli's new union) and destroyed other UHW property in an effort to hamstring their soon-to-be competitor," Judge Alsup wrote.

SEIU's case against the former UHW leaders went to trial in U.S. District Court in San Francisco before Judge Alsup and a federal jury. After 10 days of testimony, the jury delivered a verdict that found Rosselli and 15 of his top lieutenants including John Borsos, Barbara Lewis, Ralph Cornejo, Fred Seavey, Dan Martin, and John Vellardita liable for their acts. The federal jury imposed damages of about $1.5 million against Rosselli and 15 other defendants, as well as the National Union of Healthcare Workers.

The verdict by an impartial and independent jury that heard

> ## UHW "did engage in financial malpractice."

evidence and arguments from both sides was a vindication of SEIU's argument that Rosselli and his allies had abused the trust of UHW members and engaged in a scheme that harmed many innocent workers.

The jury heard evidence that Rosselli and his co-defendants secretly took and destroyed bargaining and grievance documents needed to protect members' rights and to support the workers' fight for raises, healthcare, and other benefits.

Before ruling against Rosselli and NUHW, the jury heard evidence on other issues, including:

- Violence and Intimidation. Witnesses testified that Rosselli and his followers used violence and intimidation as part of their efforts to hold onto power.
- Making UHW "Ungovernable." Defendant Barbara Lewis wrote a memo in 2008 about how to use members to "create an ungovernable situation" and sabotage their own union in order to weaken UHW to the benefit of the rival union they planned to launch.
- Stolen Lists. Rosselli and others developed secret databases and planned to operate computers to connect with the union server without the union knowing. They also established a private email system to communicate about their schemes without being detected or leaving incriminating emails on the UHW servers.

The jury also heard that Rosselli and the other defendants began plotting as early as 2007—long before the trusteeship—about how they would smear SEIU, resist democratic decisions made by SEIU delegates and elected leaders, and launch their new rival union using the resources of UHW.

Mary Kay Henry, shortly before she became SEIU president, sat in the courtroom throughout the trial. "I was struck watching UHW members get up on the stand and hold their former leaders accountable for their betrayals," she noted after the verdict. "The members themselves faced down the people they once trusted to protect their union and they held them accountable for their actions."

Erica Boddie, a UHW member at Kaiser San Francisco, attended the trial and strongly criticized Rosselli and NUHW when the verdict came in. "They lied to us," she said. "They stole from us. They put our contracts and our families' financial security at risk, and they got caught red-handed."

It is the rare union trusteeship that is not controversial. Often these strong interventions in which leaders are removed are upsetting to members and controversial in their communities. Most SEIU trusteeships have ended in the return to a democratically elected leadership after fixing the problems and instituting changes that result in a more effective local going forward.

That was the case in Local 25, now part of SEIU Local 1. It became one of the three largest and most effective property service locals—having won major contract gains for its members.

Local 32BJ, which was trusteed in 1999, not only is known on the East Coast as a voice for New York City workers, but over the following decade under President Mike Fishman used its bargaining clout to improve the lives of property services and security officers from Rhode Island to Virginia.

A similar positive outcome was expected at United Healthcare Workers West where leaders worked in early 2010 to cope with the serious misconduct by the ousted former officials. Even with those problems, the local quickly shifted to a member-focused union that was winning major gains for its members.

UHW concluded a new two-year contract in Sacramento County, California, for 18,000 home care workers in February 2010, for example, that improved their healthcare, protected employees' wages, and ensured that seniors and people with disabilities continued to receive services they need to live independently in their homes.

# CHAPTER 32

# The Tough Struggle For Immigration Reform
## SEIU Seeks Legal Path To Citizenship

In the late spring of 2000, more than 20,000 people gathered at the Los Angeles Sports Arena for what was, at the time, the largest immigrant rights event ever held in the United States.

One of the major speakers that day was Eliseo Medina, a Mexican American who had risen through the labor movement to become one of SEIU's top leaders. He spoke passionately about the injustice of an American immigration system that allowed greedy employers to prey upon the vulnerable status of undocumented workers.

"Immigrants—documented and undocumented—are making enormous contributions to the economic well-being and to the cultural and civic institutions of this country," Medina said at the rally. "But what too many receive in return is poverty wages, few if any benefits, and terrible working conditions."

"Our immigration policies no longer protect the working people of this country or their fight to form a union," Medina told the crowd, saying that the deportation of workers "not only breaks organizing drives, it breaks families. That's wrong and we need to do something about it."

Medina had come to the United States from Mexico at the age of 10 with his mother and siblings to join their father, who was an immigrant farm worker. His career as a labor activist began when, as a 19-year-old grape-picker, he participated in the historic United Farm Workers' strike in Delano, California. Over the next 13 years, he worked alongside the legendary labor leader and civil rights activist César Chávez. Medina honed his skills as a union organizer and political strategist, eventually

serving as a United Farm Workers national vice president before beginning his work with SEIU in 1986.

Though far larger than most, the Los Angeles rally was representative of the scores of demonstrations, protests, prayer vigils, and other events that SEIU had begun organizing in the wake of Reagan-era immigration policies and laws. The 1986 Immigration Reform and Control Act had been billed as a way to punish employers who knowingly hired undocumented workers. But its practical effect was to allow some employers to exploit immigrants and take advantage of their vulnerable legal status.

After working for years to pave the way for organized labor to throw its support behind legalization of citizenship for hard-working immigrant workers, SEIU had emerged as a key player in the national movement for progressive and comprehensive reform of immigration laws. The union helped to coordinate and organize the pro-immigration reform campaign of a broad group of labor, religious, and community allies.

Prior to the June 2000 rally in Los Angeles, delegates to SEIU's convention held in Pittsburgh in May 2000 had adopted a resolution calling for repeal of the 1986 law. Taking action on that resolution, SEIU leaders including Medina and Dennis Rivera, then president of 1199/SEIU, helped to convene a series of forums sponsored by the AFL-CIO. In New York City, Chicago, Atlanta, Los Angeles, and other locations, SEIU spearheaded the organizing of the forums, reaching out to labor, church, civic, and community groups.

At these forums, workers as well as religious, labor, and community leaders drove home the point that, rather than sticking with the status quo of policies that end up exploiting and punishing immigrant workers, the solution was a set of laws and policies that would:

- recognize the right of all workers—documented or undocumented—to unite and form unions;
- raise the federal minimum wage; and
- discourage U.S. corporations from exploiting workers in other countries.

They said it was the only way to ensure that low-wage workers, whether native-born or immigrant, would be able to earn enough money to support their families and pursue the American Dream.

Assuming a leading role in the quest for the rights of immigrant workers seemed to be SEIU's destiny. The union had been founded in 1921 by a small group of immigrant janitors in Chicago. And from those early days forward, the union had reached out to—and been strengthened by—immigrant workers from every corner of the globe.

By 2010, with 2.2 million members, SEIU represented more immigrant workers than any other union in the United States. While large numbers of the union's immigrant workers were Latino (and the union's signature rally cry was "¡Sí Se Puede!  Yes We Can!"), members of SEIU came from scores of different countries.  Languages spoken by SEIU members included Spanish, French, Polish, Chinese, Tagalog, Korean,

Mary Kay Henry, a few months before she became SEIU president, spoke out in favor of the nomination of Sonia Sotomayor to become the first Latina Justice of the United States Supreme Court. Key immigration issues, such as Arizona's restrictive laws, are expected to be resolved by the Court.

Italian, Greek, Vietnamese, Arabic, Japanese, Creole, Hmong, and Portuguese among others.

And on any given day, a snapshot of SEIU's members would include people such as Luz Portillo, a Boston janitor who had come to the United States from El Salvador; Mahira Selimbegovic, a Chicago service worker who had come to the United States in 1996 with her husband and two children to escape the war in Bosnia; and Dr. Lorraine Williams, a native of Trinidad and Tobago, who joined SEIU during her medical residency.

When the English film director Ken Loach decided in the late 1990s to make a film about the struggles of immigrant workers in the United States, he turned to SEIU for expert assistance. He based his movie *Bread and Roses* on the work and lives of SEIU janitors in Los Angeles. Many SEIU janitors and organizers were featured in the film as actors and extras.

Two members who played parts in the film were Local 1877 members Maria Ortega and Ernesto Vega of Los Angeles. Some scenes in the movie mirrored Ortega's hardscrabble life of cleaning offices under the gaze of an unscrupulous supervisor. When she refused his sexual advances, she was fired. As she said in media interviews after her part in the film, "Thank God, because we have a union, we have won better conditions."

Over the decades, SEIU's position on immigration remained clear and unwavering. It was simply this: unity, not division and anti-immigrant hysteria, holds the promise of a better life for America's low-wage workers. The failure of those workers to earn better salaries stems not from competition from immigrant workers, but from the greed of employers who profit from underpaid labor.

In the spring of 2001, SEIU once again renewed its call for comprehensive immigration reform, and helped to lead a national grassroots coalition of religious, labor, and community groups called "Reward Work!"

There were rallies and demonstrations in the streets of Boston; Chicago; Providence, Rhode Island; and Newark, New Jersey. In June 2001, SEIU President Andy Stern joined with a dozen immigrant janitors in front of the U.S. Capitol for a 24-hour fast and vigil for immigration reform. At the time, President George W. Bush was pushing for an expansion of the guest worker program, which created a revolving workforce of underpaid immigrant workers.

"We don't need a new guest worker program," Stern said. "We need a 'legalized worker' program for those who are already here."

At concurrent events, thousands of SEIU janitors marched and rallied in front of the U.S. Immigration and Naturalization Service building in Los Angeles, and hundreds more rallied in front of the Federal Plaza Building in New York City.

Despite those and other efforts by SEIU and the Reward Work! coalition, Congress failed to respond to the call for legal reforms that would give hardworking, taxpaying immigrant workers a pathway to legal status in the United States.

And then came September 11, 2001. In the aftermath of that day's terror attacks on the World Trade Center and the Pentagon, anti-immigrant sentiment in the United States rose to new levels, and the fight for immigration reform became even more difficult. The years that followed did little to improve prospects for reform. The United States was fighting wars in Afghanistan and Iraq and the U.S. economy nearly collapsed in 2008. The uphill battle to win political support for immigration reform got steeper still.

But in 2009, with President Barack Obama in the White House and a Democratic majority in Congress, SEIU members and leaders pushed forward with the union's decades-long cry for immigration reform.

In April 2009, the union put technology to use, launching an online campaign to stop the deportation of high-achieving immigrant students. The campaign saved Walter Lara and several other students from deportation to countries they barely knew. They had entered the United States as small children, became academic achievers, yet faced deportation because they had no path to legalized citizenship. The campaign by SEIU convinced U.S. officials to delay their deportation.

In 2010, SEIU joined with faith, labor, and other immigrant rights advocates to launch the largest and most coordinated field operation in the history of the immigration reform movement. Holding nearly 100 rallies at district offices, vigils, watch parties, and press events across the country, activists said the time had come, once and for all, to get comprehensive immigration reform passed by Congress and signed into law.

The diverse Reform Immigration for America (RI4A) coalition—which included law enforcement, faith leaders, labor

SEIU members and other immigrant rights supporters marched on the White House as part of demonstrations urging immigration reform on April 30, 2009.

activists, and business—organized an "immigration week of action" in January 2010 to present its vision of the elements of successful immigration reform.

Eliseo Medina, who led SEIU's fight for immigration reform, laid out the union's view in a response to harsh new anti-immigrant measures in Arizona in May 2010.

He attacked the "enforcement-only mandates" that waste billions of taxpayer dollars on border walls and worksite round-ups and divert attention from the practical immigration solutions America needs.

He said Congress should enact a balanced, comprehensive bill that gets undocumented immigrants into the system and under the rule of law; provides for smart enforcement on the border and in workplaces; and creates a visa system that protects labor rights and meets the economic needs of the future.

"A comprehensive solution would couple enforcement at the border and in the workplace with a path to earned legalization for all hard-working immigrants," Medina said. "It will also replace guest worker programs with a system that guarantees immigrant workers full labor and civil rights protections and a path to U.S. citizenship.

"Done together, these reforms will finally restore the rule of law and eliminate the informal labor market that drives down wages and labor protections for all U.S. workers."

SEIU's work on immigration reform was guided by the set of principles that the union's members and leaders had developed over the years. As those principles so eloquently noted, "The need for comprehensive reform is urgent, not just for immigrants, but for all of us. Until it is enacted, the absurdities of our current system will continue to drag our economy downward and claim an ever-growing list of victims, including workers who suffer depressed wages...and families separated from their loved ones."

Taking the long-term view of how to fix the broken system of U.S. immigration laws, the principles called for expanding both the union's and the nation's partnerships with immigrant-producing countries. "The long-term solution to uncontrolled immigration," the principles stated, "is to encourage real economic development and sustainable jobs in immigrant-producing countries, so that workers in those countries don't have to leave their native country in order to support themselves and their families."

As Julia Marroquin, the 19-year-old daughter of a Local 26 member in Minnesota, said at an SEIU-sponsored immigration reform rally in her city, "This is our moment to put behind us the failures of the past and to reform the U.S. immigration system once and for all, so that it supports all U.S. workers and strengthens this country that we love."

# SEIU Expands Fight For Fair Labor Laws

Two years into his job as a security officer in Miami's South Beach, always on the watch for shoplifters, pan-handlers, drunken brawlers or worse, Richard Ruiz got himself fired.

Out of a job, just like that.

And it was 2009, smack in the middle of the worst and biggest economic recession the United States had seen in decades.

His "crime"? Talking publicly about the frustrating process he and his co-workers were going through in their as yet unsuccessful effort to form a union.

Nearly 75 percent of his 50 or so fellow security officers had signed union cards six months earlier. To them, the choice seemed clear. They were stuck in jobs paying $10 an hour, with no benefits, and they wanted something better: improved wages and benefits, and more training. They believed that joining together in SEIU, which represents thousands of security officers across the United States, would help them reach those goals.

The immediate impact of their signing union cards, however, was a round of intimidation, scare tactics, and harassment from the employer. And when Ruiz spoke out publicly about the harassment, he was fired.

"Employers shouldn't stop decent people from trying to have a better life, " Ruiz said later.

But they do. Even though it is illegal under U.S. labor laws, employers do fire union supporters, all the time.

Ruiz is but one of thousands of workers harassed, intimidated, and subjected to delaying tactics each year by employers who don't want to see their workers join unions. A May 2009 study by a Cornell University labor professor showed that, in the previous two decades, employer opposition to union organizing had been on the increase.

The study, "No Holds Barred: The Intensification of Employer Opposition to Organizing," examined 1,004 union organizing campaigns. In 34 percent, pro-union workers had been fired; in 47 percent, employers had made threats to cut wages and benefits.

Forming unions was not prohibited in the United States prior to 1935, but Congress took the step that year of writing organizing and collective bargaining rights into law. As Harley Shaiken, a professor specializing in labor and the global economy at the University of California–Berkeley, wrote in 2007, the Wagner Act put Congress "squarely on the side" of the democratic right to form unions. In fact, the National Labor Relations Board's original interpretation of the act was that employers were *required* to remain neutral in organizing campaigns. The result, Shaiken notes, was that millions of workers poured into unions.

But in the 1940s, with the political climate shifting, the Taft-Hartley Act was approved. Employers soon claimed the "free speech" right to get involved in union campaigns. The law also took away the NLRB's right to certify unions without an election. This, Shaiken said, "set the stage for the modern anti-union campaign." That change plus Ronald Reagan's infamous decision in 1981 to allow the "permanent replacement" (which is to say, firing) of striking federal air traffic controllers played a big role— along with globalization, the changing economy, and other factors—in the long decline of labor.

By the early 2000s, fewer than 15 percent of U.S. workers were union members, putting a drag on wages and benefits for all workers, and making it increasingly hard for SEIU members and other union workers to hold on to their hard-earned improvements.

In 2006, SEIU—working with other unions and allies—set out to revamp the labor laws through new legislation called the Employee Free Choice Act (EFCA).

As the progressive organization American Rights at Work noted, EFCA would help restore the balance between workers and employers in organizing campaigns by:

- Strengthening penalties against employers who break the law.
- Allowing employers or employees' unions to resolve their first contracts through arbitration if they're unable to successfully conclude negotiations.
- Giving workers the right to form a union through "majority sign-up," an efficient and fair process where the NLRB certifies a union when a majority of employees sign written union authorization forms. Employees, and not employers, would be able to choose either the NLRB election process or a majority sign-up process.

"No workers, including healthcare givers, should face cruelty, abuse, or firing just because we exercise our right to form a union," said Michelle Collins, a member of SEIU United Healthcare Workers West in California and one of the thousands of union members who took part in rallies and visited their members of Congress on behalf of EFCA.

In addition to strong and widespread support from union members, EFCA had backing from some small business owners, students, veterans, farmers, and environmentalists.

And in stark contrast to the previous years under anti-

worker President George W. Bush, EFCA had strong backing from President Barack Obama and Labor Secretary Hilda Solis. Testifying before Congress in early 2010, Solis said that union workers earned $908 a week, compared to $710 for nonunion workers.

"These numbers make it clear that union jobs are good jobs," said Solis, affirming her support for EFCA.

Further support for labor law reform legislation came from the White House Task Force on the Middle Class headed by Vice President Joe Biden in its 2010 annual report, which stated:

"The (Obama) Administration has supported the Employee Free Choice Act as a way to rebalance the union organizing playing field…One underappreciated reason for the negative trends portrayed in our economic analysis of middle-class families is the loss of worker bargaining power.

"While raising the unionized share of the workforce would not close the gap between income and productivity, it would help to provide low- and middle-income workers with some of the clout they need to claim a fairer share of the fruits of their labors."

Although opposition was loud and harsh from the big-business lobby and other anti-union forces, public support for EFCA was strong.

In 2009, EFCA was reintroduced and, as of 2010, was still awaiting action. SEIU and other backers remained determined to push through the long-overdue overhaul of the nation's labor laws.

SEIU Local 26 in Minnesota campaigned for green jobs in its 2010 contract negotiations.

# CHAPTER 33

# SEIU Leads Push For Green Jobs

## Union Fights To Protect Environment

With scientific evidence of global warming mounting at the turn of the 21st century, SEIU put itself firmly in the "green economy" camp.

The union pushed Congress and the White House to invest in jobs that would promote energy efficiency and lay the groundwork for new industries based on renewable resources.

The union's property services members were in the forefront of these efforts. In New York City, Local 32BJ, the nation's largest local union of property services workers, led by President Mike Fishman, established a fund in 2005 to train 1,000 "green superintendents" in building efficiency.

With studies showing that 77 percent of New York's greenhouse gases came from buildings, increasing their energy efficiency stood to make a huge difference—the equivalent of taking 150,000 cars off the road.

The program got a boost in 2010 with a $2.8 million grant from the U.S. Department of Labor. The funds gave Local 32BJ the ability to train an additional 1,200 superintendents, with 200 getting the opportunity for advanced building training through the City University of New York. The full range of topics required to operate buildings in the most efficient way possible was covered, including insulation, heating, air sealing, and water conservation.

The Department of Labor also awarded a $4.6 million grant that year to the Healthcare Career Advancement Program (H-CAP), a national partnership of SEIU healthcare unions and major employers. The funds helped train 3,000 healthcare environmental services workers (often called housekeepers) in methods of tracking and reducing the use of energy, water, and

waste. The ultimate goal was to make the industry safer and healthier for patients and workers alike.

SEIU janitors in Minneapolis were also taking up the cause of green jobs. In December 2009, as they headed into negotiations for new contracts covering 4,000 janitors in the Minneapolis-St. Paul metro area, they marched through downtown Minneapolis in support of "green cleaning." Joined by community activists, the mayors of St. Paul and Minneapolis, and Minnesota Congressman Keith Ellison, they chanted, "What do we want?" and answered with, "Green jobs!"

One of the major energy-saving proposals they put forward was quite simple: Janitors should work more day shifts, which would significantly reduce lighting and heating costs in the commercial buildings they cleaned. They also proposed other "green jobs" practices, such as using safer, less toxic cleaning chemicals.

As Local 26 President Javier Morillo-Alicea said: "With our economy in a recession, we all need to think about ways to make our work smarter. We want to help make this industry part of our new green economy by increasing the use of green cleaning products with safer chemicals, recycling more trash, and supporting the transition to day-shift cleaning that can reduce energy use and reduce the carbon footprint of hundreds of buildings in our region."

SEIU's push for well-paying green jobs also included efforts on the national and international fronts.

In 2006, with its membership growing rapidly and the need for meeting and staff space growing as well, SEIU moved its headquarters offices from 1313 L Street, NW, in Washington, D.C., to a larger building at 1800 Massachusetts Avenue, NW.

The union's leaders used the move as an opportunity to put real substance into SEIU's green philosophy. The 1800 Massachusetts building, originally constructed in 1979, was converted into a state-of-the-art "green" building.

Located in D.C.'s thriving Dupont Circle neighborhood, and just blocks from the White House, SEIU's new environmentally conscious International headquarters won "gold" LEED-EB status from the U.S. Green Building Council. LEED-EB is the council's designation for "leadership in energy and environmental design of an existing building." As of 2009, only 14 buildings nationwide had won that status.

The building has two "green roofs" that help to filter water pollutants and manage storm water. It was renovated with

SEIU Local 32BJ President Mike Fishman and New York City Mayor Mike Bloomberg helped create a "Green Buildings" program that will train building superintendents in energy efficient practices.

a focus on recycling, indoor air quality, lighting performance, and energy and water efficiency.

In December 2009, SEIU leaders were part of a Blue Green Alliance delegation to the United Nations Climate Change Conference held in Copenhagen. At the "COP 15" meetings, they urged the adoption of a strong international agreement to address climate change with a goal of creating millions of good, green jobs across the world.

The Blue Green Alliance is a national partnership of labor unions and environmental organizations dedicated to expanding the number and quality of jobs in the green economy. It was launched by the United Steelworkers and the Sierra Club in 2006.

SEIU Executive Vice President Gerry Hudson, who headed SEIU's team in Copenhagen, noted that the United States, with a population that is just 5 percent of the global total, is responsible for 30 percent of the greenhouse gas emissions in the atmosphere.

"President Obama's willingness to address and establish long-term solutions to our deepening environmental problems is a night-and-day difference from the Bush Administration's era of climate change deniers," said Hudson.

With the United States and world economies facing turbulent times, and with conservative politicians and activists still attempting to cast doubt on the scientific evidence of global warming, the Copenhagen conference ended with only slight progress toward addressing the enormous environmental issues facing the planet.

But SEIU's members, from coast to coast, remained determined to press forward for a greener, healthier economy.

Minnesota janitor Marie Flores put it best when she said: "We are willing to do our part to make our work safer and better for the environment....Going green should be a win-win for everybody."

# SEIU Custodian Pushes School Trash Recycling

Matt Edgerton, a public school custodian from Marysville, Washington, was a man on a mission. He wanted to do something about all the trash his school cafeteria produced.

"My 'aha!' moment was me, inside the dumpster jumping on garbage bags, trying to make room to put more garbage bags in....I'm thinking there's got to be a better way than this!" he recalled. In 2009, Edgerton wrote the winning essay for an SEIU public division contest about his idea to replace the 180,000 Styrofoam trays his middle school used each year with something more environmentally sustainable.

Matt knew involving the middle school students would be integral to the program's success. A "Green Team" made up of students, teachers, managers, and parents helped build support for the project. Now students separate their own lunch waste into different containers for garbage, combined recyclables, and compostables—in the process reducing cafeteria waste from 56 bags a day to just 5.

Edgerton's ideas for reducing the environmental impact of his school kept the equivalent of six school buses of trash out of the landfill in 2009 alone, saved his school district $5,000 on its utility bill, and gave hundreds of children firsthand experience with recycling and conservation. Science classes analyzed how much waste they were saving, and took field trips to the solid waste dump so students could see their impact directly. Students took leadership in figuring out how to implement the project.

"I'm not surprised what our folks come up with," said Jim Baxter, executive director of finance at the school district in 2010. "They're the ones doing the work. They're the ones that face the challenges each day. I think, as administrators, we have a responsibility to listen a little bit more than maybe is the norm."

The district built off Edgerton's initiative and moved to expand the program to other schools and ultimately districtwide. And though custodians and other classified school employees aren't always seen as having much political clout, Matt's initiative won new respect for the work that he and other SEIU school employees do.

"At a recent school board election, I had school board candidates vying for an endorsement from the SEIU chapters," said Edgerton, a member of Local 925. "And the reason that they were stating that they were desperate for this endorsement was because of the recycling project."

SEIU President Andy Stern described the union's campaign on behalf of healthcare reform to activists who participated in Melanie's March in February 2009. The march from Philadelphia to Washington, D.C., honored Melanie Shouse, an Obama campaign volunteer, who died from breast cancer after she, like thousands of others, could not find affordable health insurance.

# CHAPTER 34

# SEIU Helps Pass Historic Healthcare Reform
## Coverage Extended To 32 Million Lacking Insurance

Loretta Johnson had to quit a job with good pay and benefits as a deputy courthouse clerk in Lebanon, Virginia, to care for her terminally ill husband.

After he died, she became an SEIU personal care assistant who worked "at the bedside every day giving people the same type of care I gave my husband." But Johnson herself lost health insurance when she changed jobs and had to rely on a smaller paycheck to cover her own healthcare needs.

About 32 million Americans like Loretta Johnson who faced each day without health insurance got a lifeline thrown to them when President Obama signed into law the historic healthcare reform bills in March 2010 that had been the top legislative goal of SEIU for years.

It was a landmark moment that will rank with major legislative achievements such as the passage of Social Security, Medicare, and the Civil Rights Act.

President Obama called SEIU President Andy Stern to thank union members shortly after the House of Representatives voted 219 to 212 to pass healthcare reform despite every Republican voting against the legislation. On March 23, 2010, at the White House signing ceremony, President Obama told Stern the century-long battle to achieve nearly universal healthcare could not have been won without SEIU members' hard work on its behalf.

SEIU played such a crucial role in winning passage of the legislation in part because, as the largest union of healthcare workers in North America, no group knew the sorry state of the healthcare system better. Every day, more than one million nurses, home healthcare providers, nursing home aides, medical technicians, doctors, and other healthcare workers who are SEIU members deliver quality care to millions of patients.

But those SEIU healthcare providers on the front lines also saw the huge failures of a system in which more than 47 million people lacked health insurance and another 47.5 million were underinsured. Despite bargaining victories that had provided health coverage for many members, there were still tens of thousands of SEIU workers who lacked affordable, quality coverage for their families and themselves.[212]

As the political debate over healthcare reform was playing out in 2009-2010, Americans were spending more money per capita on healthcare than any other country in the world. Yet the United States ranked 38th among other nations in major health indicators, including life expectancy. At the same time, healthcare premiums had increased four times faster than workers' wages. And 8 out of 10 of those without insurance were from working families.[213]

Even insured Americans found themselves unable to pay their growing share of hospital bills, their co-pays and deductibles, and the cost of filling their prescriptions. Consider the following:

- Fewer than one in four middle-class families could cope financially with a typical medical emergency.
- From 1990 to 2007, the number of families declaring bankruptcy because of a health emergency rose by 2,000 percent.
- A study released during the legislative debate on healthcare reform found that half of all bankruptcy cases were connected to medical bills.

• Healthcare costs pressured business as well, with the average Fortune 500 company projected to spend as much for healthcare in 2008 as it made in profits.

All the statistics and the harsh Congressional debate about reining in healthcare costs at times obscured the human costs of failing to enact reform. But SEIU and its allies repeatedly focused national attention on those who had suffered unbearable pain from the failures of a healthcare system dominated by private insurance companies concerned too often only about their bottom-line profits.

SEIU Secretary-Treasurer Anna Burger told the story of SEIU Healthcare 775NW member Pat DeJong. Her husband Dan, a fourth-generation rancher from just outside Libby, Montana, died from Hodgkin's lymphoma.

"During his treatment, the medical bills became so unbearable, Dan and Pat were forced to sell their family's farm and apply for Medicaid and food stamps," Burger recalled. After Dan died, Pat still had no health insurance from her job as a home care worker and no ranch to sell if she developed her own health problems.

Loretta Johnson, an SEIU personal care assistant, joined U.S. Senate Majority Leader Harry Reid and Senators Tom Harkin and Christopher Dodd at a Capitol Hill press conference in December 2009 to unveil the elements of the healthcare reform legislation that later became law. Johnson called for an end to the lack of accountability of the big insurance companies.

Georgeanne Koehler, an SEIU member and hospital worker in Pittsburgh, came to the Capitol steps on a frigid day in December 2009—her third visit in three months—to tell the story of how her brother, William, died.

He was a 57-year-old pizza deliveryman who was found slumped over his steering wheel after his defibrillator battery ran out. He couldn't afford to replace the expensive battery after losing his health insurance when he was laid off in 2003 from his job as an electronics technician. With his arrhythmia viewed as a pre-existing condition, no insurance company would cover him.

Georgeanne Koehler carried a bag filled with her brother's EKG charts as she visited Congressional offices as part of SEIU's lobbying effort for healthcare reform. She also carried around a folding chair as part of her own "No More Empty Chairs" campaign during the holiday season. "This Christmas we're going to have an empty chair at the dinner table," she said.

The SEIU Healthcare Pennsylvania member was not allowed to unfold the chair by the Capitol police, but did deliver about 1,000 holiday healthcare postcards urging the Senate to pass healthcare reform.

About the same time Koehler made her way to the offices of Pennsylvania's Senators and Representatives, Loretta Johnson also found herself on Capitol Hill pushing hard for healthcare reform.

U.S. Senate Majority Leader Harry Reid and a group of powerful Senators invited the Virginia home healthcare worker to join them at a crowded press conference to unveil core elements of the bill that later passed. Johnson, the only speaker who was not a Senator, appeared as a representative of SEIU and its 2.2 million members.

When Majority Leader Reid introduced her at the podium, she praised the Senators for a bill that put America one step closer to real healthcare reform, but then said: "Now, in my opinion, there's probably some room for improvement." She called for an end to the huge control of insurance companies over the healthcare system and urged passage of legislation that would make sure "people can afford the care they need."

It was a moment in the long debate that recognized both SEIU's role for many years as a driving force in advocating a progressive healthcare system and, at the same time, highlighted the plight of so many Americans, such as Johnson, who lacked any health insurance coverage and suffered as a result.

The new healthcare reform legislation did not include all the provisions urged by SEIU, but many elements supported by the union did end up in the bill.

The law put new pressures on insurance companies, for example, preventing denials of coverage due to pre-existing conditions such as diabetes, asthma, or high blood pressure. It also banned annual and lifetime limits on insurance coverage and contained guaranteed issue and renewal requirements.

Young adults were able to stay on their families' insurance plans until age 26, rather than lose coverage after they left home or graduated from college.

The new law provided for the creation of insurance exchanges at the state level where the uninsured and self-employed could purchase coverage that fit their needs. A guaranteed package of benefits including free preventive care had to be included in all those plans.

Medicaid was expanded under healthcare reform to provide health insurance to an additional 16 million low-income people.

SEIU fought successfully for an end to sex discrimination in health insurance. Previously, women could be charged more than men for the same coverage under individual policies.

The new law provided increased investments to train nurses, primary care doctors, and public health professionals. It also created state-level consumer assistance programs to help patients understand and defend their new rights.

Some experts estimated the legislation would create or save more than 2.5 million jobs through 2020, in part by reducing healthcare costs for employers.

SEIU advocated major healthcare reforms throughout much of its history. It had encouraged President Clinton's effort to develop legislation, but that initiative failed to gain traction during his first term in the early 1990s. In 2002, SEIU established Americans for Health Care (AHC), a project that sought to unite healthcare workers, consumers, small business owners, and others to push for broad-based healthcare reforms.

AHC, which became the largest grassroots healthcare reform organization in the country, ran state-based campaigns in 20 states and signed up nearly half a million healthcare voters nationwide. The group was critical in passing landmark healthcare legislation in Maryland, New Hampshire, and Maine.

In addition to work at the state level, SEIU and its allies made some progress during the administration of President George W. Bush, although much of the effort involved blocking actions that would have made the healthcare system even worse. Several victories that did advance reforms included:

- Pushing Congress to provide additional help to states that had funding shortfalls for State Children's Health Insurance Programs so eligible children didn't lose coverage.

- Passage of the Genetic Non-Discrimination Act, which protects workers from discrimination based on the results of genetic testing.

- Reauthorization of the Ryan White Act in 2007 that gave support to many effective state programs to prevent and treat HIV/AIDS.

- Giving new authority to the Food and Drug Administration to make sure drugs that are approved are actually safe.

- Requiring hospitals and nursing homes to publicly report additional quality measures in an effort to help patients and their families compare facilities.

SEIU had strongly opposed Bush in the 2000 campaign in part because he dismissed the need for real healthcare reform. The union's early backing of Howard Dean in the 2004 race for

SEIU pushed all the presidential candidates in 2007 to provide detailed plans for healthcare reform. Barack Obama unveiled his initiative at the University of Iowa Hospital and Clinics in Iowa City where he met with SEIU members.

the Democratic presidential nomination grew out of the fact that Dean was a medical doctor committed to pushing healthcare reform.

Candidates campaigning in New Hampshire were greeted at the Manchester airport by a large poster of an SEIU nurse challenging them to spell out their plan to reform healthcare.

The union conducted a healthcare reform march across the Golden Gate Bridge during its 2004 convention. More than 17,000 activists—led by Stern, Burger, Mary Kay Henry, and other top leaders—signaled that the issue would be a top priority for SEIU voters in the fall.

Senator John Kerry had strong SEIU support against Bush in the general election, but the Bush victory ruled out any major healthcare reform for another four years—necessitating the smaller, incremental approach that led to the gains described above.

SEIU also used the Bush years to try to stimulate thinking about what reforms should be enacted once America had elected political leaders committed to them. SEIU President

Andy Stern wrote in 2006 in his book, *A Country That Works*, about the decline of the employer-based healthcare system and called for a new approach built around the same basic tenet as the educational system: universal access.

"If every child is guaranteed a public education, every American must be guaranteed access to affordable healthcare," Stern argued. "Then we can integrate the finest research, doctors, and hospitals in the world into a delivery system that controls costs and offers the highest quality."

Among the models Stern urged as worthy of being adapted to the broader system included the healthcare plan enjoyed by members of Congress themselves, the U.S. Defense Department's healthcare program known as TRICARE that covers more than nine million members of the military and their families, and the Medicare system, which could be expanded to cover everyone.

Stern described the large number of countries that have some form of universal healthcare and also report better health outcomes at lower cost. Signaling the growing frustration felt by many, the SEIU president wrote:

"If all of these nations can figure out universal plans that meet their nations' interests, why can't America do the same? Americans deserve *a fair debate, not an endless one* on how best to provide universal, affordable, quality healthcare."[214]

In July 2006, SEIU wrote a letter to every Fortune 500 CEO asking them to make healthcare reform a national priority. A surprising number responded. While they did not agree with many of the specifics that progressive healthcare reformers advocated, it was becoming clear that major corporations faced huge outlays for their workers' healthcare as costs continued to escalate. Inflation in healthcare costs cut into the bottom line, hurting profits and raising labor costs without improving actual benefits.

Following long discussions among Stern, Secretary-Treasurer Burger, Executive Vice President Mary Kay Henry,

SEIU Healthcare leader Dennis Rivera, and other top officials, SEIU released its *Vision for Reform* in 2007. It outlined 10 fundamental principles to guide the union's work to promote healthcare solutions:

- It is time for our nation to guarantee affordable health-care coverage for all Americans. Piecemeal reform is not a solution.

- The current employer-based healthcare system is not the foundation for 21st century healthcare reform, particularly given the competitive challenges of a global economy.

- A universal healthcare system must ensure a choice of doctors and healthcare plans without gaps in coverage or access, and the delivery system must meet the needs of at-risk populations.

- A universal healthcare system must include a core health-care benefit similar to one that is available to federal employees.

- Preventive care must be part of any basic benefit plan to promote health, control costs, and eliminate economic and racial disparities.

- Any plan for healthcare reform must control costs by pro-viding care that is cost-efficient and medically effective.

- Secure electronic medical records that consumers control are necessary to increase quality and reduce costs.

- Hospital and physician quality, outcome, and cost data must be available to consumers.

- A universal healthcare system must integrate long term care service, reduce out-of-pocket costs, and maximize oppor-tunities for individuals to receive assistance in home- and community-based settings, rather than in hospitals and nursing homes.

- Employers, individuals, and government must share re-sponsibility for financing the system.

With the union's set of principles for healthcare reform in place, SEIU activists set out to make America's grow-ing healthcare crisis a major issue in the 2008 presidential cam-paign (see Chapter 27). The kickoff occurred in March 2007 in Nevada, where SEIU organized a forum sponsored by the Uni-versity of Nevada–Las Vegas (UNLV). It was the first national healthcare debate of the campaign. Seven of the Democratic candidates outlined their views and faced tough questioning from some of the hundreds of SEIU workers who were there.

The gauntlet thrown down by SEIU was simple: any presi-dential candidate hoping to get the official support of more than two million members had to offer a detailed, comprehensive plan to provide healthcare to every woman, man, and child in America. The response: all the major Democratic candidates produced healthcare plans and the issue became a major focus on the campaign trail.

Over many years, SEIU helped win gains by forming co-alitions and working closely with allies around specific issues. While agreeing to disagree on many points, SEIU saw value in partnerships on important legislative issues with both friends in the progressive community, but also with others who might be

Mary Kay Henry, then-SEIU executive vice president and head of the union's healthcare division, joined children and parents lobbying for the State Childen's Health Insurance Program (SCHIP) in 2007. President George W. Bush had vetoed two attempts to expand health coverage for uninsured children.

strange bedfellows—particularly certain business groups.

On the progressive side, SEIU joined with Healthcare for America Now (HCAN), a coalition of the nation's largest grassroots organizations, including Change to Win, AFSCME, AFL-CIO, U.S. Action, Planned Parenthood, and about 1,000 other groups representing 30 million people demanding comprehensive healthcare reform. HCAN proved to be a crucial force in the ultimate victory of healthcare reform.

While working in partnership with others, SEIU continued its own vigorous effort to make healthcare reform a top issue in the 2008 campaign. Thousands of SEIU member political organizers and staff deployed around the country during primary/caucus season working for Barack Obama, who had won SEIU's endorsement.

SEIU activists consistently found that voters talked about their problems with the healthcare system—their lack of health coverage, or high co-pays and other out-of-pocket costs, denial for previously existing health problems, and many others.

SEIU regularly ran paid television ads in targeted markets that drew sharp distinctions between the Republican and Democratic positions on healthcare and what those differences meant to working families.

As the 2008 Democratic and Republican national conventions approached, SEIU launched "The Road to American Healthcare," a nationwide bus tour. It made hundreds of stops throughout the nation, such as Tucson, Arizona, where organizers set up a canopy in the city's Main Library Place and invited passersby to take shelter from the desert sun and listen as SEIU members joined with elected officials and talked about the healthcare crisis.

"A lot of folks are hurting and one of the last things folks need is continued increases in healthcare premiums, co-pays, and deductibles—but that's what's happening," said Dave Mitchell, president of SEIU Arizona's Pima County chapter. "People are skimping on preventive care because they can't afford it, or they delay going to the doctor. We've become a nation of the walking wounded."

In Springfield, Missouri, the Road to American Healthcare Tour held a forum for veterans from Iraq, Korea, Vietnam, and World War II who spoke out against Senator McCain's consistent record of voting to deny funds for veterans' healthcare.

"If we're going to send our soldiers to war, and we're going to spend billions of dollars a day on a war, then we need to take care of the soldiers who go and fight those wars," said Akeam Ashford, an Iraq war veteran. He pointed out that McCain voted against full funding for veterans' healthcare in 2004, 2005, 2006, and 2007.

In August 2008, SEIU conducted a series of nationwide actions questioning health insurance industry tactics. The union's big purple bus played a role in Oregon where it pulled up to the state Capitol in Salem for a press conference at which the union and its ally, Oregon Action, presented evidence indicting the health insurers there. They outlined how the insurance industry used deliberate tactics designed to maximize profits by raising premiums, co-pays and deductibles; refusing coverage or charging exorbitant rates to people with pre-existing conditions; and even retroactively denying coverage to people with insurance.

In Spokane, Washington, members of SEIU Local 925 joined the bus tour in front of health insurer Premera Blue Cross seeking greater transparency into the firm's finances and rejection rates. "I'm so glad we did that!" said Paula Hall, a child care worker from Spokane and Local 925 member. "The way I see it, health insurance companies are answering to their shareholders, so they focus more on profits than on patient care. This has to change."

Even before Barack Obama's victory in November 2008, SEIU had launched its "100 Days for Change" campaign aimed at pushing through the union's post-election legislative priorities, with healthcare reform at the top of the list.

Medical doctors who belonged to SEIU Healthcare's Committee of Interns and Residents joined the union's Road to American Healthcare tour in August 2008. The union doctors saw every day on the job the huge problems of a healthcare system in dire need of reform.

Much of the normal work of the union was set aside, including a number of important organizing drives, so that more than half of the International Union staff and about 40 percent of all local union staff (excluding organizers) could work on post-election accountability. Locals also engaged their members in the effort, which was run similar to a political campaign, with doorknocking and phonebanking, house parties and meet-ups, town hall meetings, and outreach to community and religious coalition partners. The goal was to ratchet up pressure on Congress to build support for healthcare reform and other SEIU legislative priorities, such as the Employee Free Choice Act.

The effort evolved into SEIU's major national campaign called "Change That Works" that kicked off in January 2009 with a state-by-state effort to pass comprehensive healthcare reform, ensure approval of the economic recovery package, and guarantee workers the freedom to choose a voice at work.

SEIU targeted 35 states and hired campaign directors for each of those states. The union created a "war room" at its headquarters in Washington, D.C. Bruce Colburn coordinated the health reform effort.

"If we're going to revive the American Dream, we have to build an economy that works for everyone," SEIU Secretary-Treasurer Burger said as the campaign was launched. She said the union would push strongly for healthcare reform as President Obama pledged to see it through Congress at the onset of his new Administration.

Change That Works helped build strong pressure in target states in 2009, but momentum for healthcare reform on Capitol Hill slowed as President Obama deferred to certain Congressional leaders to craft the specifics of the legislation.

Democrats who chaired relevant committees in both the Senate and the House chose to engage in long, drawn-out discussions with Republicans over the healthcare reform bills' details. Months and months of talks to win at least a few Republican votes for the legislation led nowhere, even after a number of huge compromises that disappointed progressive forces.

Advocates of a single-payer healthcare system, similar to those of many other countries that deliver quality care at a lower cost, were angered when Democrats rejected the concept before the debate had begun.

Later, the debate shifted to a "public option" through which a government-funded health insurance plan would compete with private insurance companies to help keep premiums and other costs more reasonable. Consumers in a number of states faced insurance monopolies in which only one or two companies controlled the local market for health insurance. SEIU supported the public option, which was included in the House bill passed in late 2009, but it was not in the Senate version of the legislation that became the basis for the final healthcare reform law.

Much of the debate in late 2009 was shaped by the fact that Democrats supporting healthcare reform needed 60 votes out of the 100-member Senate in order to force an end to debate and bring a bill to an actual vote. Senate rules provided for a filibuster that meant 41 Senators could block passage of legislation even though a majority of Senators favored that legislation.

The drive for healthcare reform suffered a major setback in

August 2009 when Senator Edward Kennedy, the leading advocate of universal healthcare, died after a 15-month struggle with brain cancer.

A small group of very conservative Democrats in the Senate, including Senators Ben Nelson of Nebraska and Blanche Lincoln of Arkansas, refused to commit to voting to end the filibuster and allow the reform bill to come to a vote. They sought special favors at the expense of the broader public and at times seemed to carry out the agenda of the insurance companies that had inflicted so much damage on their constituents.

But finally the Senate adopted a healthcare bill that fell short of what SEIU had wanted, but nevertheless appeared to mean that reform would become the law of the land. All that remained was to conform that Senate bill and the version passed weeks earlier by the House.

When Congress recessed for the holidays in December, President Obama and the Democratic and Republican leaders in the House and Senate indicated the final compromises in the House and Senate versions were likely to be finalized shortly after Congress returned to business in early 2010.

Scott Brown's upset victory in January 2010 over Martha Coakley in the election to fill the U.S. Senate seat in Massachusetts—vacant due to the death of Senator Edward Kennedy—sent shockwaves through Washington, D.C.

The Republican upset in the special election meant the GOP had 41 Senate votes to sustain a filibuster and block future legislation. Many pundits and political observers thought healthcare reform was dead.

Insurance companies, which spent millions of dollars on lobbyists to try to shape healthcare reform to their liking, believed they had won a victory with the stalling of the legislative process. They moved immediately with huge rate increases across the country. Anthem Blue Cross of California (owned by for-profit WellPoint Inc.) announced it would be raising indi-

vidual premiums as much as 39 percent. Anthem also sought massive premium hikes in Connecticut, including 24 percent for individual policies (rejected by the state) and in Maine, where the company sought a 23 percent increase.

Anthem's greed was not alone. Rate hikes by insurance companies that had been proposed during the healthcare reform debate included Blue Cross/Blue Shield of Michigan, which sought premium hikes of 56 percent. Regency Blue Cross/Blue Shield in Oregon demanded a 20 percent increase.

These incredible rate increases provoked particular outrage in the midst of the deep economic recession in which many people had lost their employer-provided health insurance and had been forced to seek individual coverage that was the core of the proposed rate hikes.

And the insurance firms' rate hikes came while they were reporting huge profits. WellPoint, UnitedHealth Group, Cigna, Aetna, and Humana together took in $12.2 billion in profits in 2009, up 56 percent over 2008.[215] From 2000 through 2009, profits for the 10 largest insurance companies increased 250 percent—10 times faster than inflation.

The raw greed of the insurance companies, unleashed by the apparent defeat of healthcare reform, provoked a massive backlash that helped to breathe new life into the legislative effort.

Republicans continued their effort to scrap the legislation, which had been debated for a year before being passed with only one Republican vote in the House and no Republican votes in the Senate. The outcome occurred even though a number of Republican proposals had been included in the Senate version as part of Democrats' attempts to attract bipartisan support.

Democrats finally adopted healthcare reform in March, 2010, but Republicans vowed to repeal the historic healthcare bill even before President Obama signed it into law in front of a White House audience including SEIU President Stern, SEIU Healthcare leader Dennis Rivera, 1199/SEIU United Healthcare Workers-East President George Gresham, and other SEIU activists.

President Obama's sincere thanks to SEIU leaders and members for the crucial role they played in winning the most important social legislation since the passage of Medicare in the 1960s underscored how far the union had come.

From a small group of underpaid and overworked janitors in Chicago nearly 90 years earlier, SEIU had evolved into a 2.2 million-member powerhouse that delivered at the bargaining table, the ballot box, and in the halls of Congress.

One mark of the union's effectiveness was the increasingly shrill volume of attacks from right-wing talk show hosts such as Glenn Beck and Rush Limbaugh, whose hate-filled attacks on Stern, Mary Kay Henry, and SEIU became a staple of their programming in 2010.

But for every snarl from a Glenn Beck, there was a smile from an SEIU member such as Loretta Johnson, who with the healthcare reform law could finally look forward to living without the fear of having no health insurance. So, too, could 32 million Americans who lacked healthcare coverage before SEIU and so many other allies worked together to change history for the better.

Thousands attended a Labor Day rally for healthcare reform in Boston on September 7, 2009.

# CHAPTER 35

Mary Kay Henry was sworn in as the 10th SEIU president after her election by
the International Executive Board on May 8, 2010.

# Mary Kay Henry Becomes SEIU's 10th President
## Retirement of Andy Stern Ends An Era

SEIU's success throughout the years came in part because the union seemed always to be led by the right person for the times.

William Quesse had the perseverance to pull flat janitors in Chicago together to form the union in the early 20th century. David Sullivan's commitment to social justice fit well with President Kennedy in the early 1960s.

George Hardy brought an organizing culture while John Sweeney fought the anti-unionism of the Reagan era. And Andy Stern restructured SEIU to focus big new resources that allowed the union to more than double in size to 2.2 million members.

As Mary Kay Henry became the 10th SEIU president in May 2010, the union yet again seemed to have the right leader for a new time.

Henry, who had been organizing director and rose in 2004 to become executive vice president and head of the union's healthcare division, replaced Andy Stern. He retired after more than 14 years as SEIU president and became president emeritus.

"This moment marks a renewed commitment to our union's core mission: to improve the lives of all workers who are struggling to make ends meet in this economy," Henry said May 8, 2010, when the 73-member International Executive Board elected her president.

She secured the presidency when Secretary-Treasurer Anna Burger withdrew her candidacy after a number of large local unions announced support for Henry.

Stern praised Henry's election: "For 30 years, I have worked side-by-side with Mary Kay Henry and witnessed her extraordinary passion for justice and the natural gift that can only be called her way with people. She will be an incredible president of our union, as well as an important and impassioned voice for working people."

Henry won a reputation for working closely with SEIU members—meeting with them at 3 a.m. on night shifts in hospitals, walking picket lines, and leading members in contract bargaining.

"Mary Kay doesn't just come by to give a speech and she doesn't just come by to shake hands—she's one of us," said Loretta Reddy Blauvel, an SEIU Healthcare Florida member who has worked with Henry on multiple campaigns. "She is always in the trenches with us."

Henry, the eldest sister of 10 siblings, grew up in and around Detroit, Michigan. After graduating from Michigan State University in 1979, Henry joined SEIU as a research specialist and worked on campaigns in California for child care and public sector workers. Assigned next to Minneapolis, she participated in all aspects of bargaining, organizing, and legislative advocacy.

Henry's leadership enabled SEIU to achieve groundbreaking agreements with Beverly Enterprises, Catholic Healthcare West, Tenet, and HCA that united tens of thousands of members in SEIU. She helped create the Labor-Management Partnership at Kaiser Permanente and played a critical role in the fight to extend state health insurance coverage to children.

She earned a reputation as a strong advocate for immigrant rights and also was a founding member of SEIU's gay and lesbian Lavender Caucus.

Mary Kay Henry is the first woman to serve as SEIU president.

# Mission Statement

## of the
## Service Employees International Union (SEIU)

We are the Service Employees International Union, an organization of more than two million members united by the belief in the dignity and worth of workers and the services they provide and dedicated to improving the lives of workers and their families and creating a more just and humane society.

We are public workers, healthcare workers, building service workers, office workers, professional workers, and industrial and allied workers. We seek a stronger union to build power for ourselves and to protect the people we serve.

As a leading advocacy organization for working people, it is our responsibility to pursue justice for all.

People of every race, ethnicity, religion, age, physical ability, gender, gender expression and sexual orientation, we are the standard-bearers in the struggle for social and economic justice begun nearly a century ago by janitors who dared to dream beyond their daily hardships and to organize for economic security, dignity, and respect.

Our vision is of a society:

Where all workers and their families live and work in dignity.

Where work is fulfilling and fairly rewarded.

Where workers have a meaningful voice in decisions that affect them.

Where workers have the opportunity to develop their talents and skills.

Where the collective voice and power of workers is realized in democratic and progressive unions.

Where union solidarity stands firm against the forces of discrimination and hate and the unfair employment practices of exploitative employers.

Where government plays an active role in improving the lives of working people.

To achieve this vision:

We must organize unorganized service workers, extending to them the gains of unionism while securing control over our industries and labor market.

We must build political power to ensure that workers' voices are heard at every level of government to create economic opportunity and foster social justice.

We must provide meaningful paths for member involvement and participation in strong, democratic unions.

We must develop highly trained and motivated leaders at every level of the union who reflect the membership in all its diversity.

We must bargain contracts that improve wages and working conditions, expand the role of workers in workplace decision-making, and build a stronger union.

We must build coalitions and act in solidarity with other organizations who share our concern for social and economic justice.

We must engage in direct action that demonstrates our power and our determination to win.

To accomplish these goals we must be unified—inspired by a set of beliefs and principles that transcends our social and occupational diversity and guides our work.

We believe we can accomplish little as separate individuals, but that together we have the power to create a just society.

We believe unions are the means by which working people build power—by which ordinary people accomplish extraordinary things.

We believe our strength comes from our unity, and that we must not be divided by forces of discrimination based on gender, race, ethnicity, religion, age, physical ability, sexual orientation, or immigration status.

We believe our power and effectiveness depend upon the active participation and commitment of our members, the development of our leaders, and solidarity with each other and our allies.

We believe we have a special mission to bring economic and social justice to those most exploited in our community—especially to women and workers of color.

We believe our future cannot be separated from that of workers in other parts of the world who struggle for economic justice, a decent life for their families, peace, dignity, and democracy.

We believe unions are necessary for a democratic society to prevail, and that unions must participate in the political life of our society.

We believe we have a moral responsibility to leave the world a better place for our children—and everyone's children.

# A Selected SEIU Bibliography

Prepared By SEIU Archivist Louis Jones, PhD, CA
Walter P. Reuther Library of Labor and Urban Affairs
Wayne State University

Beadling, Tom et al. A Need for Valor: The Roots of the Service Employees International Union, 1902-1992. Washington, D.C.: Service Employees International Union, 1992.

Boris, Eileen C. and Klein, Jennifer. "Organizing Home Care: Low-Wage Workers in the Welfare State." *Politics and Society* 34 (March 2006): 81-107.

Building Service Employees International Union. "Going Up!": The Story of Local 32B. New York: Building Service Employees International Union, 1955.

Delp, Linda and Quan, Katie, "Homecare Organizing in California: An Analysis of a Successful Strategy," *Labor Studies Journal* 27 (2002): 1-23

Erem, Suzan. Labor Pains: Inside America's New Union Movement. New York: Monthly Review Press, 2001.

Fink, Leon and Greenberg, Brian. Upheaval in the Quiet Zone: 1199SEIU and the Politics of Health Care Unionism. Chicago: University of Illinois Press, 2009.

Fisk, Catherine et al., "Union Representation of Immigrant Janitors in Southern California: Economic and Legal Challenges," in Milkman, Organizing Immigrants: the Challenge for Unions in Contemporary California. Ithaca: ILR Press, 2000, pp. 199-224.

Hearn, Albert G. Building a Dream: The History of a Union for Canadian Service Workers, 1943-1988. Washington, D.C.: Service Employees International Union, 1988.

Jentz, John B. "Citizenship, Self-Respect, and Political Power: Chicago's Flat Janitors Trailblaze the Service Employees International Union, 1912-1921." *Labor's Heritage* 9, No. 1 (Summer 1997): 4-23.

Jentz, John B. "Labor, the Law, and Economics: The Organization of the Chicago Flat Janitor's Union, 1902-1917." *Labor History* 38, no. 4 (Fall 1997): 413-431.

Jentz, John B. "Unions, Cartels, and Political Economy of American Cities: the Chicago Flat Janitors' Union in the Progressive Era and 1920s." *Studies in American Political Development*, 14 (Spring 2000): 51-71.

Jones, Louis (Curator) of on-line exhibit titled, *SEIU District 925: Organizing for Raises, Rights and Respect* located at http://www.reuther.wayne.edu/925/Raises.html

Lopez, Steven. Reorganizing the Rustbelt: An Inside Story of the American Labor Movement. Berkeley: University of California Press, 2004.

Palladino, Grace. "'When Militancy Isn't Enough': The Impact of Automation on New York City Building Service Workers, 1934-1970." *Labor History* 28 (1987): 196-220.

Ransom, David. 'So Much to be Done': George Hardy's Life in Organized Labor. Washington, D.C.: Service Employees International Union, 1980.

Slater, Joseph Elijah. "Ground-Floor Politics and the BSEIU in the 1930s" in Joseph Slater, Public Workers: Government Employee Unions, the Law, and the State, 1900-1962. Ithaca: Cornell University Press, 2004.

Stern, Andrew. A Country That Works: Getting America Back on Track. New York: Simon & Schuster. 2006.

Tait, Vanessa. Poor Workers' Unions: Rebuilding Labor from Below. Cambridge: South End Press, 2005.

Takahashi, Beverly. "Home Care Organizing in California." WorkingUSA 7, No. 9 (Winter 2003-2004): 62-87.

Williams, Jane. "Restructuring Labor's Identity: The Justice for Janitors Campaign in Washington, D.C." in Ray M. Tillman, Michael Cummings (eds.) The Transformation of U.S. Unions: Voices, Visions, and Strategies from the Grassroots. Boulder: Lynne Rienner Publishers, 1999.

Witwer, David Scott. "The Scandal of George Scalise: A Case Study in the Rise of Labor Racketeering in the 1930s." Journal of Social History 36 (Summer 2003): 917-941.

Yu, Kyoung-Hee. "Between Bureaucracy and Social Movements: Careers in the Justice for Janitors." Ph.D. diss., Massachusetts Institute of Technology, 2008.

# Photo And Artwork Credits

CHAPTER 22
Page 163, photo by David Bacon ©2007.

CHAPTER 23
Page 164, 167, 168, photos by Meenu Bhardwaj ©2010.
Page 175, photo by Dave Sanders/SEIU32BJ.

CHAPTER 24
Page 178, photo by Andrew Cutraro ©2006.
Page 181, photo by Jason Frizzelle ©2008.
Page 182, photo by Kaveh Sardari/Page One from *SEIU Action* ©2001.

CHAPTER 25
Page 184, photo by Eric Brunetta/SEIU.
Page 187, photo by Kaveh Sardari/Page One ©2000.

CHAPTER 26
Page 194, photo by Bill Fitzpatrick ©2008.
Page 195, photo by Bill Burke/Page One.
Page 196, photo by Keith Mellnick ©2008.
Page 197, photo by Bill Auth ©2008.
Page 198, photo by Bill Fitzpatrick ©2008.
Page 201, photo by Keith Mellnick ©2008.

CHAPTER 27
Page 202, photo by Anne Hamersky ©2007.
Page 204, photo by Bill McAllen ©2007.
Page 205, photo by Ryan Donnell ©2008.
Page 206, photo by Jay Reiter ©2007.
Page 208, photo by Bill Burke/Page One ©2008.
Page 209, photo by Jim Wilkinson ©2008.
Page 211, photo by Kris Price/SEIU.

CHAPTER 28
Page 215, left column, photo by William Melton Jr./SEIU ©2008.
Page 215, right column, photo by Nathan Ames ©2008.
Page 216, photo by Angel Ruiz ©2010.
Page 217, Thomas Padilla.

CHAPTER 29
Page 218, photo by Ricardo Figueroa ©2009.
Page 220, photo by Manolo Coss ©2009.
Page 222, photo by Javier Rodriguez ©2009.
Page 223, Mairym Ramos/SEIU ©2009.

CHAPTER 30
Page 224, Belinda Gallegos/1199SEIU ©2010.
Page 226, David Sachs/SEIU ©2009.
Page 228, photo by Kate Thomas/SEIU.

CHAPTER 31
Page 232, photo by Keith Mellnick ©2008.

CHAPTER 32
Page 242, photo by Brian Liu.
Page 243, photo by David Sachs.
Page 244, photo by Kaveh Sardari/Page One from *SEIU Action*.
Page 245, photo by Anna Maria Mendez Ritchie ©2009.
Page 247, photo by William Melton Jr./SEIU ©2009.

CHAPTER 33
Page 250, photo by Clark Jones.
Page 251, photo by Nancy Louie.

CHAPTER 34
Page 252, photo by David Sachs/SEIU ©2009.
Page 253, photo by Kris Price/SEIU ©2009.
Page 256, photo by Ryan Donnell ©2008.
Page 257, photo by Keith Mellnick ©2008.
Page 259, photo by Bill Burke/Page One.
Page 261, photo by Aaron Donovan ©2009.

CHAPTER 35
Page 262, photo by Kris Price/SEIU ©2010.

As with many historical works, the passage of time can make it difficult to ascertain the names of the photographers or artists whose images defined SEIU history, particularly in the early years. We have made diligent efforts to track down and credit as many as possible, but early recordkeeping often left little to go on. Most of the photos in the book come from photo files at SEIU and at the Walter P. Reuther Library at Wayne State University in Detroit and were originally taken for use by SEIU for its publications, such as *SEIU Action*, or in the union's printed materials. If you can provide more information on any of the images in the book, please email: seiu.book@gmail.com. This will help us update credits in future editions. Our thanks go to David Sachs, who researched photo credits and did a superb job of providing many of the excellent photos in the book, and to Louis Jones, the SEIU archivist at the Reuther Library, who spent countless hours assisting with photos, particularly of the union's early years.

# Endnotes

1 Beadling,Tom, Palladino, Grace, and Cooper, Pat. *A Need for Valor: The Roots of the Service Employees International Union.* Washington, D.C.: Service Employees International Union, 1992, p. 2. The pre-1992 history of the union in this book is an updated and edited version of SEIU's earlier editions of *A Need for Valor*, the first of which appeared in 1984 and the second in 1992. *Stronger Together* relies heavily on the work of Beadling, Palladino, Cooper, and others who were commissioned by SEIU to write the predecessor volumes. This pre-1992 material is edited, condensed, and otherwise reworked from the *Valor* editions, and all three volumes are copyrighted by SEIU. For more on the 1902 flat janitors' charter, see the *Chicago Federationist*, April 19, 1902, and the *Building Service Employee*, April 1942, p. 8.

2 *The New York Times*, August 24, 1903; March 27, 1905; December 5, 1904.

3 *Chicago Record-Herald*, July 15, 1905; 1928 AFL convention, pp. 73-75.

4 *Public Safety*, July 1930, pp. 13-14.

5 Beadling,Tom, Palladino, Grace, and Cooper, Pat. *A Need for Valor: The Roots of the Service Employees International Union.* Washington, D.C.: Service Employees International Union, 1992. p. 10.

6 Ibid, p. 11.

7 Ebell, Monique, and Ritschl, Albrecht. *Real Origins of the Great Depression: Monopolistic Competition, Union Power, and the American Business Cycle in the 1920s*, Centre for Economic Policy Research, 2007.

8 *The New York Times*, June 10, 1922.

9 *Chicago-American*, April 12 and April 20, 1924; Staley, Eugene, *History of the Illinois State Federation of Labor.* Chicago: University of Chicago Press, 1930.

10 Bambrick, James. *The Building Service Story*, New York: Labor History Press, 1930. pp. 11-12.

11 *The New York Times*, November 2, 1934, and November 4, 1934; Merritt, Walter Gordon. *Destination Unknown: Fifty Years of Labor Relations.* New York, 1951.

12 *The New York Times*, February 14, 15, 16, 17, 1935.

13 Jentz, John B. "Citizenship, Self-Respect, and Political Power: Chicago's Flat Janitors Trailblaze the Service Employees International Union, 1912-1921." *Labor's Heritage 9*, No. 1 (Summer 1997): 4-23.

14 *A Need for Valor*, p. 9.

15 William Quesse, "History of the Organization: Why and How the Flat Janitors of Chicago, Illinois Were Organized," *1919 Official Year Book*.

16 Jentz, John B. "Citizenship, Self-Respect, and Political Power: Chicago's Flat Janitors Trailblaze the Service Employees International Union, 1912-1921." *Labor's Heritage 9*, No. 1 (Summer 1997): 4-23.

17 Jentz, John B. "Citizenship, Self-Respect, and Political Power: Chicago's Flat Janitors Trailblaze the Service Employees International Union, 1912-1921." *Labor's Heritage 9*, No. 1 (Summer 1997): 4-23.

18 *The Negro in Chicago: A Study of Race Relations and a Race Riot*, Chicago Commission on Race Relations. Chicago: University of Chicago, 1922, pp. 411-12, 415-16.

19 *The New York Times*, March 22, 1965.

19a *The New York Times*, March 26, 1965.

20 *Chicago Record-Herald*, July 15, 1905; 1928 AFL convention, pp. 73-75.

21 BSEIU General Executive Board, Minutes, April 14, 1961.

22 John Jeffrey writing to BSEIU President David Sullivan in a letter to the editor, *Service Employee*, March 3, 1966.

23 Beadling,Tom, Palladino, Grace, and Cooper, Pat. *A Need for Valor: The Roots of the Service Employees International Union.* Washington, D.C.: Service Employees International Union, 1992, p. 66.

24 Damon Stetson, "State Employees to Vote on New Contract Nov. 19," *The New York Times*, November 10, 1979.

25 This is drawn from an internal SEIU document written by Stephen Lerner analyzing developments in SEIU's Building Service Division over the 1985-1993 period.

26 Stern, Andy. *A Country that Works*. New York: Free Press, 2006.

27 Weinstein, Henry. "Union Seeking Boycott of 5 Atlanta Convention Events," *Los Angeles Times*, July 9, 1988.

28 Meyerson, Harold. "Street vs. Suite," *LA Weekly*, April 13, 2000.

28a Waldinger, Roger, et al. "Helots No More: A Case Study of the Justice for Janitors Campaign in Los Angeles." The Lewis Center for Regional Policy Studies Working Paper Series, UCLA School of Public Policy and Social Research, 1996.

28b Ibid.

28c Ibid.

28d Ibid.

28e Ibid.

29 Baker, Bob. "Police Use Force to Block Strike March." *Los Angeles Times*, June 16, 1990.

30 Milkman, Ruth, and Wong, Kent. "Voice From the Front Lines: Organizing Immigrant Workers in Los Angeles," Center for Labor Research and Education, UCLA, 2000.

31 Serrin, William. "Lane Kirkland, Who Led Labor in Difficult Times, Is Dead at 77." *The New York Times*, Aug. 15, 1999. For more details on this period, see *A Need for Valor*, Chapter 7.

32 Stern interview with Don Stillman, 11/11/2009.

33 *A Country That Works*, p. 62.

34 Stern interview with Don Stillman, 11/11/2009.

35 *A Country That Works*, p. 63.

36 SEIU Executive Vice President Tom Woodruff chapter in *Peter Bremme: Never work alone, Organizing – ein Zukunftsmodell für Gewerkschaften (A Future Model for the Unions)*. Hamburg, VSA, 2007, S. 101.

37 Interview with Andy Stern conducted by Glenn Silber, director/producer of *Labor Day* film about SEIU's 2008 election effort.

38 *SEIU Action*, June 1997, pp. 7-9. *Stronger Together* draws heavily on SEIU materials, documents, memos, PowerPoints, websites, and publications, particularly the union's magazine *SEIU Action*. It carried union news and worker stories that appear in this book in many chapters. Our thanks to the writers and editors at SEIU for the work on which this volume has drawn.

39 *SEIU Action*, June 1997, p. 24.

40 Eaton, Adrienne, Fine, Janice, Porter, Allison, and Rubinstein, Saul. *Organizational Change at SEIU: 1996-2009*. Known as the "Rutgers Report," this independent study commissioned by SEIU examined the process of change within the union from 1996, when Andy Stern became president, through 2009. *Stronger Together* relied on the Rutgers Report in a number of areas and wishes to thank Eaton, Fine, Porter, and Rubinstein for their ideas and research. The final version of their work had not been published when *Stronger Together* went to press, so we relied on earlier versions available to us. Thanks to David Snapp, who worked with the Rutgers professors on their report.

41 Eaton, Adrienne, Fine, Janice, Porter, Allison, and Rubinstein, Saul. *Organizational Change at SEIU: 1996-2009*.

42 Eaton, Adrienne, Fine, Janice, Porter, Allison, and Rubinstein, Saul. *Organizational Change at SEIU: 1996-2009*.

43 *SEIU Action*, January-February 1998, p. 20.

44 Minutes of SEIU International Executive Board, Dec. 9-11, 1996, p. 1.

45 *A Country That Works*, p. 117.

46 SEIU Executive Vice President Tom Woodruff chapter in *Peter Bremme: Never work alone, Organizing – ein Zukunftsmodell für Gewerkschaften (A Future Model for the Unions)*. Hamburg, VSA, 2007, S. 101.

47 *SEIU Action*, January-February 1998, p. 20.

48 Eaton, Adrienne, Fine, Janice, Porter, Allison, and Rubinstein, Saul. *Organizational Change at SEIU: 1996-2009*.

49 Eaton, Adrienne, Fine, Janice, Porter, Allison, and Rubinstein, Saul. *Organizational Change at SEIU: 1996-2009*.

50 Eaton, Adrienne, Fine, Janice, Porter, Allison, and Rubinstein, Saul. *Organizational Change at SEIU: 1996-2009*.

51 *Evaluate*, SEIU President's Committee 2000, p. 21.

52 *A Country That Works*, p. 74, and Eaton, Adrienne, Fine, Janice, Porter, Allison, and Rubinstein, Saul. *Organizational Change at SEIU: 1996-2009*.

53 Eaton, Adrienne, Fine, Janice, Porter, Allison, and Rubinstein, Saul. *Organizational Change at SEIU: 1996-2009*.

54 Eaton, Adrienne, Fine, Janice, Porter, Allison, and Rubinstein, Saul. *Organizational Change at SEIU: 1996-2009*.

55 *SEIU Action*, March/April 1999, p. 20.

56 "Letters to the Editor," *SEIU Action*, July/August 2002, p. 2.

57 *SEIU Action*, June 1997, p. 19.

58   *SEIU Action*, October 1997, p. 5.

59   *A Country That Works*, see Chapter 3.

60   *A Country That Works*, p. 58.

61   *A Country That Works*, p. 69.

62   *A Country That Works*, p. 70.

63   *A Country That Works*, p. 71.

64   *SEIU Action*, April 1998, p. 10.

65   Greenhouse, Steven. "Service Unions to Merge in Bid for More Clout." *The New York Times*, January 7, 1998.

66   "Our Life and Times," *1199SEIU*, March/April 2009, p. 6.

67   "Our Life and Times," *1199SEIU*, March/April 2009, p. 5.

68   *SEIU Action*, April 1998, p. 10.

69   *SEIU Action*, April 1998, p. 10.

70   "Our Life and Times," *1199SEIU*, March/April 2009, p. 6.

71   *SEIU Action*, January-February 1999, p. 7.

72   *SEIU Action*, January-February 1999, p. 9.

73   Meyerson, Harold. "Caretakers Take Charge." *LA Weekly*, February 26-March 4, 1999.

74   Greenhouse, Steven. "In Biggest Drive Since 1937, Union Gains a Victory," *The New York Times*, October 20, 2009.

75   *SEIU Action*, March/April 1999, pp. 7-9.

76   Delph, Linda, and Quan, Katie. "Homecare Worker Organizing in California: An Analysis of a Successful Strategy." *Labor Studies Journal 27* (2002): 1-23.

77   Eaton, Adrienne, Fine, Janice, Porter, Allison, and Rubinstein, Saul. *Organizational Change at SEIU: 1996-2009.*

78   Walsh, Jess. "Creating Unions, Creating Employers: The SEIU Los Angeles Homecare Campaign." Article in *Care Work: The Quest for Security*. Geneva: International Labor Organization (2001), pp. 219-231. Our thanks to Jess Walsh, now an Australian trade union leader, who gave us permission to rely heavily on her analysis of the homecare issue.

79   Ibid p. 4, citing Cousineau, Michael R. *Providing Health Insurance to IHSS Providers: Final Report to the California HealthCare Foundation.* University of Southern California, June 2000.

80   Ibid p. 6.

81   Ibid p. 3.

82   Ibid p. 16.

83   Ibid p. 7.

84   Ibid p. 8.

85   Meyerson, Harold. "Caretakers Take Charge." *LA Weekly*, February 26-March 4, 1999.

86   Walsh, p. 11.

87   Meyerson, Harold. "Caretakers Take Charge." *LA Weekly*, February 26-March 4, 1999.

88   Walsh, p. 22.

89   *SEIU Action*, March/April 1999, p. 9

90   Shulman, Barbara. "Healthcare, Property Service, and Public Service Worker Organizing with SEIU: 1996-2009." Washington, D.C.: Service Employees International Union (2009). Our thanks to Barbara Shulman on whose work we relied heavily.

91   Carlsen, William. "Peggy Ferro." *San Francisco Chronicle*, 11/12/1998, p. C-7.

92   Ibid.

93   Ibid.

94   Ibid.

95   *SEIU Action*, December 2000, p.14.

96   *SEIU Action*, August-September 2000, pp.16-17.

97   *SEIU Action*, August-September 2000, pp.16-17.

98   There is an SEIU Local 925 in Washington state.

99   SEIU Executive Vice President Tom Woodruff chapter in *Peter Bremme: Never work alone, Organizing – ein Zukunftsmodell für Gewerkschaften (A Future Model for the Unions)*. Hamburg, VSA, 2007, S. 101. Also see *Evaluate*, President's Committee 2000 Report. Washington, D.C.: Service Employees International Union.

100  SEIU Executive Vice President Tom Woodruff chapter in *Peter Bremme: Never work alone, Organizing – ein Zukunftsmodell für Gewerkschaften (A Future Model for the Unions)*. Hamburg, VSA, 2007, S. 101.

101  *Evaluate*. President's Committee 2000. Published by Service Employees International Union, Washington, D.C. SEIU's President's Committee 2000 published three publications, *Evaluate, Imagine*, and *Decide*, in the run-up to the 2000 SEIU Convention.

102  The National Education Association (NEA) representing teachers has about 3.2 million members.

103 *SEIU 2000 Convention Proceedings*, p. 17. Published by Service Employees International Union, Washington, D.C., 2000.

104 Eaton, Adrienne, Fine, Janice, Porter, Allison, and Rubinstein, Saul. *Organizational Change at SEIU: 1996-2009*.

105 Eaton, Adrienne, Fine, Janice, Porter, Allison, and Rubinstein, Saul. *Organizational Change at SEIU: 1996-2009*.

106 SEIU Executive Vice President Tom Woodruff chapter in *Peter Bremme: Never work alone, Organizing – ein Zukunftsmodell für Gewerkschaften (A Future Model for the Unions)*. Hamburg, VSA, 2007, S. 101.

107 Eaton, Adrienne, Fine, Janice, Porter, Allison, and Rubinstein, Saul. *Organizational Change at SEIU: 1996-2009*.

108 Thomas, Kate. "SEIU Remembers September 11 Victims," SEIU Website, 9/11/2009 http://www.seiu.org/2009/09/seiu-remembers-sept-11-victims.php.

109 *SEIU Action*, October 2001, p.14.

110 SEIU's International Executive Board elected Anna Burger to replace the retiring Betty Bednarczyk at its meeting in early June 2001. Burger served as an executive vice president for the previous three years and oversaw the union's Eastern Region. At the same IEB meeting, the board elected Tom Woodruff to fill the vacancy created by Paul Policicchio, who stepped down as an executive vice president. Woodruff took on the role of handling the Central Region and also continued to be a director of SEIU organizing programs nationally. SEIU President Stern praised Bednarczyk and said: "While I will miss having Betty as a valued adviser, I speak for the entire SEIU family when I thank her for her years of leadership."

111 *SEIU Action*, November-December 2001, p. 24.

112 *SEIU Action*, November-December 2001, p. 24.

113 *SEIU Action*, May-June 2002, p. 7.

114 *SEIU Action*, January-February 2002, p. 10.

115 Bole, William. "Catholic Healthcare West's Organizing Campaign." *Our Sunday Visitor*, Catholic-Labor Network, November 1998.

116 "Unionbusting" on Wikipedia, referencing Logan, John. "The Union Avoidance Industry in the United States." *British Journal of Industrial Relations*. Blackwell Publishing Ltd. (December 2006), p. 651–675.

117 *Our Sunday Visitor*, November 1998.

118 *Our Sunday Visitor*, November 1998.

119 "CHW Caregivers Organize to Improve Patient Care." *SEIU Action*, May 2000. pp. 10-11.

120 *Our Sunday Visitor*, November 1998.

121 Filteau, Jerry. "Catholic Health System, Union Set Expedited Election Rules." *Catholic News Service*, April 10, 2001.

122 *SEIU Action*, November-December 2001, pp. 16-17.

123 Health Corporation of America merged with Columbia Hospital Corporation in 1994 and called itself Columbia/HCA. Later, it reverted to the name HCA and in 2006 the company agreed to go private in a deal led by KKR and Bain Capital.

124 Shulman, Barbara. "Healthcare, Property Service, and Public Service Worker Organizing with SEIU: 1996-2009." Washington, D.C.: Service Employees International Union (2009).

125 McElvaine, Robert S. "HNN Poll: 61% of Historians Rate the Bush Presidency Worst." *History News Network*, George Mason University, April 2008.

126 Moberg, David. "Stand Up, Al." *LA Weekly*, March 2, 2000.

127 *SEIU Action*, November 2000. p. 14.

128 Dershowitz, Alan. *Supreme Injustice: How the High Court Hijacked Election 2000*. Oxford University Press, 2001, pp. 174 and 198.

129 Hunt, Gerald, ed. *Laboring for Rights: Unions and Sexual Diversity Across Nations*. Temple University Press, 1999.

130 Eaton, Adrienne, Fine, Janice, Porter, Allison, and Rubinstein, Saul. *Organizational Change at SEIU: 1996-2009*.

131 SEIU Executive Vice President Tom Woodruff chapter in *Peter Bremme: Never work alone, Organizing – ein Zukunftsmodell für Gewerkschaften (A Future Model for the Unions)*. Hamburg, VSA, 2007, S. 101. Also see *Evaluate*. President's Committee 2000 Report, Washington, D.C.: Service Employees International Union.

132 SEIU Executive Vice President Tom Woodruff chapter in *Peter Bremme: Never work alone, Organizing – ein Zukunftsmodell für Gewerkschaften (A Future Model for the Unions)*. Hamburg, VSA, 2007, S. 101. Also see *Evaluate*. President's Committee 2000 Report, Washington, D.C.: Service Employees International Union.

133 Andy Stern's keynote address to 2004 SEIU convention. *SEIU 2004 Convention Proceedings*. Washington, D.C., Service Employees International Union, 2004.

134 *A Country That Works*, p. 79.

135 "Framework for SEIU Role in Building a Stronger Movement." Internal SEIU document, written January 2005.

136 Lerner, Stephen. "An Immodest Proposal." *New Labor Forum*, Summer 2003, pp. 9-30. Lerner deserves credit for much of the analysis and writing about changes needed to revitalize the American labor movement in the years leading up to the debate about AFL-CIO reform.

137 Milkman, Ruth. "Divided We Stand." *New Labor Forum*, May 2006.

138 Menendez, Ana. "While Shalala Lives In Luxury, Janitors Struggle." *Miami Herald*, March 1, 2006. Menendez did a superb job of covering the Miami janitors' struggle. Her excellent novel *The Last War* (unrelated to the janitors' dispute) appeared in 2009. Another good account of the Miami janitors' struggle was written by Randy Shaw in his book, *Beyond the Fields: Cesar Chavez, the UFW, and the Struggle for Justice in the 21st Century*, University of California Press, 2008. We drew on the work of Shaw and Menendez in shaping this chapter and wish to both credit and thank them. Those interested in learning more should also see a chapter written by SEIU's Stephen Lerner, Jill Hurst, and Glenn Adler that appears in *The Gloves-off Economy: Workplace Standards at the Bottom of America's Labor Market*, edited by Annette Bernhardt, Heather Boushey, Laura Dresser, and Chris Tilly, Cornell University Press/ILR Press, 2008.

139 Lewine, Edward. "An Academic Retreat." *The New York Times Magazine*. February 12, 2006.

140 Menendez, Ana, "While Shalala Lives In Luxury, Janitors Struggle," *Miami Herald*. March 1, 2006.

141 Levenson, Michael. "Women, scientists on wish list for Harvard." *The Boston Globe*. February 26, 2006.

142 "University of Miami vs. UNICCO Universities With Union Representation," SEIU Local 11 flyer. Miami, 2006.

143 Bierman, Noah. "Union Boosters." *Miami Herald*. December 20, 2005.

144 "Why is the University of Miami Ignoring its Cleaning Company's Dirt?" SEIU advertisement in the *Miami Herald*. March 20, 2006.

145 "Workplace Health and Safety Dirty Dozen Report," The National Council for Occupational Safety and Health news release, April 25, 2006.

146 "Batay Ouvriye Protests UM President Donna Shalala's Health Care Hypocrisy in Haiti," Batay Ouvriye press release. Petionville, Haiti, March 11, 2006.

147 "Ashe Tuesday." Picketline Blog. March 29, 2006. Online resource, available: http://picketline.blogspot.com/2006/03/ashe-tuesday.html.

148 Rapriccioso, Robert. "Hungry for Recognition." *Inside Higher Ed*. April 11, 2006.

149 "Janitors at Second Major South Florida University to Strike UNICCO," SEIU Local 11 news release, April 10, 2006.

150 Gerstein, Josh. "Ex-Aide to Clinton Is at the Center of Labor Dispute." *The New York Sun*. April 14, 2006.

151 Goodnough, Abby, and Greenhouse, Steven. "Anger Rises on Both Sides of Strike at University of Miami." *The New York Times*. April 18, 2006.

152 Greenhouse, Steven. "Walkout Ends at University of Miami as Janitors' Pact Is Reached." *The New York Times*. May 2, 2006.

153 Boodhoo, Niala. "UM Janitors End 2-Month Strike." *Miami Herald*. May 2, 2006.

154 Albright, Jason. "Contending Rationality, Leadership, and Collective Struggle: The 2006 Justice for Janitors Campaign at the University of Miami." *Labor Studies Journal*, 33.1 (March 2008), 63-80.

155 Chalfie, Deborah, et al. "Getting Organized." National Women's Law Center, February 2007.

156 Ibid p. 14.

157 Ibid p. 15.

158 Bai, Matt. "The New Boss." *The New York Times Magazine*, January 30, 2005.

159 *Wal-Mart Counter Annual Report*. By Don Stillman for Wal-Mart Watch, 2005.

160 Thomas, Kate. "SEIU Janitors and Business Leaders Unveil New Model for Making Health Care More Accessible and Affordable for Thousands of Low-Wage Workers." SEIU.org, published on December 17, 2008.

161 Perin, Monica. *Houston Business Journal*. "Health Clinic for Janitors to Be Unveiled," December 16, 2008.

162 Fred Feinstein testimony before House Judiciary Subcommittee on Immigration, May 23, 2007.

163 Harkinson, Josh. "A Victory for Janitors in Houston, with Thanks to a Humble Martyr." *Mother Jones* Blog, Nov. 21, 2006. Available at http://motherjones.com/mojo/2006/11/victory-janitors-houston-thanks-humble-martyr.

164 Moreno, Sylvia, and Russakoff, Dale. "Labor's Gambit in Houston." *The Washington Post*, November 17, 2006.

165 "Janitors to Walk Off the Job to Protest Pay." *Houston Business Journal*, Oct. 23, 2008.

166 Moreno, Sylvia, and Russakoff, Dale. "Labor's Gambit in Houston." *The Washington Post*, November 17, 2006.

167 "Big Arrests (at) Houston Cleaners Protest." Labornet, Nov. 17, 2006.

168 Scott, Judith. "Standing Up for the Real 'Joe the Plumbers,'" Yale Law School: Preiskel-Silverman Lecture, February 7, 2009. Scott has served as SEIU general counsel since 1997. By way of full disclosure, *Stronger Together* author Don Stillman is her spouse. Scott recused herself and legal review of the book was coordinated by Norm Gleichman and conducted by Orrin Baird, John Sullivan, Maryann Parker, Dora Chen, and Alvin Velazquez.

169 Moreno, Sylvia, and Russakoff, Dale. "Labor's Gambit in Houston." *The Washington Post*, November 17, 2006.

170 Moreno, Sylvia, and Russakoff, Dale. "Labor's Gambit in Houston." *The Washington Post*, November 17, 2006.

170a Harkinson, Josh. "A Victory for Janitors in Houston, with Thanks to a Humble Martyr." *Mother Jones* Blog, Nov. 21, 2006. Available at http://motherjones.com/mojo/2006/11/victory-janitors-houston-thanks-humble-martyr.

171 Shulman, Barbara. "Healthcare, Property Service, and Public Service Worker Organizing with SEIU: 1996-2009." Washington, D.C.: Service Employees International Union (2009).

172 Technically, a memorandum of understanding with the county.

173 *SEIU Annual Report*, 2006.

174 SEIU 2008 Convention Proceedings. Published by SEIU, Washington, D.C., 2008.

175 "SEANC-SEIU Pack Political Punch." *North Carolina Capitol Monitor*, February 2, 2010.

176 So-called "right-to-work" laws prohibit unions and employers from making union membership or payment of union dues or "fees" a condition of employment.

177 "Justice for All." Recommendations to the SEIU 2008 Convention, p. 6.

178 Ibid p. 8.

179 Eaton, Adrienne, Fine, Janice, Porter, Allison, and Rubinstein, Saul. *Organizational Change at SEIU: 1996-2009*.

180 Annelle Grajeda resigned as executive vice president in 2009 and Mitch Ackerman was elected to that post.

181 *Labor Day*, a film by Glenn Silber and Claudia Vianello. Catalyst Media Productions, New York. 2009. Some quotes/material in this chapter come from the film, which was partially financed by SEIU. For more information on Silber and Vianello's film, see: http://www.labordaythemovie.com/.

182 Greenhouse, Steven. "A Union With Clout Boldly Stakes Its Claim on Politics." *The New York Times*, October 30, 2007.

183 2008 Democratic National Convention proceedings.

184 "McCain: Economy Still 'Strong.'" MSNBC, Sept. 15, 2008.

185 *Labor Day*, a film by Glenn Silber and Claudia Vianello. Catalyst Media Productions, New York. 2009.

186 Economic Policy Institute, 2008. Jared Bernstein found that U.S. Census Bureau data revealed that real median household income declined in the 2000-2007 period.

187 *SEIU 2004 Convention Proceedings*, p. 25. Published by Service Employees International Union. Washington, D.C., 2004.

188 Eaton, Adrienne, Fine, Janice, Porter, Allison, and Rubinstein, Saul. *Organizational Change at SEIU: 1996-2009*.

189 *SEIU Annual Report*, 2006, p. 13.

190 Eaton, Adrienne, Fine, Janice, Porter, Allison, and Rubinstein, Saul. *Organizational Change at SEIU: 1996-2009*.

191 *SEIU Annual Report*, 2008.

192 Bogardus, Kevin. "SEIU, AFL-CIO Battle Puerto Rico's Governor over Looming Layoffs." *The Hill*, October 17, 2009.

193 Frumin, Ben. "SEIU Health Care Chair: 300K To 400K Protesters in Puerto Rico Today." *Talking Points Memo LiveWire*, October 15, 2009.

194 "Governor of Puerto Rico Signs Union Law." *Reuters*, published in *Orlando Sentinel*, February 26, 1998.

195 *SEIU Action*, February/March/April 2000, p. 12.

196 Burger, Anna. "Crash the Bankers' Party in Chicago." *The Huffington Post*, October 22, 2009.

197 Thornton, Emily. "Gluttons at the Gate." *Business Week*, October 30, 2006.

198 *Behind the Buyouts*, p. 11. Published by Service Employees International Union, Washington, D.C., 2007.

199 Study by Emmanuel Saez and Thomas Piketty, cited in *Behind the Buyouts*, p. 10.

200   A portfolio company is one in which a private equity or buyout firm invests.

201   *Behind the Buyouts*, p. 30.

202   Duhigg, Charles. "At Many Homes, More Profits and Less Nursing." *The New York Times*, September 23, 2007.

203   Ibid.

204   "SEIU to Lead Comprehensive Ethics Reform Initiative," SEIU press release, September 3, 2008.

205   In the Matter of the Trusteeship of Local 25, Case No. 96-3(T), Hearing Officer Marc Earls, International Vice President.

206   Greenhouse, Steven. "Ex-Union Chief's Private Palace; Rank and File Get a Glimpse of Bevona's Penthouse." *The New York Times*, February 9, 1999.

207   Ibid.

208   Ibid.

209   Greenhouse, Steven. "Chief of Building Workers' Union Leaves with $1.5 Million." *The New York Times*, February 3, 1999.

210   In the Matter of the Trusteeship of SEIU Local 5000 (NAGE), October 26, 2001, p. 25.

211   "Tyrone Freeman Permanently Banned from Holding SEIU Membership or Office." SEIU press release, November 26, 2008.

212   *SEIU Healthcare Reform Playbook 2009*, p. 2. Internal document of Service Employees International Union, Washington, D.C.

213   *SEIU: Building a New American Health Care System*, p. 3. Published by Service Employees International Union, Washington, D.C.

214   *A Country that Works*, p. 158.

215   "Insurance Companies Prosper, Families Suffer: Our Broken Health Insurance System." Department of Health and Human Services, February 2010.

# About The Author

Don Stillman first wrote about SEIU issues when he covered the growing militancy of nurses in 1966 on the front page of *The Wall Street Journal*. He now directs Labor Rights Now, a human rights group that campaigns for the release of jailed worker activists worldwide.

He served as director of governmental and international affairs for the United Auto Workers union for more than 20 years. Earlier, Stillman worked for Jock Yablonski when he opposed Tony Boyle for the presidency of the United Mine Workers and, following Yablonski's murder, joined in creating Miners for Democracy. He helped topple the UMWA's corrupt leadership in 1972.

Stillman's work as editor of the *United Mine Workers Journal* won it the National Magazine Award. He also was the recipient of the Research and Writing Award from the John D. and Catherine T. MacArthur Foundation and the Samuel Gompers Award from the CUNY Graduate School.

Stillman has taught at Oxford University where he served as a visiting fellow at Magdalen College. He was founding editor of *WorkingUSA*, an academic journal dealing with issues of labor, class, and gender. In addition to *The Wall Street Journal*, Stillman's work has been published in *The Washington Post*, *Life* magazine, *Progressive*, *Columbia Journalism Review*, and other publications.